Utilizing AI Tools in Academic Research Writing

Anugamini Priya Srivastava
Symbiosis Institute of Business Management Pune, Symbiosis International University, Pune, India

Sucheta Agarwal
Institute of Business Management, GLA University, Mathura, India

A volume in the Advances in Educational Technologies and Instructional Design (AETID) Book Series

IGI Global
PUBLISHER of TIMELY KNOWLEDGE

Published in the United States of America by
IGI Global
Information Science Reference (an imprint of IGI Global)
701 E. Chocolate Avenue
Hershey PA, USA 17033
Tel: 717-533-8845
Fax: 717-533-8661
E-mail: cust@igi-global.com
Web site: http://www.igi-global.com

Library of Congress Cataloging-in-Publication Data

Names: Srivastava, Anugamini, 1987- editor. | Agarwal, Sucheta, 1986- editor.
Title: Utilizing AI tools in academic research writing / edited by Anugamini Srivastava, Sucheta Agarwal.
Description: Hershey, PA : Information Science Reference, 2024. | Includes bibliographical references and index. | Summary: "This book delves into the practical dimensions of AI integration, showcasing how AI aids in identifying research topics and ideas, streamlining research design and methodology selection, empowering data collection and analysis, and enhancing the rigor of literature reviews"-- Provided by publisher.
Identifiers: LCCN 2024002038 (print) | LCCN 2024002039 (ebook) | ISBN 9798369317983 (hardcover) | ISBN 9798369317990 (ebook)
Subjects: LCSH: Academic writing. | Academic writing--Technological innovations. | Research--Methodology. | Research--Technological innovations. | Artificial intelligence--Educational applications.
Classification: LCC LB2369 .U75 2024 (print) | LCC LB2369 (ebook) | DDC 808.02--dc23/eng/20240207
LC record available at https://lccn.loc.gov/2024002038
LC ebook record available at https://lccn.loc.gov/2024002039

This book is published in the IGI Global book series Advances in Educational Technologies and Instructional Design (AE-TID) (ISSN: 2326-8905; eISSN: 2326-8913)

British Cataloguing in Publication Data
A Cataloguing in Publication record for this book is available from the British Library.

For electronic access to this publication, please contact: eresources@igi-global.com.

Advances in Educational Technologies and Instructional Design (AETID) Book Series

Lawrence A. Tomei
Robert Morris University, USA

ISSN:2326-8905
EISSN:2326-8913

Mission

Education has undergone, and continues to undergo, immense changes in the way it is enacted and distributed to both child and adult learners. In modern education, the traditional classroom learning experience has evolved to include technological resources and to provide online classroom opportunities to students of all ages regardless of their geographical locations. From distance education, Massive-Open-Online-Courses (MOOCs), and electronic tablets in the classroom, technology is now an integral part of learning and is also affecting the way educators communicate information to students.

The **Advances in Educational Technologies & Instructional Design (AETID) Book Series** explores new research and theories for facilitating learning and improving educational performance utilizing technological processes and resources. The series examines technologies that can be integrated into K-12 classrooms to improve skills and learning abilities in all subjects including STEM education and language learning. Additionally, it studies the emergence of fully online classrooms for young and adult learners alike, and the communication and accountability challenges that can arise. Trending topics that are covered include adaptive learning, game-based learning, virtual school environments, and social media effects. School administrators, educators, academicians, researchers, and students will find this series to be an excellent resource for the effective design and implementation of learning technologies in their classes.

Coverage

- Instructional Design
- Social Media Effects on Education
- Higher Education Technologies
- Collaboration Tools
- Classroom Response Systems
- Educational Telecommunications
- Adaptive Learning
- Virtual School Environments
- E-Learning
- Online Media in Classrooms

IGI Global is currently accepting manuscripts for publication within this series. To submit a proposal for a volume in this series, please contact our Acquisition Editors at Acquisitions@igi-global.com or visit: http://www.igi-global.com/publish/.

The Advances in Educational Technologies and Instructional Design (AETID) Book Series (ISSN 2326-8905) is published by IGI Global, 701 E. Chocolate Avenue, Hershey, PA 17033-1240, USA, www.igi-global.com. This series is composed of titles available for purchase individually; each title is edited to be contextually exclusive from any other title within the series. For pricing and ordering information please visit http://www.igi-global.com/book-series/advances-educational-technologies-instructional-design/73678. Postmaster: Send all address changes to above address.

Titles in this Series

For a list of additional titles in this series, please visit:
http://www.igi-global.com/book-series/advances-educational-technologies-instructional-design/73678

Addressing Issues of Learner Diversity in English Language Education
Thao Quoc Tran (HUTECH University, Vietnam) and Tham My Duong (Ho Chi Minh City University of Economics and Finance, Vietnam)
Information Science Reference • © 2024 • 357pp • H/C (ISBN: 9798369326237) • US $235.00

AI-Enhanced Teaching Methods
Zeinab E. Ahmed (Department of Computer Engineering, University of Gezira, Sudan & Department of Electrical and Computer Engineering, International Islamic University Malaysia, Malaysia) Aisha A. Hassan (International Islamic University of Malaysia, Malaysia) and Rashid A. Saeed (Taif University, Saudi Arabia)
Information Science Reference • © 2024 • 405pp • H/C (ISBN: 9798369327289) • US $245.00

Effective and Meaningful Student Engagement Through Service Learning
Sharon Valarmathi (Christ University, India) Jacqueline Kareem (Christ University, India) Veerta Tantia (Christ University, India) Kishore Selva Babu (Christ University, India) and Patrick Jude Lucas (Christ University, India)
Information Science Reference • © 2024 • 293pp • H/C (ISBN: 9798369322567) • US $275.00

Integrating Cutting-Edge Technology Into the Classroom
Ken Nee Chee (Universiti Pendidikan Sultan Idris, Malaysia) and Mageswaran Sanmugam (Universiti Sains Malaysia, Malaysia)
Information Science Reference • © 2024 • 425pp • H/C (ISBN: 9798369331248) • US $300.00

Embracing Technological Advancements for Lifelong Learning
Mahmoud M. Kh. Hawamdeh (Al-Quds Open University, Palestine) and Faiz Abdelhafid (Al-Istiqlal University, Palestine)
Information Science Reference • © 2024 • 365pp • H/C (ISBN: 9798369314104) • US $230.00

Unlocking Learning Potential With Universal Design in Online Learning Environments
Michelle Bartlett (Old Dominion University, USA) and Suzanne M. Ehrlich (University of North Florida, USA)
Information Science Reference • © 2024 • 286pp • H/C (ISBN: 9798369312698) • US $240.00

Navigating Innovative Technologies and Intelligent Systems in Modern Education
Madhulika Bhatia (Amity University, India) and Muhammad Tahir Mushtaq (Cardiff Metropolitan Univesity, UK)
Information Science Reference • © 2024 • 307pp • H/C (ISBN: 9798369353707) • US $245.00

IGI Global
PUBLISHER of TIMELY KNOWLEDGE

701 East Chocolate Avenue, Hershey, PA 17033, USA
Tel: 717-533-8845 x100 • Fax: 717-533-8661
E-Mail: cust@igi-global.com • www.igi-global.com

Table of Contents

Detailed Table of Contents

The growing power of artificial intelligence (AI) is fundamentally altering the landscape of academic research. AI-powered tools are streamlining tasks like literature reviews, manuscript drafting, and reference generation, empowering researchers to delve deeper into their work and foster innovation within their fields. Natural language processing (NLP) capabilities of AI tools facilitate rapid and comprehensive literature reviews, identifying emerging trends, gaps, and interconnected themes. This integration of AI in academic research signifies a paradigm shift, offering unprecedented opportunities for exploration and discovery. However, as AI tools become more commonplace, reviewers and editors must maintain vigilance. While these tools enhance efficiency, there's a risk that their use may compromise the scientific integrity of research. Therefore, striking a balance between leveraging AI's advantages and preserving the rigor of scientific discourse is imperative.

Wisdom cannot be replaced by AI tools. AI tools can save time spent on a pre-draft research. AI tools can open the door to create a better writing outcome. AI tools can boost productivity. Writing produced by AI tools still needs a human touch. Academic writing has undergone a revolution as a result of AI. Writing a book, a research grant, or even an academic journal article can be done by using AI techniques. Additionally, there are several AI-powered applications that can assist researchers in editing their publications and use English correctly.

In the context of agricultural science, the academic writing is of great importance, as articles of academicians and scientists make available all their developments available for studying the experiences around the world. This contributes not only to the exchange of experience, but also to expand the practical knowledge in agrarian topics to different continents and countries, spreading the developments of economical agriculture for solving problems with food on a global scale. Therefore, the use of artificial intelligence in the field of agrarian academic writing can be as positive results, so has risks of incorrect research of certain issues. This chapter sets itself the goal of considering the pros and cons of using artificial intelligence tools in academic writing with an agronomic focus, taking into account the specifics of the basic concept of academic writing and new artificial intelligence tools. The novelty of this work lies in the fact that developments of Ukrainian scientists can serve as interesting theoretical material for foreign colleagues.

Preface

Welcome to the dawn of a new era in academic research and writing. As you hold this book in your hands, you are about to embark on a journey that will revolutionize the way you approach scholarly endeavors. *Utilizing AI Tools in Academic Research Writing*, authored by Anugamini Priya Srivastava and Sucheta Agarwal, is not just another addition to the library of academic literature; it is a beacon illuminating the path toward innovation, efficiency, and integrity in the realm of academic pursuits.

Meticulously crafted to cater to the diverse needs of academic audiences, spanning from budding researchers to seasoned scholars, this comprehensive reference book offers a roadmap for harnessing the power of AI in pursuit of knowledge and discovery.

Chapter 1: Role of AI in Academic Research

The journey begins with an exploration of the foundational concepts in Chapter 1. Here, we elucidate the pivotal role of AI in academic research. AI is not merely a tool but a transformative force shaping the landscape of scholarly pursuits. It has the potential to augment human capabilities, enhance research methodologies, and revolutionize the way knowledge is generated and disseminated.

Chapter 2: Evolution of AI in Academic Research

Tracing the evolution of AI in scholarly pursuits, Chapter 2 provides invaluable insights into its trajectory. From its inception to its current state, AI has undergone remarkable advancements, driven by interdisciplinary collaboration and technological innovation. Understanding this evolution is essential for comprehending the breadth and depth of AI's impact on academic research.

Chapter 3: Augmenting Research: The Role of Artificial Intelligence in Recognizing Topics and Ideas

Chapter 3 delves into the practical implications of AI in research augmentation. Here, we explore how AI can assist researchers in recognizing topics and generating ideas. By leveraging advanced algorithms and natural language processing techniques, AI tools can analyze vast amounts of data, identify relevant themes, and inspire novel research directions, thereby accelerating the pace of discovery.

Chapter 4: AI Tools for Efficient Writing and Editing

In Chapter 4, we unveil the transformative potential of AI in streamlining writing and editing processes. AI-powered tools offer researchers unprecedented efficiency and precision in articulating their ideas, refining their arguments, and polishing their manuscripts. From grammar and style suggestions to automated citation management, these tools empower researchers to produce high-quality written work with ease and confidence.

Chapter 5: The Use of Artificial Intelligence Tools in Academic Writing With Agronomic Direction

Chapter 5 shines a spotlight on the intersection of AI and agronomic research. Here, we demonstrate how AI tools can revolutionize the landscape of agricultural science. By harnessing the power of AI-driven data analysis, predictive modeling, and decision support systems, researchers in agronomy can optimize crop yields, mitigate environmental impact, and address global food security challenges more effectively.

Chapter 6: The Role of Generative AI-Assisted Literature Reviews in Transforming Academic Research

Chapters 6 illuminate the role of generative AI in literature reviews and hypothesis development. In Chapter 6, we explore how AI can catalyze breakthroughs in knowledge synthesis by assisting researchers in conducting comprehensive and systematic literature reviews. By automating the process of information retrieval, synthesis, and analysis, AI enables researchers to uncover insights, identify trends, and make informed decisions more efficiently.

Chapter 7: AI-Enhanced Hypothesis Development and Research Questions

Chapter 7 delves into AI-enhanced hypothesis development and research questions. Here, we showcase how AI tools can facilitate the formulation of hypotheses and research questions by analyzing large datasets, identifying patterns, and generating testable hypotheses. By leveraging AI-driven analytics and predictive modeling, researchers can refine their research objectives, design more rigorous experiments, and generate novel hypotheses with greater precision and confidence.

Chapter 8: AI-Powered Data Collection and Analysis

In the era of big data, Chapters 8 and 9 present AI-powered solutions for data collection, analysis, and interpretation. Chapter 8 offers insights into AI-driven data collection methodologies, ranging from web scraping and social media analytics to sensor networks and Internet of Things (IoT) devices. These techniques enable researchers to gather large volumes of data from diverse sources, providing a rich and comprehensive foundation for analysis and interpretation.

Chapter 9: AI Tools for Efficient Writing and Editing in Academic Research

Chapter 9 revisits the theme of AI tools for efficient writing and editing, focusing on their application in the context of academic research. Here, we delve deeper into the capabilities of AI-powered writing assistants, citation management tools, and collaborative editing platforms. By harnessing these tools, researchers can streamline the writing process, enhance the quality of their manuscripts, and facilitate collaboration with colleagues and peers.

Chapter 10: Enlightening Cases: Utilization of Exemplary AI-Enhanced Research Endeavors

Through enlightening case studies in Chapter 10, we witness firsthand the transformative impact of AI-enhanced research endeavors. These case studies exemplify the diverse applications of AI in academic research, spanning across disciplines and domains. From healthcare and finance to education and environmental science, AI is revolutionizing the way research is conducted, insights are generated, and solutions are implemented.

Chapter 11: The Researcher's Sidekick: Unleashing ChatGPT's Potential in Academic Research

Chapter 11 introduces ChatGPT as the researcher's sidekick, unlocking its potential as a versatile and intelligent assistant in academic research. By harnessing the power of conversational AI, researchers can engage in real-time dialogue with ChatGPT to brainstorm ideas, clarify concepts, and overcome challenges in their research endeavors. ChatGPT serves as a valuable companion, offering insights, suggestions, and guidance throughout the research process.

Chapter 12: Transformative Horizons: Exploring ChatGPT's Impact on Scientific Research

In Chapter 12, we explore the transformative horizons of ChatGPT's impact on scientific research. Here, we navigate the dual dimensions of efficiency and ethics in the age of AI-driven discovery. By embracing ChatGPT as a tool for collaboration, communication, and creativity, researchers can unlock new avenues for exploration, accelerate the pace of discovery, and uphold ethical principles in their scholarly pursuits.

Chapter 13: Navigating the Ethical Landscape: AI's Impact on Academic Research and Integrity

Amidst these technological advancements, it is essential to acknowledge the ethical dimensions of AI integration in academic research. Chapter 13 delves into the ethical considerations and societal implications, urging researchers to navigate the terrain of AI-driven discovery with mindfulness and integrity. By fostering a culture of responsible AI utilization and ethical research practices, we can ensure that AI serves as a force for good, advancing knowledge and benefiting society as a whole.

Chapter 14: AI in Research Challenges and Future Directions

In Chapter 14, we confront the challenges and future directions of AI in research. Here, we explore the barriers to adoption, the limitations of current AI technologies, and the potential risks and pitfalls associated with AI integration in academic research. By addressing these challenges head-on and charting a course toward responsible AI utilization, we can harness the full potential of AI to advance knowledge, foster innovation, and address pressing societal challenges.

Chapter 15: Future Trends in AI and Academic Research Writing

As we peer into the future in Chapter 15, we envision the emerging trends and possibilities that lie ahead. Here, we explore the cutting-edge developments in AI technologies, the transformative impact on academic research methodologies, and the evolving role of researchers in the age of AI-driven discovery. By staying abreast of these trends and embracing a mindset of continuous learning and adaptation, we can navigate the ever-changing landscape of academic research with confidence and fores.

Anugamini Priya Srivastava
Symbiosis Institute of Business Management, Symbiosis International University, Pune, India

Sucheta Agarwal
Institute of Business Management, GLA University, Mathura, India

Chapter 1
Role of AI in Academic Research

Hari Kishan Kondaveeti
https://orcid.org/0000-0002-3379-720X
VIT-AP University, India

Valli Kumari Vatsavayi
https://orcid.org/0000-0002-7252-8301
Andhra University, India

Samparthi V. S. Kumar
VIT-AP University, India

Preethi Ananthachari
Woosong University, South Korea

Atchuta Venkata Naga Manusree
VIT-AP University, India

ABSTRACT

Artificial intelligence (AI) is rapidly transforming academic research, accelerating discovery, improving efficiency, and opening up new avenues across various disciplines. This chapter introduces AI and discusses its broad range of applications, both within and outside of academia. The chapter then presents the applications of AI in academic research. It covers various AI tools, such as Scite, Elicit, etc., and a comparative analysis of their capabilities and limitations. The chapter also discusses some ethical issues that must be considered when using AI in academic research. It concludes with a discussion on the future of AI in academic research and the potential benefits and challenges that lie ahead. This chapter is intended for a broad audience, including academic researchers, students, and those who are interested in learning more about the role of AI in academic research.

INTRODUCTION

The term Artificial Intelligence (AI) is used for the first time in the book called McCarthy 1956 (Russel et al., 2010). In 1950, Alan Turing published "Computer Machinery and Intelligence", from this AI was introduced to this new era. AI in academic research is like having a research assistant with us which never gets tiered. AI is built by fields like computer science and engineering, neuroscience, cognitive science, philosophy, and economics. Learning and understanding the AI techniques has to be adopted and used for educational purposes ethically. Academicians and students are using AI for research, learning, and improving purposes.

DOI: 10.4018/979-8-3693-1798-3.ch001

AI plays different types of roles in academics like Automated Grading and Assessment (Richardson et.al.,2021), Personalized Learning (Pataranutaporn et.al.,2021), Virtual Teaching Assistants (Wang et.al.,2021), Content Creation and Recommendation (Ip et al.,2023), Research and Data Analysis (Loai et al., 2016), Language Translation and Accessibility (Sarayrah et al.,2021), Administrative Efficiency (Grzebyk et al.,2021), Plagiarism Detection (Gao et al.,2022), Early Intervention for Student Support (Nurshatayeva et al.,2020), Professional Development (Randhawa et al.,2020) and Predictive Analytics for Enrolment and Resource Planning (Fahd et al.,2023).

AUTOMATED GRADING AND ASSESSMENT AI

AI is helpful to give grades to the students when they submit the quizzes or exams to the professors in online mode then AI scans the data and verifies it This AI is useful whether there is a high number of students or the complexity of the quizzes or exams. Because of this AI, we can get immediate results after the quizzes or exams. Automated grading ensures a high level of consistency in evaluation because the algorithms apply the same criteria to all submissions. This helps in fair grading. Many educational institutions integrate automated grading systems with their learning management systems, creating a seamless experience for both instructors and students. (Fleming et al., 2010).

Personalized Learning AI

AI is helpful for students to directly talk or chat with a chatbot AI clarifies doubts and can learn lessons with the help of AI (Pataranutaporn et.al.,2021). In this Personalized Learning AI, AI first scans the personality of the student or user and then helps with his problems or queries according to them. Personalized learning AI, relies on data analytics to collect data and analyze students' progress. Instructors use this data to make informed decisions about identifying areas of improvement, adjusting instructional strategies, and offering extra support when it is needed. Personalized Learning AI, often involves giving students choices in how they demonstrate their understanding of concepts and encouraging them to pursue topics that align with their interests. These platforms use AI and machine learning to analyze students' interactions with educational content and dynamically adjust the difficulty and pace of instruction to match individual needs (Zhang et al., 2020), (Shemshack et al., 2020).

Virtual Teaching Assistants AI

AI is helpful for AI chatbots and Virtual Teaching Assistants (VTA) can handle normal inquiries, freeing up educators to focus on more complex interactions (Wang et.al.,2021). These assistants can answer questions of users or students provide information, and offer guidance on different academic issues. VTAs seamlessly integrate with learning management systems, making it easy for educators to deploy them within existing online course structures. VTAs can assist in the assignment submission process, provide guidelines on assignments, and offer automated grading for assessments that have clear criteria. This helps streamline administrative tasks for educators. VTAs can analyze the progress of individual students and tailor learning paths accordingly. This adaptability ensures that students receive content at an appropriate difficulty level, accommodating various learning styles. Unlike human teaching assistants, VTAs can operate around the clock, providing support and assistance to students regardless of time zones. This enhances accessibility and addresses the diverse schedules of online learners. VTAs can send automated updates and announcements to students, keeping them informed about changes in the course schedule, upcoming assignments, or any other important information. VTAs can send automated updates and announcements to students, keeping them informed about changes in the course schedule, upcoming assignments, or any other important information. VTAs can send reminders to students about upcoming deadlines, exams, or important events. This helps students stay organized and on track with their coursework (Kim et al., 2019).

Content Creation and Recommendation AI

AI can help educators in creating and cleric educational content (Ip et al.,2023). It can recommend relevant materials, textbooks, and resources based on the curriculum, student progress, and emerging trends in the field. AI tools can computerize the process of content creation, producing educational materials such as quizzes, assessments, and even basic instructional content. This helps educators save time and ensures a consistent quality of materials. AI can create adaptive learning paths by analyzing students' performance data. Based on individual strengths and weaknesses, the system generates personalized content recommendations to address specific learning needs.

Natural Language Processing (NLP), a subset of AI, enables machines to understand and generate human-like language. AI-driven content creation tools can use NLP to generate coherent and contextually relevant educational content. AI can create personalized learning paths for individual students based on their performance, preferences, and learning styles. This ensures that learners receive content that is tailored to their unique needs and abilities. AI employs semantic analysis to understand the context and meaning of educational content. This enables more accurate recommendations by identifying the relevance and relationships between different pieces of content. Content recommendation systems can dynamically update suggestions based on changes in the curriculum, emerging trends, or the introduction of new learning materials. This ensures that the content remains current and relevant. Content recommendation systems often integrate seamlessly with learning management systems, making it easy for educators to deploy personalized content within existing course structures. AI can optimize the use of educational resources by recommending content that is aligned with specific learning objectives, ensuring that time spent on learning is focused and efficient. In summary, AI-driven content creation and recommendation systems contribute to the effectiveness and efficiency of educational processes. By tailoring content to individual learners, these technologies support personalized learning experiences and help educators make informed decisions about the educational materials they provide (Xiao et al., 2019).

Research and Data Analysis AI

AI plays a significant role in research and data analysis, revolutionizing the way researchers extract insights, identify patterns, and draw conclusions from vast datasets AI tools can automatically collect, aggregate, and organize data from various sources, including online databases, websites, and sensors (Loai et al., 2016). This accelerates the data collection process and ensures a more comprehensive dataset. AI algorithms assist in cleaning and preprocessing raw data by identifying and correcting errors, handling missing values, and standardizing formats. This ensures that the data is accurate and ready for analysis. AI-driven predictive analytics models leverage machine learning algorithms to forecast future trends and outcomes based on historical data. This is applicable in various fields, from finance to healthcare, where predictive modeling can assist in decision-making.

NLP enables machines to understand and analyze human language. In research, NLP is employed for sentiment analysis, summarization of textual data, and extracting insights from unstructured data such as research papers, articles, and social media content. AI algorithms can analyze medical images to identify patterns, aiding in diagnostics and research. Machine learning algorithms can classify data or clusters based on patterns and similarities. This is beneficial for grouping similar entities, identifying trends, and making sense of complex datasets. Analysis to understand patterns and trends over time. This is crucial in fields such as finance, environmental science, and economics.

AI tools can analyze social network data to identify relationships, influencers, and patterns within a network. This is valuable in sociology, marketing, and other fields where understanding social connections is essential. AI algorithms can automate the process of hypothesis testing by analyzing data and determining statistical significance. This accelerates the research process and allows researchers to focus on interpreting results. (Cui et al., 2021), (Elish et al., 2018).

Language Translation and Accessibility AI

AI can break down language barriers, making information more accessible and fostering communication across linguistic differences (Sarayrah et al.,2021),. AI-driven machine translation tools, such as Google Translate and Microsoft Translator, use Neural Machine Translation (NMT) algorithms to provide more accurate and contextually relevant translations between languages. AI facilitates real-time translation services, enabling users to translate spoken or written language instantly. This is particularly useful in scenarios like international conferences, meetings, or online communication.

AI models can be trained on domain-specific terminology, enhancing the accuracy and relevance of translations in specialized fields such as legal, medical, or technical domains. AI models are constantly improving and expanding language pairs, allowing for translation between a broader range of languages and dialects. AI algorithms aim to understand context and nuances in language, improving the quality of translations by considering the meaning of words within specific contexts. Some AI translation tools allow users to customize the tone and style of translations to better align with the intended communication. Text-to-Speech (TTS) and Speech-to-Text (STT) technologies, convert written text into spoken language and vice versa. This benefits individuals with visual or auditory impairments. AI-driven screen readers use natural language processing to read aloud the content of digital screens, making websites, documents, and applications accessible to individuals with visual impairments. AI-driven language understanding models assist in interpreting and responding to user input, benefiting individuals who may have difficulty using traditional interfaces. (Strobel et al., 2023),(Liebling et al., 2020).

Administrative Efficiency AI

The use of artificial intelligence technologies to streamline and optimize administrative processes within organizations (Grzebyk et al.,2021). AI can be applied to various administrative tasks, automating routine activities, improving decision-making, and enhancing overall operational efficiency. AI-powered tools can automate data entry tasks, reducing the time and effort required for manual data input. This improves accuracy and minimizes errors in administrative databases. AI-based document management systems can organize, categorize, and retrieve documents more efficiently (Engstrom et al., 2020).

Optical Character Recognition (OCR) technology enables the extraction of information from scanned documents. AI-driven chatbots provide instant and automated responses to customer queries, freeing up human resources for more complex tasks. This enhances customer support efficiency and responsiveness.

AI algorithms can optimize appointment scheduling processes by analyzing calendars, preferences, and availability. This is particularly useful in scenarios like healthcare or service-oriented industries.

AI can automate expense tracking and management, simplifying the reimbursement process for employees. This includes the extraction of relevant information from receipts and invoices. AI can be employed to automate email categorization, prioritization, and responses. This helps in managing email overload and ensures that important messages receive prompt attention (Barth et al., 1999).

Plagiarism Detection AI

Plagiarism involves the unauthorized use or reproduction of someone else's work, ideas, or intellectual property without proper attribution (Gao et al.,2022). AI-driven plagiarism detection tools help educational institutions, publishers, and content creators maintain academic integrity and originality. Plagiarism detection tools compare the text in a document with a vast database of academic papers, articles, books, and other sources. Advanced algorithms analyze similarities and identify potential matches. Machine learning models are trained to recognize patterns associated with plagiarism. These models can detect not only exact matches but also paraphrased or reworded content that may still constitute plagiarism. Plagiarism detection systems maintain extensive databases of academic and non-academic content. Indexing and regularly updating this database ensure that the system has access to a comprehensive range of sources for comparison. AI algorithms can analyze citation patterns to identify whether proper credit has been given to the sources. (Khalil et al., 2023).

Early Intervention for Student Support AI

Early Intervention for Student Support AI refers to the use of artificial intelligence technologies to identify and address academic, behavioral, or emotional challenges faced by students at an early stage (Nurshatayeva et al.,2020). The goal is to provide timely and targeted interventions that can help students overcome difficulties and achieve academic success. AI systems analyze student performance data, including grades, assessment scores, and engagement metrics. Early warning systems use predictive analytics to identify students at risk of falling behind. AI tools can analyze behavioral data, including attendance records, participation in class activities, and interactions with learning materials. Unusual patterns or signs of disengagement can trigger alerts for early intervention. AI-driven predictive models analyze historical data to predict future outcomes. In education, this could involve predicting a student's likelihood of success, dropout risk, or the need for additional support based on various factors. NLP algorithms can analyze written communication, such as essays or forum posts, to detect signs of emotional distress or challenges in understanding the material. This helps identify students who may need additional support. AI-powered adaptive learning systems tailor educational content based on individual student progress and performance. These platforms can identify areas where a student is struggling and provide targeted resources or exercises for improvement. AI-driven early warning systems use a combination of academic and behavioral data to identify students who may be at risk of academic challenges or dropping out. Educators receive alerts to intervene proactively. AI can generate personalized feedback for students, highlighting their strengths, areas for improvement, and specific actions they can take to enhance their learning experience (Ford et al., 1996).

Professional Development AI

Professional development AI refers to the use of artificial intelligence technologies to enhance and streamline the process of continuous learning and skill development for professionals in various fields (Randhawa et al.,2020). These AI applications aim to provide personalized, efficient, and effective learning experiences tailored to individual needs. AI analyses individual learning preferences, performance, and career goals to create personalized learning paths. This ensures that professionals receive relevant and targeted content based on their specific needs. AI tools can conduct skill gap analyses by assessing current skills against desired competencies. This information helps professionals and organizations identify areas for improvement and design targeted training programs. AI-powered adaptive learning platforms adjust the difficulty and content of courses based on the user's progress and performance. This ensures that professionals are consistently challenged and engaged. AI-driven recommendation engines suggest relevant courses, articles, and resources based on an individual's learning history, preferences, and career aspirations. AI can map competencies and skills to specific job roles, helping professionals understand the skills needed for career advancement. This information guides them in choosing appropriate professional development opportunities. AI facilitates the creation of microlearning modules, delivering small, focused pieces of content that professionals can consume quickly, fitting into their busy schedules. NLP algorithms analyze feedback provided by professionals, mentors, or peers. This helps identify areas for improvement and suggests relevant learning resources (Randhawa et al., 2020).

Predictive Analytics for Enrolment and Resource Planning Using AI

Predictive analytics for enrolment and resource planning using AI involves leveraging advanced data analysis and machine learning algorithms to forecast future trends, patterns, and demands in educational institutions (Fahd et al.,2023). This application of AI helps educational institutions optimize their resource allocation, anticipate enrolment fluctuations, and enhance overall operational efficiency. AI models analyze historical enrolment data, demographic trends, and external factors to predict future enrolment numbers. This helps institutions plan for capacity, allocate resources effectively, and anticipate changes in student demographics. Predictive analytics can assess factors contributing to student retention or attrition. By identifying at-risk students early, institutions can implement interventions to improve retention rates. AI models predict the demand for specific courses based on historical data, student preferences, and industry trends. This assists institutions in optimizing course offerings and resource allocation. Predictive analytics helps optimize the allocation of resources such as classrooms, faculty, and support services. Institutions can adjust staffing levels and facilities usage based on anticipated demand. AI-driven predictive models assist in budget planning by forecasting future resource needs. This includes estimating expenditures for staffing, infrastructure, technology, and other resources. Predictive analytics helps streamline admissions processes by identifying patterns in applicant data, predicting acceptance rates, and optimizing admission criteria. AI models can predict the demand for financial aid and assess the impact of various aid programs on enrolment. This helps institutions allocate financial aid resources more effectively (Votto et al., 2021).

AI IN ACADEMIC RESEARCH

Artificial intelligence has emerged as a transformative force in academic research, revolutionizing the way scholars conduct investigations, analyze data, and draw conclusions. The integration of AI technologies in academic research brings unprecedented opportunities for efficiency, innovation, and the exploration of complex scientific questions. This introduction delves into the key aspects of AI's role in academic research. In academia, AI automates routine tasks such as grading assessments, enabling educators and researchers to focus on more complex aspects of their work. Machine learning algorithms ensure consistent and unbiased evaluation. AI empowers researchers to engage in data-driven discovery by efficiently processing and analyzing massive datasets. This capability is particularly valuable in fields such as genomics, environmental science, and social sciences, where large-scale data is prevalent. AI has become a cornerstone in reshaping the landscape of academic research. From data-driven insights to enhanced experimentation and collaboration, the integration of AI technologies offers unprecedented opportunities for researchers to advance knowledge, address complex challenges, and drive innovation across diverse academic disciplines. As the field continues to evolve, embracing AI responsibly and ethically remains crucial for ensuring the integrity and impact of academic research (Bergen. et al., 2019).

Various AI Tools

AI tools play a crucial role in various stages of academic research, offering solutions for data analysis, literature review, collaboration, and more. Here are some AI tools commonly used in academic research,

SCITE

Scite (https://scite.ai/) is a platform designed to help researchers discover and evaluate scientific articles using a unique approach. Scite utilizes deep learning and natural language processing to analyze scholarly articles and provide insights into the credibility and context of research findings. Scite goes beyond traditional citation analysis. It provides users with the citation context, showing whether a citing paper provides supporting or contrasting evidence to the cited work. The platform uses "smart citations" to highlight whether a citation is a supporting or disputing reference. This helps researchers quickly assess the impact and reliability of a given article. Scite extracts and categorizes citation statements, allowing users to see how a paper has been cited in terms of whether it provides evidence for or against a particular claim. The platform includes visualizations that help users understand the citation relationships between papers, providing a graphical representation of the scholarly discourse around a specific topic. Scite aims to assist in evaluating the reproducibility of research. It can highlight whether a study has been confirmed, disputed, or mentioned in subsequent research. Scite continuously expands its database of scholarly articles, covering a wide range of disciplines. Scite is designed to integrate into researchers' workflows, making it a valuable tool during literature review processes and when evaluating the reliability of scientific literature. Scite aims to contribute to the open access movement by providing free access to some of its features, making scholarly information more accessible to the research community (Brody. et al., 2021).

ELICIT

Elicit (Kung et al.,2023) is made for students, researchers from academic and independent organizations. Elicit, a no-cost AI research assistant developed by Ought, an American non-profit Machine Learning (ML) research lab, streamlines researchers' workflows using language models. Elicit effectively synthesizes evidence and extracts text, drawing from Semantic Scholar to accelerate literature reviews. Simply type your research question into the search bar, and elicit will identify top-tier papers in that field. Elicits capabilities extend beyond keyword matching, enabling it to summarize key takeaways from papers and extract crucial information into a research matrix. It is mainly used by researchers. Elicit works on different web browsers like Chrome, Microsoft Edge, Firefox. It is a tool that produces the literature review process by checking eight papers and likely to answer, extracting, and summarizing important elements based on user choice. Elicit offers a different tool that asks scholar literature in a brief format to help users by conducting literature reviews and find relative articles to find the answers for research questions (Kung et al., 2023).

TRINKA

Trinka AI (https://www.trinka.ai/) is used for grammar checking and language correction. It can check your grammar, spelling, style, and consistency, and it can also provide suggestions for how to make your writing more clear, concise, and effective. Trinka is also a useful tool for paraphrasing and summarizing text. It can help you to rephrase complex sentences into simpler ones, and it can also summarize long documents into shorter, more concise summaries. Trinka is available as a web-based application, as well as a plug-in for Microsoft Word and Google Docs. It is also available for use with LaTeX documents. Trinka is specifically designed for academic and technical writing, so it can understand the nuances of these styles of writing and provide feedback that is tailored to your needs (Petare et al., 2023).

SCHOLARCY

Scholarcy AI (https://www.scholarcy.com/) is a platform that uses artificial intelligence to assist with academic writing, summarization, and research. Scholarcy AI is designed to help researchers, students, and academics save time by automating certain aspects of the research and writing process. Scholarcy AI employs Natural Language Processing (NLP) algorithms to automatically generate concise summaries of academic papers, making it easier for researchers to quickly grasp the main points of a document. The platform identifies and highlights key information within academic papers, helping users focus on essential concepts, findings, and arguments. Scholarcy AI can assist in extracting and formatting citations, streamlining the process of compiling references for research papers. The platform helps users organize and structure their content by providing suggestions for section headings and highlighting key elements to include in different sections of a document. Scholarcy AI extracts relevant keywords from academic papers, aiding researchers in understanding the main themes and topics covered in a document. Scholarcy AI may offer integrations with reference management tools, making it convenient for users to manage and organize their references. The platform may provide writing assistance by suggesting improvements in language, style, and clarity, enhancing the overall quality of research papers. Scholars and researchers can use Scholarcy AI to expedite the literature review process by obtaining concise summaries and key insights from a large volume of academic papers. Scholarcy AI may prioritize user-friendly interfaces to ensure accessibility for a wide range of users, including those who may not have extensive technical expertise. Some versions of Scholarcy AI may include collaborative features, allowing multiple users to work on a document simultaneously or share insights. The platform may use AI-driven algorithms to analyze and understand the content of academic papers, enabling more sophisticated summarization and extraction capabilities (Howat. et al., 2021).

SEMANTIC SCHOLAR

Semantic Scholar (https://shorturl.at/ghHX8) is an academic search engine that utilizes artificial intelligence and natural language processing to provide more contextually relevant and meaningful search results in the field of scientific research. Developed by the Allen Institute for Artificial Intelligence (AI2), Semantic Scholar aims to help researchers, scientists, and academics discover and navigate scholarly literature more efficiently. Semantic Scholar uses advanced algorithms to understand the semantics of research papers, going beyond keyword matching to provide more contextually relevant search results. The platform employs NLP techniques to extract and understand the meaning of text within research papers. This enables more accurate summarization and contextualization of content. Semantic Scholar can identify and recognize entities such as authors, institutions, and key concepts within research papers, enhancing the user's ability to navigate and understand scholarly content.

The AI algorithms in Semantic Scholar extract key phrases and terms from research papers, aiding in the identification of important concepts and topics. Semantic Scholar may use graph-based representations to showcase relationships between research papers, authors, and topics. This helps users explore related work and understand the academic landscape. The platform incorporates citation analysis, allowing users to see how research papers are connected through citations. This feature helps in understanding the influence and impact of specific papers within a research domain. Semantic Scholar provides an indicator for open access papers, helping users quickly identify freely accessible content.

Researchers can use Semantic Scholar to streamline the literature review process. The platform provides insights into related work, recent publications, and key contributions in a specific field. Semantic Scholar generates author profiles, aggregating information about an author's publications, citations, and contributions, offering a comprehensive overview of their academic impact.

Semantic Scholar introduced a dedicated COVID-19 Research Explorer to help researchers navigate and discover relevant studies related to the COVID-19 pandemic. The platform may use machine learning algorithms to improve the ranking of search results, ensuring that the most relevant and impactful papers appear prominently (Fricke. et al., 2018), (Wade.et al., 2022).

CHALLENGES AND LIMITATIONS

A comparative analysis of AI capabilities and limitations provides insights into the strengths and challenges associated with artificial intelligence technologies. Let's explore in both aspects:

- Lack of Understanding and Common Sense and difficulties in handling situations that require intuitive understanding.
- *Data Bias and Discrimination:* AI models can inherit biases present in training data
- *Ethical Concerns:* AI raises ethical dilemmas, especially in decision-making processes.

Table 1. Comparative analysis of AI tools for academic research

Name of the Tool	List of Features	Free\Paid	Advantages	Disadvantages
Scite	• Citation analysis • Similarity checking	Free	• Provides context to citations • Offers visualizations for citation impact	• Limited features in the free version • Not as comprehensive as some paid alternatives
Elicit	• Find papers • Extract data from PDF • Citation information	Free\Paid	• Increased discoverability • Access to a wide range of papers • Advanced search and filtering options	• Access limitations • Cost implications • Incomplete coverage
Trinka	• Writing assistance • Plagiarism detection	Paid	• Advanced plagiarism detection • Grammar and writing suggestions	• Subscription-based model might be costly for some users • Dependency on internet connection
Scholarcy	• Automated Summarization • Reference extraction	Free	• Helps in summarizing research papers • Extracts key references	• Freemium version has limitations • May not be suitable for complex documents
Semantic Scholar	• Advanced search Capabilities • Citation network analysis	Free	• Access to a vast database of scholarly articles • Semantic search functionality	• Limited collaboration features • Some advanced features may require other tools

- *Interpretability and Explainability:* Some AI models, especially deep neural networks, lack interpretability.
- *Resource Intensive:* Training complex AI models requires significant computational resources.
- *Security Risks:* AI systems may be vulnerable to adversarial attacks and security breaches.
- *Overreliance and Job Displacement:* Widespread adoption of AI may lead to job displacement in certain sectors.
- *Limited Contextual Understanding:* AI may struggle to understand nuanced or ambiguous situations.
- *Regulatory and Legal Challenges:* The legal and regulatory framework for AI is still evolving.
- *Dependence on Data Quality:* AI models are highly dependent on the quality and representativeness of training data. (Koubaa. et al., 2023).

ETHICAL ISSUES

The integration of AI in academic research brings about various ethical considerations that need careful attention. Here are some of the key ethical issues associated with the use of AI in academic research:

- *Bias and Fairness:* AI models may inherit biases present in the training data, leading to unfair and discriminatory outcomes and the concern is the unintentional perpetuation of biases in research findings, affecting fairness and equity.
- *Transparency and Explainability: S*ome AI models, especially complex deep learning models, lack transparency and are challenging to interpret and the concern is difficulty in explaining re-

search outcomes to peers, stakeholders, or the public, raising questions about accountability and trust.

- *Informed Consent:* AI tools may process personal data without individuals' explicit consent and the concern is a violation of privacy and ethical norms, emphasizing the importance of obtaining informed consent for data collection and analysis.
- *Data Privacy:* AI systems often require access to sensitive data, raising concerns about privacy breaches, and the concern is safeguarding confidential information and ensuring compliance with data protection regulations.
- *Algorithmic Accountability:* Lack of clarity regarding who is responsible for the outcomes of AI systems and the concern is defining clear lines of responsibility and accountability for the ethical use of AI in research.
- *Security Risks:* AI applications may be vulnerable to adversarial attacks and security breaches and the concern is ensuring the robustness and security of AI systems to prevent unauthorized access and manipulation.
- *Reproducibility and Rigor:* Lack of transparency in AI models may hinder the reproducibility of research findings and the concern is upholding scientific rigor and ensuring that research can be independently validated.
- *Dual-Use Concerns*: Research outcomes and technologies developed with AI may have dual uses, including potentially harmful applications and the concern is ensuring responsible use and preventing unintended negative consequences or misuse.
- *Equitable Access to AI Tools:* Unequal access to AI technologies and resources may contribute to disparities in research capabilities and the concern is promoting equitable access to AI tools, particularly for researchers in underrepresented regions or institutions.
- *Collaboration and Open Science:* AI models trained on proprietary datasets may limit collaboration and open sharing of research and the concern is balancing the need for proprietary information with the principles of collaboration and open science.
- *Ethics in AI Research Publication:* Ethical considerations related to AI research may not always be explicitly addressed in publications and the concern is encouraging researchers to transparently report ethical considerations, potential biases, and limitations in their AI-based studies.
- *Long-Term Impact on Education and Learning:* Overreliance on AI in education may impact traditional learning experiences and the concern is balancing the integration of AI in educational settings with maintaining the human and ethical aspects of teaching and learning (Wang. et al., 2018) (Ouchchy. et al., 2020) (Stahl. et al., 2021).

FUTURE DIRECTIONS IN ACADEMIC RESEARCH

The future directions of AI in academic research are likely to be shaped by ongoing technological advancements, evolving research methodologies, and the integration of AI tools across diverse disciplines. Here are some potential future directions for AI in academic research:

- *Explainable AI (XAI)*: Enhancing the interpretability and explainability of AI models and this impact as addressing the "black box" nature of certain AI algorithms, fostering trust, and facilitating a deeper understanding of model decisions (Borboni et al,2023).

- *Ethics and Responsible AI:* Continued emphasis on ethical considerations and responsible AI practices and this impact as development of comprehensive ethical frameworks, guidelines, and standards for the ethical use of AI in research, ensuring transparency, fairness, and accountability (Jobin et al.,2019).
- *AI for Scientific Discovery:* Leveraging AI for accelerating scientific discovery and hypothesis generation and this impact as using AI to analyze complex scientific datasets, identify patterns, and discover novel relationships, potentially leading to breakthroughs in various scientific domains (Wang et al.,2023).
- *AI-Augmented Research Tools:* Integration of AI into existing research tools and platforms and this impact enhancing the capabilities of researchers by providing AI-driven assistance in literature reviews, data analysis, and experiment design (Battina et al.,2016).
- *Cross-Disciplinary Collaboration:* Facilitating increased collaboration between AI researchers and experts from various disciplines and this impact as joint efforts to address interdisciplinary challenges, combining AI expertise with domain-specific knowledge to drive innovation (Liao et al.,2020).
- *AI for Personalized Learning:* Expanding the use of AI in educational research to personalize learning experiences and this impact as tailoring educational content and strategies to individual student needs, optimizing learning outcomes (Somasundaram et al.,2020).
- *AI in Reproducible Research:* Utilizing AI to enhance the reproducibility of research findings and this impact as implementing AI-driven tools to ensure transparent and reproducible research practices, reducing the "replication crisis" (Gundersen et al.,2018).
- *AI-Driven Experimentation:* Automation of experimental design and execution using AI and this impact as accelerating the pace of experimentation, optimizing resource allocation, and improving the efficiency of research processes (Gupta et al.,2023).
- *AI in Multimodal Data Integration:* Integrating AI techniques to analyze and interpret multimodal data (e.g., text, images, and sensor data) this impact as enabling a more comprehensive understanding of complex phenomena by combining information from diverse sources (Luan, H. et al., 2020) (Zhang. et al., 2021).

CONCLUSION

The future directions of AI in academic research are likely to be shaped by ongoing technological advancements, evolving research methodologies, and the integration of AI tools across diverse disciplines. Here are some potential future directions for AI in academic. In conclusion, the integration of AI in academic research represents a transformative force with significant implications for how research is conducted, analyzed, and disseminated. The multifaceted applications of AI in academia have reshaped traditional research methodologies, offered new opportunities, and addressed challenges across various disciplines. As we reflect on the impact of AI in academic research, several key points emerge as AI tools have streamlined various aspects of the research process, from literature reviews and data analysis to experimental design and content creation. This increased efficiency allows researchers to focus more on the core aspects of their work. AI's capacity to analyze vast datasets has enabled researchers to uncover patterns, correlations, and insights that might be challenging to identify through traditional methods. This data-driven approach has the potential to accelerate scientific discovery across disciplines.

AI catalyzes collaboration between experts in AI and researchers from diverse fields. This interdisciplinary collaboration fosters the development of innovative solutions to complex problems and opens new avenues for research exploration.

The adoption of AI in academia has raised ethical considerations, including issues related to bias, transparency, and responsible use. Addressing these challenges is crucial to ensure the ethical application of AI technologies in research. AI's role in education and personalized learning has created more adaptive and customized learning experiences. It has the potential to revolutionize pedagogical approaches and cater to the individual needs of learners. AI contributes to the promotion of open science by facilitating collaboration, sharing research findings, and enhancing accessibility to knowledge. Open access initiatives, coupled with AI-driven tools, contribute to a more inclusive and collaborative research ecosystem. The future of AI in academic research is marked by ongoing technological advancements, including developments in explainable AI, quantum computing, and the integration of AI with other emerging technologies. Staying abreast of these advancements is crucial for researchers and institutions. The collaborative synergy between humans and AI systems is becoming increasingly pronounced. Researchers are leveraging AI as a complementary tool, enhancing human capabilities and contributing to more effective problem-solving. AI has the potential to address global challenges, ranging from healthcare and environmental sustainability to social issues. The collaborative and interdisciplinary nature of AI research positions it as a key player in addressing complex societal problems. The responsible use of AI in academic research requires robust governance frameworks, ethical guidelines, and ongoing discussions within the academic community. Ensuring that AI aligns with ethical principles and societal values is paramount.

REFERENCES

Advanced Grammar Checker for Academic & Professional Writing - TRINKA. (2021, July 24). https://www.trinka.ai/

AI for Research - scite.ai. (n.d.-c). scite.ai. https://scite.ai/

Al-Sarayrah, W., Al-Aiad, A., Habes, M., Elareshi, M., & Salloum, S. A. (2021, March). Improving the deaf and hard of hearing internet accessibility: JSL, text-into-sign language translator for Arabic. In *International Conference on Advanced Machine Learning Technologies and Applications* (pp. 456-468). Cham: Springer International Publishing. 10.1007/978-3-030-69717-4_43

Barth, T. J., & Arnold, E. (1999). Artificial intelligence and administrative discretion: Implications for public administration. *American Review of Public Administration*, *29*(4), 332–351. doi:10.1177/02750749922064463

Battina, D. S. (2016). AI-Augmented Automation for DevOps, a Model-Based Framework for Continuous Development in Cyber-Physical Systems. *International Journal of Creative Research Thoughts (IJCRT).*

Benedetto, L., Cremonesi, P., & Parenti, M. (2019). A virtual teaching assistant for personalized learning. *arXiv preprint arXiv:1902.09289.*

Bergen, K. J., Johnson, P. A., de Hoop, M. V., & Beroza, G. C. (2019). Machine learning for data-driven discovery in solid Earth geoscience. *Science, 363*(6433), eaau0323. doi:10.1126/science.aau0323 PMID:30898903

Borboni, A., Reddy, K. V. V., Elamvazuthi, I., AL-Quraishi, M. S., Natarajan, E., & Azhar Ali, S. S. (2023). The Expanding Role of Artificial Intelligence in Collaborative Robots for Industrial Applications: A Systematic Review of Recent Works. *Machines, 11*(1), 111. doi:10.3390/machines11010111

Brody, S. (2021). Scite. *Journal of the Medical Library Association: JMLA, 109*(4), 707. doi:10.5195/jmla.2021.1331 PMID:34858110

Cui, Z., Jing, X., Zhao, P., Zhang, W., & Chen, J. (2021). A new subspace clustering strategy for AI-based data analysis in IoT system. *IEEE Internet of Things Journal, 8*(16), 12540–12549. doi:10.1109/JIOT.2021.3056578

Daubner, S. C., Gutierrez, V., & Rodriguez, M. (2018). Introducing Students to Biochemistry Through An Inquiry-Based Curriculum Documented Using Electronic Notebooks on SciNote. *The FASEB Journal, 32*(S1), 663–667. doi:10.1096/fasebj.2018.32.1_supplement.663.7

Elish, M. C., & Boyd, D. (2018). Situating methods in the magic of Big Data and AI. *Communication Monographs, 85*(1), 57–80. doi:10.1080/03637751.2017.1375130

Engstrom, D. F., Ho, D. E., Sharkey, C. M., & Cuéllar, M. F. (2020). Government by algorithm: Artificial intelligence in federal administrative agencies. *NYU School of Law*, Public Law Research Paper, (20-54).

Erickson, L. B., Young, J. R., & Pinnegar, S. (2011). Endnote. *Studying Teacher Education, 7*(2), 215–216. doi:10.1080/17425964.2011.591192

Exner-Stöhr, M., Kopp, A., Kühne-Hellmessen, L., Oldach, L., Roth, D., & Zimmermann, A. (2017). *The potential of Artificial Intelligence in academic research at a Digital University*. Gesellschaft für Informatik.

Fahd, K., & Miah, S. J. (2023). Designing and Evaluating a Big Data Analytics Approach for predicting students' success factors. *Journal of Big Data, 10*(1), 159. doi:10.1186/s40537-023-00835-z

Fleming, A. D., Goatman, K. A., Philip, S., Prescott, G. J., Sharp, P. F., & Olson, J. A. (2010). Automated grading for diabetic retinopathy: A large-scale audit using arbitration by clinical experts. *The British Journal of Ophthalmology, 94*(12), 1606–1610. doi:10.1136/bjo.2009.176784 PMID:20858722

Ford, J., & Sutphen, R. D. (1996). Early intervention to improve attendance in elementary school for at-risk children: *A pilot program. Children & Schools, 18*(2), 95–102. doi:10.1093/cs/18.2.95

Fricke, S. (2018). Semantic scholar. *Journal of the Medical Library Association: JMLA, 106*(1), 145. doi:10.5195/jmla.2018.280

Gao, C. A., Howard, F. M., Markov, N. S., Dyer, E. C., Ramesh, S., Luo, Y., & Pearson, A. T. (2022). Comparing scientific abstracts generated by ChatGPT to original abstracts using an artificial intelligence output detector, plagiarism detector, and blinded human reviewers. BioRxiv, 2022-12. doi:10.1101/2022.12.23.521610

Ghufron, M. A., & Rosyida, F. (2018). The role of Grammarly in assessing English as a Foreign Language (EFL) writing. *Lingua Cultura, 12*(4), 395–403. doi:10.21512/lc.v12i4.4582

Grzebyk, M., Pierscieniak, A., & Stec, M. (2021). Assessment of Management Efficiency in Local Administrative Offices: Case Study Poland. *Lex Localis, 19*(2), 329–351. doi:10.4335/19.2.329-351(2021)

Gundersen, O. E., Gil, Y., & Aha, D. W. (2018). On reproducible AI: Towards reproducible research, open science, and digital scholarship in AI publications. *AI Magazine, 39*(3), 56–68. doi:10.1609/aimag.v39i3.2816

Gupta, V., & Gupta, C. (2023). Leveraging AI technologies in libraries through experimentation-driven frameworks. *Internet Reference Services Quarterly, 27*(4), 1–12. doi:10.1080/10875301.2023.2240773

Henning, V., & Reichelt, J. (2008, December). Mendeley-a last. fm for research? *In 2008 IEEE fourth international conference on eScience* (pp. 327-328). IEEE.

Howat, A. M., Mulhern, A., Logan, H. F., Redvers-Mutton, G., Routledge, C., & Clark, J. (2021). Converting Access Microbiology to an open research platform: Focus group and AI review tool research results. *Access Microbiology, 3*(4). Advance online publication. doi:10.1099/acmi.0.000232 PMID:34151179

Ip, K. (2023). Revolutionising content recommendation: The impact of AI in marketing. *Journal of AI. Robotics & Workplace Automation, 2*(4), 382–389.

Jobin, A., Ienca, M., & Vayena, E. (2019). The global landscape of AI ethics guidelines. *Nature Machine Intelligence, 1*(9), 389–399. doi:10.1038/s42256-019-0088-2

Khalil, M., & Er, E. (2023). Will ChatGPT get you caught? Rethinking of plagiarism detection. *arXiv preprint arXiv:2302.04335*. doi:10.1007/978-3-031-34411-4_32

KhanM. J.MahadeA. Investigation to Improve Decision Support Systems with the Help of Artificial Intelligence in Higher Education. *Available at* SSRN 4530480. doi:10.2139/ssrn.4530480

Kim, J., Merrill, K., Xu, K., & Sellnow, D. D. (2020). My teacher is a machine: Understanding students' perceptions of AI teaching assistants in online education. *International Journal of Human-Computer Interaction, 36*(20), 1902–1911. doi:10.1080/10447318.2020.1801227

Koubaa, A., Boulila, W., Ghouti, L., Alzahem, A., & Latif, S. (2023). Exploring ChatGPT Capabilities and Limitations: A Survey. *IEEE Access*. kssNvYB7y66y. (2023b, September 5). *Online Summarizing Tool | Flashcard Generator & Summarizer | Scholarcy*. Scholarcy | the Long-form Article Summariser. https://www.scholarcy.com/

Kung, J. Y. (2023). Elicit. *The Journal of the Canadian Health Libraries Association, 44*(1), 15.

Liao, H. T., Wang, Z., & Liu, Y. (2020, April). Exploring the cross-disciplinary collaboration: A scientometric analysis of social science research related to Artificial Intelligence and Big Data application. []. IOP Publishing.]. *IOP Conference Series. Materials Science and Engineering, 806*(1), 012019. doi:10.1088/1757-899X/806/1/012019

Liebling, D. J., Lahav, M., Evans, A., Donsbach, A., Holbrook, J., Smus, B., & Boran, L. (2020, April). Unmet needs and opportunities for mobile translation AI. *Proceedings of the 2020 CHI conference on human factors in computing systems.* 10.1145/3313831.3376261

Loai, A. T., Mehmood, R., Benkhlifa, E., & Song, H. (2016). Mobile cloud computing model and big data analysis for healthcare applications. *IEEE Access : Practical Innovations, Open Solutions, 4*, 6171–6180. doi:10.1109/ACCESS.2016.2613278

Luan, H., Geczy, P., Lai, H., Gobert, J., Yang, S. J., Ogata, H., Baltes, J., Guerra, R., Li, P., & Tsai, C. C. (2020). Challenges and future directions of big data and artificial intelligence in education. *Frontiers in Psychology, 11*, 580820. doi:10.3389/fpsyg.2020.580820 PMID:33192896

Malik, A. R., Pratiwi, Y., Andajani, K., Numertayasa, I. W., Suharti, S., Darwis, A., & Marzuki. (2023). Exploring Artificial Intelligence in Academic Essay: Higher Education Student's Perspective. *International Journal of Educational Research Open, 5*, 100296. doi:10.1016/j.ijedro.2023.100296

Maney, K. (2003). *The maverick and his machine: Thomas Watson, Sr. and the making of IBM*. John Wiley & Sons.

Miller, T. (2019). Explanation in artificial intelligence: Insights from the social sciences. *Artificial Intelligence, 267*, 1–38. doi:10.1016/j.artint.2018.07.007

Nurshatayeva, A., Page, L. C., White, C. C., & Gehlbach, H. (2020). Proactive student support using artificially intelligent conversational chatbots: The importance of targeting the technology. *EdWorking paper, Annenberg University https://www. edwor kingp apers. com/sites/defau lt/files/ai20-208. pdf.*

Ouchchy, L., Coin, A., & Dubljević, V. (2020). AI in the headlines: The portrayal of the ethical issues of artificial intelligence in the media. *AI & Society, 35*(4), 927–936. doi:10.1007/s00146-020-00965-5

Pataranutaporn, P., Danry, V., Leong, J., Punpongsanon, P., Novy, D., Maes, P., & Sra, M. (2021). AI-generated characters for supporting personalized learning and well-being. *Nature Machine Intelligence, 3*(12), 1013–1022. doi:10.1038/s42256-021-00417-9

Petare, P. A. (2023). 13 Artificial Intelligence Tools for Education: Exploring The New Horizons For Teaching Learning Process. *Exploring New Horizons*, 77.

Randhawa, G. K., & Jackson, M. (2020, January). The role of artificial intelligence in learning and professional development for healthcare professionals. *Healthcare Management Forum, 33*(1), 19–24. doi:10.1177/0840470419869032 PMID:31802725

Richardson, M., & Clesham, R. (2021). Rise of the machines? The evolving role of Artificial Intelligence (AI) technologies in high stakes assessment. *London Review of Education, 19*(1), 1–13. doi:10.14324/LRE.19.1.09

Russell, S. J., & Norvig, P. (2010). *Artificial intelligence a modern approach.*

Semantic Scholar | AI-Powered Research Tool. (n.d.-b). https://shorturl.at/ghHX8

Shemshack, A., & Spector, J. M. (2020). A systematic literature review of personalized learning terms. *Smart Learning Environments, 7*(1), 1–20. doi:10.1186/s40561-020-00140-9

Somasundaram, M., Junaid, K. M., & Mangadu, S. (2020). Artificial intelligence (AI) enabled intelligent quality management system (IQMS) for personalized learning path. *Procedia Computer Science*, *172*, 438–442. doi:10.1016/j.procs.2020.05.096

Stahl, B. C., & Stahl, B. C. (2021). Ethical issues of AI. Artificial Intelligence for a better future: An ecosystem perspective on the ethics of AI and emerging digital technologies, 35-53.

Strobel, G., Schoormann, T., Banh, L., & Möller, F. (2023). Artificial Intelligence for Sign Language Translation–A Design Science Research Study. *Communications of the Association for Information Systems*, *52*(1), 33. doi:10.17705/1CAIS.05303

Toğaçar, M. (2022). The Contribution of AI-Based Approaches in the Determination of CO. *Artificial Intelligence for Renewable Energy and Climate Change*, 173.

Votto, A. M., Valecha, R., Najafirad, P., & Rao, H. R. (2021). Artificial intelligence in tactical human resource management: A systematic literature review. *International Journal of Information Management Data Insights*, *1*(2), 100047. doi:10.1016/j.jjimei.2021.100047

Wade, A. D. (2022, April). The semantic scholar academic graph (s2ag*). In Companion Proceedings of the Web Conference 2022* (pp. 739-739). Academic Press.

Wang, H., Fu, T., Du, Y., Gao, W., Huang, K., Liu, Z., Chandak, P., Liu, S., Van Katwyk, P., Deac, A., Anandkumar, A., Bergen, K., Gomes, C. P., Ho, S., Kohli, P., Lasenby, J., Leskovec, J., Liu, T.-Y., Manrai, A., ... Zitnik, M. (2023). Scientific discovery in the age of artificial intelligence. *Nature*, *620*(7972), 47–60. doi:10.1038/s41586-023-06221-2 PMID:37532811

Wang, Q., Saha, K., Gregori, E., Joyner, D., & Goel, A. (2021, May). Towards mutual theory of mind in human-ai interaction: How language reflects what students perceive about a virtual teaching assistant. In *Proceedings of the 2021 CHI conference on human factors in computing systems* (pp. 1-14). 10.1145/3411764.3445645

Wang, W., & Siau, K. (2018). Ethical and moral issues with AI.

Xiao, W., Zhao, H., Pan, H., Song, Y., Zheng, V. W., & Yang, Q. (2019, July). Beyond personalization: Social content recommendation for creator equality and consumer satisfaction. *In Proceedings of the 25th ACM SIGKDD International Conference on Knowledge Discovery & Data Mining* (pp. 235-245). 10.1145/3292500.3330965

Yildirim, T. M., Khoramnia, R., Masyk, M., Son, H. S., Auffarth, G. U., & Mayer, C. S. (2020). Aesthetics of iris reconstruction with a custom-made artificial iris prosthesis. *PLoS One*, *15*(8), e0237616. doi:10.1371/journal.pone.0237616 PMID:32790803

Zawacki-Richter, O., Marín, V. I., Bond, M., & Gouverneur, F. (2019). Systematic review of research on artificial intelligence applications in higher education–where are the educators? *International Journal of Educational Technology in Higher Education*, *16*(1), 1–27. doi:10.1186/s41239-019-0171-0

Zhang, K., & Aslan, A. B. (2021). AI technologies for education: Recent research & future directions. *Computers and Education: Artificial Intelligence*, *2*, 100025. doi:10.1016/j.caeai.2021.100025

Zhang, L., Basham, J. D., & Yang, S. (2020). Understanding the implementation of personalized learning: A research synthesis. *Educational Research Review*, *31*, 100339. doi:10.1016/j.edurev.2020.100339

Chapter 2
Evolution of AI in Academic Research

Mansi Batra Kawatra
https://orcid.org/0009-0004-2146-8662
GLA University, India

ABSTRACT

The progression of artificial intelligence (AI) in academic study is a fascinating exploration of the past, characterized by important achievements, revolutionary advancements, and a relentless pursuit to expand the limits of human understanding. Within the present academic environment, artificial intelligence (AI) has a ubiquitous influence that can be found in a variety of fields, including instruction, research, and administration. Individualized learning experiences are provided by intelligent tutoring systems, which are powered by machine learning algorithms. These systems are able to adjust to the specific requirements of each learner. Applications of artificial intelligence in data analysis, predictive modeling, and pattern recognition are beneficial to research processes because they speed up the discovery of scientific knowledge across an array of fields. The primary aim is to explore the historical development, pivotal contributions, emerging trends, and future directions of AI within the academic realm.

1. INTRODUCTION

The domain of artificial intelligence (AI) has made significant progress since its origin, transitioning from the realm of speculative fiction to a progressively essential technology that is revolutionizing various industries and impacting lives on a global scale. Because to advancements in machine learning, natural language processing, and computer vision, artificial intelligence (AI) has transitioned from being a futuristic aspiration to a present-day actuality (Marr, B.,2023).

The increasing fascination of scholars and practitioners in AI has led to a wide range of study subjects being investigated in large volumes of scholarly material published in top research publications (Yogesh K. et al, 2023).

The progression of Artificial Intelligence (AI) in academic study is a fascinating exploration of the past, characterized by important achievements, revolutionary advancements, and a relentless pursuit to

DOI: 10.4018/979-8-3693-1798-3.ch002

expand the limits of human understanding. This chapter explores the extensive history of AI at academic institutions, explaining its development, impact on research, and its role in establishing the future of AI in academia.

2. THE EMERGENCE OF AI IN ACADEMIA

The origins of artificial intelligence can be traced back to the early 20th century, coinciding with the introduction of computer science and the earliest emergence of machine intelligence. Conversely, the 1950s and 1960s marked the emergence of artificial intelligence as a distinct academic discipline.

- **Alan Turing and the Turing Test:** Alan Turing, via his pioneering research on computing and the development of the Turing machine, established the fundamental principles of artificial intelligence. His work serves as the bedrock for the advancement of machine intelligence. The Turing Test, proposed by Turing, serves as a benchmark in the area to assess a machine's capacity to demonstrate intelligence similar to that of a person.
- **John McCarthy and Dartmouth Workshop:** John McCarthy, a pioneer of artificial intelligence, is credited with coining the term "Artificial Intelligence" in 1956. McCarthy is recognized as a pioneer in the subject. McCarthy, together with a number of other scholars, organized the Dartmouth Workshop, which is widely regarded as the birthplace of artificial intelligence. The goal of the workshop was to look into the possibilities of building intelligent robots.
- **Early Research and Symbolic AI**: The initial AI community in academics mostly focused on symbolic AI, aiming to create intelligent computers through symbolic manipulation and logical reasoning. Researchers were the inventors of expert systems, knowledge representation techniques, and rule-based systems. During this period, John McCarthy developed LISP, a computer language that played a pivotal role in the field of artificial intelligence.

3. AI WINTER AND THE RISE OF MACHINE LEARNING

An AI winter refers to a phase in the history of artificial intelligence when there is a decline in financial support and enthusiasm for research in the field of artificial intelligence (AI Expert Newsletter, 9 November 2013). field has seen multiple cycles of exaggerated excitement, subsequent disillusionment and critique, further reductions in financial support, and subsequent revival of interest, occurring years or even decades later.

The 1970s and 1980s were marked by a phenomena known colloquially as the "AI winter." As a result of unmet expectations, the area of AI saw a significant drop in funding and interest during this time period. Academia had an important role in reviving AI by refocusing emphasis on machine learning, neural networks, and statistical techniques.

- **The AI Winter:** The AI winter was a challenging period for AI research as the initial expectations of creating intelligent robots were not realized. Financial support diminished, leading to a prevailing feeling of hopelessness among scholars. This stage pushed AI researchers to reassess their methodologies and transition towards more practical and data-centric approaches.

- **Machine Learning Resurgence**: Academic researchers initiated an investigation into machine learning and its several subfields, including supervised and unsupervised learning. There is a growing interest among individuals in utilizing data to train computers for the purpose of making predictions and judgments. This change in viewpoint laid the foundation for several advancements in artificial intelligence that followed.
- **Geoffrey Hinton and Neural Networks:** Scholar and academic researcher Geoffrey Hinton was instrumental in the resurgence of neural networks in the late 20th century. His pivotal contributions to the advancement of backpropagation and deep learning were instrumental in driving the deep learning revolution, a profound paradigm shift in the field of artificial intelligence.

4. THE DEEP LEARNING REVOLUTION

With the turn of the 21st century came the deep learning revolution, an enormous paradigm upheaval in the study of artificial intelligence. A substantial progression in computational hardware capabilities and the availability of vast datasets occurred during this period, facilitating the training of intricate neural networks. Academic researchers have achieved significant progress in fields including image recognition, natural language processing, and reinforcement learning, often in collaboration with industry.

- **Image Recognition**: The field of image identification was transformed by deep learning, specifically convolutional neural networks (CNNs). Academic researchers have established models in conjunction with technology enterprises that have effectively attained levels of performance comparable to those exhibited by humans in tasks like object recognition and image categorization.
- **Natural Language Processing**: Deep learning techniques, such as transformers and recurrent neural networks (RNNs), have brought about a significant paradigm shift in the domains of natural language processing (NLP), encompassing language production, sentiment analysis, and machine translation. Owing to scholarly research in this domain, algorithms capable of comprehending and generating text that closely resembles human language have been developed.
- **Reinforcement Learning**: Reinforcement learning made significant advancements during the period of deep learning. Institutions and university researchers have developed algorithms that have outperformed human capabilities in challenging games like Go and video games.
- **Frameworks for Deep Learning:** In academia, TensorFlow and PyTorch, two open-source frameworks designed for deep learning, have been implemented extensively. These instruments empowered researchers to construct and evaluate complex neural network architectures.

5. AI ETHICS AND FAIRNESS

The widespread adoption of AI technology in various fields has made it crucial for academia to play a central role in addressing the ethical issues associated with AI. Academic institutions have launched inquiries into the ethical implications of artificial intelligence, namely examining justice, accountability, transparency, and the mitigation of bias.

- **Fairness and Bias Mitigation**: The academic community has developed methodologies to identify and mitigate any biases that might exist within AI systems. This is particularly crucial in fields like criminal justice, lending, employment, and recruitment, where biased AI algorithms have the capacity to perpetuate socioeconomic disparities.
- **AI Ethics Guidelines**: Academic institutions, along with industry and governmental entities, have established AI ethical principles and frameworks to ensure the responsible progress and application of AI technologies. These frameworks place a high importance on ensuring that artificial intelligence is used in a responsible and ethical manner, with a focus on accountability and transparency, across many applications.

6. INTERDISCIPLINARY RESEARCH

The field of academic AI research has experienced substantial advancement, becoming a highly interdisciplinary realm that integrates knowledge from computer science, mathematics, neuroscience, psychology, linguistics, and other related fields. Interdisciplinary cooperation have helped the development of AI applications in diverse disciplines like as healthcare, economics, social sciences, and environmental conservation.

Healthcare: Academic researchers have been leading the way in implementing artificial intelligence (AI) in healthcare, working along with medical practitioners. Machine learning is utilized in health monitoring, drug discovery, diagnostics, and individualized treatment regimens.

In the field of **economics and social sciences**, artificial intelligence (AI) has been utilized to provide support in policy recommendations, data analysis, and modeling. AI is employed in academic study across several fields to get a more profound comprehension of complex economic and social systems.

Environmental Conservation: AI researchers collaborate with environmental scientists to utilize machine learning for the analysis and prediction of ecological changes, wildlife observation, and climate pattern monitoring. The application of AI shows potential in assisting the mitigation of environmental problems.

7. CHALLENGES AND CONSIDERATIONS

Pursuing AI research in university might be challenging. As the field continues to evolve, several significant concerns and focal points have emerged:

Funding: Sustaining financial support for AI research is challenging. Academic institutions consistently encounter a predicament: they require increasingly larger funds to sustain research, gather data, and stay abreast of the latest computer systems.

Ethical Considerations: It is imperative to closely monitor the ethical ramifications of AI, such as privacy infringement, transparency, and prejudice. Universities play a significant role in educating policymakers and academics about the ethical dilemmas associated with AI research and development.

Rapid advancements in technology significantly impact the field of AI research, posing a constant challenge for academics to stay abreast of the latest discoveries.

Quantum Computing: Quantum computing is an emerging field that has the potential to revolutionize the study of artificial intelligence. It has inspired computer scientists, engineers and physicists, and the potential of its application is undeniably altering the current information technology (IT) landscape (Corcoles, A.D., et. al .2020) Academics are now researching quantum algorithms, quantum machine learning, and their implications for tackling complex issues.

Ensuring the safety and security of AI technologies is of paramount importance, particularly when they are employed in critical systems. Academic academics are currently investigating methods to safeguard AI systems against cyber threats and develop robust AI programs that are impervious to failure.

International collaboration is essential in the field of AI due to the global nature of AI research. Increasingly, scholars worldwide are disseminating knowledge, resources, and optimal methodologies.

AI for Social Good: Universities are dedicated to utilizing artificial intelligence (AI) to address societal challenges such as poverty, inequality, limited access, and crisis response. Artificial intelligence experts and humanitarian organizations are increasingly collaborating.

The future of AI in academia has great promise. Researchers from several disciplines are collaborating to explore novel approaches and address ethical and social challenges in AI, while also investigating emerging technology.

CONCLUSION

The continuous advancement of artificial intelligence (AI) in academic research is an intricate and ever-changing procedure that encompasses the possibilities and responsibilities that come with this groundbreaking technology. Academic institutions have been pivotal in the development of the area of artificial intelligence, from its early stages with symbolic AI to the recent deep learning revolution and the careful improvement of AI systems. The field of academic AI research is advancing towards the creation of intelligent systems that enhance human existence, address global challenges, and shape the trajectory of future human knowledge. The presence of artificial intelligence (AI) in academia is marked by the merging of collaboration, ethical considerations, and creativity. It has the potential to create a promising future filled with limitless possibilities.

REFERENCES

Corcoles, A. D., Kandala, A., Javadi-Abhari, A., McClure, D. T., Cross, A. W., Temme, K., Nation, P. D., Steffen, M., & Gambetta, J. M. (2020). Challenges and opportunities of near-term quantum computing systems. *Proceedings of the IEEE, 108*(8), 1338–1352. doi:10.1109/JPROC.2019.2954005

Dwivedi, Y. K., Sharma, A., Rana, N. P., Giannakis, M., Goel, P., & Dutot, V. (2023). Evolution of artificial intelligence research in Technological Forecasting and Social Change: Research topics, trends, and future directions, *Technological Forecasting and Social Change*, 192. https://www.sciencedirect.com/science/article/pii/S0040162523002640 doi:10.1016/j.techfore.2023.122579

Marr, B. (2023). The Evolution Of AI: Transforming The World One Algorithm At A Time. Retrieved from https://bernardmarr.com/the-evolution-of-ai-transforming-the-world-one-algorithm-at-a-time/

Chapter 3
Augmenting Research: The Role of Artificial Intelligence in Recognizing Topics and Ideas

Vivek Agrawal
https://orcid.org/0000-0001-7665-7103
Institute of Business Management, GLA University, Mathura, India

Shivam Bhardwaj
https://orcid.org/0000-0001-5327-7802
Institute of Business Management, GLA University, Mathura, India

Neeraj Pathak
Institute of Business Management, GLA University, Mathura, India

Jitendra Kumar Dixit
Institute of Business Management, GLA University, Mathura, India

Sucheta Agarwal
https://orcid.org/0000-0001-6525-3007
Institute of Business Management, GLA University, Mathura, India

Mujtaba M. Momin
https://orcid.org/0000-0003-2601-1480
College of Business Administration, American University of the Middle East, Kuwait

ABSTRACT

The growing power of artificial intelligence (AI) is fundamentally altering the landscape of academic research. AI-powered tools are streamlining tasks like literature reviews, manuscript drafting, and reference generation, empowering researchers to delve deeper into their work and foster innovation within their fields. Natural language processing (NLP) capabilities of AI tools facilitate rapid and comprehensive literature reviews, identifying emerging trends, gaps, and interconnected themes. This integration of AI in academic research signifies a paradigm shift, offering unprecedented opportunities for exploration and discovery. However, as AI tools become more commonplace, reviewers and editors must maintain vigilance. While these tools enhance efficiency, there's a risk that their use may compromise the scientific integrity of research. Therefore, striking a balance between leveraging AI's advantages and preserving the rigor of scientific discourse is imperative.

DOI: 10.4018/979-8-3693-1798-3.ch003

1. INTRODUCTION

The world of academic research stands at the precipice of a significant paradigm shift driven by the growing power of AI (Gendron et al., 2022). No longer relegated to the realm of futuristic fantasies, AI tools are rapidly becoming integral to the research workflow, empowering researchers with unprecedented capabilities to navigate vast information oceans and identify both research gaps and burgeoning trends (Pigola et al., 2023). This chapter delves into the transformative potential of AI in recognizing topics and ideas, a cornerstone of the research process.

Traditionally, the identification and definition of research topics have relied on a confluence of existing knowledge, intuition, and painstaking manual literature review (Ahmad et al., 2022). While fundamental, this approach can be time-consuming and susceptible to the inherent limitations of human cognition. AI, on the other hand, presents a compelling alternative by leveraging its ability to analyze massive text datasets and unearth patterns, connections, and hidden themes (Chiu et al., 2023). This adeptness at recognizing topics and ideas within vast information troves empowers researchers to expand the scope of inquiry, identify emerging trends, and refine research questions.

The academic landscape is experiencing an information deluge. The sheer volume of published research articles continues to explode exponentially, making it increasingly challenging for researchers to stay abreast of current developments within their fields (Golan, 2023). Traditional methods of literature review, the cornerstone of effective research, are buckling under the pressure. Manual searching, once a viable approach, becomes increasingly inefficient with each passing year. Keyword-based searches, while seemingly efficient, often miss relevant studies due to the inherent limitations of keywords capturing the nuances of research topics (Adams and Chuah, 2022). This information overload creates a significant bottleneck, hindering researchers' ability to identify the most impactful work, uncover hidden connections across disciplines, and ultimately, propel their research endeavors forward.

In this situation, AI offers a beacon of hope, promising to revolutionize research workflows by leveraging its capabilities in Natural Language Processing (NLP) (Altmäe et al., 2023). AI-powered tools equipped with NLP can automate tedious tasks like literature search, information extraction, and even preliminary analysis. The study envisions a world where AI can scour vast databases of research articles, identify relevant studies based on specific research questions, and even summarize key findings – all within a fraction of the time it would take a human researcher (Gilat and Cole, 2023). This newfound efficiency frees up valuable time for researchers to delve deeper into the intricacies of their chosen field, explore innovative research avenues, and ultimately contribute to the advancement of knowledge.

The study will embark on an exploration of the diverse AI techniques employed for topic recognition, including text analysis, topic modeling, and the intricacies of natural language processing (NLP) (Chen et al., 2020). It will meticulously dissect the strengths and limitations of these techniques, while simultaneously elucidating how they can be effectively woven into the research workflow. Furthermore, it will address the ethical considerations surrounding AI-assisted research, such as the potential for biases within datasets and algorithms (Salvango et al., 2023). By critically evaluating the role of AI in recognizing topics and ideas, the study aspires to contribute to the creation of a more efficient, comprehensive, and profoundly innovative research landscape.

2. THE EVOLUTION OF ARTIFICIAL INTELLIGENCE (AI) AND ITS INTEGRATION WITH ACADEMIC RESEARCH

The evolution of AI spans several decades, beginning with its conceptualization in the 1950s and progressing through various stages of development (Cain, 2023). In the 1950s, the foundation of AI was laid with the introduction of the Turing Test, marking the formalization of AI research during the Dartmouth Conference in 1956, led by pioneers like John McCarthy and Marvin Minsky (Dönmez et al., 2023). During the 1960s-1970s, the focus shifted towards expert systems, aiming to replicate human expertise in specific domains. The 1980s-1990s witnessed significant advancements in knowledge representation and natural language processing. The late 1990s to the 2000s saw a resurgence of machine learning techniques, and the 2010s marked a pivotal moment with the widespread adoption of deep learning methods, particularly neural networks. Key advancements in this era include models such as BERT and GPT, which have made substantial progress in understanding context, semantics, and nuances in language (Kasneci et al., 2023). These state-of-the-art AI models leverage sophisticated architectures, enabling them to excel in recognizing various themes and concepts with exceptional accuracy and efficiency.

This continuous journey of innovation and refinement has culminated in the development of advanced models capable of sophisticated language understanding and recognition tasks, fundamentally altering academic methodologies (Kenwright, 2024). AI-powered tools streamline tasks like literature reviews, manuscript drafting, and reference generation. This integration of AI simplifies the intricate processes involved in academic research, freeing researchers to delve deeper into their work and foster innovation within their fields (Thompson et al., 2023).

Natural language processing (NLP) capabilities of AI tools facilitate rapid and comprehensive literature reviews, identifying emerging trends, gaps, and interconnected themes (Roberts, 2023). They excel at uncovering hidden patterns within vast datasets, enabling researchers to identify unexplored areas and anticipate the trajectory of their disciplines. Personalized research recommendations, driven by machine learning algorithms, understand researchers' preferences and past interests (Khabib, 2022). This approach enables AI systems to suggest relevant articles, conferences, and potential collaborators, fostering discoveries and interdisciplinary connections. Semantic search powered by AI provides precise and contextually relevant results, while knowledge graphs map intricate relationships between concepts, offering a holistic understanding of research domains (Mohammed et al., 2023).

3. THE EVOLVING LANDSCAPE OF ACADEMIC RESEARCH

The explosion of research publications in recent years has fundamentally altered the research landscape. Scientific databases like Scopus, Web of Science, etc. showcase this exponential growth, making it increasingly challenging for researchers to stay abreast of current developments within their fields. This information overload creates difficulties in filtering relevant information from vast datasets and identifying the most impactful research.

Traditional methods of literature review, such as manual searching and keyword-based approaches, often struggle to keep pace with the ever-increasing volume of research output. Keyword-based searches, for instance, can miss relevant studies due to variations in terminology, while manual searching becomes increasingly inefficient with the ever-growing body of research. The integration of AI in academic research signifies a paradigm shift, offering unprecedented opportunities for exploration and discovery (Chen et al., 2020). By harnessing AI's capabilities, scholars can propel their research endeavors into new realms, fostering a future where the synergy between human ingenuity and AI reshapes the landscape of knowledge creation.

However, as AI tools become more commonplace, reviewers and editors must maintain vigilance. While these tools enhance efficiency, there's a risk that their use may compromise the scientific integrity of research (Jaiswal et al., 2021). Therefore, striking a balance between leveraging AI's advantages and preserving the rigor of scientific discourse is imperative. Responsible and judicious use of AI tools requires ongoing attention to ensure the quality and reliability of scientific publications remain uncompromised amidst technological advancements (Garbuio and Lin, 2021). However, challenges and ethical considerations, including data privacy, algorithmic biases, and transparency in AI-driven processes, must be addressed.

4. ARTIFICIAL INTELLIGENCE FOR RESEARCH: A GAME CHANGER

AI is poised to revolutionize research workflows by offering a powerful toolkit for analyzing and understanding the vast amount of textual data available (Zawacki-Richter et al., 2019; Dergaa et al., 2023). Natural Language Processing (NLP), a subfield of AI, equips machines with the ability to process and understand human language. This empowers AI-powered tools to perform a variety of tasks crucial to research.

One key area of impact is text classification and topic modelling (Golan et al., 2023). AI algorithms can automatically categorize research articles based on their topics, making it easier for researchers to identify relevant themes and trends within a specific field. Additionally, AI can extract key concepts, ideas, and entities (like names, locations, and dates) from research articles. This information extraction and entity recognition provides researchers with a deeper understanding of the content they're studying. AI can even analyze the overall sentiment or opinion expressed within research literature through sentiment analysis, offering insights into the prevailing attitudes or controversies surrounding a particular topic.

The applications of AI in recognizing research topics and ideas are extensive (Hoffman, 2017). AI can automate literature searches based on keywords and research questions, efficiently searching vast databases and identifying relevant articles with higher accuracy than traditional methods. AI can also summarize key findings and extract key concepts from retrieved literature, saving researchers valuable time and effort. Looking beyond literature reviews, AI can analyze vast datasets of research articles to identify emerging trends and future directions within specific fields. This trend analysis helps researchers stay ahead of the curve and pinpoint potential research gaps or areas for further investigation (Duymaz and Tekin, 2024). AI can even uncover hidden connections and relationships between seemingly disparate research topics, fostering interdisciplinary collaboration and innovation.

AI can also assist researchers in gaining a deeper understanding of complex research concepts by analyzing a broad range of research articles on a particular topic (Dönmez et al., 2023). This concept exploration allows researchers to identify various perspectives, interpretations, and related concepts. They can leverage AI to discover relevant resources and scholarly works, enriching their understanding and exploration of a specific concept. Perhaps most interestingly, AI can potentially assist researchers in formulating research questions and hypotheses. By analyzing relationships and patterns within existing research, it can suggest novel research questions based on unexplored areas or conflicting findings. It can also highlight potential connections between seemingly unrelated research areas, sparking new research avenues and fostering innovative thinking (Ginting et al., 2023). Furthermore AI can significantly improve the discoverability of relevant research and facilitate the exploration of research topics within a broader context through knowledge organization. It can even be used to build knowledge graphs that map intricate relationships between research concepts and findings. These knowledge graphs provide researchers with a holistic understanding of a particular field and its interconnected knowledge base.

5. STEPS TO USE AI FOR RECOGNIZING TOPICS AND IDEAS IN ACADEMIC RESEARCH

(i). Define Your Research Focus:

- ◦ **Brainstorm Broadly:** Before diving into the AI, spend some time brainstorming potential research areas or questions. Jot down anything that sparks your interest within your field.
- ◦ **Refine and Narrow:** Once you have a broad list, choose a specific area or question you'd like to explore further. This provides a starting point for the AI tool and ensures your research stays focused.

(ii). Select the Right AI Tool:

- ◦ **Consider Your Needs:** Different AI content generators have varying strengths (Refer to Table 1).

(iii). Craft a Tailored Prompt:

- ◦ **Start with Background:** Briefly introduce your chosen research area or question.
- ◦ **Specify Your Request:** Clearly state how you want the AI to assist you. Here are some specific prompts based on your needs:
  - ▪ **Keyword and Topic Generation:** "Generate a list of 10 keywords or subtopics related to [your research area]".
  - ▪ **Research Summary:** "Summarize the key findings from recent research on [your research question]". (Specify a timeframe if needed)
  - ▪ **Identify Research Gaps:** "Analyze current research on [your research area] and identify any potential gaps or unexplored areas".
  - ▪ **Brainstorm Research Questions:** "Based on current trends in [your research area], suggest 5 new research questions for further investigation".
- ◦ **Refine Based on Outputs:** Start with a basic prompt and adjust it based on the AI's initial response. The AI might suggest interesting new angles or refine your initial topic focus.

(iv). Analyze and Evaluate the AI Outputs:

- ◦ **Relevance Assessment:** Carefully evaluate whether the generated ideas or topics align with your initial research focus.
- ◦ **Accuracy Check:** Don't blindly accept information, especially statistics or specific claims. Fact-check these using credible academic sources.
- ◦ **Completeness Understanding:** Recognize that AI outputs are a starting point, not a finished product. You'll likely need to conduct further research to develop strong arguments and evidence for your chosen topic.

Table 1. AI tools for academic research

AI Tool	Category	Specific Uses
Scholarcy	Literature Review & Knowledge Management	Summarizes & extracts key information, identifies figures & tables, recognizes concepts, citation management
Scite	Literature Review & Citation Management	Analyzes articles, checks citation accuracy, visualizes citation landscape, suggests citation formats
Trinka	Writing & Editing	Grammar & language correction for academic writing
Mendeley	Reference Management & Collaboration	Manages & organizes PDFs, creates bibliographies, facilitates note-taking & annotation, collaborative research projects
Zotero	Reference Management & Collaboration	Like Mendeley, user-friendly for organizing papers, citations, and collaboration
Research Rabbit	Literature Review & Discovery	Research paper discovery & organization, categorized collections ("research Spotify")
Elicit	Literature Review & Trend Analysis	Analyzes articles to identify research gaps, trends, and connections between topics
Consensus	Literature Review & Knowledge Synthesis	Compiles information from research & peer-reviewed articles, offers a comprehensive understanding of a topic
Mendeley	Reference Management & Collaboration	Manages & organizes PDFs, creates bibliographies, facilitates note-taking & annotation, collaborative research projects
Zotero	Reference Management & Collaboration	Similar to Mendeley, user-friendly for organizing papers, citations, and collaboration
OpenRead	Reading & Comprehension	Interactive platform for engaging with academic formats, Q&A systems, "Paper Espresso" for faster literature reviews
Writeful	Writing & Editing	AI-powered writing assistant for academic research, checks grammar, plagiarism, and style
Paperpile	Reference Management & Citation Management	Organizes PDFs, creates bibliographies, integrates with Google Docs and other writing platforms
Quillbot	Paraphrasing & Summarization	Rewrites sentences and paragraphs while maintaining meaning, helps avoid plagiarism
Grammarly	Writing & Editing	Grammar and plagiarism checker, offers suggestions for clarity and style improvement
ChatGPT	Large Language Models (LLMs) for Creative Exploration & Brainstorming	Generates different creative text formats to brainstorm research ideas and explore diverse angles within your study area.
Gemini	Large Language Models (LLMs) for Creative Exploration & Brainstorming	Offers strong text generation, Integrates with Google Scholar for research-oriented brainstorming.

Source: Created by authors

(v). Leverage AI for Deeper Exploration:

- **Targeted Analysis:** Once you have a list of potential topics, use the AI tool to delve deeper into specific areas.
  - For example, ask the AI to analyze a recent article related to an interesting topic you identified.
  - Use the AI to explore connections between seemingly disparate research areas within your domain.
- **Refine Your Research Question:** As you explore with the AI, your research question might become more refined or even shift direction entirely. This is a natural part of the research process. Don't be afraid to adapt your initial question based on new insights.

(vi). Maintain a Critical and Curious Mind:

- **Don't Be Overly Reliant:** Remember, AI is a tool to assist you, not replace your critical thinking skills. Question the AI's outputs and conduct your research to verify information and develop your ideas further.
- **Embrace New Discoveries:** The AI might lead you down unexpected paths – embrace them! New discoveries can often lead to groundbreaking research.
- **Document Your Process:** Keep track of your interactions with the AI tool, including the prompts you used and the outputs you received. This will help you stay organized and reference the AI's contribution to your research journey.

6. BENEFITS AND CHALLENGES OF AI-AUGMENTED RESEARCH

While AI integration in research offers a multitude of benefits, challenges also need to be addressed. On the positive side, AI automates tedious tasks like literature search and information extraction. This frees up researchers' valuable time to focus on higher-level analysis and creative endeavors. Additionally, AI-powered tools can analyze vast amounts of data with greater accuracy and completeness compared to traditional methods. This leads to more comprehensive and insightful research findings (Chen et al., 2020). Furthermore, AI can help researchers uncover hidden patterns and connections within data. This has the potential to lead to the discovery of new research questions, unexplored areas, and innovative solutions (Golan et al., 2023). AI can also facilitate collaboration across disciplines by enabling researchers to discover connections between seemingly disparate fields. Additionally, AI tools can streamline knowledge sharing by automatically organizing and summarizing research findings. Finally, AI excels at analyzing large datasets, uncovering hidden patterns, and identifying relationships that might be missed by human researchers. This allows researchers to gain a more comprehensive understanding of their field and explore new research avenues.

However, alongside these benefits, there are challenges to consider. The effectiveness of AI tools heavily relies on the quality and representativeness of the data used to train them. Biases within the training data can be reflected in the AI's outputs, potentially leading to skewed results or missed opportunities (Lund et al., 2023). While AI can be a powerful tool, researchers must maintain a healthy balance. Over-reliance on AI for tasks like literature review or hypothesis generation can lead to a decline in critical thinking skills and a reduced ability to independently evaluate research findings (Mijwil et al., 2023). The use of AI in research also raises ethical concerns regarding transparency and explainability of AI outputs (Curtis, 2023). Researchers need to understand how AI arrives at its conclusions and ensure that the tools they use are unbiased and ethically sound (Jobin et al., 2019). Finally, access to advanced AI tools can be a barrier for some researchers, particularly those affiliated with institutions with limited resources.

7. THE FUTURE OF AI IN RESEARCH

The future of AI in research is brimming with exciting possibilities that promise to revolutionize the way we approach discovery. A key area of focus will be on improving the accuracy and explainability of AI models for recognizing research topics and ideas. This will allow researchers to have more trust in the information AI generates, while also gaining valuable insights into the reasoning behind AI's recommendations (Liu et al., 2021).

Furthermore, as AI technology continues to mature, we can expect to see the development of specialized tools tailored to the specific needs of different research disciplines. These tools will leverage in-depth knowledge of each field to provide researchers with even more targeted and effective support. Imagine AI assistants that can analyze legal documents for a law researcher or decipher complex protein structures for a biologist. The possibilities are truly endless.

The future of research won't be defined by AI replacing researchers, but rather by a powerful collaboration between human and machine intelligence (Wachter et al., 2020). AI will excel at processing massive datasets and identifying patterns, while researchers will continue to leverage their critical thinking skills to evaluate findings, formulate research questions, and generate creative solutions. This seamless integration of AI with existing research tools and platforms will create a more holistic research experience, empowering researchers to achieve greater success. In essence, the future of research lies in a partnership between human intuition and the immense potential of AI.

8. KEY TAKEAWAYS

The ever-increasing volume of research literature presents a significant challenge for researchers. AI offers a powerful solution, with AI-powered tools equipped with NLP capabilities revolutionizing research workflows by automating tasks and recognizing research topics and ideas. AI can assist with literature reviews, identify emerging trends, facilitate concept exploration, and even support hypothesis generation. These capabilities offer numerous benefits, including increased efficiency, improved accuracy, and the potential for groundbreaking discoveries. However, it's crucial to address challenges like data bias and ethical considerations. As AI continues to evolve and becomes more integrated with research practices, the future holds immense promise for a collaborative approach that leverages the strengths of both human and AI to reshape the landscape of knowledge creation.

ACKNOWLEDGMENT

The authors would like to acknowledge the use of an AI-powered grammar checker tool for enhancing the language and grammatical accuracy of the presented work.

REFERENCES

Adams, D., & Chuah, K. M. (2022). Artificial intelligence-based tools in research writing: Current trends and future potentials. *Artificial intelligence in higher education*, 169-184.

Ahmad, S. F., Alam, M. M., Rahmat, M. K., Mubarik, M. S., & Hyder, S. I. (2022). Academic and administrative role of artificial intelligence in education. *Sustainability (Basel)*, *14*(3), 1101. doi:10.3390/su14031101

Altmäe, S., Sola-Leyva, A., & Salumets, A. (2023). Artificial intelligence in scientific writing: A friend or a foe? *Reproductive Biomedicine Online*, *47*(1), 3–9. doi:10.1016/j.rbmo.2023.04.009 PMID:37142479

Cain, W. (2023, March). GPTeammate: A design fiction on the use of variants of the GPT language model as cognitive partners for active learning in higher education. In *Society for Information Technology & Teacher Education International Conference* (pp. 1293-1298). Association for the Advancement of Computing in Education (AACE).

Chen, L., Chen, P., & Lin, Z. (2020). Artificial intelligence in education: A review. *IEEE Access : Practical Innovations, Open Solutions*, *8*, 75264–75278. doi:10.1109/ACCESS.2020.2988510

Chiu, T. K., Xia, Q., Zhou, X., Chai, C. S., & Cheng, M. (2023). Systematic literature review on opportunities, challenges, and future research recommendations of artificial intelligence in education. *Computers and Education: Artificial Intelligence*, *4*, 100118. doi:10.1016/j.caeai.2022.100118

Curtis, N. (2023). To ChatGPT or not to ChatGPT? The impact of artificial intelligence on academic publishing. *The Pediatric Infectious Disease Journal*, *42*(4), 275. doi:10.1097/INF.0000000000003852 PMID:36757192

Dergaa, I., Chamari, K., Zmijewski, P., & Saad, H. B. (2023). From human writing to artificial intelligence generated text: Examining the prospects and potential threats of ChatGPT in academic writing. *Biology of Sport*, *40*(2), 615–622. doi:10.5114/biolsport.2023.125623 PMID:37077800

Dönmez, İ., Sahin, I., & Gülen, S. (2023). Conducting academic research with the ai interface chatgpt: Challenges and opportunities. *Journal of STEAM Education, 6*(2), 101-118.

Duymaz, Y. K., & Tekin, A. M. (2024). Harnessing artificial intelligence in academic writing: Potential, ethics, and responsible use. *European Journal of Therapeutics*, *30*(1), 87–88. doi:10.58600/eurjther1755

Garbuio, M., & Lin, N. (2021). Innovative idea generation in problem finding: Abductive reasoning, cognitive impediments, and the promise of artificial intelligence. *Journal of Product Innovation Management*, *38*(6), 701–725. doi:10.1111/jpim.12602

Gendron, Y., Andrew, J., & Cooper, C. (2022). The perils of artificial intelligence in academic publishing. *Critical Perspectives on Accounting*, *87*, 102411. doi:10.1016/j.cpa.2021.102411

Gilat, R., & Cole, B. J. (2023). How will artificial intelligence affect scientific writing, reviewing and editing? The future is here…. *Arthroscopy*, *39*(5), 1119–1120. doi:10.1016/j.arthro.2023.01.014 PMID:36774329

Ginting, P., Batubara, H. M., & Hasnah, Y. (2023). Artificial intelligence powered writing tools as adaptable aids for academic writing: Insight from EFL college learners in writing final project. *International Journal of Multidisciplinary Research And Analysis*, *6*(10), 4640–4650. doi:10.47191/ijmra/v6-i10-15

Golan, R., Reddy, R., Muthigi, A., & Ramasamy, R. (2023). Artificial intelligence in academic writing: A paradigm-shifting technological advance. *Nature Reviews. Urology*, *20*(6), 327–328. doi:10.1038/s41585-023-00746-x PMID:36829078

Hoffman, S. G. (2017). Managing ambiguities at the edge of knowledge: Research strategy and artificial intelligence labs in an era of academic capitalism. *Science, Technology & Human Values*, *42*(4), 703–740. doi:10.1177/0162243916687038

Jaiswal, A., & Arun, C. J. (2021). Potential of Artificial Intelligence for transformation of the education system in India. *International Journal of Education and Development Using Information and Communication Technology*, *17*(1), 142–158.

Jobin, A., Ienca, M., & Vayena, E. (2019). The global landscape of AI ethics guidelines. *Nature Machine Intelligence*, *1*(9), 389–399. doi:10.1038/s42256-019-0088-2

Kasneci, E., Seßler, K., Küchemann, S., Bannert, M., Dementieva, D., Fischer, F., Gasser, U., Groh, G., Günnemann, S., Hüllermeier, E., Krusche, S., Kutyniok, G., Michaeli, T., Nerdel, C., Pfeffer, J., Poquet, O., Sailer, M., Schmidt, A., Seidel, T., ... Kasneci, G. (2023). ChatGPT for good? On opportunities and challenges of large language models for education. *Learning and Individual Differences*, *103*, 102274. doi:10.1016/j.lindif.2023.102274

Kenwright, B. (2024). Is it the end of undergraduate dissertations?: Exploring the advantages and challenges of generative ai models in education. In *Generative AI in teaching and learning* (pp. 46–65). IGI Global.

Khabib, S. (2022). Introducing artificial intelligence (AI)-based digital writing assistants for teachers in writing scientific articles. *Teaching English as a Foreign Language Journal*, *1*(2), 114–124. doi:10.12928/tefl.v1i2.249

Lund, B. D., Wang, T., Mannuru, N. R., Nie, B., Shimray, S., & Wang, Z. (2023). ChatGPT and a new academic reality: Artificial Intelligence-written research papers and the ethics of the large language models in scholarly publishing. *Journal of the Association for Information Science and Technology*, *74*(5), 570–581. doi:10.1002/asi.24750

Mijwil, M. M., Hiran, K. K., Doshi, R., Dadhich, M., Al-Mistarehi, A. H., & Bala, I. (2023). ChatGPT and the future of academic integrity in the artificial intelligence era: A new frontier. *Al-Salam Journal for Engineering and Technology*, *2*(2), 116–127. doi:10.55145/ajest.2023.02.02.015

Mohammed, O., Sahib, T. M., Hayder, I. M., Salisu, S., & Shahid, M. (2023). ChatGPT Evaluation: Can It Replace Grammarly and Quillbot Tools? *British Journal of Applied Linguistics*, *3*(2), 34–46. doi:10.32996/bjal.2023.3.2.4

Pigola, A., Scafuto, I. C., da Costa, P. R., & Nassif, V. M. J. (2023). Artificial Intelligence in academic research. *International Journal of Innovation*, *11*(3), e25408–e25408. doi:10.5585/2023.25408

Roberts, L. W. (2023). Addressing the Novel Implications of Generative AI for Academic Publishing, Education, and Research. *Academic Medicine*, 10–1097. PMID:38451086

Salvagno, M., Taccone, F. S., & Gerli, A. G. (2023). Can artificial intelligence help for scientific writing? *Critical Care*, *27*(1), 75. doi:10.1186/s13054-023-04380-2 PMID:36841840

Thompson, K., Corrin, L., & Lodge, J. M. (2023). AI in tertiary education: Progress on research and practice. *Australasian Journal of Educational Technology*, *39*(5), 1–7. doi:10.14742/ajet.9251

Zawacki-Richter, O., Marín, V. I., Bond, M., & Gouverneur, F. (2019). Systematic review of research on artificial intelligence applications in higher education–where are the educators? *International Journal of Educational Technology in Higher Education*, *16*(1), 1–27. doi:10.1186/s41239-019-0171-0

Chapter 4
AI Tools for Efficient Writing and Editing

Rashmi Rani Samantaray
https://orcid.org/0000-0002-9696-3404
HKBK College of Engineering, India

Abdul Azeez
https://orcid.org/0000-0002-4009-0958
HKBK College of Engineering, India

ABSTRACT

Wisdom cannot be replaced by AI tools. AI tools can save time spent on a pre-draft research. AI tools can open the door to create a better writing outcome. AI tools can boost productivity. Writing produced by AI tools still needs a human touch. Academic writing has undergone a revolution as a result of AI. Writing a book, a research grant, or even an academic journal article can be done by using AI techniques. Additionally, there are several AI-powered applications that can assist researchers in editing their publications and use English correctly.

INTRODUCTION

Streamlining the research workflow with AI involves utilizing artificial intelligence technologies to enhance and optimize various stages of the research process, from data collection and analysis to result interpretation and dissemination. AI-powered tools and techniques assist researchers in managing vast amounts of data, automating tedious tasks, deriving insights, and ultimately accelerating the pace of research advancements. Artificial Intelligence (AI) is revolutionizing the way research is conducted across various disciplines, significantly streamlining workflows and boosting productivity. Researchers now have access to advanced AI-powered tools that provide invaluable assistance in handling the complexities of modern research. These tools help in data collection, organization, analysis, and interpretation, allowing for more efficient and precise research outcomes.

DOI: 10.4018/979-8-3693-1798-3.ch004

One of the key areas where AI has made a substantial impact is in data collection and pre-processing. AI algorithms can sift through massive amounts of data, extracting relevant information and filtering out noise. For instance, in biomedical research, AI can analyze diverse datasets such as genetic information, clinical records, and medical imaging to identify patterns and correlations that could be crucial for understanding diseases and designing targeted treatments. This substantially expedites the initial data processing phase, which is often a time-consuming and resource-intensive aspect of research.

Furthermore, machine learning algorithms, a subset of AI, can be trained to recognize complex patterns within data. This is particularly useful in scenarios where data is too extensive for manual analysis. For example, in climate science, AI models can analyze meteorological data to predict weather patterns, assess climate change impact, and optimize renewable energy usage. By automating pattern recognition, researchers can focus more on deriving insights from the patterns identified by AI systems.

Incorporating AI into the research workflow significantly enhances data analysis. AI can process vast datasets and generate meaningful insights that might have been overlooked using traditional methods. In social sciences, AI can be used to analyse sentiments from social media data to understand public opinion on various topics. Natural Language Processing (NLP) techniques, a branch of AI, can extract insights from a vast corpus of research papers, providing a comprehensive view of existing research and potential gaps.

Moreover, AI facilitates automation in routine and repetitive tasks, enabling researchers to allocate their time and expertise more efficiently. For instance, in astronomy, AI algorithms can autonomously analyse astronomical images to detect celestial bodies, aiding astronomers in their research. This automation not only saves time but also allows researchers to focus on the critical aspects of their work that require human intuition and decision-making(Rahman,2023).

AI-powered literature review tools help researchers stay updated with the latest advancements in their field. These tools can scan and summarize a vast number of research papers, making it easier for researchers to keep track of the most relevant and influential works. Additionally, AI algorithms can suggest potential collaborators based on research interests and past collaborations, fostering interdisciplinary partnerships and enhancing the research ecosystem.

Furthermore, AI contributes to refining models and simulations. AI algorithms can optimize parameters in complex models, enhancing accuracy and predictive capabilities. This is crucial in fields like finance, where AI can enhance risk assessment models, or in drug discovery, where AI can predict molecular properties for potential drug candidates.

Another remarkable application of AI in research is in virtual laboratories. AI-driven virtual labs simulate real-world experiments, allowing researchers to conduct virtual trials, make predictions, and refine hypotheses before conducting physical experiments. This not only accelerates the research process but also saves resources.

In conclusion, integrating AI into the research workflow holds immense potential to revolutionize how research is conducted and accelerate progress across diverse domains. AI's ability to handle vast amounts of data, derive insights, automate repetitive tasks, and optimize models significantly enhances research efficiency and efficacy. As AI technologies continue to advance, their role in research is expected to become increasingly prominent, shaping the future of scientific discovery and innovation. Researchers must embrace and adapt to this evolving landscape to harness the full potential of AI in advancing knowledge and solving complex problems.

1. The Role of AI in Academic Writing: Enhancing Productivity, Creativity, and Quality

Case Study: ChatGPT

In recent years, artificial intelligence (AI) has made significant strides, revolutionizing various fields, including the realm of academic writing. ChatGPT, developed by OpenAI, is a cutting-edge AI tool that employs deep learning to generate human-like text based on the provided input. This essay explores the multifaceted role of ChatGPT in academic writing, emphasizing how it can enhance productivity, foster creativity, and improve the overall quality of academic output.

Enhancing Productivity

One of the primary advantages of employing ChatGPT in academic writing is its potential to enhance productivity through efficient idea generation and organization. Academic writers frequently grapple with the challenge of initiating the writing process and organizing their thoughts effectively. ChatGPT can serve as a valuable aid in brainstorming ideas and structuring them coherently, ultimately streamlining the writing process (Ang, 2023).

Idea Generation

ChatGPT's capacity to generate text based on specific prompts or inquiries significantly aids in brainstorming sessions. By providing a seed topic or research question, writers can obtain a plethora of related ideas, concepts, or arguments from ChatGPT. This not only kick-starts the writing process but also allows for exploration of diverse perspectives and potential research directions.

Structural Assistance

ChatGPT can assist in creating outlines and structuring academic papers. Writers can input key points they wish to cover, and ChatGPT can suggest optimal ways to organize these points logically. This collaborative outlining approach ensures a systematic and cohesive flow of ideas, contributing to the overall efficiency of the writing process.

Fostering Creativity

ChatGPT's ability to simulate human-like conversation and generate creative text is instrumental in academic writing by infusing creativity into the content. Academic papers often tend to be formal and monotonous, potentially disengaging readers. ChatGPT can inject creativity into the content, making it more captivating and ensuring reader engagement.

Engaging Introductions and Conclusions

ChatGPT can assist in crafting engaging introductions and conclusions that captivate the readers' interest. By providing innovative opening statements and thought-provoking closing remarks, ChatGPT helps in creating a compelling narrative that entices readers to delve deeper into the academic discussion.

Language Refinement

ChatGPT aids in refining language and improving clarity by suggesting synonyms, offering rephrased sentences, and providing explanations. This feature is particularly beneficial for non-native English speakers and those seeking to enhance the quality and accessibility of their writing.

Improving Quality Through Real-Time Assistance

ChatGPT augments the writing process by functioning as a virtual writing assistant, offering real-time feedback and suggestions during the drafting phase. This feedback helps writers enhance their ideas, correct errors, and elevate the overall quality of the academic paper(Lund,2023).

Real-time Feedback

By inputting segments of their draft into ChatGPT, writers can receive immediate feedback on their writing style, coherence, and grammar. ChatGPT can highlight areas for improvement and offer suggestions for rephrasing or restructuring sentences, ultimately enhancing the readability and quality of the paper.

Collaboration and Peer Review

ChatGPT facilitates collaboration and peer review by simulating a peer's perspective. Writers can input their work and receive simulated feedback, enabling them to identify strengths and weaknesses in their arguments. This simulated peer review process assists in refining the paper before formal submission.

ChatGPT emerges as a promising tool for enhancing productivity, fostering creativity, and improving the quality of academic writing. Its capabilities in idea generation, outline creation, creative content generation, and real-time feedback make it a valuable asset for academic writers. As AI technologies continue to advance, integrating ChatGPT into the academic writing process is poised to become standard practice, enhancing the efficiency and output of academic work. However, it is imperative to use ChatGPT as a complementary tool and uphold critical thinking and academic rigor throughout the writing process.

AI TOOLS FOR ENHANCING ACADEMIC WRITING AND EDITING RESEARCH PAPERS

1. Introduction

In the contemporary academic landscape, researchers are increasingly utilizing artificial intelligence (AI) tools to augment and refine their research papers. AI can significantly enhance the editing and writing process by providing automated assistance in grammar checking, language refinement, citation management, and overall document organization. This essay explores various AI tools and technologies that can aid researchers in editing research papers, ultimately enhancing the quality and impact of their scholarly output.((Golan,2023),(Dubose,2023),(Giray,2023),(Fok,2023)).

2. Grammar Checking and Proofreading

AI-powered grammar checking tools offer researchers a robust means to identify and correct grammatical errors and inconsistencies within their research papers.

Grammarly

Grammarly is a widely-used AI tool that provides real-time grammar checking, contextual spellchecking, and style suggestions. It helps researchers maintain an error-free and polished writing style, contributing to the overall quality of the research paper.

Grammmarly Communication Assistance, Built for researcher:

Go beyond fixing mistakes so that you, your team, or your entire organization can communicate with speed, skill, and confidence.

Assistance comes to you through seamless integration on desktop and mobile, across thousands of websites and applications. Discover the possibilities of writing with an AI co-creator—built with privacy and security in mind.

3. ProWritingAid

ProWritingAid offers in-depth grammar and style checking, helping researchers improve sentence structure, readability, and coherence. It also provides detailed reports on various aspects of writing, facilitating targeted editing efforts.

ProWritingAid: Enhancing Academic Writing and Editing Efficiency

ProWritingAid is an advanced artificial intelligence (AI) tool designed to aid writers and researchers in enhancing the quality of their written work. With its comprehensive suite of features, ProWritingAid offers valuable assistance in grammar checking, style analysis, readability enhancement, and more. This essay delves into the capabilities and benefits of ProWritingAid in the context of academic writing and editing research papers.

Grammar and Style Analysis

ProWritingAid excels in grammar checking and style analysis, providing writers with detailed insights into their writing style and language usage.

Real-Time Grammar Checking

The tool identifies and highlights grammatical errors, including spelling, punctuation, and sentence structure issues. By providing real-time suggestions and corrections, ProWritingAid aids researchers in maintaining error-free research papers.

Style Suggestions and Consistency

ProWritingAid offers suggestions for improving writing style, ensuring consistency in tone, vocabulary, and phrasing. This consistency is crucial for presenting a professional and polished academic document.

Readability Enhancement

Ensuring that the research paper is easily understandable to a broader audience is essential. ProWritingAid offers features to enhance the readability of the text.

Readability and Sentence Structure

The tool analyzes sentence structure, sentence length, and readability metrics, providing suggestions to improve clarity and coherence. It aids in simplifying complex sentences and ensures that the paper is accessible to readers.

Vocabulary Enhancement

ProWritingAid suggests alternative words and phrases to enhance vocabulary and avoid repetition. This feature contributes to the richness and variety of language used in the research paper.

Citation and Referencing

Efficiently managing citations and references is a fundamental aspect of academic writing, and ProWritingAid offers features to streamline this process.

Citation and Referencing Consistency

ProWritingAid checks the consistency and accuracy of citations and references, ensuring that they adhere to the specified academic style (APA, MLA, Chicago, etc.). This feature aids in maintaining a professional and standardized format for references.

Plagiarism Checking

The tool has built-in plagiarism detection capabilities, allowing researchers to ensure the originality of their work and avoid unintentional plagiarism, a critical ethical consideration in academia.

Document Organization and Structure

ProWritingAid facilitates the organization and structuring of the research paper, aiding in maintaining a logical and coherent flow of ideas.

Document Outline and Structure Analysis

The tool provides insights into the overall document structure, offering suggestions to enhance the organization and arrangement of content. This helps in presenting a well-structured and cohesive research paper.

Section and Subsection Analysis

ProWritingAid highlights sections and subsections, ensuring that each part of the research paper is adequately developed and organized, contributing to a more effective presentation of ideas.

ProWritingAid stands as a powerful AI tool for researchers seeking to improve the quality and efficiency of their academic writing and research paper editing. Its diverse range of features, from grammar checking to readability enhancement and citation management, make it a valuable asset for academic writers. By incorporating ProWritingAid into their editing process, researchers can streamline their editing efforts, refine their language and style, and ultimately produce research papers that are clear, polished, and impactful. However, it's crucial to use ProWritingAid as a complement to human expertise, ensuring that the essence and rigor of academic writing are preserved.

4. Language Refinement and Clarity

AI can assist in refining the language and clarity of research papers, ensuring that the content is clear, concise, and easily comprehensible.

Hemingway Editor

The Hemingway Editor analyzes text, highlighting complex sentences, common errors, and suggesting simpler alternatives. It promotes clear and effective communication of research findings to a broader audience.

Readable

Readable assesses the readability of the text, offering suggestions to simplify language and enhance clarity. It assists researchers in tailoring their language to match the target audience's comprehension level.

CITATION AND REFERENCE MANAGEMENT

Managing citations and references is a crucial aspect of academic writing. AI tools can automate and streamline this process.

5. Zotero

Zotero is an AI-powered reference management tool that helps researchers organize, cite, and generate bibliographies effortlessly. It facilitates seamless integration of references into the research paper.

Zotero is an excellent tool for researchers, academics, and students to manage and organize their research materials efficiently. Here's how researchers can make the most of Zotero for their work:

1. **Collecting and Organizing References**:

Use Zotero to collect and organize references from various sources such as academic databases, library catalogs, websites, and more. It helps in creating a centralized repository for all your research materials.

2. **Tagging and Categorizing**:

Utilize tags and categories to organize your references into meaningful groups. Tags help in quickly identifying and retrieving specific types of references or themes.

3. **Storing Full Text and Attachments**:

Attach PDFs, documents, images, or any other relevant files to your references within Zotero. This feature helps in keeping all associated materials in one place.

4. **Automatic Metadata and PDF Retrieval**:

Zotero automatically fetches metadata and information about the references, saving you time in manual entry. It can also retrieve PDFs for many references, ensuring a comprehensive database.

5. **Creating Bibliographies and Citations**:

Use Zotero to generate accurate citations and bibliographies in various citation styles. It seamlessly integrates with word processors like Microsoft Word and Google Docs, making the citation process effortless.

6. **Collaboration and Sharing**:

Collaborate with other researchers by sharing your Zotero library or specific collections. It's a great way to work on projects collectively and keep everyone updated on the latest research.

7. **Annotating and Highlighting**:

Annotate PDFs directly within Zotero to add notes, highlights, or comments to important sections. This is especially useful for in-depth analysis and review of research materials.

8. **Advanced Search and Filtering**:

Utilize the advanced search and filtering options in Zotero to quickly find specific references based on criteria such as author, year, tags, or keywords.

9. **Integration with Research Tools**:

Integrate Zotero with other research tools and software to enhance your workflow. For example, it can be used alongside text analysis or data visualization tools.

10. **Regular Backups and Syncing**:

Ensure regular backups of your Zotero library to prevent data loss. Take advantage of Zotero's syncing feature to keep your library updated across multiple devices.

By leveraging these features and functionalities, researchers can optimize their research workflow, improve organization, enhance collaboration, and streamline the citation and bibliography creation process.

6. EndNote

EndNote allows researchers to manage references efficiently, automatically formatting citations according to various academic styles. It simplifies the citation and referencing process, saving researchers valuable time(Jarrah,2023).

EndNote: Streamlining Citation Management for Researchers

EndNote is a powerful reference management software designed to assist researchers in organizing and managing references, citations, and bibliographies efficiently. This essay explores the features and benefits of EndNote, highlighting how it streamlines the citation management process for researchers and enhances the overall quality of academic writing(Bakla,2023).

Centralized Reference Management

EndNote allows researchers to consolidate all their references in one centralized location, providing a structured and organized database of sources.

Import and Export Capabilities

Researchers can easily import references from various sources like databases, library catalogs, and PDFs. EndNote also supports exporting references to different citation styles and formats, simplifying the bibliography creation process.

Customization and Organization

The software enables researchers to categorize references into folders, add tags, and apply custom labels, ensuring a systematic and intuitive organization of the vast array of sources.

Citation Insertion and Formatting

EndNote facilitates the seamless integration of citations and references within research papers, ensuring accuracy and consistency.

Integration with Word Processors

EndNote integrates smoothly with popular word processors like Microsoft Word, enabling researchers to insert citations and generate bibliographies effortlessly within their manuscripts.

Citation Styles and Formatting

Researchers can choose from a wide range of citation styles, including APA, MLA, Chicago, and more. EndNote automatically formats the citations and bibliography according to the selected style, saving time and ensuring adherence to specific formatting guidelines.

Enhanced Collaboration and Sharing

EndNote promotes collaboration among researchers by allowing them to share references and collaborate on projects.

Sharing Libraries

Researchers can share their entire reference libraries with colleagues, facilitating collaborative research efforts and ensuring that everyone has access to the same set of references.

Sync and Cloud Storage

EndNote offers cloud storage options, enabling seamless synchronization of libraries across multiple devices. This ensures that researchers can access their references and work on their research from anywhere.

Searching and Discoverability

EndNote provides researchers with powerful search capabilities, enhancing the discoverability of relevant literature.

Integrated Database Search

The software allows researchers to search online databases within the interface, retrieving references and directly importing them into their EndNote library, streamlining the research process.

Full-Text PDF Search

EndNote permits full-text PDF searches, assisting researchers in finding specific information within their saved PDF documents.

Conclusion

EndNote is a valuable tool that significantly simplifies the citation management process for researchers. By centralizing reference management, offering various customization options, and seamlessly integrating with word processors, EndNote optimizes the citation and bibliography creation process. Additionally, its collaboration features and search capabilities enhance efficiency and productivity for researchers. As a comprehensive reference management tool, EndNote proves to be an essential asset for researchers seeking to manage their references effectively and produce high-quality academic papers.

AI TOOLS FOR DOCUMENT ORGANIZATION AND STRUCTURE

AI tools can aid in organizing the research paper, ensuring a logical and coherent structure..

Document Organization and Structure Tools for Academic Research

Efficient organization and structure are essential for creating well-organized academic research documents. Here, we explore various tools that can aid researchers in achieving effective document organization and structure, enhancing the quality and impact of their research output(Nazari,2021).

1. Microsoft Word

Microsoft Word remains a fundamental tool for document organization and structure in academic research.

- **Styles and Headings**: Utilize built-in styles and headings to organize sections and subsections, creating a hierarchical structure for the document.
- **Table of Contents**: Generate an automated table of contents based on the defined styles, providing an organized overview of the document's structure.
- **Outline View**: Use the Outline View to organize and rearrange the document's sections and headings, aiding in a coherent structure.

2. Google Docs

Google Docs offers collaborative and intuitive features for document organization and structure.

- **Headings and Subheadings**: Utilize headings and subheadings to create a structured hierarchy, improving document readability.
- **Document Outline**: Access the Document Outline feature to navigate through headings and sections, ensuring a well-organized layout.
- **Comments and Collaborative Editing**: Collaborate with peers, advisors, or colleagues using comments and real-time editing, streamlining the feedback and revision process.

3. Scrivener

Scrivener is a specialized tool designed for managing complex writing projects.

- **Hierarchical Structure**: Create a hierarchical structure with folders, subfolders, and files for different sections, facilitating easy navigation and organization.
- **Research Repository**: Store and manage research materials directly within the tool, keeping all relevant resources accessible and organized.
- **Outline and Corkboard Views**: Visualize and rearrange the document's structure using outline and corkboard views, aiding in structural adjustments.

4. Notion

Notion is a versatile tool that can be adapted for various organizational needs in research.

- **Database and Tables**: Create databases and tables to organize research notes, references, and related information systematically.
- **Hierarchical Structure**: Establish a hierarchical structure using pages, sub-pages, and toggles, allowing for a well-organized layout.
- **Integration with Other Tools**: Integrate Notion with tools like Zotero or EndNote for seamless citation and reference management.

5. Mendeley

Mendeley is a reference manager and academic social network that facilitates document organization.

- **Reference Library**: Create a well-structured library to organize and manage references, PDFs, and annotations.
- **Tags and Folders**: Use tags and folders to categorize and sort documents, enhancing accessibility and organization.
- **Citation Plugin**: Utilize the citation plugin to easily insert citations and generate bibliographies within the research document.

6. Trello

Trello is a project management tool that can aid in organizing and structuring research tasks and milestones.

- **Lists and Cards**: Create lists and cards for different research tasks, allowing for a visual representation of the project's progress and structure.
- **Due Dates and Labels**: Assign due dates and labels to organize tasks based on priority or category, aiding in task management.
- **Collaboration**: Collaborate with team members by sharing boards and working on tasks collaboratively, promoting efficient teamwork.

Utilizing appropriate tools for document organization and structure is crucial for researchers to streamline their research processes and present their findings in a clear and effective manner. Whether it's hierarchical structuring, collaborative editing, or reference management, the right tool can significantly enhance the quality and organization of academic research documents. Researchers should choose the tools that align with their specific needs and preferences to optimize their document organization and enhance the impact of their research.

7. Scrivener

Scrivener provides a platform for organizing research notes, outlines, and drafts. It enables researchers to structure their research papers effectively and maintain a cohesive flow of ideas throughout the document.

FEW MORE TOOLS FOR AI EDITING

• Outline AI

Outline AI helps in creating clear and organized outlines for research papers, ensuring that all essential points are adequately covered and logically structured.

Outline AI: A Tool for Streamlining Research Document Outlining

Outline AI is an innovative tool designed to assist researchers in creating well-structured outlines for their research documents. Its advanced features aid in organizing ideas, arranging content hierarchically, and facilitating a logical flow of information. In this essay, we will explore the capabilities and benefits of Outline AI in the context of academic research document outlining.

- **Automated Outlining**

Outline AI utilizes automation to generate outlines based on the input provided by the user.

- **Topic Analysis**

The tool performs a thorough analysis of the research topic, identifying key themes, concepts, and subtopics that form the basis of the outline.

- **Hierarchical Structuring**

Outline AI creates a hierarchical structure, categorizing main topics, subtopics, and supporting details to present a clear and organized outline.

- **Customizable and Interactive Interface**

Outline AI offers a user-friendly interface that allows for customization and interactivity in the outlining process.

- **Drag-and-Drop Functionality**

Researchers can easily rearrange and reorganize the outline using a simple drag-and-drop interface, ensuring flexibility and adaptability.

- **Real-time Updates**

The tool provides real-time updates as modifications are made, enabling researchers to visualize the outline dynamically.

- **Collaboration and Sharing**

Outline AI promotes collaboration among researchers by facilitating easy sharing and collaborative outlining.

- **Shareable Outlines**

Researchers can share the generated outline with colleagues, collaborators, or advisors, fostering collaborative efforts in refining and finalizing the document structure.

- **Real-time Collaboration**

Multiple users can work on the same outline simultaneously, providing a collaborative environment for refining and improving the document's structure.

- **Integration with Writing Tools**

Outline AI seamlessly integrates with various writing tools, enhancing the writing and editing process.

- **Export and Integration**

The tool allows for easy export of the generated outline to popular word processors, enabling a smooth transition from outlining to drafting.

- **Compatibility**

Outline AI is compatible with a range of writing tools, ensuring that researchers can use their preferred writing environment.

- **Enhanced Efficiency and Productivity**

Outline AI streamlines the outlining process, saving researchers time and effort while enhancing productivity.

- **Automated Formatting**

The tool automatically formats the outline based on predefined styles and formatting options, maintaining consistency and saving time.

- **Quick Generation**

Outline AI swiftly generates an outline, allowing researchers to focus more on content creation and less on structural planning.

Outline AI is a valuable tool for researchers seeking to optimize their research document outlining process. By automating the creation of well-structured outlines, providing customization options, supporting collaboration, and seamlessly integrating with writing tools, Outline AI significantly enhances the efficiency and productivity of researchers. Utilizing Outline AI in the outlining phase enables researchers to establish a clear and organized document structure, paving the way for a successful and impactful research paper.

AI tools have become indispensable aids for researchers seeking to enhance the quality and efficiency of editing their research papers. From grammar checking to language refinement, citation management, and document organization, AI technologies offer a range of valuable capabilities. By incorporating these AI tools into their editing process, researchers can refine their papers, optimize clarity and coherence, and ultimately present their research findings in a more impactful and accessible manner. However, it is crucial to use these AI tools judiciously, complementing them with human judgment and expertise to maintain the integrity and rigor of academic writing.

Here are some AI tools that can be used by researcher at various stages of research:

RESEARCH PLANNING

GanttPRO A research planning tool to create a timeline, tasks, follow progress and deadlines. https://ganttpro.com/

Research planning is a critical aspect of any academic or professional research project. GanttPRO is an online project management tool that can be effectively used for research planning, scheduling, and tracking progress. Here's how you can utilize GanttPRO for efficient research planning(Lingard,2023).

1. Project Setup:
   - **Create a New Project:** Open GanttPRO and start a new project dedicated to your research. Give it a clear and descriptive title to reflect the research's focus.
   - **Define Objectives and Deliverables:** Clearly outline the project's objectives and expected deliverables. This will help in setting specific goals for the research.
2. Task Breakdown:
   - **Identify Tasks:** Break down the research project into smaller, manageable tasks. This includes literature review, data collection, analysis, writing, revision, etc.
   - **Task Dependencies:** Establish dependencies between tasks to ensure that the research follows a logical sequence. For example, data collection must precede data analysis.
3. Timeline and Scheduling:
   - **Estimate Task Durations:** Estimate the time needed for each task. This helps in scheduling and allocation of resources appropriately.
   - **Allocate Resources:** Assign team members or resources to each task. This ensures that responsibilities are clear and everyone is aware of their role.
   - **Set Milestones:** Define significant milestones in the research process, such as completing the literature review, finishing data collection, or submitting the final draft.
4. Gantt Chart Creation:
   - **Use Gantt Chart View:** Utilize GanttPRO's interface to create a Gantt chart. Input all the tasks, task durations, task dependencies, and milestones.
   - **Visualize the Timeline:** The Gantt chart will visually represent the project timeline, task sequences, and their respective durations.
5. Resource Management:
   - **Track Resource Utilization:** Monitor the workload of each team member to ensure even distribution and prevent overloading.
   - **Resource Leveling:** Adjust task assignments to balance resource allocation and optimize productivity.
6. Progress Tracking:
   - **Update Task Progress:** Regularly update the progress of tasks in GanttPRO. This allows you to track the project's actual progress against the planned schedule.
   - **Compare Planned vs. Actual:** Analyze how the research is progressing by comparing planned timelines with actual progress. Adjust the plan if needed to stay on track.
7. Collaboration and Communication:
   - **Share the Project:** Share the Gantt chart with the research team to ensure everyone is on the same page regarding project progress and deadlines.
   - **Collaboration Features:** Use GanttPRO's collaboration features for discussions, comments, and file sharing to facilitate effective communication within the team.

GanttPRO proves to be a valuable tool for research planning, aiding in efficient project management, and ensuring that research goals are met within the defined timelines and resources.

Finding and Synthesizing Literature

- Semantic Scholar:

Get access to 200 million research papers, discover links between topics, get recommendations based on recent searches and generate summaries. https://lnkd.in/dKkGMeXw

Semantic Scholar is an academic search engine designed to help researchers discover and access scientific articles. It utilizes artificial intelligence and natural language processing to understand and extract meaning from scholarly content. Here's how you can effectively use Semantic Scholar for finding and synthesizing literature for your research:

1. Search and Discovery:
    - **Focused Search Queries:** Begin with a specific research topic or question in mind. Use precise search queries related to your research to retrieve relevant academic papers.
    - **Keyword Optimization:** Incorporate relevant keywords, phrases, and synonyms to enhance search results and discover a broad spectrum of related literature.
    - **Use Filters:** Utilize filters to narrow down your search based on criteria such as publication date, authors, journals, and more, focusing on the most recent and reputable sources.
2. Review and Evaluation:
    - **Abstract and Title Review:** Read the abstract and title of each paper to quickly gauge its relevance to your research topic. This helps in screening out irrelevant studies.
    - **Keywords and Topics:** Pay attention to the keywords and topics associated with the paper to understand its main focus and relevance to your research.
    - **Authors and Affiliations:** Consider the reputation and expertise of the authors and their affiliations. Established researchers or reputable institutions often produce high-quality research.
    - **Citations and References:** Check the citations and references in each paper to discover related research. This can lead you to seminal works and foundational literature in your field.
3. Organizing and Synthesizing:
    - **Literature Organization:** Use tools like Zotero, EndNote, or Mendeley to organize and manage the literature you find. These tools help in creating a centralized database of references.
    - **Note-Taking and Annotations:** While reading each paper, take detailed notes, highlight important sections, and annotate key findings. Organize these notes by themes or topics.
    - **Synthesize Information:** Compare and contrast the information from different papers. Identify patterns, trends, and gaps in the existing literature, and synthesize the information to develop a coherent understanding of the topic.
4. Utilizing Semantic Scholar's Features:
    - **Advanced Search Options:** Leverage Semantic Scholar's advanced search options to refine your search based on various parameters, including publication date, journal, and field of study.
    - **Topic Extraction:** Explore Semantic Scholar's topic extraction feature to understand the main themes and concepts associated with a specific research paper.
    - **Related Papers:** Take advantage of the "Related Papers" feature to discover additional papers that are related to the one you are currently reading, expanding your literature base.

Semantic Scholar, with its AI-powered capabilities, can significantly assist researchers in efficiently finding, organizing, and synthesizing relevant literature for their research projects. By effectively leveraging its features and combining it with other reference management tools, researchers can streamline the literature review process and enhance the quality of their scholarly work.

- **Scholarcy**

AI powered article summarizer which identifies key info like participants, data analysis, main findings and limitations. https://lnkd.in/d-n_yEHn

Creates a Referenced Summary

Scholarcy summarises the whole paper with references, rewriting statements in the third person, making it easier to cite the information correctly in your report, essay or thesis.

The summarisation process is fully customisable: choose the number of words, the level of highlighting and level of language variation(Forester,2023).

Finds the References

No more trawling the web trying to find the papers in the references – Scholarcy does that for you, locating open-access PDFs from Google Scholar, arXiv and elsewhere. Scholarcy enlists the excellent UnPaywall API to help with this.

You can also download the entire bibliography in BibTex or .RIS format, so you can import each entry into your favourite reference management tool.

Extracts Tables and Figures

Need to check the numbers? Scholarcy finds the tables in a PDF or Word document and lets you download them in Excel format, so you can run your own calculations on the results.

Scholarcy can be configured to give you thumbnails of each figure in the PDF, cross-referenced in the text, so you can easily jump to the corresponding figure while you are reading.

Highlights Important Points

Scholarcy's unique Robo-Highlighter™ automatically highlights important phrases and contributions made by the paper. No more printing off papers and manually going over them with a marker pen – Scholarcy's advanced AI has learnt how academic papers are written and can identify when an important point is being made.

- Paper Digest

Creates 3-minute summaries of research papers by extracting key ideas and sentences. https://lnkd.in/d7TsH96f

It summarizes and finds paper,grants,funds,patents for last 5 years related information.

- Content Mine

Enables you to find, download, analyze, and extract knowledge from academic papers. https://lnkd.in/dQ73C2Af

Contentmine is a leading text and data mining company, with headquarters in Cambridge, England. They specialize in building open source tools to enable clients to find facts hidden in the information.

- **Elink.io**

Enables you to save the content from around the web: articles, videos, cloud files, social media posts and share them with peers. https://elink.io/

- **Elicit**

Another AI tool which helps you find relevant papers without perfect keyword match, summarize takeaways from the paper specific to your question, and extract key information from the papers. https://elicit.org/

It helps in Get one sentence abstract summaries from research paper. Select relevant papers and search for more like them. Extract details from papers into an organized table

- **Scite**

Allows researcher to see how publication has been cited by providing the context of citation and discover supporting and contrasting evidence for each paper. https://scite.ai/

Scite is an acknowledged resource for finding and assessing scientific articles with Smart Citations. By providing the context of the citation and a classification indicating whether it offers supporting or contradictory evidence for the referenced assertion, Smart Citations enable users to see how a publication has been cited.

- **SciSpace Co-pilot**

A multi-lingual AI tool, is helps you comprehend the paper (and the math and tables in it), seek answers to your queries, turn lengthy texts and sections into easy to consume summaries. https://typeset.io/

This helps in briefing abstract,Introduction,methods used, data used, more related papers about the title, briefly describing the conclusion etc. .

Researcher may take help of this tool using website https://typeset.io/.This enhances their understanding ability as well streamline their literature review time.Thus,this AI tool helps in research editing and research paper writing .

AI Tools for Data Analysis

- Excel Formula Bot

Converts your text instructions into spreadsheet formula. https://lnkd.in/dRFKeC25!

Typically, these tools provide guidance, suggestions, or automation to help users create, understand, or optimize Excel formulas(Kennelly,2023). They might offer features like suggesting formulas based on input, explaining functions, checking for errors, or assisting in formula creation. Excel formula plays a significant role in data analysis.

ACADEMIC WRITING

- Trinka

A grammar checker and language correction AI tool for academic and technical writing; finds errors unique to academic writing that other grammar checker tools may miss. https://www.trinka.ai/

Trinka is a language enhancement tool designed for academic writing. It offers assistance with grammar, syntax, style, and structure to help users improve the quality of their academic papers, research articles, and other scholarly writing.

Trinka uses artificial intelligence to provide suggestions and feedback that align with academic writing standards and guidelines. It aims to help users communicate their ideas effectively and professionally, particularly in the academic and research domains.

- Lex

A text editor which helps you neatly store and format documents with simple prompts including references, headers and bulleted list. https://lex.page/

Lex is basically a word processor that comes equipped with artificial intelligence – meaning its always there to help you write better, faster, and help escape writer's block.

ery simply LEX. page is a web-based AI writing tool that helps you generate content quickly and easily.

- AI paraphrasing tools

Ø QuillBot, Inc.:

QuillBot, Inc. is a company that has developed an AI-powered paraphrasing tool called QuillBot. QuillBot is designed to help users rewrite and rephrase sentences, paragraphs, or articles while retaining the original meaning.

The tool uses artificial intelligence to understand the context of the input text and suggests alternative phrasings to improve clarity, coherence, and originality. It's often used by writers, students, and professionals who need assistance in creating original content or avoiding plagiarism(Huang Z.,2023).

For the most current and detailed information about QuillBot, Inc. and their products or services, I recommend visiting their official website or checking the latest online sources for updates.

Ø Writesonic:

Writesonic is an AI-powered copywriting tool. It's designed to assist users in creating various types of written content, including marketing copy, blog posts, ad copy, social media posts, and more. Writesonic utilizes artificial intelligence to generate content based on user inputs and preferences.

Users typically provide prompts or describe the type of content they need, and Writesonic's algorithms generate text accordingly, aiming to match the desired tone, style, and purpose. It's a tool used by businesses, marketers, writers, and others looking to streamline the content creation process.

For the most up-to-date and detailed information about Writesonic, I recommend visiting their official website or checking the latest online sources for any updates or changes.

Ø Grammarly:

Grammarly is a widely used AI-powered writing assistant tool. It's designed to help users improve their writing by identifying and correcting grammar, punctuation, spelling, and style mistakes. Grammarly is available as a web-based application, a browser extension, a Microsoft Word add-in, and a mobile ap p(Seufert,2021),(Ilieva,2022),(Busch,2023),(Yan,2023),(Straunme,2022)).

Grammarly offers features such as grammar and spell checking, style and tone suggestions, sentence structure improvements, vocabulary enhancements, and plagiarism detection. It's a valuable tool for students, professionals, writers, and anyone looking to enhance the quality of their written content.

Ø Anyword:

It resonates most with product marketers and content managers.

It helps to social media managers, product managers, growth marketers, cmo,content managers .It increase conversions.

Ø Google Docs: Same time google docs is editable by a group of people who is given with access .It increases productivity and saves time.

SURVEY ON AI TOOLS FOR SCIENTIFIC, RESEARCH WRITING AND EDITING

A Study has been done for a total count of 61 people mixed mass of students, academicians and other professionals for the usage and effectiveness of AI tools and their writing of research paper and other editing work. For this study ten questions are framed and their responses are tabulated in five different categories as follows. The responses of this are shown in table I and table II(Carneiro, 2022),Cuneryr, 2023),(Lin,2023),(Gayd,2022),(Abd-Elsalam,2023)).

Note:

SA:Strongly Agree

A:Agree

N:Neutral

D:Disagree

SD:Strongly disagree

Questions:

CONCLUSION

Integrating AI tools into the research paper writing process can lead to enhanced efficiency, improved quality, and valuable insights.AI tools can streamline various aspects of the research paper writing process. They assist in tasks like literature review, data analysis, and even generating drafts. This efficiency

Table 1. Response in percentage

Sl no	Questions	Responses %				
		SA	A	N	D	SD
Q1	AI-based learning tools improve my writing skills.	53	40	6	2	0
Q2	AI-based learning tools improve my performance.	55	36	5	2	0
Q3	AI-based tools help me in achieving writing objectives.	56	38	5	0	0
Q4	AI-based tools improve the quality of my writing.	54	41	3	0	0
Q5	AI-based tools are easily accessible.	51	38	12	0	0
Q6	AI-based tools have various features.	56	40	3	0	0
Q7	AI-based tools saves my time.	61	38	3	0	0
Q8	AI-based tools features quickly follow the instruction .	58	33	8	0	0
Q9	Organization and presentation is very good	50	42	8	0	0
Q10	I am eager and motivated to use AI-based tools.	43	43	12	0	0

Table 2. Each question aggregate response in percentage.

	Q1	Q2	Q3	Q4	Q5	Q6	Q7	Q8	Q9	Q10
SA	32	34	34	33	31	34	37	35	30	28
A	24	22	23	25	23	24	23	20	25	26
N	3	3	3	2	7	2	2	5	5	6
DA	1	1	0	0	0	0	0	0	1	0
SDA	1	1	1	1	1	1	1	1	0	1
%	87.87	88.52	89.18	89.18	88.20	89.51	93.11	88.85	87.54	86.23

can save researchers valuable time and resources. By harnessing the capabilities of AI, researchers can access advanced data analysis, language optimization, and even plagiarism checks. This contributes to a higher standard of quality in research papers, ensuring accuracy and reliability.AI tools can uncover patterns and trends in data that might be challenging for humans to identify. This can lead to new perspectives and insights, enriching the depth of research and its potential impact.

While AI can be a powerful ally, it's essential to maintain a balance. Human intuition, critical thinking, and creativity are irreplaceable. Researchers should use AI tools as aids, not substitutes, ensuring the human touch remains integral to the research process. The integrity of research is paramount. Researchers must be vigilant about the potential biases or errors in AI algorithms and validate their findings through traditional research methods. This ensures that the results are robust and trustworthy. The landscape of AI is ever-evolving. Researchers need to stay informed about the latest advancements, ensuring that their use of AI aligns with ethical standards. Awareness of the limitations and potential biases in AI systems is crucial to making informed decisions.

REFERENCES

Abd-Elsalam, K. A., & Abdel-Momen, S. M. (2023). Artificial Intelligence's Development and Challenges in Scientific Writing. *Egyptian Journal of Agricultural Research*, *101*(3), 714–717. doi:10.21608/ejar.2023.220363.1414

Ang, T. L., Choolani, M., See, K. C., & Poh, K. K. (2023). The rise of artificial intelligence: Addressing the impact of large language models such as ChatGPT on scientific publications. *Singapore Medical Journal*, *64*(4), 219. doi:10.4103/singaporemedj.SMJ-2023-055 PMID:37006087

Busch, P. A., & Hausvik, G. I. (2023). Too Good to Be True? An Empirical Study of ChatGPT Capabilities for Academic Writing and Implications for Academic Misconduct.

Carneiro, A. S. R. (2022). Following the path of otherwise: Subalternized subjects, academic writing and the political power of discomfort. *Journal of Multicultural Discourses*, *17*(2), 138–157. doi:10.1080/17447143.2022.2113886

Curry, N., Kasparkova, A., Ganobcsik-Williams, L., & Gustafsson, M. (2023). Thinking outside the academic writing box. *Journal of Academic Writing*, *13*(1), ii–v. doi:10.18552/joaw.v10i1.968

Dubose, J., & Marshall, D. (2023). AI in academic writing: Tool or invader. *Public Services Quarterly*, *19*(2), 125–130. doi:10.1080/15228959.2023.2185338

Fok, R., & Weld, D. S. (2023). What Can't Large Language Models Do? The Future of AI-Assisted Academic Writing. In In2Writing Workshop at CHI.

Forrester, C., Boothe, K., & Generative, A. I. (n.d.). *Academic Writing*. Ethical Recommendations.

Gayed, J. M., Carlon, M. K. J., Oriola, A. M., & Cross, J. S. (2022). Exploring an AI-based writing Assistant's impact on English language learners. *Computers and Education: Artificial Intelligence*, *3*(100055), 100055. doi:10.1016/j.caeai.2022.100055

Giray, L. (2023). Prompt engineering with ChatGPT: A guide for academic writers. *Annals of Biomedical Engineering*, *51*(12), 2629–2633. doi:10.1007/s10439-023-03272-4 PMID:37284994

Golan, R., Reddy, R., Muthigi, A., & Ramasamy, R. (2023). Artificial intelligence in academic writing: A paradigm-shifting technological advance. *Nature Reviews. Urology*, *20*(6), 327–328. doi:10.1038/s41585-023-00746-x PMID:36829078

Huang, Z., & Winkel, W. (n.d.). Automated Feedback: An AI-powered Tool to Scale Micro-level Feedback for Better Academic Writing.

Ilieva, R., & Tonchev, A. (2022). Adapting the Teaching of Academic Writing to the Emergence of Natural Language Generators. In 2022 V International Conference on High Technology for Sustainable Development (HiTech) (pp. 1–4). IEEE. 10.1109/HiTech56937.2022.10145549

Jarrah, A. M., Wardat, Y., & Fidalgo, P. (2023). Using ChatGPT in academic writing is (not) a form of plagiarism: What does the literature say. *Online J. Commun. Media Technol.*

Kennelly, I., & Donnelly, R. (2023). AI Supporting Student Academic Writing in Higher Education.

Lingard, L. (2023). Writing with ChatGPT: An illustration of its capacity, limitations & implications for academic writers. *Perspectives on Medical Education*, *12*(1), 261–270. doi:10.5334/pme.1072 PMID:37397181

LiuZ.YaoZ.LiF.LuoB. (2023). Check me if you can: Detecting ChatGPT-generated academic writing using CheckGPT. Retrieved from http://arxiv.org/abs/2306.05524

Lund, B. D., Wang, T., Mannuru, N. R., Nie, B., Shimray, S., & Wang, Z. (2023). ChatGPT and a new academic reality: Artificial Intelligence-written research papers and the ethics of the large language models in scholarly publishing. *Journal of the Association for Information Science and Technology*, *74*(5), 570–581. doi:10.1002/asi.24750

Maruashvili, E. (2023). Criteria For Academic Writing. Georgian Academy of Business Sciences. *MOAMBE*, *1*, 60–64.

Nazari, N., Shabbir, M. S., & Setiawan, R. (2021). Application of Artificial Intelligence powered digital writing assistant in higher education: Randomized controlled trial. *Heliyon*, *7*(5), e07014. doi:10.1016/j.heliyon.2021.e07014 PMID:34027198

Rahman, M. A., Terano, H. J., Rahman, N., Salamzadeh, A., & Rahaman, M. S. (2023). ChatGPT and Academic Research: A review and recommendations based on practical examples. Journal of Education. *Management and Development Studies*, *3*(1), 1–12. doi:10.52631/jemds.v3i1.175

Seufert, S., Burkhard, M., & Handschuh, S. (2021). Fostering Students' Academic Writing Skills: Feedback Model for an AI-enabled Support Environment. In Association for the Advancement of Computing in Education (pp. 49–58). AACE.

Straume, I., & Anson, C. (2022). Amazement and trepidation: Implications of AI-based natural language production for the teaching of writing. *Journal of Academic Writing*, *12*(1), 1–9. doi:10.18552/joaw.v12i1.820

Yan, D. (2023). Impact of ChatGPT on learners in a L2 writing practicum: An exploratory investigation. *Education and Information Technologies*, *28*(11), 1–25. doi:10.1007/s10639-023-11742-4

Chapter 5
The Use of Artificial Intelligence Tools in Academic Writing With Agronomic Direction

Nadezhda Anatolievna Lebedeva
https://orcid.org/0000-0003-4095-2631
International Personnel Academy, Germany

ABSTRACT

In the context of agricultural science, the academic writing is of great importance, as articles of academicians and scientists make available all their developments available for studying the experiences around the world. This contributes not only to the exchange of experience, but also to expand the practical knowledge in agrarian topics to different continents and countries, spreading the developments of economical agriculture for solving problems with food on a global scale. Therefore, the use of artificial intelligence in the field of agrarian academic writing can be as positive results, so has risks of incorrect research of certain issues. This chapter sets itself the goal of considering the pros and cons of using artificial intelligence tools in academic writing with an agronomic focus, taking into account the specifics of the basic concept of academic writing and new artificial intelligence tools. The novelty of this work lies in the fact that developments of Ukrainian scientists can serve as interesting theoretical material for foreign colleagues.

INTRODUCTION

Academic writing is a traditional type of language competence, which in our rapidly developing century has become especially relevant due to the global development of science and international academic relations. As Ukraine is one of the most agronomical developed countries, agrarian science constantly provides its achievements to the world community not only in the form of innovations in agricultural products but also a description of its scientific achievements, experiences and developments. As a result, the progress and improvement of academic writing with an agronomic focus occurs. In particular, students are trained to write scientific works on agricultural specialities not only in their native language but also

DOI: 10.4018/979-8-3693-1798-3.ch005

in a foreign language in the course "Foreign Language for Professional Orientation." They learn to read, understand, format and structure their work to present it at student scientific conferences and publish in collections of articles. For international student conferences, works with agronomic focus are written in English. Thus, practical knowledge of academic writing is the most important factor for successful studies at an agricultural university. The appearance of artificial intelligence in our reality has become a breakthrough in all areas of human knowledge, naturally affecting scientific writing. The advantages and disadvantages of using artificial intelligence in academic writing with an agronomic focus will be discussed in this chapter.

At the beginning of 2023, a huge event happened - this was the spread of information about the ChatGPT artificial intelligence tool, the release of which took place back in November 2022. University education faced the threat of the actual disappearance of such types of works as essays, abstracts, and even diploma and master's theses and dissertations (Ostapovych, 2023; Soroka, 2023; Balyk & Shmyger, 2023). ChatGPT is a chatbot with artificial intelligence that can work with text, create images, work with formulas and tables - and generate everything it is asked. Therefore, the possibilities for its use are practically limitless, the chatbot is capable of simplifying the work and increasing the efficiency of employees in almost any field of human activity. As scientists write (Ostapovych, 2023), the use of machine learning algorithms to analyze the entered text and generate answers that are designed to imitate human conversation allows to use this chatbot for anything, even answering notes, providing information, communicating with various languages, means of conversation. There is a need to observe the ethical principles of higher education and academic integrity in the scientific community and among students (Ostapovych, 2023, p. 201). Artificial intelligence has many definitions (Khoroshaylo, & Kochergina, 2023); Gureeva (2021). If to summarize these definitions, it would be that artificial intelligence is a broad term used to describe a set of technologies that can solve and perform tasks to achieve any goals without human guidance. There was a need to support artificial intelligence in the higher education system of Ukraine to make universities better adapted to the needs of modern society. This is especially relevant for agronomic science, which is constantly developing and needs a description of its activities.

The purpose of this chapter is a theoretical description of the possibilities of using artificial intelligence tools in agricultural academic writing.

The following tasks are set during the study:

- generalization of information about the possibilities of using artificial intelligence in the field of agricultural science, education and teaching based on modern scientific literature;
- to highlight the main directions for the development of writing skills for further application in professional activities based on existing programs and scientific sources;
- consideration of the scope of application of existing knowledge for agricultural universities, as well as highlighting the problems, advantages and disadvantages of artificial intelligence in the field of academic writing in agriculture.

The novelty of the work is to describe the Ukrainian experience of teaching academic writing at the Agricultural University based on scientific sources and existing programs. Methodology. This study is an analysis of the literature and practical results for several years. During the preparation of the chapter, the following methods were used: analysis, synthesis, the philosophical method of generalization and the method of a systematic approach. Figures were created by the author of this chapter showing the problems.

BACKGROUND

Let's note once again that academic writing on agrarian topics acquires a need for its further development precisely because agriculture feeds people and its development spreads thanks to scientific achievements on a global scale. A foreign language course for professional orientation in agricultural universities of Ukraine causes a lot of difficulties for students and future scientists. Artificial intelligence can be a good helper in this case. Until now, the possibility of artificial interest has largely remained outside the attention of researchers. It is noted that the neural network can be useful if a person needs to replenish the vocabulary, "tell about new words and expressions, give definitions of unknown words and examples of use, offer contextual tasks to make sure of your understanding; give advice on the correct use of grammatical structures of a foreign English language, explanations on complex grammatical rules; improving spelling and translation. The neural network can translate texts in English and another foreign language into any language it is trained to, which allows understanding the meaning of words and phrases and even prepares the student for exams" (Samoilenko, 2023).

This is, to a certain extent, a fairly simple level of understanding the problem, since with such everyday tasks in learning a foreign language, according to information (Ostapovych et al., 2023) it is much more effective and with less about the number of errors, Google translate advises. With regard to the professional training of a specialist in agronomy, animal and bioengineering or plant quarantine, it can be argued that a correctly formulated request to ChatGPT helps in professional activity to edit highly specialized, terminologically saturated texts translated by him into or from a foreign language according to the relevant context bases to native. One of the key advantages of artificial intelligence in education, according to Horoshaylo & Kochergyna (2023), is its ability to personalize learning. "Artificial intelligence algorithms can track student progress and provide personalized feedback, helping students identify their strengths and weaknesses, as well as pay more attention to those issues that need improvement" (Horoshaylo & Kochergyna, 2023, p. 123). Such a personalized approach to learning, according to the mentioned scientists, is more effective than traditional teaching methods and leads to better student results. The author of this chapter fully agrees with the statement, as she was in the war zone herself, and was forced to leave her country and switch to online teaching, that "the advantage of artificial intelligence in education is its potential to overcome inequality and improve access to quality education. Artificial intelligence can help overcome geographical and financial barriers, allowing students with disabilities, refugees (those Ukrainians who were forced to leave Ukraine due to the state of war, but intend to continue their studies at native universities), those who live in communities, where hostilities are taking place, people from remote or occupied territories have access to the same high-quality higher education that students from other regions have" (Horoshaylo & Kochergyna, 2023, p. 123). In such a case in future, teachers will receive sets of data, with which they can analyze and understand the needs of individual students and automatically adapt their program to the pace of learning of each specific student of agricultural topics in a foreign language. The use of artificial intelligence in an agricultural university in general and the teaching of foreign languages in a professional direction, in particular, is a relevant topic about the analysis of the challenges, advantages and risks that artificial intelligence carries. Although it has many positive applications in the educational space, there are some ethical issues that we will focus on in this chapter.

The professional language of agrarians is not a linguistically independent system within the framework of a national language. On the contrary, it arose by differentiation and expansion of the writing. The

Figure 1. Features of agriculture special language (summarized by the author of the chapter)

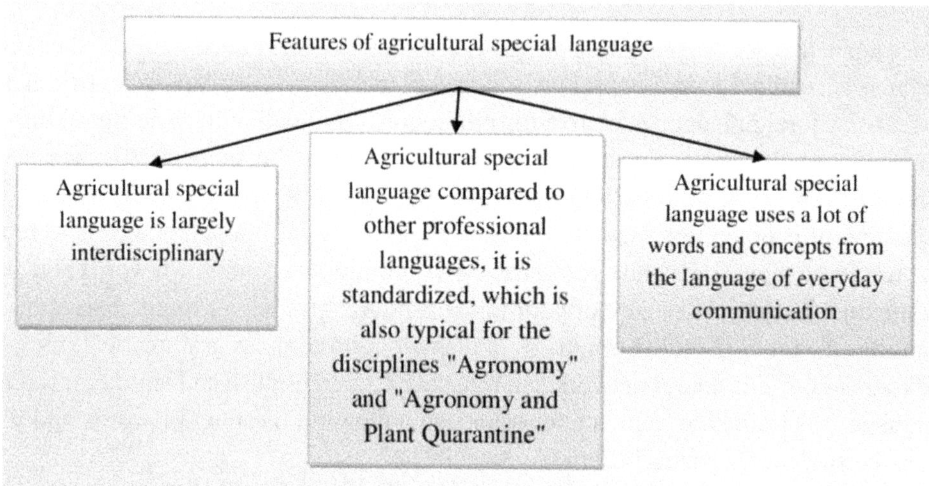

national, or literary, language creates the lexical basis and grammatical structure for any professional language. Thus, the professional language of agrarians has the following features, which are shown in Figure 1.

Researchers Kornienko (2013), Zhazanova (2015), Lebedeva (2018; 2021; 2022; 2023), Shor and Gauliullina (2021) note that for students to master a special dictionary and be able to use it, it is necessary to determine the volume of such a dictionary, its organization as a system, and communicate clearly to those who master it. However, the subject matter of agrarian is limited to the levels shown in Figure 2.

To educate students, along with methodological recommendations developed by universities, teaching aids in a foreign language of professional orientation are widely used. The training course helps to improve the speech skills of the English language in the field of agronomy and plant quarantine. For students Bazanova (2016) regarding the preparation for bachelor's and master's notes the tasks of mastering the professional speech culture, which is achieved by using writing in the classroom.

Figure 2. Levels of the specialty "Agronomy" subject study (summarized by the author of the chapter)

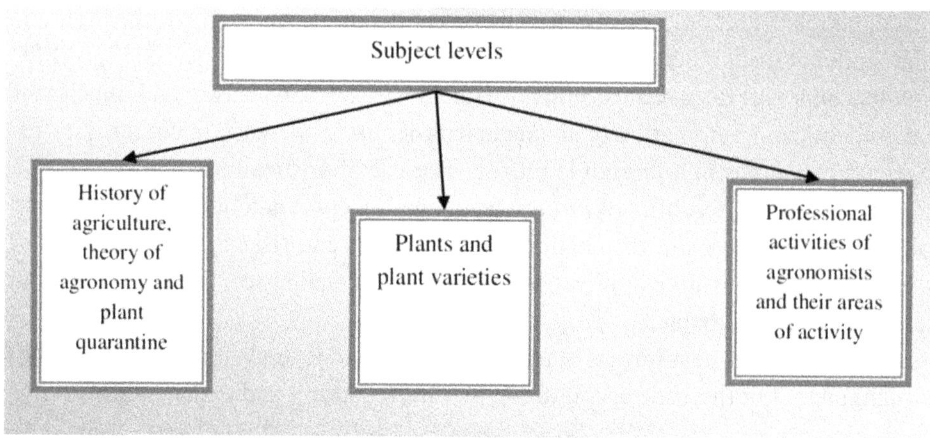

The researcher notes: *"Here we focus on the term "culture" in any interpretation that implies the process and result of continuous improvement. Competences based on the knowledge of the culture of written scientific speech are formed in the study of all disciplines. In the process of studying, students master the glossary on each topic, develop the ability to work with dictionaries, read scientific texts, and gain experience in compiling notes, writing annotations and abstracts, essays, articles and reports, reviews, and reviews. They have skills and experience in editing, compiling a bibliography, etc."* (Bazanova, 2016, p. 21).

According to Takanova (2008), a foreign language for students of agrarian specialities must correspond to professional skills, and certain qualification characteristics, which are fixed by the university curriculum.

"Professional-oriented education is understood as education based on taking into account the needs of students in learning a foreign language, dictated by the characteristic features of the profession or speciality, which, in turn, require its study. This is what determines the main difference between professionally-oriented learning and language learning for general educational purposes. Each component of the professionally oriented education system integrates several subsystems depending on the sphere of future professional activity of students" (Takanova, 2008, p. 50).

For students studying animal and bioengineering, Kherson scientists Pasechko and Lebedeva developed a 3-language dictionary of special terms (Lebedeva & Pasechko, 2017).

MAIN FOCUS OF THE CHAPTER

1. Academic Writing in the Agrarian Science: General Characteristics

As already noted in the introduction of this chapter, academic writing at an agricultural university is the basic language competence of a successful specialist, allowing him to read, understand, structure and create his scientific texts. In the course of teaching a foreign language with a professional orientation to students of agricultural universities in Ukraine, a significant amount of time is devoted specifically to teaching academic writing skills. Scientists have described in detail the genres of academic writing. In general, it is well known that a genre is a form of organization of speech material within the framework of a particular style of speech. Scientific academic writing is the richest in this aspect, due to the presence of many types of texts. According to researchers, speech genres are defined as relatively stable, thematic, compositional and stylistic types of statements. Traditionally, academic genres are divided into primary and secondary. Primary ones include a scientific article, academic review, monograph, or dissertation, secondary ones include an abstract, theses, abstract, specialized encyclopaedic article, scientific discussion, and description of a scientific project. Any young scientist should have an idea and master each of them (Tretyakova & Akimova, 2018). An abstract is a condensed description of the source. It lists the main issues of the source's subject matter, and in some cases characterizes its structure (Kiselova & Zavalska, 2023, p. 22). An abstract is a brief presentation that includes the main provisions of the content of the primary text. The abstract reflects the main information contained in the source, new information, and essential data contained in the main text (https://publishing_dictionary.academic.ru/842/Abstract.) Scientific discussion is a way of discussing and searching for truth in the process of studying scientific problems. It is carried out by putting forward, contrasting and critically discussing different points of view (Klobukova, 1998). A scientific article is an author's work published in a scientific publication that describes the results of an intermediate or completed original scientific research (primary scientific article) or is devoted to the consideration of previously published scientific articles related to a common topic (systematic review) (Kiselova & Zavalska, 2023, p. 22). An academic (scientific) review is a written analysis of a scientific text (article, diploma work and dissertation for the academic degree of candidate/doctor of science), containing a critical assessment (https://www.hse.ru/review/journalreview) A dissertation is a qualifying work for the award of an academic or scientific degree and qualification (Big Encyclopedic Dictionary, 1991, p. 395). Kuular M. (2021) defines a monograph as "a scientific, popular science or production-practical publication that presents a complete, comprehensive and in-depth examination of one topic, problem or issue in the form of scientific research results, or an exhaustive generalization of theoretical material on one scientific problem with critical analysis, determination of significance, formulation of new concepts, written by one or more authors, aimed mainly at specialists" (Kuular, 2021, p. 82).

Genres of academic writing differ in composition, volume content, and linguistic design. They have a specific internal vocabulary (for example 3-language dictionary of special terms by Lebedeva & Pasechko, 2017). What they have in common is the expression of precise scientific thought. Academic writing genres follow the precise choice of words and phrasing characteristic of academic style and adhere to traditional structure, spelling, punctuation, and grammar. Compositionally, academic writing is most often characterized by a simple structure: introduction, body, and conclusion. In the main part, references are made to other scientific works, and one's own opinion is substantiated. A conclusion is a completion that summarizes the key points made in a scientific essay. In the final part, research prospects related to the issues considered are outlined. A significant difference between academic writing and other writing genres is based on citation and referencing. If a scientist expresses a judgment about something within the framework of the genres of academic writing, then he confirms his own opinion through connection with the published works of other scientists (Paltridge et al., 2009); Yiğitoğlu, & Reichelt, (2014); Tretyakova & Akimova, 2018; Kiselova & Zavalska, 2023). References to the works of other authors occupy a central place in the academic literature of agronomical orientation as they show that the researcher has read the literature, understands the hypotheses and methodology, has integrated the problems and has taken into account the prospects for future work. "In academic writing, rules of punctuation and grammar are always followed, because if the reader does not understand something, then he will not be able to read the author's thoughts. Therefore, the presentation of the problem must be clear and precise" (Tretyakova & Akimova, 2018). To summarize the general concepts of academic writing about agronomic specialities, the author of this chapter notes that the course of teaching academic writing at Ukrainian agricultural universities is carried out within the framework of the subjects "Foreign language of professional orientation" and "Business Ukrainian language". Academic writing in the agricultural field is a language competence, the knowledge of which allows the researcher to read, understand and describe his experiments in scientific texts. Genres of academic writing are divided into certain types and have several features. They are characterized by a simple structure (introduction, main part, and conclusion), citing and references to the works of other scientists, clarity and accuracy of statements, and following the rules of punctuation, grammar and spelling. Since there is a direct connection between academic writing with an agronomic focus and teaching a foreign language with a specialized focus, the possibilities of translation using artificial intelligence are a pressing issue that the author will consider in this chapter.

Figure 3. Several types of translation exercises (summarized by the author of the chapter)

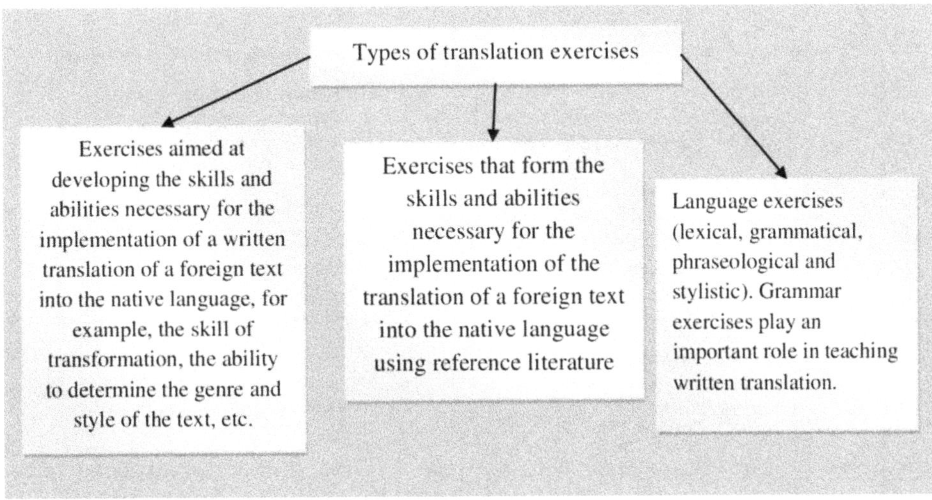

Because the lesson at the university is limited in time, it is more reasonable to teach the written translation of foreign texts into the native language as part of additional classes. However, since written translation contributes to the improvement of a foreign language, it is advisable to introduce elements of written translation in the planned classes, that is, to ask students to translate texts on special agricultural topics.

The experience of Abramova and Ananieva (2010) is also interesting, where a writing project was created, which is designed for the fourth year of a bachelor's degree or the first year of a master's degree and was carried out as part of the educational process in parallel with the study of the main program. The author of this article used some aspects of studying a specialized foreign language for students of a master's program in the speciality "Agriculture". Abramova and Ananieva's (2010) initial experience included several stages: 1) a comparative analysis of the styles of written scientific text in English and native languages; 2) the creation of a scientific article in the native language based on the material of the student's term paper in the main speciality; 3) adaptation of this article, taking into account the requirements for English-language scientific texts; 4) translation of an adapted article into English with a pre-translation analysis and a detailed commentary on translation transformations; 5) design and presentation of written work, reflecting all stages of the project. A comparative analysis of the styles of written scientific text in English and native a language, even though it is not a written task, is an important stage, since its results determine the quality of the final text. In most cases, students create a reference text in their native language and then mechanically translate it. At the same time, they do not take into account the fact that the laws on which the Ukrainian text is built do not apply to the text in a foreign language. Errors in translation into a foreign language are superimposed on the shortcomings of the source text. As a result, there is a complete loss of meaning (Abramova and Ananyeva, 2010, p. 96).

To avoid mistakes, a thorough study of the creation of written scientific texts in two languages is suggested. Here, the logical structure, style, and grammar are taken into account, special attention is paid to specialized vocabulary. Thus, students learn the skill of creating a full-fledged scientific article that will represent the results of their research in the future and meet the requirements for scientific papers around the world. A feature of such a written project is that it *"allows students to develop not only*

Figure 4. Assistance in the process of completing academic writing assignments (summarized by the author of the chapter)

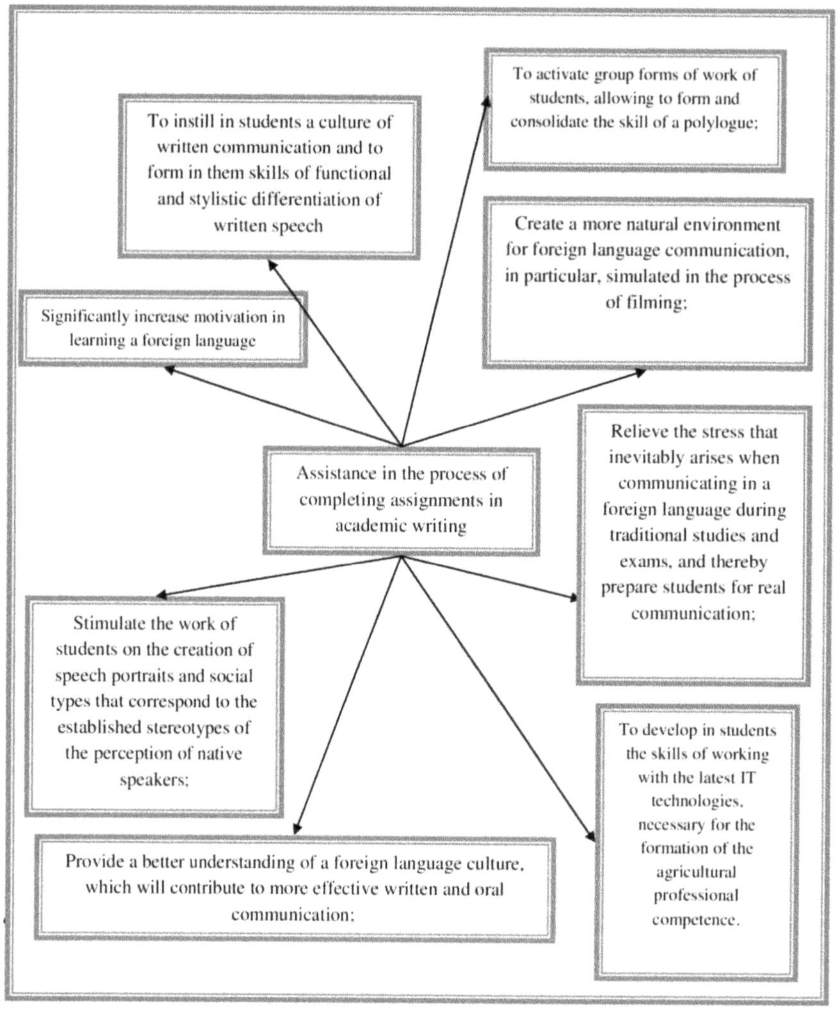

the skills of academic writing but also the basic skills of professionally oriented translation, which can become an important competitive advantage for a modern graduate. Students should be aware that in our time it is written texts (letters, applications for grants, essays for admission to foreign universities, resumes, etc.) that perform a contact-establishing function, make it possible to form an impression of a potential interlocutor or partner and determine the nature of subsequent communication" (Abramova and Ananyeva, 2010, p. 97).

Based on the foregoing, the author of this chapter comes to the understanding that teaching writing in a foreign language of a specialized orientation to students of agricultural universities in construction specialities must necessarily include a written translation.

Another essential aspect of mastering writing in a specialized foreign language is writing annotations and summarizing. Students of agrarian specialities of agricultural universities learn to annotate and abstract specialized materials in a foreign language and master the appropriate terminology, as well as grammatical and lexical means characteristic of foreign documents and scientific correspondence. Shevchenko and Mitchell note that in the course of studying a special course, students receive theoretical knowledge and acquire practical skills in working with documents and deciphering drawings. With the help of abstract writing and summarizing, students develop and improve basic special language skills and skills in the field of professional activity (Shevchenko and Mitchell, 2013, p. 128).

One more important aspect of academic writing is to familiarize students with educational values such as academic culture and integrity, respect for intellectual property and copyright. This aspect of academic writing in Ukraine is analyzed in detail in the work of Skidan and Efimchuk (2019). Their study analyzed the manifestations of academic dishonesty among students. This is cheating on each other, appropriation of other people's results (including during the writing of independent works, analysis of literary and Internet sources; envy of the subjects of study who received the best results of current control, dishonest attitude of students towards each other) (Skidan & Efimchuk, 2019, p. 242). Unfortunately, similar manifestations also occur among teachers. Ulyanova and Baaji (2023) studied the problem in their study and described it in their scientific article. Scholars have noted the fact that academic integrity is encouraged and implemented through a wide range of international, regional and national initiatives. An important role is also played by the developed academic integrity policies of individual educational, scientific and management institutions and their practical measures for the implementation of these policies. "In the modern educational and scientific environment both in Ukraine and abroad, issues of academic integrity and trust often turn into issues of monitoring, control and coercion in both online and offline formats. In the context of the introduction of a large number of online resources, and the development of distance learning, a variety of software products are being actively used, which act as tools for measuring the level of integrity, monitoring or checking education seekers and scientists. The leading place today should be occupied by preventive measures to prevent academic dishonesty and inculcate zero tolerance towards its manifestations. Currently, the introduction of new and improvement of already existing effective mechanisms for the prevention of academic offences in face-to-face and remote forms of the educational-scientific process requires active implementation" (Ulyanova and Baadzhi, 2023, p. 102).

For the agronomic direction, it is important to use experimental data and their description, therefore the culture of scientific text design is an indisputable factor in the process of writing articles in the agronomic direction and teaching academic writing. It is mandatory in the learning process to become familiar with the rules for citing and formatting references to bibliographic sources.

2. Problems of Using Artificial Intelligence Tools in Academic Writing in Agronomic Areas

As mentioned above, at the end of 2022, the academic community was shocked by the launch of a tool such as ChatGPT1 - a chatbot with artificial intelligence and extensive automatic text generation capabilities. ChatGPT is capable of not only generating answers to questions that mimic human ones but also remembering search queries and learning on its own by analyzing user messages. A chatbot has unique capabilities due to its ability to understand, which allows it to answer questions, complete tasks, create creative texts, imitate the author's writing style, do linguistic translation from one language to another, create pictures and much more (Soroka, 2023; Ostapovich & et al.2023, Balik, & Schmiger, 2023). ChatGPT is a natural language processing (NLP) technology that makes computers to understand input of a human. Proficiency in AI tools like natural language processing (NLP), machine learning, and data analytics is crucial for academic writing in agronomy. It involves understanding and utilizing these technologies effectively. Additionally, the ability to gather, analyze, and interpret agronomic data is essential, given AI's reliance on substantial datasets for generating insights. From the works (Zhou et al., 2020; Resnik, & Lin, 2010; Strubell et al., 2019; DeYoung et al., 2019; Kang et al., 2020; Feng et al., 2021; Olujimi, Ade-Ibijola, 2023) it follows that NLP is a field of artificial intelligence that aims to enable computers to understand and process the natural language that people use to communicate with each other. NLP is used in areas where it is necessary to process and analyze large volumes of text information. NLP as a science is at the intersection of computer linguistics and machine learning technology. Using natural language processing, computers learn to conduct conversations, answer questions, translate text into different languages, or generate them from scratch. You can delegate routine tasks to machines, such as asking them to automatically categorize support tickets by topic or language in which they are written, sending them straight to the right person. NLP can be used to solve many problems related to natural language processing. The computer can translate voice speech into text. This is required for any application that performs voice commands or chats with a person. Another aspect is natural language generation. Translation of structured, that is, tabular, data into text in natural language. We can say that this task is the opposite of speech recognition. Determining the meaning of a word. A computer can accurately determine the meaning of a word after semantically analyzing a sentence. For example, the word "lock" can have different meanings: "a mechanical device for locking doors" or "a building with fortifications." The task of NLP is to determine what meaning this word has in the text. However, natural language processing algorithms can extract subjective characteristics from text, such as emotions. When text is analyzed, it is broken down into tokens—small fragments, such as individual words. In further analysis, it is necessary to preserve and take into account their relationship. (Olujimi & Ade-Ibijola, 2023).

Thus, the scientific community in the field of academic writing acquires, on the one hand, a valuable assistant, but on the other, several problems associated with academic integrity. In general, artificial intelligence is characterized as a tool that enables machines to learn from experience, adapt to new inputs and carry out tasks given by humans. Most examples of artificial intelligence, as shown in the work of Gureev (2021), are widely known and have been good assistants until now (computers that play chess, autonomous cars, and assistants in learning a foreign language. With the advent of ChatGPT, the situation has taken on a slightly different character. For educational purposes, as can be seen from the study by Soroka, (2023). ChatGPT answers basic questions, accompanying the answers with logical explanations. Sometimes it makes unexpected errors in mathematical calculations but modifies the result of the request as a response to human prompts.

In the scientific work "Implementation of artificial intelligence in education by using ChatGPT" (Balik, & Shmyger, 2023) regarding Ukrainian education note the fact that ChatGPT can perform the following tasks in an educational context: write abstracts, essays, articles; write lesson plans; develop a curriculum plan; write requirements for the training program, training goals; create a quiz / test questions; write a script for a podcast or video; to provide instructions for educational activities; act as a learning agent; write e-mails to students; annotate the text you insert into ChatGPT (for example, a transcript of a video/podcast); write a text for students to read, which is designed for a certain level of vocabulary and contains a certain vocabulary; write adventure stories that you choose yourself; create examples to help students learn; create scenarios for role-playing games and simulations; create mathematical and natural problems, try to solve them; identify potential misconceptions of students about the content; to give low-quality and high-quality examples of writing (works); provide advice on how to personalize/

differentiate training; create prompts for discussion in the audience; provide individual training or coaching, etc. It is known how important it is to have a mentor and an expert who will help you develop your career. In this context, we will consider how to use the OpenAI ChatGPT language model as a personal mentor that will help students and teachers in professional development (Balyk, & Shmyger, 2023, p. 143). "In other words, in cases where it initially failed to match a problem to the correct solution method, ChatGPT corrected itself after receiving the appropriate hint from a human expert. As a result, ChatGPT passed the final exam for the MBA program" (Soroka, 2023, p. 275).

Scientists' optimism about artificial intelligence is that artificial intelligence is expected to become an effective tool for personalizing education as an individual assistant. At the same time, the main thing remains the motivation of the one who studies. ChatGPT helps quickly to master a new area of knowledge, in this case, agronomics. Using short dialogues, the student can find interesting research questions and formulate the first hypotheses. If we talk about teachers, then, according to Soroka (2023), ChatGPT is a tool for preparing classes, and it is proposed to be used for assessing written work.

"This is a short-term perspective that should be thought about and should be worked out methodically. In addition to evaluating what has been written, artificial intelligence can provide constructive feedback, pointing out errors, shortcomings and opportunities to improve work, which until now only a teacher could do" (Soroka, 2023, p. 275).

According to the author of this chapter, the prospect of such a future may carry the threat of job loss for a teacher, although the idea of lifelong self-education in the field of agricultural science, when technologies for agriculture are also rapidly developing, can be realized by providing valuable feedback and opening up opportunities for further development. Another positive aspect of using ChatGPT in academic writing with an agronomic focus is that it is possible to analyze, for example, large financial statements of agricultural holdings, companies involved in advertising agricultural products, as well as economic indicators of the agricultural market and the like. ChatGPT offers a huge number of possibilities for this. For example, opening the window of version 4 of ChatGPT, select Data Analytics. In this mode, you can see documents, work with PDF files, and, if necessary, analyze an Excel table. You just need to drag this table onto the monitor screen. There are many industrial tasks (i.e. instructions for setting up a task for a chatbot) for analytics of an advertising company, for financial analysis) and if ChatGPT produces a certain pattern or task, then it will cope with this task. You can replace analytics with end-to-end analytics. That is, if ChatGPT is provided with a certain statistical pattern in the form of numbers, it will also cope with this task. This is a very valuable quality for writing scientific papers with an agronomic focus since it saves a lot of time for the researcher. However, there is a risk of inaccuracy in the conclusion, since if there is only a limited amount of data available for analysis, and most of it is hidden from public access, then the study will be incomplete. In this case, it is necessary to indicate that the data was taken, for example, from the open access of the Internet or a database of a certain agricultural company. In such cases, options for the unfair use of artificial intelligence are not discussed. Scientists have yet to strategize how to legally use tools like ChatGPT. If we return to the problem of academic writing with an agronomic focus in a foreign language, we will note a software product based on artificial intelligence that helps to work with English text, such as Grammarly (www.grammarly.com). In the scientific work, Horoshailo, O. S., & Kochergina, S. S. (2023) noted that the writing checker Grammarly (www.grammarly.com) entered the market offering spelling and grammar checking with the ability to analyze clarity and understandability of the text, its coherence.

"Grammarly also offers linguistic recommendations and adaptations for text based on given parameters regarding target group (reader), level of formality (informal, neutral, formal), domain (academic, business, general, email, casual, creative), tone (neutral, confident, joyful, optimistic, friendly, urgent, analytical, respectful) and intention (inform, describe, persuade, tell a story)" (Horoshaylo, & Kochergina, 2023, p. 123).

According to Horoshailo & Kochergina (2023), since the text must first be written by someone, before translating and analyzing it, the necessary skill of professional academic writing in the neater all, students not only receive an overall grade for initial performance, but Grammarly also offers them textbook-like explanations of various lexical and grammatical phenomena. Thus, these narrow AIs are paradoxically holistic language (writing) learning tools that focus not only on shortcomings but also on the potential for improvement in various areas related to ELT, such as vocabulary, grammar acquisition, as well as productive skills" (Horoshaylo, & Kochergina, 2023, p. 124) native language is needed. And in this case, artificial intelligence is not a cause for concern.

According to Soroka (2023), ChatGPT offers similar functionality, helping to present text in English correctly. "It can be said that this is good news for those who prepare scientific articles for publication in English-language journals. In this case, the artificial intelligence checks the grammar but does not create a scientific text itself. And here you can predict both the decline of writing skills and their development. And again, a lot depends on the person and his motivation. Artificial assistants can show errors, offer options and thus help to learn, and can work instead of a person, creating texts based on questions and hints of users, replacing authors. For teachers, this means that such usual forms of assessment of the abilities of students as an essay, a report or a report lose their meaning, because ChatGPT creates an average quality imitation of the content on a given topic. At the same time, such an imitation easily passes plagiarism tests" (Soroka, 2023, p. 275.) ChatGPT is the most versatile AI chatbot for English teachers. It can help with tasks such as writing e-mails, research and provide suggestions for improving course materials, and help create interactive exercises for students to practice their writing skills. For example:

- create discussion questions for students of English on the topic of «The History of Agriculture»;
- write multiple choice comprehension questions with one correct option and four wrong options about this text;
- write fill-in-the-gaps exercises for agronomy students of English to practise the topic "Food Products";
- write sentences about the ecology for agronomy students of English using the word "field".

Thus, we can see that the implementation of artificial intelligence in education can often be divided into interrelated categories, when artificial intelligence focuses on the student (used to teach students), artificial intelligence focuses on the teacher (to support the work of teachers, including the automation of routine tasks for reduction of the teacher's workload, training analytics, use and facilitation of innovative pedagogical methods and detection of plagiarism.

3. Ethical Considerations

Ostapovych O., Ostapovych N., Mazurenko propose to solve the problem of plagiarism (2023). In their opinion, such types of educational tasks as writing home works, essays or translations in a foreign language in the age of artificial intelligence may disappear into oblivion (because they provoke the student to plagiarize or use an online machine translator, and recently - "advanced", trained neural networks), then you can combine artificial intelligence with academic integrity. "In this context, a special memo on the use of ChatGPT students, developed by the Department of World Literature of the Zaporizhzhya National University (Ostapovych et al., 2023), placed in public access, deserves unconditional attention and approval, where, despite practical advice on the academically virtuous use of artificial intelligence tools, based on large language models, examples of violations of norms of academic integrity and indicators of their detection are given" (Ostapovych et al., 2023, p. 203). The author of this chapter also got acquainted with the above-mentioned note and concluded that it is a really useful tool that deserves the attention of researchers. Here are some important statements from this document: "1. Can I use Chat GPT while working on the course? Yes, you can. However, it is worth remembering the limitations of Chat GPT as a working tool: Chat GPT does not recognize context well, and its "logic" is based on statistical correlations rather than empirical experience. Accordingly, his "understanding" of the situation often turns out to be wrong, in particular, when working with artistic sources (Note, 2023 in Ostapovich et al., 2023, p. 203). 2. Is it plagiarism to use excerpts of ChatGPT-generated text in written work that I submit on my behalf? Yes, if you do not specify the source of the text. All fragments generated by ChatGPT must be appropriately marked up in the text of your work. In addition to the standard check for plagiarism, all written works will undergo an additional check for the use of artificial intelligence using software tools OpenAI AI Text Classifier, OpenAI GPT-2 Output Detector Demo, GPTZeroX by Edward Tian (Princeton University), DetectGPT by Stanford University. Perplexity, author individualization and activity/frequency fluctuations (burstiness) will serve as key metrics. Written works submitted by the student during the previous semester will serve as an additional reference for identifying the author's style (Note, 2023 in Ostapovych et al., 2023, p. 203).

"If the probability of creation of the text by artificial intelligence is determined to be high, but there are no references to fragments generated by artificial intelligence in the text, the work will not be evaluated. 3. How can I link to fragments generated by ChatGPT? This is how ChatGPT itself answers it (OpenAI, 2023)" (Ostapovych et al., 2023, p. 203): "If you want to link to snippets generated by me, please follow these guidelines: Indicate that the fragment was generated by Artificial Intelligence. For example: "According to the information generated by ChatGPT Artificial Intelligence..." (Note, 2023 in Ostapovich et al., 2023, p. 203). The link can be inserted directly into the text or in parentheses after the fragment. For example: "According to data generated by ChatGPT (https://openai.com/blog/chat-gpt-3-language-generator/),..." If the fragment is generated using a specific model, mention its name. For example: "According to the information generated by the GPT-3 model (https://openai.com/blog/chat-gpt-3-language-generator/)..." Specify the date to which the models were trained. If you are using information generated before this date, it is worth noting this. For example: "According to the information generated by ChatGPT Artificial Intelligence (trained until September 2021)..." (Note, 2023 in Ostapovich et al., 2023).

"If you are writing a research paper, follow the citation and referencing rules established by your institution or the scientific journal to which you are submitting your paper. For example, when using a snippet generated by ChatGPT Artificial Intelligence, you can link to the project's web page: https://openai.com/blog/chat-gpt-3-language-generator/" (Open AI, 2023)" (Note, 2023 in Ostapovych et al., 2023, p. 203).

The author of this chapter considers these recommendations to be completely professionally correct and worth applying. *"The involvement of ChatGPT as a reference source with properly designed vocations completely removes the ethical dilemma of compliance with the norms of academic integrity"* (Ostapovych et al., 2023, p. 203). To prevent the tendency of ChatGPT to invent non-existent facts in agricultural sciences based on statistical probabilities, denial of information and self-repetition, it should be remembered that "the uncritical use of ChatGPT leads to obtaining distorted information, and also takes more time to evaluate the results than a simple query even in Google Translate, no matter how sceptical it was at the beginning of its work" (Ostapovych et al., 2023, p. 204). According to Ostapovych et al., (2023), there is no reason to *"blindly trust apocalyptic predictions that artificial intelligence may soon completely displace the translation profession, unless the emphasis is shifted to editing activities. However, the increase in labour productivity can, as it always happens with any scientific and technical progress, reduce the purely quantitative demand for such specialists. Therefore, it is also irrational to ignore the challenges associated with the development of neural networks*" (Ostapovych et al., 2023, p. 204).

4. The Problem of Human Talent And Artificial Intelligence

Everything mentioned above affects almost every aspect of the learning process. However, writing scientific papers can also be interpreted as a creative act of a scientist. Not all students remain in science. Those who decide to devote their lives to further scientific developments in the agricultural field of human activity are very few. From this point of view, talented people remain in science. Talent belongs to man, not to machine.

The Britannica Dictionary gives the following definition for a word "talent": "1) a special ability that allows someone to do something well; 2) a person or group of people with a special ability to do something well; 3) people who are sexually attracted" (The Britannica Dictionary, 2024).

"Every scientist, regardless of his scientific status, periodically faces the question of how to find an idea that would form the basis of a planned research work, dissertation or invention. Many believe that the ability to see a new idea is a talent, a natural gift of insight that cannot be developed or compensated for by hard training" (Sharabchiev, 2016, p. 23).

Sharabchiev (2016), in his scientific work on talent in science, noted that the revival, development and prosperity of any society and nation are largely due to the presence of a large number of outstanding personalities who form a special era of prosperity, for example, the Renaissance. The history of many countries and peoples is replete with facts of the emergence of a whole galaxy of outstanding cultural and scientific figures which play a decisive role in the revival of the nation.

"The theory of genetic determination of genius was developed by the English anthropologist F. Galton (1822-1911), although this idea was expressed by many, starting with Plato. Studying the aristocratic families of England, as well as the history of outstanding families in other countries over the centuries, F. Galton came to the conclusion that high-level abilities (talent, genius) are passed on from generation to generation, the level of talent in the family tends to increase evenly and, reaching peak, begins to decline in subsequent generations" (Sharabchiev, 2016, p. 24).

> *"The theory of the genetic determination of genius was developed by the English anthropologist F. Galton (1822-1911), although this idea was expressed by many, starting with Plato. Studying the aristocratic families of England, as well as the history of outstanding families in other countries over the centuries, F. Galton came to the conclusion that high-level abilities (talent, genius) are passed down from generation to generation, the level of giftedness in the family tends to increase evenly and, reaching a peak, begins to decline in subsequent generations" (Sharabchiev, 2016, p. 24).*

According to the scientist, an integral part of talent is the brain's ability to form and maintain for a long time in a state of arousal "a neural model of the task currently being solved by the researcher. For the first time, the idea of a dominant focus of arousal was put forward by academician A.A. Ukhtomsky, who identified two main properties of the dominant: increased excitability of a group of nerve cells, due to which stimuli coming from different sources are summed up; and a persistent delay in arousal after" (Sharabchiev, 2016, p. 24).

The ability to perceive images and form neural models (the code designation of an object or event in the cerebral cortex) and subsequent manipulation of them is the most important property of the brain, allowing to see something new in something that has been familiar for a long time. The ease of generating ideas, their depth, as well as the ability to foresee are the main characteristics of research talent (Sharabchiev, 2016, p. 27).

The most famous in the field of agriculture are such talented scientists as: K. A. Timiryazev (Torshin, 2018), Pylypenko (Kherson Chamber of Commerce, 2017), Falz-Fein (Shergalin, 2020).

In 2020 the 100-th Anniversary of the death of the founder of the first reserve in the Kherson region, but also the unique and "famous ascetic in the cause of nature conservation, breeder and ornithologist Friedrich Eduardovich Falz-Fein (1863-1920). Friedrich Eduardovich von Falz-Fein was born on April 16, 1863 in Askania-Nova into a large and wealthy family of German landowners and cattle breeders. He was the eldest son in the family and grew up with five brothers and one sister" (Shergalin, 2020, p. 1009)

> *"Friedrich Eduardovich was a born naturalist. A love for nature awoke in him from a very young age. As a ten-year-old child, he was already interested in songbirds and loved to lie in wait for their roosting places, in order to catch the birds with his hands while they slept. Thus, the first finch was caught, bringing the birder an inexhaustible source of joy with its loud singing, and soon, as a reward for successfully passing the exam for admission to the gymnasium, the boy received permission from his father to build a large aviary in the garden" (Shergalin, 2020, p. 1012).*

A huge amount of literature has been written about the founder of the unique man-made acclimatized garden and reserve in the steppe of the Kherson region, Friedrich Falz-Fein (Chaplai and Lebedeva, 2017), he was highly appreciated by the Russian Tsar Nicholas II. The scientist was known and respected in European scientific circles (Shergalin, 2020). In the bare steppe, where nothing grew, with the help of an irrigation system he invented, which was built by hand, he created an amazing garden where plants from more than 150 countries of the world were collected. This is one example of talent in the field of agriculture.

Scientists and philosophers of all times and peoples have written about talent. Although Kant distinguished between scientists and artists, saying that through hard work (Jeff Searlei, 2017), a person can become a scientist, in our time, talent, love and dedication to science are also needed. But artificial intelligence does not have this because its creator is a Human. Consequently, according to the author of the chapter, a person can still write an extraordinary scientific works. Studying and loving plants and the earth, he is inspired by the new ideas, which later come to life in his experiments with plants. It is human feelings that can create an agronomic masterpiece in science. But Artificial intelligence will help scientists save time by processing more data in different languages of the world to create new discoveries.

CONCLUSION

Thus, having summarized information about the possibilities of using artificial intelligence in the field of academic writing of agricultural science, education and teaching, the author of this chapter makes the following conclusions. Academic writing with an agronomic focus is characterized by generally accepted genres: abstract, scientific article, scientific discussion, academic review, dissertation, and monograph. They are different in composition, volume and content, but have a specific internal vocabulary. References to the works of other authors occupy a central place in the academic literature of agronomical orientation as they show that the researcher has read the literature, understands the hypotheses and methodology, has integrated the problems and has taken into account the prospects for future work. In academic writing, rules of punctuation and grammar are always followed. Since there is a direct connection between academic writing with an agronomic focus and teaching a foreign language with a specialized focus, the possibilities of translation using artificial intelligence are a relevant aspect. Another positive side of using ChatGPT in academic writing with an agronomic focus is that it is possible to analyze large financial statements of agricultural holdings, companies involved in advertising agricultural products, as well as economic indicators of the agricultural market and the like. ChatGPT offers a huge number of possibilities for this. There are many industrial tasks (i.e. instructions for setting up a task for a chatbot) for analytics of an advertising company, for financial analysis) and if ChatGPT produces a certain pattern or task, then it will cope with this task. You can replace analytics with end-to-end analytics. That is, if ChatGPT is provided with a certain statistical pattern in the form of numbers, it will also cope with this task. This is a very valuable quality for writing scientific papers with an agronomic focus since it saves a lot of time for the researcher. However, there is a risk of inaccuracy in the conclusion, since if there is only a limited amount of data available for analysis, and most of it is hidden from public access, then the study will be incomplete. In this case, it is necessary to indicate that the data was taken, for example, from the open access of the Internet or a database of a certain agricultural company. In such cases, options for the unfair use of artificial intelligence are not discussed. Scientists have yet to strategize how to legally use tools like ChatGPT. For accuracy and academic integrity, there are guidelines for citations when citing artificial intelligence work that is made publicly available on the Internet. Artificial intelligence certainly has enormous potential, but it lacks human qualities, which allows the author in this chapter to be optimistic about the further development of this field of science.

ACKNOWLEDGMENT

This research received no grant from any organization.

REFERENCES

Abramova, I. E., Ananyina, A. V. (2010). Modernization of the language teaching system at the university. *Higher education in Russia,* (8-9), 93-98.

Balik, N. R., & Shmyger, H. P. (2023). Implementation of artificial intelligence in education through the use of ChatGPT. *Current aspects of the development of STEAM education in the conditions of European integration: a collection of materials of the International Scientific and Practical Internet Conference,* 147-149.

Bazanova, E. M. (2016). Scientific publication: write in English or translate? *Science editor and publisher,* 1(1-4), 17-24.

Big Encyclopedic Dictionary. (1991). *Soviet encyclopedia* (Vol. 1). Author.

Chaplai, I. V., & Lebedeva, N. A. (2018). Realization of UNESCO goals for sustainable government management in Ukraine (preservation of land ecosystems – reserve "Askania-Nova"). PR and mass media in Kazakhstan: collection of scientific works. – PR and mass media in Kazakhstan: scientific work set / comp. and Ch. ed. L.S. Akhmetova, 44-53.

DeYoung, J., Jain, S., Rajani, N. F., Lehman, E., Xiong, C., Socher, R., & Wallace, B. C. (2019). ERASER: A benchmark to evaluate rationalized NLP models. *arXiv preprint arXiv:1911.03429*

Emiratli, A., Marchuk, M., & Osadcha, K. (2017). The problem of formation of academic writing skills among future programmers. *Ukrainian Journal of Educational Studies and Information Technology,* (3), 25–30.

Feng, S. Y., Gangal, V., Wei, J., Chandar, S., Vosoughi, S., Mitamura, T., & Hovy, E. (2021). A survey of data augmentation approaches for NLP. *arXiv preprint arXiv:2105.03075.* doi:10.18653/v1/2021.findings-acl.84

Filipenko, L. V., Dumanskyi, O. V., & Kozak, O. V. (2023). Academic integrity in the scientific and educational environment of educational institutions of Ukraine: a view through the prism of the presence of artificial intelligence. *Academic visions,* (19). 120-130.

Gayevska, O., & Shvidkiy, D. (2023). Implementation of the Scientific Research Project Method Using Artificial Intelligence in Teaching Japanese Language to Philology Students. *Scientific Bulletin of Uzhhorod University. Series: "Pedagogy. Social Work,* (2 (53)), 34–39.

Gorchynskyi, S. V., Sofilkanych, M. I., & Gorbenko, I. F. (2023). The quality of Ukrainian education and academic integrity: the impact of the use of artificial intelligence. *Academic Visions, (20).* https://academy-vision.org/index.php/av/article/view/407

Gureeva, M. Y. (2021). Enterprise management in the context of digitalization of the economy based on the use of artificial intelligence. Master's thesis of specialty 073 "Management", educational program "Business Administration", Poltava University of Economics and Trade.

Hakopyants, N. M. (2023). Using ChatGPT in the process of learning English: advantages and opportunities. *Bulletin of the National Technical University "KhPI". Series: Actual problems of the development of Ukrainian society*, (1), 69-72.

Horoshaylo, O. S., & Kochergina, S. S. (2023). The use of artificial intelligence to improve the quality of teaching foreign languages in a higher educational institution. *Scientific journal of the M. P. Drahomanov NPU. Series 5. Pedagogical sciences: realities and prospects*, 123—127.

Ishchenko, O., & Chernysh, A. (2022). Essay as a Priority Genre of Academic Writting. *Philological Treatises*, *14*(2), 47–55.

Jeff Searlei. (2016). Kant on genius. https://jeffsearle.blogspot.com/2017/11/kant-on-genius.html

Kang, Y., Cai, Z., Tan, C. W., Huang, Q., & Liu, H. (2020). Natural language processing (NLP) in management research: A literature review. *Journal of Management Analytics*, *7*(2), 139–172. doi:10.1080/23270012.2020.1756939

Kherson Chamber of Commerce. (2017). Pylypenko Yury Vladimirovich https://www.tpp.ks.ua/rus/khersonshchina-v-litsakh/784-pilipenko.html

Kherson Region News. (2017). Joseph Konpadovych Pachockiy https://kherson-news.info/main-news/hersonshina-krai-talantlivyh-ychenyh/

Kiselyova, A., & Zavalska, L. (2023). Basics of academic writing: teaching method manual. National Odesa University law academy.

Klobukova, L. P. (1998) Scientific discussion as an act of communication (linguistic aspect). Language, cognition, communication: Sat. of articles.

Komova, G. V., Rubtsova, V. V., & Salionovych, L. M. (2018). PBL as a means of forming written academic competence. *Scientific Bulletin of Kherson State University. Ser.: Translation studies and intercultural communication*, 27-31.

Kornienko, O. P. (2008). Terminological specificity of English texts of the sublanguage of architecture and construction. *Proceedings of the Russian State Pedagogical University*, 63-100.

Kuular, M. Ch. (2021). Terminological Analysis of the Concept "Monography". *Bibliosphere*, (3), 72–82. doi:10.20913/1815-3186-2021-3-72-82

Kuznetsova, N. G., Zaitseva, I. E., & Stepicheva, O. N. (2016). The Professional Language of Architects: A Systematic Approach to the Dictionary (Based on English, German and French). *Philological Sciences. Questions of theory and practice, 6-2*(60), 98-107.

Lebedeva, N. A. (2018). Teaching English in the field of knowledge "Public management and administration" in an agrarian higher educational institution. *European dimension of reforming public administration in Ukraine: materials of the International Scientific and Practical Conference*. Kyiv "Publishing House "Personal", 60-62.

Lebedeva, N. A. (2022). Consequences of the Pandemic for Ukrainian Agriculture in the Context of Public Administration. In A. Pego (Ed.), *Handbook of Research on Global Networking Post COVID-19* (pp. 173–188). IGI Global. doi:10.4018/978-1-7998-8856-7.ch009

Lebedeva, N. A. (2022). Teaching of Foreign Language in the Educational Process of Public Administration Personnel in Ukraine. In O. Kulaç, C. Babaoğlu, & E. Akman (Eds.), *Public Affairs Education and Training in the 21st Century* (pp. 294–310). IGI Global. doi:10.4018/978-1-7998-8243-5.ch019

Lebedeva, N. A. (2023). *Improving the Lexical and Grammatical Skills of Students Specializing in Hydraulic Engineering and Water Resources by Means of Writing. Cases on Error Analysis in Foreign Language Technical Writing*. IGI Global. doi:10.4018/978-1-6684-6222-5.ch007

Lebedeva, N. A., & Pasechko, V. V. (2017). Ukrainian-Russian-English dictionary of livestock terms. *Scientific forum: Innovative science: collection. Art. based on materials of the VII international. scientific-practical conf. No. 6(7).* https://nauchforum.ru/conf/philology/x/26238 https://nauchforum.ru/files/2017_10_26_inno/6%287%29.pdf

Matveeva, K. V. (2023). The use of artificial intelligence tools in writing scientific research: an ethical aspect. *XIII International scientific and technical conference of students, postgraduates and young scientists "Scientific Spring 2023"*, 246-248.

Nikolenko, K. V., Protas, O. L., & Yarmolenko, T. A. (2023). Innovative technologies of artificial intelligence to ensure academic integrity in educational institutions of Ukraine. *Perspectives and innovations of science ("Pedagogy" Series, "Psychology" Series, "Medicine" Series)*, (30), 393-406.

Olujimi, P. A., & Ade-Ibijola, A. (2023). NLP techniques for automating responses to customer queries: A systematic review. *Discov Artif Intell*, *3*(1), 20. doi:10.1007/s44163-023-00065-5

Ostapovych, O., Ostapovych, N., & Mazurenko, Yu. (2023). ChatGPT in the training of philologists and translators. challenges and prospects. *Scientific notes of the National University "Ostroh Academy": Series. Philology*, *17*(85), 200–205.

Pasko, O., Staurskaya, N., Tokareva, O., Cebral, P., Lebedeva, N., & Majiid, S. M. (2020). *Analysis of the Vegetation State of the Territory of Central Iraq Using Landsat Data. Handbook of Research on Agricultural Policy, Rural Development, and Enterpreneurship in Contemporary Economies. IGI Global.*

Pavlenko, T. B. (2021). Academic integrity of a student. Electronic data School of leadership for postgraduate students of KhNMU.

Pryhodii, M. A., Hurzhii, A. M., Radkevych, O. P., Kononenko, A. H., & Humennyi, O. D. (2022). *The technology of creating a digital portfolio of vocational (vocational and technical) and professional prehigher education: methodical recommendations.* Institute of Vocational Education of the National Academy of Educational Sciences of Ukraine.

Resnik, P., & Lin, J. (2010). Evaluation of NLP systems. The handbook of computational linguistics and natural language processing, 271-295.

Rudych, O. O., Ostapenko, E. M., & Cherednyk, L. M. (2023). Artificial intelligence and academic integrity: challenges, risks and opportunities for fraud prevention. Innovative pedagogy, 59, 250-254.

Sharabchiev, Yu. T. (2016). How to become a scientist and achieve success in science: creative talent and activation of scientific creativity. *Medical news. No. 5 (260).* https://cyberleninka.ru/article/n/kak-stat-uchenym-i-dobitsya-uspeha-v-nauke-tvorcheskaya-odarennost-i-aktivatsiya-nauchnogo-tvorchestva

Shergalin, E. E. (2020). Friedrich Eduardovich Falz-Fein (1863-1920) - member of the Russian ornithological committee (on the 100th anniversary of his death*). Rus. ornithol. Journal, 1895.* https://cyberleninka.ru/article/n/fridrih-eduardovich-falts-feyn-1863-1920-chlen-russkogo-ornitologicheskogo-komiteta-k-100-letiyu-so-dnya-smerti

Shevchenko, M. A., & Mitchell, P. D. (2013). Training of military translators in a civilian university (experience of the National Research Tomsk State University). *Language and Culture*, (1(21)), 125–131.

Skidan, V. V., & Yefimchuk, G. V. (2019). Innovative educational approaches in teaching technical disciplines in institutions of higher education. *Scientific notes*, (65), 238-242.

Soroka, V. V. (2023). ChatGPT: Opportunities for education. Science and education in the conditions of war. *Hlukhiv National Pedagogical University named after Oleksandr Dovzhenko: materials of the reporting scientific-practical conference*, 275.

Strubell, E., Ganesh, A., & McCallum, A. (2019). Energy and policy considerations for deep learning in NLP. *arXiv preprint arXiv:1906.02243*. doi:10.18653/v1/P19-1355

Takanova, O. V. (2008). Vocational-oriented teaching of a foreign language in non-linguistic universities. *Agroengineering*, (6), 49–51.

Tereshchuk, V. I., Ilchenko, A. M., & Semenyshina, I. V. (2023). Innovative learning technologies in institutions of higher education. *Academic visions*, (16), 234-238.

The Britannica Dictionary. (2024). https://www.britannica.com/dictionary/talent

Torshin, S. P. (2018). To the 175th anniversary of the birth of K.A. Timiryazev. *Agrochemical Bulletin. No. 3.* https://cyberleninka.ru/article/n/k-175-letiyu-so-dnya-rozhdeniya-k-a-timiryazeva

Tretyakova, I. V., & Akymova, A. S. (2018). Academic writing: genres and features. *Dnevnyk nauki, 5,* 1-6.

Ulyanova, G. O., & Baadzhi, N. P. (2023). Academic integrity as the basis of academic success. *Legal position, 4(37),* 98–103.

Vakulenko, V. L., & Boyarchuk, S. V. (2022). Key aspects of academic integrity: preventing plagiarism. *Scientific journal "Humanities studies: pedagogy, psychology, philosophy", 13(4),* 26-34.

Zhou, M., Duan, N., Liu, S., & Shum, H. Y. (2020). Progress in neural NLP: Modeling, learning, and reasoning. *Engineering (Beijing)*, *6*(3), 275–290. doi:10.1016/j.eng.2019.12.014

Chapter 6
The Role of Generative AI-Assisted Literature Reviews in Transforming Academic Research

Nitin Simha Vihari
Middlesex University, Dubai, UAE

Amandeep Kaur
Jaypee Institute of Information Technology, India

ABSTRACT

The chapter explores the transformative impact of generative artificial intelligence (AI) technologies on the traditional process of conducting literature reviews in academic research. Initially, it traces the historical evolution of literature reviews, highlighting their significance in shaping research across various fields. Generative AI technologies have revolutionized literature reviews by automating and enhancing information-gathering and synthesis. This democratizes the literature review process, making it more inclusive and accessible to researchers with limited resources. However, this advancement also brings challenges and ethical considerations regarding academic integrity and the reliability of AI-generated content. The chapter also discusses different types of literature reviews, their methodologies, strengths, and limitations, providing a comprehensive understanding of how generative AI can be integrated into these review types.

1. INTRODUCTION

Historically, the literature review is regarded as "the cornerstone of academic research, weaving the existing knowledge of a specific research topic" (Khademi, Diab, Kodaz, & Baban, 2010). The role of literature reviews in shaping academic discourse and guiding research agendas in various fields is well documented, from seminal reviews in the mycorrhiza research over the years (Koide & Mosse, 2004) to

DOI: 10.4018/979-8-3693-1798-3.ch006

the evolution of the systematic review through periods of foundation, institutionalization, and diversification (Hong & Pluye, 2018). As academic discourse has evolved alongside new paradigms in research methods, we have witnessed a movement from the traditional to the futuristic, enabled, in part, by technologies such as digital databases, online journals, and advanced search algorithms (Stebletsova, 2021) that have culminated in the era of generative AI, featuring technologies such as generative adversarial networks and AI models like ChatGPT and Stable Diffusion (Gozalo-Brizuela & Garrido-Merchán, 2023) that have come to revolutionize the landscape of literature review by automating and augmenting the process of gathering and synthesizing information.

Generative AI technologies can process vast amounts of data, identify patterns, and generate coherent and comprehensive reviews. They are not only changing the speed and efficiency with which literature reviews can be completed but also influencing the depth and breadth of the reviews themselves. These technologies enable researchers to access a broader range of literature, including publications in various languages and from diverse geographical regions, thus expanding the scope of literature reviews. By automating time-consuming tasks and providing sophisticated analytical capabilities, generative AI tools are democratizing the process of conducting literature reviews. This is particularly beneficial for researchers who may not have extensive resources or access to large databases. Moreover, the integration of AI in literature reviews is fostering a more inclusive research environment where diverse perspectives and studies can be easily incorporated. However, with these advancements come challenges and ethical considerations, particularly regarding academic integrity and the reliability of AI-generated content (Perkins, 2023).

The central thesis of this book chapter argues that the integration of Generative Artificial Intelligence (Gen AI) technologies in conducting literature reviews significantly enhances the efficiency, depth, and comprehensiveness of academic research. It posits that Gen AI tools can automate the identification, synthesis, and analysis of vast amounts of literature more quickly and accurately than traditional methods. It might further assert that these technologies can uncover patterns, trends, and gaps in the literature that might not be evident through manual review methods, thus driving forward the boundaries of knowledge and facilitating a more nuanced understanding of research topics.

2. UNDERSTANDING GENERATIVE AI TECHNOLOGIES

Generative AI is a type of artificial intelligence that creates new content. It learns from lots of data to understand patterns and details. Then, it can make new things that are similar to what it learned. There are two main kinds of tools it uses. Generative Adversarial Networks have two parts. One part makes content, and the other part judges it. The maker tries to create things that look real, while the judge decides if they seem like they were made by humans or not. They work together so that the maker gets better at creating realistic stuff. VAEs (Variational Autoencoders) work by shrinking data down so it's easier to handle, and then expanding it back to its original form. This helps the AI understand the data better and allows it to create new content that resembles the original data.

Generative AI, on the other hand, tries to learn from examples to create new things that are similar to the ones it has been trained on. That could be anything from images, to words, to pretty much any other kind of data you want to work with. One of the most significant is the improvement of GANs. These have become more sophisticated, capable of generating high-quality text, images and videos that are exceptionally realistic, afford a variety of their fields. In art, for example, they can now create new visual content. They are useful in the film and gaming industries, generating people and environments that are much more realistic. Similarly, natural language processing (NLP) models like transformer-based architectures, have come on at a pace. These can generate text that is much more human-like than before. That has made them invaluable tools for content creation, translation, and in some instances, even coding. They now also understand the context of a sentence. That means, the sentence they generate will be just as coherent and contextually appropriate as those generated by humans. Deep learning models can now produce music, too. Others are better at voice synthesis, where they generate a voice that sounds lifelike. Composing music and any number of other potentially useful applications, if not in entertainment and the arts, are relevant for virtual assistants and educational resources too.

In academic settings, these technologies are beginning to have a transformative effect. One of the main areas in which they are being applied is in research and literature review. AI models are able to analyze large volumes of text, pull out necessary information and even craft sections of academic papers or literature reviews. This will significantly reduce the amount of time and effort that researchers need to spend on these tasks, freeing them up to focus on analysis and interpretation. Generative AI is also being used to craft educational materials, creating tailored textbooks, study guides, and interactive learning materials. This can help open up educational resources and make the educational experience more accessible and tailored to the learning styles and needs of the individual. In the space of data analysis, AI models are being trained to both analyze data and generate hypotheses and new research paths. This could bring about more innovative and exploratory research, helping to push the boundaries of traditional disciplines. Generative AI does raise concerning and challenging questions in academic settings, however. One major concern is around authorship and originality. As AI is capable of creating content that is almost indistinguishable from human writing, the lines between human-generated and machine-generated content are becoming increasingly blurred. This leads to ethical questions about how these tools should be used in academic writing, and the potential problems that could arise from their misuse – from plagiarism and the generation of biased and misleading information to the generation of completely false information. Another challenge is ensuring the accuracy and reliability of AI-generated content. While these models are able to analyze so much information, they are only as good as the data they've been trained on. Incorrect or biased training data could lead to incorrect and biased outputs, which is a problem in academic research where accuracy and objectivity is paramount.

In healthcare, generative AI applications span medical imaging, protein structure prediction, clinical documentation, diagnostic assistance, and drug design, indicating its potential to revolutionize clinical diagnosis, data reconstruction, and drug synthesis. This overview also highlights the importance of future research to address current limitations (Shokrollahi et al., 2023). Generative AI aids economists by improving productivity through ideation, writing assistance, background research, data analysis, and coding. This demonstrates the broad applicability of generative AI across various stages of academic research, suggesting significant potential for efficiency gains in economic research (Korinek, 2023).

3. TRADITIONAL LITERATURE REVIEWS

A researcher cannot perform significant research without first understanding the literature in the field" (Boote and Beile, 2005). Defined as "a systematic method for identifying, evaluating, and interpreting work produced by researchers, scholars, and practitioners" (Fink, 1998), a literature review is essential. Without it, "the writer will not acquire an understanding of their topic, of what has already been done on it, how it has been researched, and what the key issues are." A literature review serves as a thematic synthesis of theoretical and empirical findings on a particular topic. An effective literature review focuses more on 'synthesizing' than 'summarizing'. While summarizing involves identifying key elements and condensing important information into one's own words - essentially, telling what's important - synthesizing goes a step further. It is not just about restating important points from the text; rather, it involves combining ideas and fostering an evolving understanding of the text. In other words, it's about putting pieces together to see them in a new way. The clarity, validity, and audibility with which a literature review (LR) is developed are crucial tests of how systematic the LR process is, irrespective of whether it is a simple scoping, a traditional narrative, or a more comprehensive systematic review (Booth et al, 2021). There's a significant risk of bias, where papers proposing an alternative argument may be unfairly rejected. Given that resources and time are often constraints, it is vital to fully outline any limitations in the chosen approach.

Literature reviews are an integral part of the scholarly work that researchers conduct. However, these reviews vary widely, in their methods and purpose. They are not just a collection of work that has been done in a particular field of study. In fact, a well-done literature review is critical, for information that it can provide about a given subject area, for critical analysis and synthesis. Because of the family of uses to which literature reviews can be put, different types of reviews can be undertaken, depending on the nature of research question, the stage of a particular field of study, and/or particular researchers' aims. In this paper, we take readers through a classification of types of literature reviews, and in so doing, examine the numerous strengths and weaknesses of this array of types review. With each being presented in order of least to most systematic, the classification includes: 1) narrative review; 2) scoping review; 3) systematic structured review; 4) systematic quantitative literature review; 5) meta-analytical review. These differences illuminate particular types of bias that each has, and the potential for different contributions that can be made with each. As a result, we encourage readers to consider carefully what they aim to achieve with their literature review and to select a type of review that will lead to fulfillment of their aims.

4. AI-ASSISTED LITERATURE REVIEWS

Technically, generative AI tools (such as GANs) are now fundamental in content creation, information appraisal, content personalization, post-production workflows, and data compression in literature reviews. They can algorithmically expedite every stage of the literature review process that will decentralize Design Science Research and broaden the discourse about shaping the future of AI-assisted Literature Reviews (AILRs) (Wagner, Lukyanenko, & Paré, 2021). These tools can generate photorealistic images or paragraphs of text from a sea of internet data, although quality decreases with the number of times AI-generated data is used as training data (Martínez Ruiz de Arcaute et al., 2021). Image generation in AI-assisted literature reviews But in AI-assisted literature reviews (in particular) we find platforms like GitHub Copilot is able to significantly enhance the productivity of human coders by completing their tasks 55.8% faster than when they were without AI assistance (Peng et al., 2023). These technologies have been used in healthcare to assist with diagnoses to predict disease spread and customize treatment paths (Secinaro et al., 2020). Now, AI platforms continue to yield varying success in evidence synthesis in health sciences and others more broadly and this is still the subject of broad evaluation around the extent to which they improve efficiency and quality in the literature review process (e.g., Blaizot et al.,

Table 1. Types of literature reviews

Type of Review	Description	Strengths	Limitations
Narrative Review	Focuses on clearly defined research questions and covers a wide range of issues on a given topic (Saunders, 2019).	Broad coverage of a topic; flexible in approach.	Can be subjective; higher risk of bias.
Scoping Review	Examines emerging evidence when it is unclear what more specific questions can be posed for systematic review (Mann and Peters et al., 2018).	Useful for new, emerging fields; helps in identifying gaps.	Less rigorous than systematic reviews; can be broad and unfocused.
Systematic Review	Uses explicit methods to methodically search, critically appraise, and synthesize literature on a specific issue (Collins and Fauser, 2005).	Reduces bias; reproducible and objective criteria.	Time-consuming; requires strict adherence to methods.
Structured Review	Scientifically structured based on widely used methods, theories, and constructs, often presented in tables and figures.	Provides insightful, organized information.	May overlook emerging or unconventional theories.
Framework Based Review	Utilizes a structured framework such as the 6 W Framework (Callahan, 2014).	Offers a systematic approach to review.	Limited by the constraints of the chosen framework.
Bibliometric Review	Focuses on authors' affiliations, countries, citations, and co-citations, using tools like VoS-Viewer.	Analyses publication patterns and impact.	Less emphasis on content and theoretical contributions.
Hybrid Review	Combines elements of bibliometric and structured reviews.	Integrates quantitative and qualitative analysis.	Complexity in merging different review types.
Review for Theory Development	Develops theoretical models and testable hypotheses but does not necessarily test them.	Aids in theory building and conceptual understanding.	Does not provide empirical validation of theories.
Theory Based Review	Focuses on analyzing the role of a specific theory in a field (e.g., Kozlenkova et al., 2014; Gilal et al., 2019).	Deepens understanding of a particular theory.	Limited to the scope of one theory.
Method Based Review	Synthesizes literature that uses a specific methodology, either quantitative or qualitative (Voorhees et al., 2016).	Provides in-depth analysis of methodological approaches.	Focuses only on methodological aspects, not content.
Meta-Analytical Review	A quantitative technique assessing prior empirical research on a specific topic using weighted average techniques (Klier et al., 2017).	Offers statistical assessment of effect sizes and directions.	Limited to quantitative studies; complex statistical methods.

2020; Leis et al., 2020). More so, generative mechanisms in literature reviews bring concepts and theories together in novel ways that sometimes contribute to the more "reveal[ing of] the cumulative character of academic knowledge" (Vaujany, Mitev, Smith, & Walsh, 2014).

4.1 Advantages of AI in Literature Reviews

AI applications significantly accelerate the review process, enabling the swift identification and synthesis of relevant literature from expansive databases. This technological leverage is poised to mitigate the traditionally labor-intensive nature of literature reviews, thereby enhancing productivity and efficiency in academic endeavors (Wagner, Lukyanenko, & Paré, 2022). Furthermore, AI-driven tools promise an improvement in the quality and accuracy of literature reviews. By automating the extraction and analysis of data, these tools minimize human errors, ensuring a more reliable and consistent review outcome (Checco et al., 2021)..

Table 2. Key Characteristics of generative AI for comprehensive literature searches

Sno	Characteristics	Description
1	Organizing Literature	Generative AI plays a significant role in organizing literature into approachable blocks, facilitating understanding of evolving areas and providing accessible entry points to vast literatures (Bissoto, Valle, & Avila, 2019).
2	Identifying Topics	It aids in topic identification by selecting words from a distribution over topics, enhancing the efficiency of document sorting (Griffiths & Steyvers, 2004).
3	Eliminating Biases	Generative AI helps discover mixed-membership communities in co-authorship graphs, thereby reducing biases introduced by citations and web searches (Eliassi-Rad & Henderson, 2009).
4	Ethical Argumentation	It can find publicly available sources to produce ethical arguments, aiding in authorship and literature exploration (Zohny, McMillan, & King, 2023).
5	Expediting Review Process	AI accelerates individual steps in literature reviews, thereby improving both quality and speed (Wagner, Lukyanenko, & Paré, 2021).
6	Quality and Trustworthiness	Generative AI enhances the trustworthiness of literature reviews by providing specific methodologies to address common pitfalls (Snyder, 2019).
7	Rapid Generation of Text Responses	Platforms like ChatGPT demonstrate the capability of generative AI to rapidly generate knowledgeable text responses, expediting the literature review process (Pavlik, 2023).
8	Increasing Persuasiveness	Generative AI can enhance the persuasiveness of literature reviews by incorporating elements like benevolence and trustworthiness (Duerr & Gloor, 2021).
9	Efficiency	Generative AI significantly increases efficiency in literature searches and reviews. For instance, tools like GitHub Copilot show that AI assistance can lead to a 55.8% increase in task completion speed, demonstrating similar potential in literature review contexts (Peng, Kalliamvakou, Cihon, Demirer, 2023).

4.2 Challenges and Ethical Considerations

Despite the promising advantages, the integration of AI into literature review processes is not devoid of challenges and ethical considerations. A paramount concern is the potential for AI systems to perpetuate and amplify biases present in the data they are trained on. The opaque nature of some AI algorithms further complicates this issue, as it obscures the decision-making process and makes it difficult to identify and rectify biases (Checco et al., 2021). Additionally, an over-reliance on AI tools may lead to a degradation of traditional research skills among academics, potentially undermining the critical thinking and analytical capabilities that are central to rigorous scholarly investigation (Lund et al., 2023). Ethical considerations also extend to data privacy concerns, especially pertinent when AI tools process sensitive or personal information contained within the literature, necessitating stringent safeguards to protect against misuse. The ethics of AI in health care have been thoroughly examined in a mapping review by Morley et al. (2020), which categorizes primary ethical risks presented by AI health and traceability concerns. The review identifies ethical issues arising at multiple levels of abstraction, including individual, interpersonal, group, institutional, societal, or sectoral. This extensive analysis underlines the importance for policymakers, regulators, and developers to consider these ethical dimensions to enable health and care systems to capitalize on the benefits of ethical AI, thereby maximizing opportunities to cut costs, improve care, and enhance the efficiency of health and care systems while proactively avoiding potential harms.

5. VARIOUS AI-ASSISTED TOOLS FOR LITERATURE REVIEWS

Each of these tools offers unique features and strengths, suitable for different aspects of conducting literature reviews. The choice depends on the specific needs of the review process, such as whether the focus is on qualitative or quantitative analysis, the scale of the literature to be reviewed, and the level of automation desired. These tools each offer unique functionalities that can be valuable at different stages of the literature review process. SEMANTIC SCHOLAR and Scite.Ai, for instance, are particularly strong in helping researchers assess the impact and credibility of papers. Tools like RAYYAN and RESEARCH RABBIT emphasize organization and discovery of related work. PAPER DIGEST and ChatGPT can be useful for quick summarization and synthesis of information. Finally, CONNECTED PAPERS provides a novel way of visualizing the interconnectedness of academic research, which can be particularly useful for understanding the context and evolution of a research field. The selection of a specific tool would depend on the needs of the research project at hand.

6. ACADEMIC INTEGRITY OF AI-ASSISTED LITERATURE REVIEWS

The use of AI in academic literature reviews has raised ethical dilemmas, particularly concerning academic integrity. The automation of tasks like literature reviews and data analysis by AI can lead to unethical practices, such as the inclusion of AI-generated text in scholarly manuscripts. This undermines the authenticity of academic work and challenges the credibility of the peer-review process and editorial oversight. To address these issues, solutions like sophisticated AI-driven plagiarism detection systems, an augmented peer-review process including an "AI scrutiny" phase, comprehensive training on ethical AI usage, and a culture of transparency recognizing AI's role in research have been suggested.

AI-assisted tools in peer reviews can reduce screening time but also require attention to potential biases and ethical implications (Checco et al., 2021). Comprehensive document searches are necessary to counteract publication bias and ensure methodological quality in systematic reviews (Wilson, 2009). The use of AI in peer review processes can expose biases and ethical concerns, such as algorithmic bias and unintended consequences (Checco et al., 2021). This necessitates a focus on ethical AI principles like transparency, privacy, accountability, and fairness (Khan et al., 2021). An ethical-mindful approach is crucial, especially in sensitive fields like biomedical research, where understanding and resolving practical problems becomes paramount (Kargl et al., 2022). Common concerns include privacy, trust, accountability, responsibility, and bias, which are prevalent in AI applications in healthcare and other domains (Murphy et al., 2021). Ethical frameworks are necessary to harness AI's potential while ensuring human control and minimizing risks (Taddeo & Floridi, 2018). Addressing algorithmic bias in AI-driven applications is crucial for ethical and responsible use, with strategies proposed to overcome these biases (Akter et al., 2021). Ethical and legal principles can mitigate bias in AI systems, emphasizing the need for fairness in design, training, and deployment (Ntoutsi et al., 2020). AI models in mental health show significant biases, underlining the importance of addressing these issues to avoid widening health inequalities (Straw & Callison-Burch, 2020).

Table 3. Summary of select AI-assisted tools

Tool	Description	Strengths	Limitations
Elicit	A platform that uses AI to accelerate research paper discovery and summarization.	Advanced summarization and discovery capabilities.	May require specific queries to get the best results.
Consensus	AI tool for finding and summarizing research papers.	Efficient at summarizing and identifying key points in papers.	Limited by the quality and availability of research papers in its database.
ASReview	Machine learning framework for systematic reviews.	Efficient in screening and identifying relevant studies; open source.	Primarily focused on titles and abstracts, may miss details in full texts.
FASTREAD	Machine-assisted reading technique for systematic literature reviews.	Highly efficient in identifying relevant studies, reducing reading time.	Might require calibration and training for specific areas of study.
SEMANTIC SCHOLAR	An AI-powered research tool that helps in finding relevant papers.	Uses AI to enhance paper discovery and offers citation context.	May have limitations in comprehensiveness of database.
RAYYAN	A web application designed for systematic review and meta-analysis.	Facilitates collaboration in review projects and has various screening features.	Interface might be less intuitive for new users.
Scite.Ai	Provides a platform to evaluate the credibility of scientific articles using AI.	Offers “Smart Citations” that show how a paper has been cited and if it’s been supported or refuted.	Database coverage and accuracy of analysis can vary.
ChatGPT	AI model that can assist in generating and summarizing content, including research papers.	Capable of synthesizing and summarizing information, useful for initial research.	Limited by the training data and knowledge cutoff.
CONNECTED PAPERS	A unique tool to find and explore academic papers and their connections.	Visualizes connections between research papers, aiding discovery of related work.	May not cover all fields equally, focusing more on certain disciplines.
PAPER DIGEST	AI tool to summarize academic papers.	Provides quick summaries of papers, helpful in initial research phases.	Summaries may not capture all critical nuances of the original research.
RESEARCH RABBIT	A tool for discovering and organizing academic papers.	Offers a visual way to explore the research landscape and find related work.	Newer tool, may have growing pains and database limitations.

7. LIMITATIONS AND FUTURE DIRECTIONS

One of the primary limitations of using AI in literature reviews is the potential compromise in quality and depth of analysis. AI may struggle to interpret complex, nuanced arguments or theoretical discussions that require human intuition and critical thinking (Wagner, Lukyanenko, & Paré, 2022). AI systems can perpetuate or even exacerbate existing biases present in the data they are trained on. This can lead to skewed or partial reviews that do not accurately represent the full spectrum of research available (Zhang et al., 2021). The ethical considerations of using AI, such as privacy issues, consent for using data, and transparency of the AI processes, remain significant challenges. Ethical guidelines for AI in literature reviews need to be established and followed to ensure the responsible use of AI technologies (Hagendorff, 2020). The implementation of AI in literature review processes involves technical complexity and requires expertise in AI technologies, which can be a barrier for researchers without a background in computer science or related fields (Morley et al., 2020). Wagner (2021) and Kaebnick

(2023) both point to the possibilities for AI, especially generative AI, transforming literature reviews and scholarly publishing more generally. AI can help to streamline the process of the literature review, Wagner suggests, while Kaebnick discusses its many applications in scholarly publishing. They are quick to underscore, however, the need to bring a responsible, critical eye to the use of AI in these practices. In medical education and primary healthcare, Preiksaitis (2023) and Štiglic (2023) likewise chart the possibilities and pitfalls of generative AI. Among those is the use of such AI to support self-directed learning and as a writing assistant. They too raise concerns about academic integrity and data accuracy. Cross-disciplinary applications for AI in literature reviews are evident across fields. Müller (2022) and Wagner (2021) share Wagner's perspective on how AI can, in Wagner's words, "dramatically accelerate the pace of literature reviews.", with Müller proposing a new tool that plugs into all of the others apps driven by AI mentioned above. Checco (2021) opines on the arrival of AI-assisted peer review, arguing that we need to pay attention to the ethical concerns and potential biases that apply. Santos (2023) finds potential for the automation of biomedical literature analyses in AI. There is little question about the explosion of possibilities prompted by AI for literature reviews, but in recent years authors have lined up to call for the ethical and methodological considerations needed to keep those possibilities poised to become actualities.

8. CONCLUSION

The integration of AI, particularly through tools like GANs and advanced NLP models, represents a paradigm shift from the traditional literature review process. By automating and enhancing information acquisition and synthesis, AI democratizes and accelerates research, making it more inclusive and accessible. This potential of AI-assisted literature reviews spans across domains, from healthcare to the humanities, indicating broad, cross-disciplinary applicability. However, as these capabilities are achieved, challenges, including ethical considerations, academic integrity, and the authority of AI-generated content have emerged as critical areas of interrogation and focus. The future of AI in literature reviews presents a landscape where efficiency, inclusivity, and innovation are central. Navigating this future effectively will necessitate the adoption of a conscientious and critical approach toward AI integration, demanding discourse and investigation of ethical considerations, transparency, and the balance between AI assistance and human stewardship. The continual evaluation of the imprint of AI upon the quality and integrity of academic work will be paramount. Further still, the development of new platforms that incorporate disparate AI applications, denote but one possible horizon of AI's applicability within the academy. The emphasis on ethical considerations in the current AI landscape and the work to reduce bias in AI-driven applications will be critical in realizing the full potential of these capabilities. In closing, as AI matures and integrates within academic research, it holds the potential to broaden the purview, agility, and accessibility of literature reviews to a global community of researchers, imparting the need for a vigilant and ethical approach to its challenges and implications. The path forward then, is one of collaborative innovation, where AI converges and partners with human intellect to redefine academic inquiry and understanding.

REFERENCES

Bissoto, A., Valle, E., & Avila, S. (2021). Gan-based data augmentation and anonymization for skin-lesion analysis: A critical review. In *Proceedings of the IEEE/CVF conference on computer vision and pattern recognition* (pp. 1847-1856). 10.1109/CVPRW53098.2021.00204

Blaizot, A., Veettil, S. P., Saidoung, P., Moreno-García, C., Wiratunga, N., Aceves-Martins, M., Lai, N., & Chaiyakunapruk, N. (2022). Using artificial intelligence methods for systematic review in health sciences: A systematic review. *Research Synthesis Methods*, *13*(3), 353–362. doi:10.1002/jrsm.1553 PMID:35174972

Boote, D. N., & Beile, P. (2005). Scholars before researchers: On the centrality of the dissertation literature review in research preparation. *Educational researcher, 34*(6), 3-15.

Callahan, J. L. (2014). Writing literature reviews: A reprise and update. *Human Resource Development Review*, *13*(3), 271–275. doi:10.1177/1534484314536705

Checco, A., Bracciale, L., Loreti, P., Pinfield, S., & Bianchi, G. (2021). AI-assisted peer review. *Humanities & Social Sciences Communications*, *8*(1), 1–11. doi:10.1057/s41599-020-00703-8 PMID:38617731

Collins, J. A., & Fauser, B. C. (2005). Balancing the strengths of systematic and narrative reviews. *Human Reproduction Update*, *11*(2), 103–104. doi:10.1093/humupd/dmh058 PMID:15618290

De Vaujany, F. X., Mitev, N. N., Smith, M., & Walsh, I. (2014). Renewing Literature Reviews in MIS Research? A Critical Realist Approach. *A Critical Realist Approach.*

Duerr, S., & Gloor, P. A. (2021). Persuasive Natural Language Generation—A Literature Review. *arXiv preprint arXiv:2101.05786.*

Fink, A. (2019). *Conducting research literature reviews: From the internet to paper*. Sage publications.

Gilal, F. G., Zhang, J., Paul, J., & Gilal, N. G. (2019). The role of self-determination theory in marketing science: An integrative review and agenda for research. *European Management Journal*, *37*(1), 29–44. doi:10.1016/j.emj.2018.10.004

Gozalo-Brizuela, R., & Garrido-Merchan, E. C. (2023). ChatGPT is not all you need. A State of the Art Review of large Generative AI models. *arXiv preprint arXiv:2301.04655.*

Griffiths, T. L., & Steyvers, M. (2004). Finding scientific topics. *Proceedings of the National Academy of Sciences of the United States of America*, *101*(suppl_1), 5228–5235. doi:10.1073/pnas.0307752101 PMID:14872004

Hagendorff, T. (2020). The ethics of AI ethics: An evaluation of guidelines. *Minds and Machines*, *30*(1), 99–120. doi:10.1007/s11023-020-09517-8

HernandezJ. A.CondeJ.ReviriegoP.de ArcauteG. M. R. (2023). Is ChatGPT capable of solving classical Communications and Networking problems? Authorea Preprints.

Hong, Q. N., & Pluye, P. (2019). A conceptual framework for critical appraisal in systematic mixed studies reviews. *Journal of Mixed Methods Research*, *13*(4), 446–460. doi:10.1177/1558689818770058

Khan, M., Mehran, M. T., Haq, Z. U., Ullah, Z., Naqvi, S. R., Ihsan, M., & Abbass, H. (2021). Applications of artificial intelligence in COVID-19 pandemic: A comprehensive review. *Expert Systems with Applications*, *185*, 115695. doi:10.1016/j.eswa.2021.115695 PMID:34400854

Korinek, A. (2023). Generative AI for economic research: Use cases and implications for economists. *Journal of Economic Literature*, *61*(4), 1281–1317. doi:10.1257/jel.20231736

Kozlenkova, I. V., Samaha, S. A., & Palmatier, R. W. (2014). Resource-based theory in marketing. *Journal of the Academy of Marketing Science*, *42*(1), 1–21. doi:10.1007/s11747-013-0336-7

Lund, B. D., Wang, T., Mannuru, N. R., Nie, B., Shimray, S., & Wang, Z. (2023). ChatGPT and a new academic reality: Artificial Intelligence-written research papers and the ethics of the large language models in scholarly publishing. *Journal of the Association for Information Science and Technology*, *74*(5), 570–581. doi:10.1002/asi.24750

Morley, J., Machado, C. C., Burr, C., Cowls, J., Joshi, I., Taddeo, M., & Floridi, L. (2020). The ethics of AI in health care: A mapping review. *Social Science & Medicine*, *260*, 113172. doi:10.1016/j.socscimed.2020.113172 PMID:32702587

Ntoutsi, E., Fafalios, P., Gadiraju, U., Iosifidis, V., Nejdl, W., Vidal, M. E., Ruggieri, S., Turini, F., Papadopoulos, S., Krasanakis, E., Kompatsiaris, I., Kinder-Kurlanda, K., Wagner, C., Karimi, F., Fernandez, M., Alani, H., Berendt, B., Kruegel, T., Heinze, C., ... Staab, S. (2020). Bias in data-driven artificial intelligence systems—An introductory survey. *Wiley Interdisciplinary Reviews. Data Mining and Knowledge Discovery*, *10*(3), e1356. doi:10.1002/widm.1356

Pavlik, J. V. (2023). Collaborating with ChatGPT: Considering the implications of generative artificial intelligence for journalism and media education. *Journalism & Mass Communication Educator*, *78*(1), 84–93. doi:10.1177/10776958221149577

Secinaro, S., Calandra, D., Secinaro, A., Muthurangu, V., & Biancone, P. (2021). The role of artificial intelligence in healthcare: A structured literature review. *BMC Medical Informatics and Decision Making*, *21*(1), 1–23. doi:10.1186/s12911-021-01488-9 PMID:33836752

Shokrollahi, Y., Yarmohammadtoosky, S., Nikahd, M. M., Dong, P., Li, X., & Gu, L. (2023). A comprehensive review of generative AI in healthcare. *arXiv preprint arXiv:2310.00795.*

Straw, I., & Callison-Burch, C. (2020). Artificial Intelligence in mental health and the biases of language based models. *PLoS One*, *15*(12), e0240376. doi:10.1371/journal.pone.0240376 PMID:33332380

Taddeo, M., & Floridi, L. (2018). How AI can be a force for good. *Science*, *361*(6404), 751–752. doi:10.1126/science.aat5991 PMID:30139858

Voorhees, C. M., Brady, M. K., Calantone, R., & Ramirez, E. (2016). Discriminant validity testing in marketing: An analysis, causes for concern, and proposed remedies. *Journal of the Academy of Marketing Science*, *44*(1), 119–134. doi:10.1007/s11747-015-0455-4

Wagner, G., Lukyanenko, R., & Paré, G. (2022). Artificial intelligence and the conduct of literature reviews. *Journal of Information Technology*, *37*(2), 209–226. doi:10.1177/02683962211048201

Zhang, B., Anderljung, M., Kahn, L., Dreksler, N., Horowitz, M. C., & Dafoe, A. (2021). Ethics and governance of artificial intelligence: Evidence from a survey of machine learning researchers. *Journal of Artificial Intelligence Research*, *71*, 591–666. doi:10.1613/jair.1.12895

Chapter 7
AI-Enhanced Hypothesis Development and Research Questions

Anugamini Priya Srivastava
https://orcid.org/0000-0003-0617-2711
Symbiosis International University, India

Swati Krutarth Shetye
https://orcid.org/0000-0001-8904-7507
Symbiosis International University, India

ABSTRACT

This chapter explores how artificial intelligence (AI) transforms research by aiding in research questions identification and hypothesis development. It aims to equip researchers with insights into leveraging AI tools effectively, driving innovation and advancing knowledge in diverse fields. AI integration revolutionizes research methodologies, offering speed and accuracy in literature review and data analysis. From natural language processing to expert systems, AI empowers researchers to formulate hypotheses grounded in theory and empirical evidence. Readers will understand AI's transformative potential in research, enabling them to uncover new insights, address complex questions, and enhance research rigor responsibly. Practical insights will empower researchers to integrate AI effectively, driving innovation and advancing scholarship.

INTRODUCTION

Welcome to the dynamic realm of research in the era of Artificial Intelligence (AI). In this chapter, we delve into the fascinating intersection of cutting-edge technology and scholarly inquiry, exploring how AI tools can reshape the landscape of research questions identification and hypothesis development. Picture a world where data flows like a mighty river, and AI algorithms serve as intrepid navigators, guiding researchers toward uncharted territories of knowledge. It's a landscape teeming with potential,

DOI: 10.4018/979-8-3693-1798-3.ch007

where traditional research methodologies converge with innovative AI-driven approaches to unlock new insights and drive scientific progress.

As we embark on this journey, it's essential to recognize the transformative power of AI in revolutionizing the research process. Gone are the days of laborious manual data analysis and painstaking hypothesis formulation. With AI as our ally, we gain access to unparalleled computational capabilities, enabling us to analyze vast datasets, uncover hidden patterns, and generate hypotheses with unprecedented speed and precision. However, amidst this technological marvel, it's crucial to tread carefully and ensure that our use of AI remains grounded in sound theoretical principles and ethical considerations (Buruk, 2023; Fyfe, 2023).

In this chapter, we'll unravel the complexities of AI-driven research questions identification and hypothesis development, offering practical insights and strategies for researchers eager to harness the full potential of AI in their scholarly pursuits. From leveraging AI-powered literature review tools to employing advanced natural language processing algorithms, we'll explore a diverse array of AI methodologies and techniques designed to streamline the research process and foster innovation. Through illuminating examples, case studies, and expert guidance, we'll navigate the intricacies of AI-driven research, empowering researchers to embark on a voyage of discovery where the boundaries of knowledge are continually pushed, and the possibilities are limitless. So, buckle up and prepare to embark on an exhilarating journey into the future of research, where AI serves as our trusty companion on the quest for knowledge and enlightenment.

What Is Hypothesis?

Ever wondered how scientists come up with those educated guesses about what might happen in their experiments? Well, that's what hypotheses are all about, and we're here to break it down for you in simple terms.

So, what exactly is a hypothesis? Think of it as a fancy way of saying "educated guess." It's like when you make a prediction about what might happen based on what you know. Scientists use hypotheses to guide their research and figure out what questions to ask.

In this chapter, we'll explore the ins and outs of hypotheses – from how they're formed to why they're so important in the world of science. Get ready to dive in and discover the fascinating world of hypotheses!

What Are the Different Types of Hypotheses?

Let's explore the different types of hypotheses with examples to illustrate each one:

Hypotheses come in various flavors, each serving a unique purpose in scientific inquiry. First up is the *null hypothesis*, often represented as "H0." Imagine a study testing whether a new teaching method improves students' test scores. The null hypothesis here would state that there's no significant difference in test scores between students who received the new teaching method and those who didn't.

On the flip side, we have the *alternative hypothesis*, denoted as "H1" or "Ha." Picture a research project investigating whether a new fertilizer increases crop yield. In this case, the alternative hypothesis would assert that there is a significant increase in crop yield among fields treated with the new fertilizer compared to those without it.

Moving on to *directional hypotheses*, let's consider a study examining the relationship between exercise and weight loss. A directional hypothesis might predict that as the amount of exercise increases, weight loss will also increase. This hypothesis implies a specific direction of the relationship between the variables, suggesting that more exercise leads to more weight loss.

Conversely, a *non-directional hypothesis* in the same study might simply propose that there is a relationship between exercise and weight loss without specifying which variable influences the other. This hypothesis acknowledges the possibility of a connection between exercise and weight loss but leaves the direction of the relationship open-ended.

Finally, let's explore *complex hypotheses*. Imagine a study investigating the factors influencing voter turnout in elections. A complex hypothesis might consider variables such as socioeconomic status, education level, and political engagement, aiming to understand how these factors interact to affect voter behavior. This hypothesis recognizes the multifaceted nature of the phenomenon under study and seeks to unravel its complexities.

In summary, hypotheses play a crucial role in guiding scientific research, and understanding the different types allows researchers to formulate educated guesses about the relationships between variables. Whether testing the absence of an effect with the null hypothesis or exploring complex interactions between multiple factors, hypotheses pave the way for uncovering new insights and advancing knowledge in diverse fields of study.

What Are the Key Challenges in Deriving a Hypothesis in Research?

Let's delve into the key challenges and prerequisites researchers should consider when deriving hypotheses in research, using simple examples to illustrate each point:

Understanding the Research Topic

Before deriving hypotheses, researchers must have a solid grasp of the research topic. This involves conducting thorough literature reviews and gaining a deep understanding of existing theories and findings . For example, if researching the effects of caffeine on memory, researchers need to familiarize themselves with previous studies on caffeine's cognitive effects.

Identifying Variables

It's crucial to identify the variables relevant to the research question. Variables are the factors that can change or be manipulated in the study. Using the same example, in the study on caffeine and memory, the variables might include the amount of caffeine consumed (independent variable) and memory performance (dependent variable).

Formulating Clear Research Questions

Clear and focused research questions lay the groundwork for deriving hypotheses. Researchers should articulate specific questions that they seek to answer through their study (Campbell *et al.*, 1982). For instance, in the caffeine and memory study, a research question might be: "Does consuming a moderate amount of caffeine improve short-term memory recall compared to no caffeine?"

Considering Practical Constraints

Researchers must consider practical constraints such as time, resources, and ethical considerations when formulating hypotheses. They need to ensure that their hypotheses are feasible and can be tested within the limitations of the study. For example, if conducting a study on the effects of a new drug, researchers need to consider factors like the availability of participants and ethical guidelines for human research.

Ensuring Testability

Hypotheses should be formulated in a way that allows them to be tested empirically. This means that researchers must be able to collect data and analyze it to determine whether the hypothesis is supported or not (Lund, 2022). Using the caffeine and memory study as an example, the hypothesis "Consuming caffeine improves short-term memory recall" is testable because memory performance can be measured after consuming caffeine.

Accounting for Confounding Variables

Researchers need to consider and control for confounding variables – factors other than the independent variable that may influence the outcome. Failure to account for confounding variables can lead to inaccurate conclusions (Scheel *et al.*, 2021). For instance, in the caffeine and memory study, factors like participants' age, gender, and baseline caffeine tolerance could act as confounding variables.

By addressing these challenges and prerequisites, researchers can derive hypotheses that are grounded in existing knowledge, clear and testable, and capable of advancing scientific understanding in their respective fields.

What Are the Steps in Hypothesis Development?

Let's delve deeper into each step of hypothesis development using the example of exploring the relationship between exercise and mood:

- **Identifying the Research Problem:**

In this step, researchers define the specific issue or question they want to investigate. For instance, they might be interested in understanding whether engaging in regular exercise affects people's moods positively. The research problem serves as the foundation for hypothesis development and guides the entire research process (Lund, 2022).

- **Reviewing Existing Literature:**

Researchers conduct a comprehensive review of existing literature to understand what previous studies have found regarding exercise and mood. They analyze research articles, books, and other sources to identify patterns, trends, and gaps in knowledge. This review helps researchers build upon existing findings and identify areas where further investigation is needed.

- **Formulating Research Questions**:

Based on the identified research problem and insights gained from the literature review, researchers formulate specific research questions to address in their study (Doody and Bailey, 2016). For example, they might ask: "How does the frequency and duration of exercise sessions relate to changes in mood?" These research questions guide the development of hypotheses and the design of the study.

- **Identifying Variables:**

Researchers identify the variables involved in their research questions. In the context of studying exercise and mood, the independent variable is exercise, which can be operationalized in terms of frequency (e.g., number of sessions per week) and duration (e.g., length of each session). The dependent variable is mood, which can be measured using validated mood assessment scales.

- **Generating Hypotheses:**

Based on the identified variables and research questions, researchers formulate hypotheses that make specific predictions about the relationship between them. For example:

Null Hypothesis (H0): "There is no significant relationship between exercise frequency/duration and mood."

Alternative Hypothesis (H1): "Higher frequency and longer duration of exercise sessions are associated with improved mood."

- **Defining Operational Definitions:**

Researchers define how they will measure and operationalize the variables in their study. For example, they may specify that exercise frequency will be measured as the number of exercise sessions per week, while exercise duration will be measured as the length of each session in minutes. Similarly, mood may be assessed using standardized mood assessment scales, such as the Positive and Negative Affect Schedule (PANAS).

By following these detailed steps, researchers can systematically develop hypotheses that guide their research efforts and contribute to advancing knowledge in the field of exercise psychology or related areas.

Relevance of Hypothesis Development in Research

The relevance of hypothesis development in research cannot be overstated, as it serves as a fundamental aspect of the scientific method, guiding researchers through the process of inquiry and discovery. Let's explore in detail why hypothesis development is essential:

- **Guiding Research Direction:** Hypotheses provide researchers with a clear direction for their investigations. By formulating specific statements or predictions about the relationship between variables, hypotheses help focus the research process and ensure that inquiries are purposeful and targeted. Without a hypothesis, researchers may find themselves aimlessly collecting data without a clear objective.

- **Structured Experimentation**: Hypotheses play a crucial role in structuring experiments. They help researchers identify the variables to be manipulated (independent variables) and measured (dependent variables), as well as the methods and procedures to be employed. This structured approach ensures that experiments are designed to test specific hypotheses and yield meaningful results.
- **Predictive Power:** Hypotheses allow researchers to make predictions about the expected outcomes of their studies. These predictions are based on existing theories, empirical evidence, or logical reasoning (Heger *et al.*, 2021). By testing these predictions through empirical investigation, researchers can evaluate the validity of their hypotheses and advance scientific knowledge.
- **Testability and Falsifiability:** A key feature of hypotheses is their testability and falsifiability. Hypotheses must be formulated in a way that allows them to be empirically tested using observable evidence (Scheel *et al.*, 2021). Through systematic data collection and analysis, researchers can assess whether the evidence supports or refutes their hypotheses (Heger *et al.*, 2021). This process of testing and potentially rejecting hypotheses is essential for refining theories and advancing scientific understanding.
- **Generating New Knowledge**: Hypotheses serve as vehicles for generating new knowledge and insights. By proposing explanations or predictions about phenomena, hypotheses stimulate curiosity and drive research efforts aimed at uncovering underlying mechanisms, patterns, or relationships. Through empirical testing, hypotheses contribute to the accumulation of evidence and the development of scientific theories.
- **Challenging Existing Theories**: Hypotheses play a crucial role in challenging and refining existing theories. When hypotheses yield unexpected or contradictory results, researchers are prompted to reevaluate existing assumptions, theories, or models. This process of theoretical refinement and revision is essential for the progress of science and the development of more accurate and comprehensive theories.
- **Communication and Collaboration**: Clear articulation of hypotheses facilitates communication among researchers and promotes collaboration. Sharing hypotheses allows researchers to exchange ideas, provide feedback, and engage in intellectual discourse. This collaborative process fosters creativity, innovation, and the exchange of diverse perspectives, ultimately enriching the scientific community.
- **Real-World Applications**: Findings resulting from hypothesis testing have practical implications and real-world applications. For example, research in medicine, psychology, or engineering often leads to the development of new treatments, interventions, technologies, or policies that improve human health, well-being, and quality of life.

In conclusion, hypothesis development is a cornerstone of scientific inquiry, providing researchers with a systematic approach to exploring phenomena, making predictions, and testing theories. By formulating clear and testable hypotheses, researchers advance knowledge, challenge existing theories, and contribute to the continuous evolution of science and understanding.

How to Avoid Errors in Hypothesis Development

Avoiding errors in hypothesis development is paramount for researchers aiming to produce reliable and valid research outcomes. Let's delve into common types of errors in hypothesis development and provide detailed strategies for scholars to circumvent them effectively:

Hypothesis development is a critical phase in the research process, laying the groundwork for empirical investigation and scientific inquiry. However, errors in hypothesis formulation can undermine the integrity and validity of research findings, leading to inconclusive results or erroneous conclusions. By understanding and addressing common pitfalls in hypothesis development, scholars can enhance the rigor and reliability of their research endeavors.

One prevalent error in hypothesis development is the formulation of ambiguous or unclear hypotheses. Ambiguous hypotheses lack specificity and clarity, making it challenging to precisely define variables and relationships under investigation (Scheel *et al.*, 2021). To avoid this error, scholars should ensure that hypotheses are clearly articulated, with precise language and unambiguous statements. Clear definitions of variables and relationships help researchers stay focused and facilitate the interpretation of research findings.

Another common error is the creation of unfalsifiable hypotheses. Hypotheses that cannot be empirically tested or falsified hinder scientific inquiry and undermine the validity of research outcomes. To prevent this error, scholars should formulate hypotheses that are testable through empirical research methods. Clear specifications of variables and operational definitions enable researchers to design experiments or studies that effectively test and falsify hypotheses, contributing to the advancement of scientific knowledge.

Overly broad or narrow hypotheses pose another challenge in hypothesis development. Hypotheses that are too broad may lack specificity, while overly narrow hypotheses may fail to capture the complexity of the phenomenon under study (Heger *et al.*, 2021). To strike a balance, scholars should tailor hypotheses to address specific aspects of the research question while remaining broad enough to encompass relevant variables and relationships (Doody and Bailey, 2016). This approach ensures that hypotheses are focused and comprehensive, facilitating meaningful research outcomes.

Ignoring confounding variables is a common error that can compromise the validity of research findings. Confounding variables, factors other than the independent variable that may influence the outcome, must be accounted for to ensure accurate conclusions. To address this error, scholars should identify potential confounding variables through literature review and pilot testing. Experimental designs or study protocols should include measures to control for confounding variables, such as randomization, matching, or statistical analysis, to minimize their impact on research outcomes (Scheel *et al.*, 2021).

Bias in hypothesis formulation is another significant concern in research. Bias can arise from selectively choosing hypotheses based on preconceived beliefs or desired outcomes, undermining the objectivity and credibility of research findings. To mitigate bias, scholars should approach hypothesis development with an open mind and a commitment to objectivity. Hypotheses should be grounded in empirical evidence, theoretical frameworks, or logical reasoning rather than personal biases or preferences (Heger *et al.*, 2021). Considering alternative explanations and viewpoints during hypothesis formulation helps researchers maintain objectivity and integrity in their research endeavors.

Practical constraints such as time, resources, and ethical considerations can also influence hypothesis development. Hypotheses that are not feasible within practical constraints may lead to unrealistic research plans or unattainable goals. To address this challenge, scholars should consider practical constraints early in the research process and ensure that hypotheses are feasible within available resources and ethical guidelines. Pilot testing of hypotheses and research designs helps identify and address potential challenges before conducting larger-scale studies, ensuring the feasibility and validity of research outcomes.

Lastly, the lack of collaboration and feedback in hypothesis development can hinder the identification and mitigation of errors. Developing hypotheses in isolation without seeking input from peers, mentors, or experts in the field may overlook important considerations or blind spots. To overcome this limitation, scholars should actively engage in collaboration and seek feedback throughout the hypothesis development process. Sharing hypotheses with colleagues, participating in peer review processes, and seeking guidance from mentors or advisors facilitate the identification and correction of errors, enhancing the quality and rigor of research endeavors.

In conclusion, avoiding errors in hypothesis development is essential for producing reliable and valid research outcomes. By understanding common pitfalls and implementing strategies to address them, scholars can enhance the rigor, credibility, and impact of their research endeavors, contributing to the advancement of knowledge in their respective fields.

Research Questions

Research questions are inquiries or queries that drive the focus and direction of a research study. They articulate what the researcher aims to investigate or explore, guiding the entire research process from conceptualization to conclusion. Research questions are typically specific, concise, and formulated to address a particular aspect of the research topic.

Spotting Research Questions

In our academic journey, understanding how to identify research questions is like finding the perfect starting point for an exciting adventure. Let me introduce you to three fascinating theories that can help us spot those crucial questions in our field.

First up, we have neglect spotting theory. Picture this: in a vast landscape of research, there are often hidden corners that haven't received much attention. Neglect spotting theory encourages us to seek out these overlooked areas. It's like being a detective, hunting for gaps in existing knowledge or perspectives that have been left in the shadows. By shining a light on these neglected spots, we can uncover new insights and contribute something fresh to the conversation (Barney, 2020). To apply this theory effectively:

- Conduct a comprehensive review of existing literature in your field, paying close attention to gaps or areas where research is sparse.
- Look for emerging topics or issues that have not yet been thoroughly explored.
- Consider alternative perspectives or marginalized voices that may have been neglected in mainstream discourse.
- Collaborate with colleagues or experts in related fields to gain insights into overlooked areas or emerging trends.
- When formulating research questions, prioritize topics that offer opportunities for original contributions or novel insights.

Next, let's talk about confusion spotting theory. Imagine navigating through a maze of research findings, only to find conflicting signposts and contradictory paths. Confusion spotting theory helps us make sense of this maze. It prompts us to identify areas where existing knowledge is unclear or where different perspectives lead to confusion. It's like untangling a knotted rope – by resolving these discrepancies, we can bring clarity and coherence to the field. To apply this theory effectively:

- Analyze existing literature critically, identifying areas where conflicting findings, unresolved debates, or contradictory theories exist.
- Consider the limitations of current research methodologies or theoretical frameworks that may contribute to confusion.
- Look for opportunities to synthesize existing knowledge or resolve discrepancies through empirical investigation or theoretical integration.
- Engage in dialogue with researchers who hold different perspectives or interpretations, seeking to clarify areas of confusion through constructive discourse.
- When formulating research questions, prioritize topics that offer opportunities to address unresolved issues or contribute to theoretical clarification and refinement.

Finally, we have application spotting theory. Think of it as connecting the dots between research and real-world impact. With application spotting theory, we look for opportunities to apply existing knowledge to practical challenges or issues (Barney, 2020). It's about finding those golden nuggets of research that can inform policy-making, improve processes, or address pressing issues in society. By focusing on practical applications, we can make our research more relevant and meaningful. To apply this theory effectively:

- Consider the broader societal or practical implications of existing research findings, looking for opportunities to address real-world challenges or inform policy-making.
- Engage with stakeholders or practitioners in relevant fields to identify pressing issues or areas where research can make a tangible impact.
- Explore interdisciplinary collaborations or translational research opportunities that bridge the gap between academic knowledge and practical applications.
- When formulating research questions, prioritize topics that offer opportunities for applied research, such as evaluating interventions, designing practical solutions, or informing decision-making processes.
- Consider the feasibility and scalability of proposed research projects, ensuring that findings can be translated into actionable recommendations or interventions.

So, there you have it – three theories that can guide us in spotting research questions. Whether we're uncovering overlooked areas, untangling confusing findings, or bridging the gap between research and practice, these theories offer valuable insights for our academic journey. As we embark on this adventure of discovery, let's keep these theories in mind as our trusty companions, helping us navigate the ever-evolving landscape of knowledge.

Role of Research Questions in Deriving Hypothesis

The role of identifying research questions in hypothesis development is pivotal, as it sets the stage for formulating clear and testable hypotheses that guide the research process effectively. Let's explore the significance of research questions, how to spot them, and recommend steps to derive hypotheses:

a. Clarify Research Objectives:

Practical Application: Before diving into hypothesis development, scholars should clearly define the objectives of their research study. This involves identifying the specific aspect of the topic they want to explore or investigate. For example, if the research topic is "the impact of social media usage on mental health," scholars may clarify their objective as understanding how different types of social media usage affect various dimensions of mental health, such as depression, anxiety, and self-esteem.

Usability: Clarifying research objectives helps scholars frame precise research questions that align with their research goals. By establishing clear objectives, scholars can ensure that their research stays focused and relevant throughout the hypothesis development process.

b. Review Existing Literature:

Practical Application: Scholars should conduct a comprehensive review of existing literature related to their research topic. This involves identifying gaps, inconsistencies, or unresolved questions in the literature that warrant further investigation. For example, in the context of social media and mental health, scholars may review studies examining the relationship between social media use and specific mental health outcomes, such as depression or loneliness.

Usability: Reviewing existing literature serves as a valuable source of inspiration for formulating research questions. By identifying gaps or unanswered questions in the literature, scholars can pinpoint areas where their research can make a meaningful contribution (Doody and Bailey, 2016). This process also helps scholars avoid duplicating existing research and ensures that their study addresses relevant and timely issues.

c. Brainstorm Potential Research Questions:

Practical Application: Scholars should engage in brainstorming sessions to generate potential research questions based on the identified gaps or areas of interest. This involves encouraging creativity and open-mindedness to explore diverse perspectives and possibilities. For example, scholars may brainstorm questions such as "How does the frequency of social media use impact feelings of loneliness?" or "What role does the type of social media platform play in moderating the relationship between social media use and depressive symptoms?"

Usability: Brainstorming potential research questions allows scholars to explore various dimensions of their research topic and consider alternative hypotheses. By fostering a collaborative and creative environment, scholars can generate a wide range of research questions that reflect different perspectives and approaches to the topic.

d. Evaluate Feasibility and Relevance:

Practical Application: Scholars should assess the feasibility and relevance of potential research questions in relation to available resources, time constraints, and the overall research objectives (Scheel *et al.*, 2021). This involves considering factors such as the availability of data, access to participants, and ethical considerations. For example, scholars may evaluate whether they have the necessary resources and expertise to conduct a longitudinal study examining the long-term effects of social media use on mental health.

Usability: Evaluating the feasibility and relevance of research questions helps scholars prioritize their research efforts and allocate resources effectively. By selecting research questions that are feasible to investigate within the scope of the study, scholars can ensure that their research is practical and achievable.

e. Refine and Narrow Down:

Practical Application: Scholars should refine and narrow down the list of potential research questions to focus on those that are most relevant, specific, and feasible. This involves considering factors such as the clarity, specificity, and potential for empirical testing of each research question. For example, scholars may refine their research question to focus specifically on the relationship between Instagram use and body image dissatisfaction among young adults.

Usability: Refining and narrowing down research questions ensures that scholars focus their efforts on addressing the most important and impactful aspects of their research topic. By selecting research questions that are clear, specific, and testable, scholars can formulate hypotheses that guide their research process effectively.

f. Formulate Hypotheses Based on Research Questions:

Practical Application: Once research questions have been identified and refined, scholars should formulate hypotheses that provide specific predictions or explanations about the expected outcomes of the study. This involves deriving hypotheses directly from the research questions and reflecting the variables and relationships under investigation. For example, scholars may formulate hypotheses such as "Increased frequency of Instagram use is positively associated with higher levels of body image dissatisfaction among young adults."

Usability: Formulating hypotheses based on research questions helps scholars translate their theoretical ideas into testable predictions that guide their research process. By clearly articulating hypotheses, scholars can design studies that empirically evaluate the relationships between variables and contribute to advancing knowledge in their field.

By applying these practical tips, scholars can effectively identify research questions and derive hypotheses that guide their research process in a focused and meaningful way. These steps help ensure that research efforts are grounded in clear objectives, informed by existing literature, and aligned with practical considerations, ultimately leading to more impactful and rigorous research outcomes.

In summary, identifying research questions serves as a critical precursor to hypothesis development, providing a clear roadmap for formulating hypotheses that guide the research process effectively. By clarifying research objectives, reviewing existing literature, brainstorming potential research questions, and refining them based on feasibility and relevance, scholars can derive hypotheses that contribute to advancing knowledge and understanding in their respective fields.

How AI Tools Can Be Used

AI tools offer invaluable assistance to scholars in exploring research problems and questions by providing efficient access to vast amounts of data, facilitating analysis, generating insights, and enhancing creativity. Here's how AI tools can help:

LITERATURE REVIEW AND ANALYSIS

Literature Review and Analysis play a crucial role in the research process, providing scholars with a foundation of existing knowledge upon which to build their investigations (Xu et al., 2021). In recent years, AI-powered tools have revolutionized the way scholars conduct literature reviews, offering unprecedented speed, efficiency, and depth of analysis (Salvagno *et al.*, 2023).

AI-powered literature review tools such as IBM Watson Discovery or Google Scholar have become indispensable resources for scholars seeking to navigate the vast landscape of academic literature. These tools employ advanced algorithms to quickly scan and analyze numerous academic papers, books, and articles related to a research problem. By automating the process of data collection and analysis, AI-powered tools can save scholars significant time and effort while providing access to a wealth of information.

One of the key capabilities of AI-powered literature review tools is their ability to identify key concepts, themes, and trends within a body of literature. Using Natural Language Processing (NLP) algorithms, these tools can extract and summarize information from a large corpus of texts, enabling scholars to gain a comprehensive understanding of existing knowledge (Salvagno *et al.*, 2023). By identifying recurring themes or patterns across multiple sources, scholars can identify areas of consensus or disagreement within the literature, helping to inform their own research questions and hypotheses.

Moreover, AI-powered literature review tools can help scholars identify gaps, contradictions, or emerging areas of interest in the literature (Salvagno *et al.*, 2023). NLP algorithms can analyze text at scale, identifying keywords, phrases, and semantic relationships that may signal areas requiring further investigation. By surfacing overlooked or underexplored topics, these tools can inspire scholars to pursue novel research directions and contribute to the advancement of knowledge in their field.

Citation analysis tools are another valuable feature of AI-powered literature review platforms. These tools can identify influential papers or authors in a given field, helping scholars trace the evolution of ideas and identify potential collaborators or experts to consult. By analyzing citation patterns and network connections within the literature, scholars can gain insights into the intellectual lineage of a research topic and identify key figures whose work has shaped the discourse.

In summary, AI-powered literature review and analysis tools offer scholars a powerful toolkit for navigating the vast landscape of academic literature. By automating the process of data collection, analysis, and synthesis, these tools enable scholars to gain a comprehensive understanding of existing knowledge, identify gaps and contradictions within the literature, and connect with other researchers working in their field (Zohery, 2023). As AI continues to advance, these tools promise to revolutionize the way scholars conduct literature reviews and accelerate the pace of discovery in academic research.

Data Mining and Analysis

In contemporary research, the proliferation of data from various sources presents both an opportunity and a challenge for scholars. With the advent of Artificial Intelligence (AI) algorithms, scholars now have powerful tools at their disposal to analyze vast datasets and derive meaningful insights relevant to their research problems.

AI algorithms are adept at handling large datasets from diverse sources, including surveys, experiments, or public repositories. This capability allows scholars to leverage data from multiple channels to gain a comprehensive understanding of the phenomena under investigation. For instance, a researcher studying the effects of climate change on biodiversity may collect data from satellite imagery, field surveys, and climate models to analyze the complex interplay of environmental factors.

Once the data is collected, AI algorithms can be employed to uncover patterns, correlations, or insights that may be hidden within the dataset. Machine learning techniques, a subset of AI, offer sophisticated tools for analyzing data. These techniques can classify data into categories based on predefined criteria, cluster similar data points together, or even predict future trends based on historical patterns (Borges *et al.*, 2021). For example, a researcher studying consumer behavior may use machine learning algorithms to categorize customers into distinct segments based on their purchasing habits, enabling targeted marketing strategies.

Moreover, AI-driven data visualization tools play a crucial role in transforming raw data into interactive visualizations that are both informative and accessible. These tools enable scholars to explore data in a visual format, making it easier to identify trends, outliers, or patterns that may not be apparent in tabular form (Borges *et al.*, 2021). For instance, a researcher analyzing healthcare data may use data visualization techniques to create interactive dashboards illustrating trends in patient demographics, disease prevalence, or treatment outcomes.

Let's consider a hypothetical scenario where a scholar is conducting research on the impact of social media usage on mental health among adolescents. The scholar begins by collecting data from various sources, including online surveys, social media platforms, and academic databases. The dataset comprises demographic information, social media usage patterns, and self-reported measures of mental health symptoms.

Next, the scholar employs AI algorithms to analyze the dataset and uncover patterns or correlations between social media usage and mental health outcomes. Using machine learning techniques, the scholar classifies participants into distinct groups based on their social media usage patterns, such as frequency of use, types of platforms accessed, and interaction patterns.

Additionally, the scholar utilizes AI-driven data visualization tools to create interactive visualizations of the data, such as scatter plots, heatmaps, or network diagrams. These visualizations allow the scholar to explore relationships between variables, such as the association between excessive social media use and symptoms of depression or anxiety, in a visually intuitive manner.

By leveraging AI algorithms and data visualization tools in this manner, the scholar can gain valuable insights into the complex relationship between social media usage and mental health outcomes among adolescents. These insights can inform the formulation of research questions, hypotheses, and future studies in the field, ultimately contributing to a deeper understanding of this important societal issue.

Text Generation and Synthesis

In the realm of scholarly research, the ability to articulate research questions, hypotheses, and literature reviews is paramount for advancing knowledge and contributing to academic discourse. With the emergence of sophisticated AI models like GPT-3 (Generative Pre-trained Transformer 3) or BERT (Bidirectional Encoder Representations from Transformers), scholars now have access to powerful tools that can assist in these critical tasks, offering innovative approaches and insights that can shape the trajectory of their research endeavors (Floridi and Chiriatti, 2020; Phillips et al., 2022).

AI models such as GPT-3 and BERT operate on natural language processing (NLP) algorithms, enabling them to generate coherent and contextually relevant text based on prompts or criteria provided by scholars. These models have been pre-trained on vast amounts of text data, allowing them to understand and mimic human language patterns with remarkable accuracy. As a result, scholars can leverage these AI models to aid in the formulation of research questions, hypotheses, or literature reviews in a variety of disciplines (Phillips et al., 2022).

Let's consider a scenario where a scholar is conducting research on renewable energy technologies and their impact on environmental sustainability. The scholar begins by providing a prompt to an AI model like GPT-3 or BERT, asking it to generate potential research questions related to the topic. The prompt may include keywords such as "renewable energy," "environmental sustainability," and "technology adoption."

Upon receiving the prompt, the AI model generates a diverse range of research questions, exploring different facets of the topic and offering alternative perspectives (Borges *et al.*, 2021). For example, it may generate questions such as "How do government policies influence the adoption of renewable energy technologies?" or "What are the socio-economic factors affecting community acceptance of wind energy projects?"

Next, the scholar may use the AI model to assist in formulating hypotheses based on the generated research questions. By providing additional context or criteria, such as specific variables or relationships of interest, the AI model can generate hypotheses that align with the research objectives. For instance, it may propose hypotheses such as "Increased government incentives for renewable energy adoption will lead to a reduction in carbon emissions" or "Community attitudes towards renewable energy technologies will vary based on proximity to existing infrastructure."

Additionally, the scholar can employ the AI model to aid in conducting a literature review by synthesizing information from multiple sources and offering insights into existing research findings (Borges *et al.*, 2021). By inputting key terms or concepts related to the research topic, the AI model can generate summaries or analyses of relevant literature, helping the scholar identify gaps, trends, or areas for further investigation.

In summary, AI models like GPT-3 and BERT offer scholars a valuable tool for generating text-based on prompts or criteria, assisting in the formulation of research questions, hypotheses, and literature reviews (Floridi and Chiriatti, 2020). By leveraging these AI models, scholars can explore different angles, synthesize information from multiple sources, and develop innovative approaches to addressing research problems, ultimately advancing knowledge and contributing to academic scholarship in their respective fields.

Semantic Scholarly Search Engines

In the digital age, scholars rely heavily on access to vast repositories of academic literature to inform their research endeavors. However, the sheer volume of scholarly publications can make navigating this sea of information a daunting task. Fortunately, AI-driven scholarly search engines like Semantic Scholar and ResearchGate have emerged as indispensable tools for scholars seeking to explore the ever-expanding landscape of academic knowledge.

These AI-driven scholarly search engines utilize advanced algorithms to parse and analyze vast amounts of textual data, enabling them to understand the context and semantics of research queries with remarkable precision. By leveraging techniques such as natural language processing (NLP) and machine learning, these tools can discern the underlying meanings and relationships embedded within scholarly texts, allowing them to deliver more relevant and precise search results to scholars.

Consider a scenario where a scholar is conducting research on the effects of artificial intelligence on workforce automation. The scholar begins by entering relevant keywords and phrases into a scholarly search engine like Semantic Scholar or ResearchGate. These keywords might include terms such as "artificial intelligence," "workforce automation," and "labor market trends."

Using advanced algorithms, the AI-driven search engine comprehends the context and nuances of the scholar's research query, enabling it to retrieve a curated selection of scholarly articles, books, and conference papers that are highly relevant to the topic at hand. Unlike traditional keyword-based search engines, which may return a plethora of irrelevant or tangentially related results, AI-driven scholarly search engines prioritize precision and relevance, ensuring that scholars can quickly access the most pertinent literature in their field.

Furthermore, these AI-driven search engines offer additional features and functionalities that enhance the research process. For instance, they can help scholars discover new connections between concepts by identifying recurring themes or patterns across multiple sources. By analyzing the co-occurrence of keywords and topics within the literature, these tools can uncover hidden relationships and insights, inspiring scholars to explore interdisciplinary perspectives and novel research directions.

Moreover, AI-driven scholarly search engines can identify emerging topics or research trends by analyzing citation patterns, publication timelines, and social media mentions. By tracking the dissemination and impact of scholarly works over time, these tools provide scholars with valuable insights into the evolution of knowledge within their field. This enables scholars to stay abreast of the latest developments and refine their research questions based on the most up-to-date findings in the literature.

In summary, AI-driven scholarly search engines like Semantic Scholar and ResearchGate play a pivotal role in empowering scholars to navigate the vast landscape of academic literature effectively. By harnessing the power of advanced algorithms, these tools provide scholars with more relevant and precise search results, facilitate the discovery of new connections and emerging trends, and ultimately enhance the quality and impact of scholarly research (Schmohl *et al.*, 2020).

Expert Systems and Knowledge Graphs

In the realm of academic research, scholars often grapple with the daunting task of navigating complex webs of domain-specific knowledge. Fortunately, AI-powered expert systems and knowledge graphs have emerged as invaluable tools for capturing, organizing, and synthesizing vast repositories of domain-specific knowledge, offering scholars a structured framework for exploring existing theories, concepts, and relationships relevant to their research problems (Schmohl *et al.*, 2020; Zohery, 2023).

Expert systems and knowledge graphs leverage advanced AI algorithms to parse and analyze a wide range of textual and structured data sources, including academic papers, textbooks, databases, and ontologies. By distilling this wealth of information into coherent knowledge representations, these AI-powered systems enable scholars to access and explore domain-specific knowledge frameworks with unprecedented efficiency and precision.

Imagine a scenario where a scholar is conducting research on the psychological factors influencing consumer behavior in the context of online shopping. The scholar begins by accessing an AI-powered knowledge graph tailored to the field of consumer psychology, which has been curated and populated with relevant theories, concepts, and relationships extracted from a comprehensive set of academic literature (Floridi and Chiriatti, 2020).

Using the knowledge graph, the scholar can explore existing theories and models related to consumer behavior, such as the Theory of Planned Behavior or the Elaboration Likelihood Model, to gain insights into the underlying psychological mechanisms driving consumer decision-making. By traversing the nodes and edges of the knowledge graph, the scholar can visualize the interconnectedness of various concepts and theories, helping to contextualize their research within the broader landscape of consumer psychology.

Furthermore, the scholar can leverage the knowledge graph to validate assumptions and refine their research questions based on established theories or models. For instance, if the scholar hypothesizes that social influence plays a significant role in online purchasing decisions, they can use the knowledge graph to explore the literature on social influence theory and its applications in the context of e-commerce. By cross-referencing their assumptions with existing knowledge, the scholar can ensure that their research questions are grounded in theoretical rigor and empirical evidence.

Moreover, AI-powered expert systems and knowledge graphs offer scholars valuable insights into emerging trends and areas of research interest within their field. By analyzing the connectivity and centrality of nodes within the knowledge graph, scholars can identify emerging theories, concepts, and relationships that may warrant further investigation. This enables scholars to stay abreast of the latest developments in their field and refine their research questions to address cutting-edge topics and gaps in the literature.

In summary, AI-powered expert systems and knowledge graphs provide scholars with powerful tools for capturing, organizing, and exploring domain-specific knowledge. By leveraging these systems, scholars can navigate complex knowledge landscapes, validate assumptions, and refine their research questions based on established theories or models, ultimately enhancing the quality and impact of their scholarly research.

By harnessing the power of AI tools in exploring research problems and questions, scholars can streamline the research process, uncover new insights, and make informed decisions, ultimately advancing knowledge and driving innovation in their respective fields.

Precautions Students Should Take While Deriving Research Questions and Hypothesis While Using AI Tools

When using AI tools to derive research questions and hypotheses, students should take certain precautions to ensure ethical conduct and avoid potential pitfalls such as plagiarism. While AI tools offer valuable assistance in the research process, it's essential for students to remain vigilant and adhere to ethical guidelines (Buruk, 2023). Here are some precautions to consider:

Understand the Tool's Functionality: Before using an AI tool, students should familiarize themselves with its functionality and limitations. Understanding how the tool operates will help students make informed decisions and interpret the results accurately.

Let's explore this concept through a different scenario. Imagine a student researcher named Alex who is conducting a study on public health perceptions related to vaccination attitudes. Alex decides to utilize an AI-powered text analysis tool to analyze online forums and social media platforms for insights into public sentiment towards vaccination.

Before proceeding with data analysis, Alex takes the time to thoroughly understand the functionality and limitations of the AI text analysis tool. Through research and experimentation, Alex learns that the tool employs machine learning algorithms to categorize text into themes such as positive, negative, or neutral sentiments regarding vaccination based on linguistic patterns and sentiment indicators.

Alex acknowledges that while the text analysis tool offers a convenient way to process large volumes of text data, it also comes with certain limitations. For example, the tool may struggle to accurately interpret nuanced language, slang, or cultural references prevalent in online discussions about vaccination. Additionally, the tool's performance may vary depending on the specificity of the research context and the quality of the data being analyzed.

With this understanding in mind, Alex proceeds with caution, implementing strategies to validate the tool's results and mitigate potential biases. Alex carefully selects a diverse sample of online discussions from various platforms and demographic groups to ensure the representativeness of the data. Additionally, Alex cross-references the text analysis results with manual coding by human raters to ensure reliability and accuracy.

Throughout the research process, Alex remains vigilant, critically evaluating the tool's output and questioning any discrepancies or inconsistencies. Alex recognizes that while AI tools can offer valuable insights, they are not without limitations and may produce errors or misinterpretations if used uncritically.

As Alex analyzes the text analysis results, interesting patterns and trends emerge in public sentiment towards vaccination. However, Alex also encounters challenges and limitations inherent in the tool's functionality. For example, the tool may struggle to distinguish between genuine concerns about vaccine safety and misinformation or conspiracy theories circulating online.

In response, Alex takes a nuanced approach, contextualizing the text analysis results within the broader socio-political context and acknowledging the tool's limitations in the research findings. By critically engaging with the functionality and limitations of the AI text analysis tool, Alex ensures the research is rigorous, transparent, and ethically sound (Miller, 2019).

This scenario underscores the importance of students familiarizing themselves with the functionality and limitations of AI tools before integrating them into their research. By doing so, students like Alex can make informed decisions, interpret results accurately, and uphold the principles of academic integrity and rigor in their scholarly pursuits.

Use Original Inputs: When using AI models like GPT-3 or BERT to generate text-based on prompts, students should provide original inputs and avoid copying text directly from existing sources. Plagiarism can occur if the generated text closely resembles existing literature without proper attribution (Zohery, 2023).

To illustrate the importance of providing original inputs when using AI models like GPT-3 or BERT to generate text-based on prompts, let's consider a hypothetical scenario involving a student named Emma who is conducting research on renewable energy technology.

Emma decides to use GPT-3 to generate potential research questions for her study. However, instead of creating her own prompts, Emma copies verbatim text from existing literature on renewable energy. She inputs these copied sentences into the AI model and requests it to generate research questions based on this content.

Unbeknownst to Emma, this approach poses significant risks of plagiarism. The generated text closely resembles the existing literature from which Emma sourced her prompts. As a result, the research questions produced by GPT-3 contain language, concepts, and structures that are nearly identical to those found in the original sources.

When Emma submits her research questions as part of her study, her academic integrity is called into question. Reviewers and peers notice the striking similarities between Emma's research questions and existing literature, raising concerns about potential plagiarism. Emma's credibility as a researcher is compromised, and her study may face rejection or retraction due to ethical violations.

In this scenario, Emma's failure to provide original inputs when using GPT-3 resulted in unintended plagiarism. To avoid such pitfalls, students must understand the ethical implications of AI-generated text and adhere to best practices for academic integrity. Providing original inputs ensures that the generated text is genuinely novel and does not infringe upon the intellectual property of others.

Furthermore, students should recognize that AI-generated text is not a substitute for independent critical thinking and scholarly inquiry. While AI models can offer valuable insights and inspiration, they should be used as tools to enhance, rather than replace, students' own creativity and analytical skills.

By providing original inputs, students like Emma can harness the power of AI models responsibly and ethically. They can generate text that is truly original and contributes to the advancement of knowledge in their respective fields. Additionally, students should always attribute sources appropriately and cite relevant literature to acknowledge the contributions of others and uphold academic integrity (Fyfe, 2023).

Cite Sources Appropriately: If students incorporate ideas or concepts generated by AI tools into their research, they should cite the sources appropriately. Even though the text is generated by AI, it's essential to acknowledge the original sources that inform the input prompts or criteria (Fyfe, 2023; Salvagno *et al.*, 2023).

To emphasize the importance of citing sources when incorporating ideas or concepts generated by AI tools into research, let's delve into a hypothetical scenario involving a student named Jason who is conducting a study on artificial intelligence in healthcare. Jason decides to use GPT-3, an AI language model, to generate potential hypotheses for his research project. He inputs a prompt related to the use of AI in diagnosing medical conditions and requests GPT-3 to generate hypotheses based on this topic. The AI model produces several hypotheses, which Jason finds insightful and relevant to his study. However, Jason neglects to cite the sources that informed the input prompt he provided to GPT-3. Although the generated hypotheses are based on Jason's input, the underlying concepts and ideas are derived from existing literature and knowledge in the field of healthcare and artificial intelligence.

As Jason incorporates these hypotheses into his research paper without proper attribution, he inadvertently commits plagiarism. Reviewers and readers familiar with the literature on AI in healthcare recognize the similarities between Jason's hypotheses and existing research findings. Without citations to acknowledge the original sources, Jason's credibility as a researcher is called into question, and his study may be subject to rejection or criticism for ethical violations.

In this scenario, Jason's failure to cite sources when incorporating AI-generated content into his research leads to allegations of academic misconduct. To avoid such repercussions, students must understand the ethical imperative of acknowledging the contributions of others, even when using AI tools. By citing the sources that inform the input prompts or criteria provided to AI models, students demonstrate integrity and transparency in their research process. They acknowledge the intellectual contributions of researchers whose work has influenced their thinking and inform the context of the AI-generated content.

Furthermore, citing sources enriches the scholarly conversation by providing readers with access to relevant literature and enabling them to trace the lineage of ideas and concepts. It fosters accountability and promotes a culture of academic honesty and integrity within the research community.

In summary, citing sources when incorporating ideas or concepts generated by AI tools into research is essential for upholding academic integrity and transparency. Students like Jason must recognize the ethical imperative of attributing the contributions of others and cite sources appropriately to avoid accusations of plagiarism and ensure the credibility of their research endeavors.

Verify Accuracy and Reliability: Students should critically evaluate the accuracy and reliability of the output generated by AI tools. While these tools can offer valuable insights, they are not infallible and may produce erroneous or misleading results. It's crucial to verify the information independently and cross-reference it with credible sources.

To underscore the necessity of critically evaluating the accuracy and reliability of output from AI tools, let's explore a hypothetical case involving a student named Maya conducting research on climate change mitigation strategies. Maya utilizes a machine learning algorithm to analyze climate data and identify potential correlations between greenhouse gas emissions and deforestation rates. The algorithm produces results suggesting a significant inverse relationship between the two variables, implying that reducing deforestation could lead to a substantial decrease in greenhouse gas emissions. Excited by these findings, Maya includes them in her research paper without further scrutiny. However, upon closer examination, Maya realizes that the output generated by the AI algorithm may be misleading. She recognizes the importance of critically evaluating the accuracy and reliability of the results before drawing any conclusions.

To verify the information independently, Maya decides to consult credible sources and cross-reference the AI-generated findings with established scientific literature on climate change and deforestation. Through her investigation, Maya discovers that while there is indeed a link between deforestation and greenhouse gas emissions, the relationship is more complex than initially suggested by the AI algorithm. Maya learns that factors such as land use change, agricultural practices, and forest degradation also play significant roles in contributing to greenhouse gas emissions. Moreover, she finds conflicting studies and expert opinions regarding the magnitude and direction of the relationship between deforestation and emissions reduction.

In light of these findings, Maya realizes the importance of approaching AI-generated results with a critical lens. While AI tools can offer valuable insights, they are not infallible and may produce erroneous or oversimplified conclusions if used uncritically. By independently verifying the information and cross-referencing it with credible sources, Maya ensures the reliability and accuracy of her research findings. This case illustrates the importance of critically evaluating the output generated by AI tools in research. Students like Maya must recognize that AI algorithms are not substitutes for human judgment and expertise. Instead, they should be viewed as tools to augment and complement the research process, subject to rigorous scrutiny and validation.

By critically evaluating AI-generated results and cross-referencing them with credible sources, students can identify potential biases, errors, or limitations in the data or algorithms used. This approach enhances the robustness and credibility of their research findings, ensuring that they contribute meaningfully to the advancement of knowledge in their respective fields. In summary, while AI tools can offer valuable insights, it's crucial for students to critically evaluate the accuracy and reliability of the output they produce. By verifying the information independently and cross-referencing it with credible sources, students can ensure the integrity and validity of their research findings, ultimately advancing scholarship in their chosen disciplines.

Avoid Overreliance on AI: While AI tools can streamline certain aspects of the research process, students should avoid overreliance on these tools. They should exercise critical thinking and independent judgment when formulating research questions and hypotheses, considering multiple perspectives and consulting with peers or mentors as needed.

Let's delve into a hypothetical scenario to illustrate the importance of avoiding overreliance on AI tools in research. Consider a student named Ethan embarking on a study examining the impact of social media on mental health. Ethan decides to utilize an AI-powered sentiment analysis tool to analyze social media posts and gauge public perceptions of mental health-related topics. The tool provides Ethan with insights into the overall sentiment surrounding mental health discussions online, categorizing posts as positive, negative, or neutral. Excited by the efficiency and convenience of the AI tool, Ethan becomes increasingly reliant on its output. He begins to formulate research questions and hypotheses solely based on the sentiment analysis results, neglecting to engage in critical thinking or consider alternative perspectives. As Ethan progresses with his study, he encounters challenges and limitations inherent in the AI tool's functionality. He realizes that while sentiment analysis can offer valuable insights, it does not provide a comprehensive understanding of the complex interplay between social media use and mental health outcomes. Moreover, the tool may overlook subtle nuances and contextual factors that influence individuals' perceptions and experiences.

Concerned about the validity and depth of his research findings, Ethan decides to seek input from peers and mentors. Through discussions with his colleagues and consultations with experts in the field, Ethan gains new insights and perspectives that challenge his initial assumptions and broaden his understanding of the research topic. With guidance from his peers and mentors, Ethan adopts a more nuanced approach to formulating research questions and hypotheses. He recognizes the importance of considering multiple perspectives and integrating diverse sources of evidence to develop a comprehensive understanding of the research problem. By incorporating feedback from his peers and mentors, Ethan enhances the rigor and validity of his study, ensuring that his research questions and hypotheses are grounded in critical thinking and independent judgment rather than solely relying on AI-generated insights.

This scenario highlights the dangers of overreliance on AI tools in research and underscores the importance of exercising critical thinking and independent judgment. While AI tools can streamline certain aspects of the research process, they should be viewed as supplements rather than substitutes for human intellect and expertise.

Students like Ethan must recognize the limitations of AI tools and actively engage in critical inquiry, considering multiple perspectives, and consulting with peers or mentors to develop robust research questions and hypotheses. By doing so, students can ensure the integrity and validity of their research findings, ultimately advancing knowledge and scholarship in their respective fields.

Consider Ethical Implications: Students should consider the ethical implications of using AI tools in their research, particularly regarding data privacy, consent, and fairness. They should ensure that their research complies with ethical guidelines and respects the rights and dignity of participants (Salvagno *et al.*, 2023).

Let's explore this concept through a critical case involving a student named Mia who is conducting research on online advertising algorithms and their impact on consumer behavior. Mia decides to use AI-powered algorithms to analyze data collected from online advertising platforms. She aims to uncover patterns and trends in consumer behavior to inform her research findings. However, Mia encounters several ethical dilemmas throughout her study.

Firstly, Mia realizes that the data she intends to use for her research may contain sensitive information about individuals' browsing habits, preferences, and demographics. She recognizes the importance of protecting participants' privacy and ensuring that their data is handled responsibly. To address this concern, Mia takes steps to anonymize the data and remove any personally identifiable information before conducting her analysis. She also obtains informed consent from participants, clearly explaining the purpose of the study and how their data will be used. By prioritizing data privacy and consent, Mia demonstrates her commitment to ethical research practices.

However, Mia faces another ethical dilemma related to fairness and bias in the AI algorithms she employs. She discovers that the algorithms may inadvertently perpetuate biases based on factors such as race, gender, or socioeconomic status. Mia realizes the importance of addressing these biases to ensure that her research findings are fair and equitable. To mitigate bias in her study, Mia implements measures such as algorithmic transparency and fairness testing. She examines the underlying algorithms for any biases or discriminatory patterns and adjusts them accordingly to promote fairness and inclusivity. Additionally, Mia diversifies her dataset to include a broader range of demographics and perspectives, reducing the risk of bias in her findings.

Through these ethical considerations and actions, Mia ensures that her research complies with ethical guidelines and respects the rights and dignity of participants. By prioritizing data privacy, informed consent, fairness, and inclusivity, Mia demonstrates her commitment to conducting ethical research that upholds the values of integrity, respect, and social responsibility.

This case underscores the importance of considering the ethical implications of using AI tools in research. Students like Mia must recognize their responsibility to uphold ethical standards and ensure that their research respects the rights and dignity of participants. By prioritizing ethical considerations throughout the research process, students can contribute to the advancement of knowledge in a manner that is both rigorous and ethically sound.

Be Transparent about AI Use: When reporting their research findings, students should be transparent about the use of AI tools and clearly communicate how these tools were employed in the research process. Transparency fosters accountability and helps readers understand the methodology behind the research.

Let's illustrate the importance of transparency in reporting research findings through a critical case involving a student named Liam conducting a study on sentiment analysis of social media data.

Liam decides to use an AI-powered sentiment analysis tool to analyze tweets related to public perceptions of climate change. He hopes to gain insights into the prevailing sentiment towards climate change discourse on social media platforms. As Liam progresses with his study, he encounters several ethical and methodological considerations related to the use of AI tools. Firstly, Liam recognizes the need for transparency in reporting his research methodology. He understands that readers should have a clear understanding of how AI tools were employed in the research process to interpret the findings accurately. Without transparency, readers may question the validity and reliability of the results. To address this concern, Liam ensures that his research paper includes a detailed description of the AI sentiment analysis tool used, including information about its functionality, limitations, and potential biases. He explains how the tool categorizes tweets as positive, negative, or neutral based on linguistic patterns and sentiment indicators. Additionally, Liam provides insights into the data collection process, including the sources of social media data, the timeframe of data collection, and any preprocessing steps applied to the data before analysis. By transparently documenting the research methodology, Liam fosters accountability and enables readers to evaluate the rigor and validity of his study.

Furthermore, Liam acknowledges the ethical considerations associated with using AI tools in research. He discusses potential risks such as privacy concerns, algorithmic bias, and the implications of relying on automated analyses. Liam emphasizes the importance of ethical conduct and ensures that his research complies with ethical guidelines and respects the rights of social media users. Through transparent reporting, Liam demonstrates his commitment to integrity and accountability in research. He enables readers to understand the intricacies of the research process and encourages critical engagement with the findings. By fostering transparency, Liam contributes to the advancement of knowledge and promotes trust and credibility in the scientific community. This case exemplifies how transparency in reporting research findings is essential for upholding integrity and accountability in research. Students like Liam must prioritize transparency and provide readers with a comprehensive understanding of how AI tools were utilized in the research process. By fostering transparency, students can ensure that their research findings are credible, reproducible, and trustworthy.

What Theoretical Understanding Is Required to Get Good and Effective Hypotheses?

In the era of Artificial Intelligence (AI), where data-driven approaches dominate research and decision-making processes, having a strong theoretical understanding remains paramount. Despite the advancements in AI technologies and their ability to process vast amounts of data, theoretical knowledge serves as the backbone for guiding AI applications effectively and ethically. In this essay, we will explore why a solid theoretical understanding is crucial in the AI era, focusing on its significance in hypothesis development and research in various domains.

The Importance of Theory in the AI Era

Contextualizing AI Algorithms: AI algorithms operate within specific theoretical frameworks or models. Understanding these theoretical underpinnings allows researchers to interpret AI outputs accurately and contextualize their implications within the broader domain. For instance, in natural language processing, theories of linguistics inform the development of AI models for text analysis, guiding researchers in interpreting linguistic nuances and cultural contexts.

Interpreting AI Outputs: AI algorithms often provide outputs without explicit explanations of their decision-making processes. A robust theoretical understanding enables researchers to interpret AI outputs critically, discerning patterns, biases, or inaccuracies that may arise due to theoretical assumptions embedded within the algorithms. This is particularly crucial in domains like healthcare and criminal justice, where AI-driven decision-making can have significant ethical implications.

Guiding Hypothesis Development: Theory guides hypothesis development by providing a conceptual framework for understanding relationships between variables. In the AI era, where data abundance can lead to hypothesis generation driven solely by data patterns, theoretical grounding ensures hypotheses are rooted in established principles and contribute to theoretical advancements. For example, in social sciences, theories of human behavior inform hypotheses about the impact of social media on mental health, guiding researchers in formulating testable predictions.

Mitigating Algorithmic Bias: AI algorithms can perpetuate biases present in the data they are trained on. A solid theoretical understanding helps researchers identify and mitigate algorithmic biases by critically assessing the theoretical assumptions underlying AI models. By recognizing how biases may manifest in AI outputs, researchers can develop strategies to address them and promote fairness and equity in AI applications.

Ethical AI Development: Theoretical knowledge is essential for ensuring ethical AI development. Understanding ethical theories and principles guides researchers in considering the broader societal implications of AI applications and anticipating potential ethical dilemmas. By embedding ethical considerations into the design and implementation of AI systems, researchers can develop technologies that align with societal values and promote ethical behavior.

The Significance of Theory in Hypothesis Development

Building on Existing Knowledge: Theory provides a foundation of existing knowledge that informs hypothesis development. By synthesizing findings from previous research, researchers can identify gaps or unresolved questions in the literature, laying the groundwork for formulating hypotheses that address these gaps. In the AI era, where data-driven insights abound, theory ensures hypotheses are not merely derived from data patterns but are grounded in theoretical understanding, enhancing the robustness of research findings

Ensuring Testability and Falsifiability: Hypotheses derived from theory are typically formulated in a way that is testable and falsifiable, allowing researchers to empirically validate or refute them. This adherence to scientific rigor ensures that research findings are reliable and reproducible, contributing to the cumulative advancement of knowledge in the field. In contrast, hypotheses derived solely from data patterns may lack theoretical justification and may be more susceptible to spurious correlations or overfitting.

Promoting Conceptual Clarity: Theory provides conceptual clarity by delineating the relationships between variables and articulating the mechanisms underlying phenomena of interest. This clarity ensures that hypotheses are well-defined and align with theoretical constructs, reducing ambiguity and facilitating the design of research studies. In the AI era, where complex algorithms may obscure the underlying logic of AI-driven insights, theoretical grounding promotes clarity and coherence in hypothesis development.

Facilitating Generalizability: Hypotheses grounded in theory are more likely to yield findings that are generalizable across contexts and populations. Theory provides a theoretical basis for understanding how relationships between variables may manifest under different conditions, allowing researchers to make broader inferences from their findings. This generalizability enhances the utility and applicability of research findings, enabling insights derived from AI-driven analyses to inform decision-making in diverse settings.

In conclusion, a solid theoretical understanding remains indispensable in the AI era, serving as a guiding framework for hypothesis development and research in various domains. Theory contextualizes AI algorithms, guides interpretation of AI outputs, and informs ethical AI development. In hypothesis development, theory ensures hypotheses are grounded in established principles, fostering scientific rigor, conceptual clarity, and generalizability. As AI technologies continue to advance, maintaining a strong theoretical foundation will be essential for harnessing the potential of AI in a manner that is ethical, reliable, and conducive to the advancement of knowledge.

SUMMARY

AI tools have revolutionized the research landscape, offering students unprecedented opportunities to streamline and enhance various aspects of the research process. However, it's crucial for students to approach the use of AI tools with caution, acknowledging both their capabilities and limitations, as well as the ethical considerations inherent in their utilization.

While AI tools undoubtedly offer valuable assistance in data analysis, text generation, and pattern recognition, they are not infallible. Students must recognize that AI-generated content should complement, rather than replace, their own critical thinking and scholarly inquiry. By leveraging AI tools as supplements to their own intellectual efforts, students can maximize the benefits of these technologies while preserving the integrity and authenticity of their research endeavors.

One of the primary considerations when using AI tools is to understand their limitations. AI algorithms are designed to process and analyze vast amounts of data efficiently, but they may struggle with nuanced language, context, or cultural subtleties. Students must critically evaluate the output generated by AI tools, recognizing that errors or biases may arise due to algorithmic limitations or data biases.

Moreover, students should be mindful of the ethical implications associated with AI utilization in research. AI tools often rely on data collected from individuals, raising concerns related to data privacy, consent, and fairness. Students must ensure that their research complies with ethical guidelines and respects the rights and dignity of participants. This includes obtaining informed consent, anonymizing sensitive data, and mitigating algorithmic biases to uphold ethical standards and protect the interests of research participants (Christou, 2023; Fyfe, 2023).

To navigate these challenges effectively, students should take precautions and exercise diligence when using AI tools in their research. This entails conducting thorough evaluations of AI algorithms and datasets, verifying the accuracy and reliability of AI-generated results, and considering the potential ethical implications of AI utilization. By approaching the use of AI tools with a critical mindset and rigorous methodology, students can harness the benefits of these technologies while mitigating associated risks.

Furthermore, students should prioritize transparency in their research practices, openly acknowledging the use of AI tools and clearly communicating how these tools were employed in the research process. Transparent reporting fosters accountability and enables readers to understand the methodology behind the research, promoting trust and credibility in the scientific community (Christou, 2023; Roe *et al.*, 2023). In summary, while AI tools offer immense potential to enhance the research process, students must approach their use with caution, recognizing both their capabilities and limitations. By taking precautions, exercising diligence, and upholding ethical standards, students can harness the benefits of AI tools while preserving academic integrity and advancing knowledge in their respective fields.

REFERENCES

Barney, J. B. (2020). Contributing to theory: Opportunities and challenges. *AMS Review*, *10*(1), 49–55. doi:10.1007/s13162-020-00163-y

Borges, A. F. S., Laurindo, F. J. B., Spínola, M. M., Gonçalves, R. F., & Mattos, C. A. (2021). The strategic use of artificial intelligence in the digital era: Systematic literature review and future research directions. *International Journal of Information Management*, *1*(April), 102225. Advance online publication. doi:10.1016/j.ijinfomgt.2020.102225

Buruk, O. (2023). Academic Writing with GPT-3.5 (ChatGPT): Reflections on Practices, Efficacy and Transparency. *ACM International Conference Proceeding Series*, 3, 144–153. 10.1145/3616961.3616992

Campbell, J. P., Daft, R. L., & Hulin, C. (1982). What to Study: Generating and Developing Research Questions. *Sage (Atlanta, Ga.)*.

Christou, P. (2023). How to Use Artificial Intelligence (AI) as a Resource, ow Methodological and Analysis Tool in Qualitative Research? *The Qualitative Report*, *28*(7), 1968–1980. doi:10.46743/2160-3715/2023.6406

Doody, O., & Bailey, M. E. (2016). Setting a research question, aim and objective. *Nurse Researcher*, *23*(4), 19–23. doi:10.7748/nr.23.4.19.s5 PMID:26997231

Floridi, L., & Chiriatti, M. (2020). GPT-3: Its Nature, Scope, Limits, and Consequences. *Minds and Machines*, *30*(4), 681–694. Advance online publication. doi:10.1007/s11023-020-09548-1

Fyfe, P. (2023). How to cheat on your final paper: Assigning AI for student writing. *AI & Society*, *38*(4), 1395–1405. doi:10.1007/s00146-022-01397-z

Heger, T., Aguilar-Trigueros, C. A., Bartram, I., Braga, R. R., Dietl, G. P., Enders, M., Gibson, D. J., Gómez-Aparicio, L., Gras, P., Jax, K., Lokatis, S., Lortie, C. J., Mupepele, A.-C., Schindler, S., Starrfelt, J., Synodinos, A. D., & Jeschke, J. M. (2021). The Hierarchy-of-Hypotheses Approach: A Synthesis Method for Enhancing Theory Development in Ecology and Evolution. *Bioscience*, *71*(4), 337–349. Advance online publication. doi:10.1093/biosci/biaa130 PMID:33867867

Lund, T. (2022). Research Problems and Hypotheses in Empirical Research. *Scandinavian Journal of Educational Research*, *66*(7), 1183–1193. doi:10.1080/00313831.2021.1982765

Miller, T. (2019). Explanation in artificial intelligence: Insights from the social sciences. *Artificial Intelligence*, *267*, 1–38. doi:10.1016/j.artint.2018.07.007

Phillips, T., Saleh, A., Glazewski, K. D., Hmelo-Silver, C. E., Mott, B., & Lester, J. C. (2022). Exploring the use of GPT-3 as a tool for evaluating text-based collaborative discourse. *Companion Proceedings of the 12th*, 54.

Roe, J., Renandya, W. A., & Jacobs, G. M. (2023). A Review of AI-Powered Writing Tools and Their Implications for Academic Integrity in the Language Classroom. *Journal of English and Applied Linguistics*, *2*(1), 22–30. doi:10.59588/2961-3094.1035

Salvagno, M., Taccone, F. S., & Gerli, A. G. (2023). Can artificial intelligence help for scientific writing? *Critical Care*, *27*(1), 75. Advance online publication. doi:10.1186/s13054-023-04380-2 PMID:36841840

Scheel, A. M., Tiokhin, L., Isager, P. M., & Lakens, D. (2021). Why Hypothesis Testers Should Spend Less Time Testing Hypotheses. *Perspectives on Psychological Science*, *16*(4), 744–755. doi:10.1177/1745691620966795 PMID:33326363

Schmohl, T., Watanabe, A., Fröhlich, N., & Herzberg, D. (2020). *How can Artificial Intelligence Improve the academic writing of students?* The Future of Education.

Xu, Y., Liu, X., Cao, X., Huang, C., Liu, E., Qian, S., Liu, X., Wu, Y., Dong, F., Qiu, C.-W., Qiu, J., Hua, K., Su, W., Wu, J., Xu, H., Han, Y., Fu, C., Yin, Z., Liu, M., ... Zhang, J. (2021). Artificial intelligence: A powerful paradigm for scientific research. *Innovation (Cambridge (Mass.))*, *2*(4), 100179. doi:10.1016/j.xinn.2021.100179 PMID:34877560

Zohery, M. (2023). ChatGPT in Academic Writing and Publishing: A Comprehensive Guide 2023. Artificial Intelligence in Academia, Research and Science: ChatGPT as a Case Study, 10–61. doi:10.5281/zenodo.7803703

Chapter 8
AI-Powered Data Collection and Analysis

Anugamini Priya Srivastava
https://orcid.org/0000-0003-0617-2711
Symbiosis International University, India

ABSTRACT

In the ever-evolving landscape of research, the integration of artificial intelligence (AI) has ushered in a new era of data collection and analysis, particularly in qualitative research. Traditionally, qualitative research has been characterized by labor-intensive processes, including manual data collection and time-consuming analysis. However, AI-powered tools have revolutionized these practices, offering researchers, including students at various academic levels, efficient and powerful methods for data collection, screening, and analysis. In this chapter, the authors embark on an exciting journey to explore myriad possibilities of utilizing different AI tools to streamline the qualitative research process.

INTRODUCTION

Welcome to the fascinating realm of research, where the integration of Artificial Intelligence (AI) is reshaping the data collection and analysis landscape, particularly in qualitative research. Traditionally, qualitative research involved laborious processes, from manually gathering data to spending hours on analysis. However, AI-powered tools have revolutionized these practices, offering researchers, from beginners to seasoned professionals, efficient and robust data collection and analysis methods (Christou, 2023).

AI tools have emerged as game-changers in research, offering simplicity, speed, and precision. They automate tedious tasks, allowing researchers to focus more on interpreting data and drawing meaningful insights (Buruk, 2023). By harnessing AI, researchers can streamline the entire research process, saving valuable time and resources (Christou, 2023; Oshiro et al., 2020).

Moreover, AI tools ensure ethical data collection and analysis. With built-in algorithms and safeguards, these tools minimize biases and errors, promoting fairness and accuracy in research findings (King, 2023). They uphold ethical standards by anonymizing sensitive information, protecting participant confidentiality, and ensuring compliance with data protection regulations (Fyfe, 2023).

DOI: 10.4018/979-8-3693-1798-3.ch008

The accessibility of AI tools empowers researchers at all levels, including students, to confidently embark on research endeavours (Golan et al., 2023). These tools provide user-friendly interfaces and intuitive functionalities, making them accessible even to those without extensive technical expertise (Schmohl et al., 2020). By democratizing access to advanced research technologies, AI promotes inclusivity and diversity in the research community (Strobl et al., 2019).

In this chapter, we embark on an exciting journey to explore the innumerable possibilities of utilizing different AI tools for qualitative research. Together, we will discover how these tools can enhance our research capabilities, foster ethical data practices, and unlock new insights. So, let's embrace the transformative power of AI and embark on a journey towards more efficient, moral, and impactful research endeavours.

How to Start Data Collection With AI Tools

When planning data collection with AI tools, navigating the process carefully and ensuring ethical standards and rigorous methodology are essential (Fyfe, 2023). Let's use simple yet convincing examples to explain the critical aspects and why they matter.

Firstly, having clear objectives is like having a map for your journey. If you're studying shopping habits, your goal might be understanding why people choose certain products. With a clear objective, you can tailor your data collection methods to gather insights that directly address your research questions.

Choosing suitable data sources is akin to selecting fresh ingredients for a recipe. Just as you wouldn't use spoiled milk in your cooking, you want to ensure the data you collect is relevant and reliable. For instance, if you're studying online shopping habits, you'd gather data from reputable e-commerce platforms known for accurate transaction records.

Ethical considerations are paramount. Imagine you're surveying shopping preferences. Before participants start answering questions, you'd explain the purpose of the study, how their responses will be used, and assure them of their privacy. This transparency builds trust and ensures participants feel respected and valued.

Quality control is like ensuring your recipe turns out just right. You'd want to check for errors and inconsistencies in your data, just as you'd taste-test your dish while cooking. This might involve verifying the accuracy of data entries, ensuring data security to protect participants' information, and maintaining transparency in your data collection methods.

Mitigating biases is crucial for fair and inclusive research. Suppose your data shows a preference for a particular brand of products. To ensure your findings aren't skewed, you might implement techniques like balanced sampling to capture a diverse range of perspectives, just as you'd adjust seasoning to balance flavours in your dish.

By incorporating these critical aspects into your data collection plan—clear objectives, careful data selection, ethical considerations, quality control, and bias mitigation—you can ensure that your AI research is ethical and rigorous, producing reliable and insightful results (Fyfe, 2023; Schmohl et al., 2020).

Data Collection: Understanding the Concept

Data collection is a fundamental and systematic research, analysis, and decision-making process across various fields, including science, social sciences, business, and healthcare. It involves the gathering and recording information or data from diverse sources to facilitate research objectives and draw meaningful conclusions.

1. Purpose of Data Collection

Data collection serves as the lifeblood of research endeavours, driving the quest for knowledge and empowering decision-makers with actionable insights. Consider the field of environmental science, where researchers utilize data collection to monitor biodiversity trends and assess the impact of climate change on ecosystems. For instance, in a study conducted in the Amazon rainforest, researchers collected extensive data on species populations, habitat characteristics, and climatic variables to understand the intricate relationships between biodiversity and environmental factors. By employing advanced data collection techniques such as remote sensing and GPS tracking, scientists were able to uncover patterns and trends essential for conservation efforts and sustainable land management (Golan et al., 2023; Schmohl et al., 2020).

In healthcare, data collection is paramount in improving patient outcomes and advancing medical research (Kung et al., 2023). Take, for example, a large-scale clinical trial investigating the efficacy of a new drug in treating a particular disease. Researchers meticulously collect data on patient demographics, medical histories, treatment protocols, and health outcomes to evaluate the drug's effectiveness and safety (Delahanty et al., 2018). Researchers can draw evidence-based conclusions through rigorous data collection and analysis, informing healthcare practitioners' decisions and potentially revolutionizing treatment practices (Garcia-Vidal et al., 2019).

Moreover, data collection is pivotal in social sciences, where researchers explore complex societal phenomena and human behaviour. Consider a longitudinal study examining the impact of socioeconomic factors on educational attainment. Researchers collect data over an extended period, tracking participants' demographic information, family backgrounds, educational experiences, and academic achievements. By analyzing this rich dataset, researchers can identify critical determinants influencing educational outcomes and formulate targeted interventions to address disparities and promote equitable access to education (Schmohl et al., 2020).

In each of these examples, data collection serves as the linchpin of research endeavours, facilitating the generation of insights and driving informed decision-making. Whether unravelling ecological mysteries in remote rainforests, advancing medical knowledge in clinical trials, or unravelling societal dynamics in educational research, systematic data collection enables researchers to delve deeper into their inquiries, uncovering patterns, trends, and correlations essential for progress and innovation. As we continue to push the boundaries of knowledge across diverse disciplines, robust data collection methodologies remain paramount, laying the foundation for transformative discoveries and meaningful change.

2. Methods of Data Collection

Data collection methods vary depending on the research goals and the nature of the data being collected. Here are some standard techniques:

- *Surveys* involve administering questionnaires or structured interviews to participants to gather responses on specific topics. They can be conducted via paper, online forms, phone interviews, or in person.

- *Observations* entail systematically watching and recording events, behaviours, or phenomena in real time. Observational data collection is prevalent in psychology, anthropology, and ecology.
- *Interviews*: Interviews involve direct interaction with individuals or groups to gather information. Depending on the research goals, interviews can be structured (with predetermined questions) or unstructured (more like a conversation).
- *Experiments*: Experiments are designed to manipulate variables under controlled conditions to observe their effects on outcomes. Data collected during experiments is often quantitative.
- *Secondary Data*: Secondary data collection involves using existing data sources, such as government reports, academic papers, databases, or historical records. Researchers analyze and interpret this pre-existing data for their research.

3. The Significance of Quality Data

The quality and accuracy of collected data are paramount. Poorly collected data can lead to incorrect conclusions, flawed decision-making, and invalidated research findings. Data reliability and validity are ensured through continuous processes throughout the research cycle.

Challenges in Data Collection

Data collection is a critical research and decision-making phase, but it has challenges. These challenges can significantly impact the quality and reliability of the collected data. Let's delve deeper into the challenges in data collection:

1. Bias

Bias refers to systematic errors or distortions in data collection that result in inaccuracies or misrepresentations of the population or phenomenon being studied. Several forms of bias can impact the integrity of collected data. One such form is selection bias, which occurs when the sample chosen for data collection does not represent the entire population. For instance, if a survey primarily gathers responses from a specific age group, it may fail to accurately capture the opinions of other age groups, leading to skewed results. Another type of bias is response bias, where respondents intentionally or unintentionally provide inaccurate or misleading information. This distortion can arise due to social desirability, where respondents alter their responses to conform to societal norms or memory recall issues.

Moreover, interviewer bias can occur when data is collected through interviews, as the interviewer's demeanour, tone, or body language may influence respondents' answers. This bias can introduce inconsistencies in data collection, compromising the reliability and validity of the findings. Recognizing and mitigating these various forms of bias is essential for ensuring the accuracy and credibility of research outcomes.

2. Errors

Data collection errors can occur at various process stages, from data entry to interpretation. Common types of errors include:

Data Entry Errors: During manual data entry, typographical or transcription mistakes can lead to incorrect data. This can be especially problematic when large datasets are involved.

Misinterpretation of Responses: Researchers may need to be more accurate to understand responses, leading to data inaccuracies. This is more likely to happen with open-ended questions that require subjective interpretation.

3. Non-Response

Non-response occurs when selected participants or respondents need to participate or complete data. Non-response can introduce bias if those who choose not to participate differ systematically from those who do. This challenge is particularly relevant in survey research and data collection involving human participants.

4. Data Security and Privacy

Ensuring data security and privacy is critical, especially nowadays, with all the stories we hear about data breaches and privacy concerns. Picture this: data breaches, where hackers get unauthorized access to collected data, can be a nightmare. It's like someone breaking into your house and rummaging through your stuff, except your personal information is being rifled through. To prevent this, researchers need to beef up security measures like fortifying the digital locks on their data (Strobl et al., 2019).

Then there's the whole deal with informed consent. You know, that legal and ethical thing where researchers have to make sure participants understand what they're signing up for. It's like signing a contract, except it's way more complicated. Researchers must explain why they're collecting data, how they will use it, and what rights participants have over their info. It's like describing the terms and conditions of a super lengthy contract, but in a way that your grandma would understand.

And let's remember data anonymization. It's all about protecting people's identities while keeping the helpful data. Imagine covering up all the personal details in a photo, like blurring faces or censoring names, but making sure the picture still makes sense. It's a tricky balancing act because even the slightest slip-up could reveal someone's identity.

Dealing with these challenges requires serious attention to detail, transparency, and sticking to ethical guidelines (King, 2023). Researchers need to put rock-solid quality control measures in place to dodge bias, reduce mistakes, boost response rates, and, most importantly, keep people's data safe and sound. Plus, they must closely monitor the data at every step to ensure it's legit and trustworthy. It's like being a data detective, constantly looking for any sneaky business that could mess things up.

5. Ethical Considerations

Ethical considerations are the cornerstone of data collection practices, requiring researchers to uphold participant privacy, informed consent, and data security principles (Fyfe, 2023). Prioritizing these ethical standards is paramount to safeguarding the rights and well-being of participants involved in research studies (King, 2023). Respecting participant privacy entails ensuring that individuals' personal information remains confidential and protected from unauthorized access. Obtaining informed consent from participants is a fundamental ethical requirement. It necessitates clear and comprehensive communication about the purpose of data collection, how their data will be used, and their rights regarding their information. Maintaining robust data security measures is also essential to prevent unauthorized access, data breaches, or misuse of collected data. By adhering to ethical guidelines, researchers demonstrate their commitment to responsible research conduct and foster trust among participants and the broader community (King, 2023). Upholding ethical standards promotes integrity and transparency in research practices. It upholds the dignity and rights of those contributing to scientific inquiry.

6. Data Collection and Research Validity

Data collection directly impacts the validity and reliability of research findings. Validity refers to the accuracy and truthfulness of the data in measuring what it's supposed to measure. Reliability refers to the consistency and stability of data over time and across different conditions.

In summary, data collection is a foundational step in the research process. It involves gathering information from various sources using appropriate methods. High-quality data collection ensures that research is valid, reliable, and ethically sound, enabling researchers and decision-makers to draw meaningful insights and make informed choices.

HOW TO GET RELEVANT RESPONSES THROUGH PROMPTS IN THE AI TOOL

When giving prompts in AI tools for data collection, several key points are crucial to ensure relevant answers:

- Clarity and Specificity: Provide clear and specific prompts to guide respondents on what information is required. Vague or ambiguous prompts may lead to irrelevant or inconsistent responses. For example, instead of asking, "Tell us about your experience," specify the aspects of the experience you're interested in, such as, "Please describe your satisfaction with the product's performance."
- Relevance to Research Objectives: Ensure that the prompts directly relate to the research objectives and the information needed to address research questions. Aligning prompts with research goals helps elicit pertinent responses to the study. For instance, if investigating customer preferences, prompts should focus on factors influencing their purchasing decisions.
- Open-ended and Probing: Use open-ended prompts that allow respondents to provide detailed and nuanced answers. Additionally, probing questions should be incorporated to delve deeper into specific topics or clarify respondents' responses. For example, follow up a general prompt about satisfaction with a probing question like, "Can you elaborate on what aspects of the product contribute to your satisfaction?"
- Contextualization: Provide context within prompts to help respondents understand the relevance of their answers. Contextual prompts can frame questions within a specific situation or scenario, facilitating more meaningful responses. For instance, when collecting feedback on a new software feature, provide context by describing its functionality and purpose.
- Avoid Leading or Biased Language: Ensure that prompts are neutral and unbiased to avoid influencing respondents' answers. Leading or biased language can skew responses and compromise the integrity of the data collected. For example, instead of asking, "Don't you agree that the new design is more user-friendly?" ask, "What are your thoughts on the usability of the new design?"

- Accessibility and Language: Tailor prompts to the target audience's language proficiency and accessibility needs. Use clear and straightforward language, avoiding jargon or technical terms that may be unfamiliar to respondents. Additionally, provide options for respondents to communicate in their preferred language if applicable.
- Ethical Considerations: Maintain ethical standards in prompt design by ensuring transparency, respecting respondents' privacy, and obtaining informed consent. Communicate the purpose of data collection and how respondents' information will be used—respect respondents' autonomy and right to withdraw from participation at any time.

By adhering to these key points when crafting prompts for AI tools in data collection, researchers can elicit relevant and insightful responses that contribute to achieving research objectives while upholding ethical standards and ensuring participant engagement.

Data Collection With AI Tools

Qualitative research often involves sifting through extensive textual data sources, such as interviews, surveys, and open-ended responses. AI can significantly simplify this process:

Example: Imagine you are researching customer feedback for a product. AI-driven sentiment analysis tools can swiftly categorize thousands of customer reviews as positive, negative, or neutral, providing you with valuable insights without manually reading each review.

How AI can be used for data collection-

1. Automated Surveys

AI can streamline the process of creating, administering, and analyzing surveys. This can be especially valuable for students conducting research or gathering project feedback.

Imagine you are a bachelor's student surveying your research project. Instead of spending hours designing paper surveys or manual online forms, you can use an AI-powered survey platform like SurveyMonkey. It offers pre-designed survey templates, automated data collection, and essential analysis tools. This saves time and ensures your survey is professional and user-friendly.

2. Data Extraction

AI can extract meaningful information from unstructured data sources like text, audio, or images. This capability can be applied to various academic scenarios.

Let's say you are a master's student in linguistics analyzing a large corpus of text documents. Instead of manually reading and categorizing texts, you can employ AI-based text analysis tools like Natural Language Processing (NLP). Tools like NLTK (Natural Language Toolkit) in Python can help you automatically identify themes, sentiment, and linguistic patterns in texts, facilitating your research.

3. Chatbots and Virtual Assistants

AI-powered chatbots and virtual assistants can engage in natural language conversations with users, making them helpful in conducting interviews, surveys, or gathering information interactively.

Suppose you are a PhD student researching public opinion on environmental policies. To engage with respondents, you can deploy an AI-powered chatbot on your research website or social media platforms. The chatbot can ask questions, provide information, and collect responses in a conversational style, making the survey experience more engaging and increasing response rates.

4. Web Scraping

AI-driven web scraping tools can automatically collect data from websites, databases, and social media platforms. This is particularly useful for students collecting data from online sources.

As a graduate student in economics, you may need to collect economic indicators from various government websites for your thesis. Instead of manually copying and pasting data from multiple sources, you can use AI-based web scraping tools like BeautifulSoup in Python. It can automate the process of extracting data from websites, saving you time and ensuring accuracy in your research.

In summary, AI offers students at all academic levels powerful tools to streamline data collection processes. Whether conducting surveys, analyzing texts, engaging with respondents, or gathering data from the web, AI can enhance efficiency, reduce manual effort, and improve the quality of data collection (Schmohl et al., 2020). These examples illustrate how AI can be harnessed for academic research and projects, making the research process more accessible and effective for students.

How to Start With Data Analysis Understanding With AI Tools

When embarking on the quest to find suitable data analysis tools via AI assistance, it's imperative to navigate the search process precisely and clearly, ensuring that the recommended tools align closely with the user's specific requirements and objectives (Chowdhury et al., 2023). To facilitate this journey, several key prompts play a pivotal role in eliciting the necessary information to guide users effectively.

First and foremost, understanding the type of analysis needed sets the foundation for the search. By prompting users to specify whether they require descriptive, predictive, or prescriptive analytics, AI tools can narrow recommendations to tools that offer the most relevant functionalities for the user's analytical needs. This ensures that users are directed towards tools that align with the nature and scope of their data analysis tasks.

Next, delving into the characteristics of the user's data source is essential for identifying compatible tools by inquiring about the format and size of the data – whether structured or unstructured and its volume – AI tools can filter out options that may not be suitable for handling the user's specific data requirements. This helps streamline the search process and directs users towards tools that can effectively process and analyze their data. Furthermore, understanding the features and functionality that users prioritize in a data analysis tool is crucial. By prompting users to specify their essential features, such as visualization capabilities, machine learning algorithms, or integration options, AI tools can tailor recommendations to match the user's desired functionalities. This ensures that users are directed towards tools that offer the necessary capabilities to meet their analytical goals (Schmohl et al., 2020).

Additionally, considering the user's level of expertise and preference for ease of use versus advanced capabilities is paramount. By inquiring about the user's skill level and usability requirements, AI tools can recommend tools that align with the user's proficiency and comfort level. This ensures that users are directed towards tools suitable for their level of expertise, whether they require user-friendly interfaces or advanced analytical functionalities.

Moreover, understanding the user's budget constraints and preferences regarding pricing models is essential. By inquiring about the user's budget and pricing preferences, AI tools can recommend tools that fall within the user's financial parameters. This ensures that users are directed towards tools that offer the best value for their budget, whether they prefer free, open-source options or subscription-based services.

By incorporating these critical prompts into the search process, AI tools can effectively guide users towards data analysis tools that best suit their needs, preferences, and constraints. This holistic approach ensures that users are equipped with the tools to tackle their data analysis tasks confidently and efficiently, ultimately driving informed decision-making and actionable insights.

Enhanced Data Analysis

AI has the capacity to transform the way qualitative data is analyzed. It can identify patterns, themes, and sentiments more efficiently than human analysts:

Example: Suppose you are researching social media data to understand public sentiment during a political event. AI-powered natural language processing algorithms can process millions of tweets and identify prevailing emotions and trending topics in real time, enabling you to capture the public's mood accurately.

Ethical Considerations

While AI offers remarkable advantages, navigating the ethical implications of AI-powered data collection and analysis is crucial. Ensuring data privacy, mitigating bias, and maintaining transparency are paramount:

Example: In an AI-assisted research project involving personal data, you must obtain informed consent and use anonymization techniques to protect participants' privacy. Additionally, auditing AI algorithms for bias is essential to ensure fair and unbiased analysis.

AI TOOLS FOR DATA UNDERSTANDING, EXPLORATION, AND COLLECTION

1. Natural Language Processing (NLP)

Natural Language Processing (NLP) is a branch of artificial intelligence that focuses on enabling computers to understand, interpret, and generate human language. NLP tools are vital for students as they can automatically analyze textual data, making it useful for various tasks. Sentiment analysis, for instance, involves using NLP to determine whether text expresses positive, negative, or neutral sentiment. This can be particularly beneficial for students researching public opinion or analyzing customer reviews. Topic modelling, another NLP technique, helps students identify underlying themes or topics within large text sets, simplifying the organization and categorization of textual data. Insights extraction, the ability to extract specific information from unstructured text, aids students in mining valuable data from sources like news articles or social media posts (Strobl et al., 2019). NLP tools can analyze and understand text data, making them invaluable for various academic tasks:

Sentiment Analysis

Sentiment Analysis, also known as opinion mining, is a branch of NLP that focuses on determining the emotional tone or sentiment expressed in a text, whether positive, negative, or neutral.

How Can Students Use Sentiment Analysis?

Public Opinion Gauge: For students conducting research in social sciences, political science, or marketing, Sentiment Analysis can be a powerful tool to gauge public opinion. Students can understand how people feel about particular issues or products by analyzing social media posts, news articles, or comments on specific topics.

User Review Analysis: In the context of product reviews, Sentiment Analysis can be applied to analyze user reviews of products or services. Students studying business or consumer behaviour can use this analysis to gain insights into customer satisfaction and identify areas for improvement.

Research Projects: Sentiment Analysis can be integrated into research projects where understanding public sentiment is essential. For example, a student researching the impact of social media on public perception can employ Sentiment Analysis to categorize and quantify sentiments expressed in social media posts.

2. Topic Modeling

Topic Modeling is an NLP technique automatically identifying topics or themes within an extensive collection of text documents. It uncovers hidden structures in textual data.

How Can Students Use Topic Modeling?

Research Organization: Students can use Topic Modeling to categorize and organize their research materials. For instance, in a literature review, Topic Modeling can automatically group research papers into thematic clusters, making it easier to identify key research areas.

Content Recommendations: In recommendation systems, Topic Modeling can be applied to suggest relevant articles, books, or resources to students based on their research interests. This is particularly valuable for students looking to expand their knowledge in specific areas.

Content Generation: Topic Modeling can also assist students in generating relevant content for their research projects. Students can gain inspiration for their writing or discover gaps in existing literature by identifying prevalent themes in a corpus of text (Oshiro et al., 2020).

3. Insights Extraction

Insights Extraction involves using NLP techniques to identify and extract specific information from unstructured text automatically. This could include extracting names, dates, locations, or other relevant data points.

How Can Students Use Insights Extraction?

Data Mining: Students in journalism or social sciences often need to extract specific information from large text datasets. For instance, a journalism student could use Insights Extraction to automatically extract names and dates from news articles to track trends or analyze historical events.

Information Retrieval: Insights Extraction can help students quickly locate and extract relevant data from research papers or articles in academic research. For example, students can automatically extract statistical data or quotes from scholarly articles to support their research.

Content Summarization: Students can use Insights Extraction to generate concise summaries of lengthy texts. This can be particularly helpful for digesting complex research papers or summarizing key points from a collection of articles.

Incorporating these NLP techniques into their academic work, students can streamline data analysis, improve content organization, and enhance their understanding of textual data, ultimately contributing to more effective and insightful research and projects.

Machine Learning Algorithms

Machine learning algorithms are designed to enable computers to learn from data and make predictions or decisions without explicit programming. For students, these algorithms offer valuable automation and analytical capabilities. Pattern recognition, one aspect of machine learning, helps students identify trends or patterns within data, simplifying the understanding and visualization of complex relationships within their datasets. Predictive modelling empowers students to make forecasts or predictions based on historical data, allowing them to anticipate trends or outcomes in their research or projects (Strobl et al., 2019). Clustering and classification techniques, also part of machine learning, help students group similar data points together or categorize data into specific classes, enhancing data exploration and organization. These machine-learning algorithms open up new avenues for students to analyze and interpret data more effectively (Roe et al., 2023).

Machine learning algorithms have emerged as powerful tools with diverse applications, making them invaluable for students, particularly when navigating complex datasets. These algorithms offer a range of capabilities, including pattern recognition, predictive modelling, clustering, and classification, enhancing students' abilities to analyze and interpret data effectively.

Pattern Recognition

Pattern recognition is a fundamental aspect of machine learning that allows algorithms to identify patterns or trends within datasets. For students, this capability is instrumental in comprehending intricate relationships within their data. Here's how it works:

When students are presented with large and complex datasets, it can be challenging to manually discern meaningful patterns or trends. Machine learning algorithms, however, excel in this task. They can automatically detect recurring patterns, relationships, or anomalies within the data (Roe et al., 2023).

For instance, imagine a student in the field of finance analyzing stock market data. They can identify recurring price patterns that signal potential buying or selling opportunities using machine learning algorithms. These patterns might not be evident to the naked eye. Still, machine learning algorithms can uncover them, aiding the student in making informed investment decisions.

Moreover, in fields like medical research, machine learning can assist in identifying patterns in patient data that lead to improved diagnostic accuracy (Kung et al., 2023). By recognizing subtle patterns in symptoms, test results, or medical histories, students can enhance their ability to detect diseases or conditions earlier (Garcia-Vidal et al., 2019; Oshiro et al., 2020).

One remarkable success story is in the field of finance. Algorithmic trading, powered by machine learning, analyzes vast datasets of financial market data in real time (Oshiro et al., 2020). These algorithms detect subtle patterns in stock prices, trading volumes, and other market variables that human traders might overlook. For instance, Renaissance Technologies, a hedge fund, achieved astonishing returns by employing machine learning algorithms to identify complex patterns in financial markets.

Predictive Modeling

Predictive modelling is a crucial application of machine learning that empowers students to make informed forecasts based on historical data. It enables them to anticipate trends, outcomes, and future events, vital for research and projects (Roe et al., 2023). Here's how it benefits students:

Students often seek to understand and predict future scenarios in various academic disciplines. For instance, a student in environmental science may want to predict the impact of climate change on a specific ecosystem. Using historical climate data and machine learning models, they can develop predictive models estimating future environmental changes.

In business and economics, predictive modelling can assist students in forecasting market trends, consumer behaviour, or financial outcomes (Strobl et al., 2019). This is essential for decision-making, whether for investment strategies or marketing campaigns.

Predictive modelling is also widely employed in healthcare, where students can use historical patient data to predict disease risks, patient outcomes, or treatment responses (Kung et al., 2023). This capability contributes to more effective healthcare strategies and interventions. Healthcare has seen remarkable success in predictive modelling. IBM's Watson for Oncology, an AI-powered system, analyzes patient medical records and research literature to suggest personalized cancer treatment options (Oshiro et al., 2020). By examining historical patient data, the system can predict which treatments will likely be most effective for individual patients, improving treatment decisions and patient outcomes (Garcia-Vidal et al., 2019).

Clustering and Classification

Clustering and classification techniques are powerful machine-learning methods for organizing and categorizing data. These methods aid students in data exploration and categorization, allowing them to make sense of large and complex datasets:

Clustering involves grouping similar data points based on shared characteristics. Students can apply clustering to identify natural clusters within their data, revealing hidden structures or relationships. For instance, in social sciences, clustering can help group survey respondents with similar demographics or preferences, aiding in the analysis of survey data.

Classification focuses on categorizing data into predefined classes or labels. Students can use classification algorithms to automatically classify data, which is valuable in fields such as image recognition, spam email detection, or medical diagnosis (Delahanty et al., 2018). For example, a student in computer science may build a classifier to classify images of animals into species categories automatically.

In e-commerce, recommendation systems utilize clustering and classification. Amazon, for instance, uses machine learning to cluster products based on user behaviour and preferences. When customers view or purchase a product, the system classifies them into groups with similar interests. This enables Amazon to make personalized product recommendations, enhancing the shopping experience and increasing sales.

In conclusion, machine learning algorithms equip students with indispensable tools for handling complex datasets. Whether recognizing patterns, making predictions, or organizing data, these capabilities empower students across various academic disciplines to conduct more sophisticated research, make data-driven decisions, and advance their understanding of complex real-world problems (Schmohl et al., 2020; Strobl et al., 2019).

Chatbots and Virtual Assistants

AI-driven chatbots and virtual assistants are interactive software applications that simulate human conversation, making them valuable for students in various ways. Data collection is simplified as chatbots can engage with survey respondents or interviewees in natural conversations, making the process more engaging and interactive. Chatbots provide quick access to research materials for students seeking information (Schmohl et al., 2020). They can answer queries related to their projects, saving time and enhancing productivity (Oshiro et al., 2020). Moreover, virtual assistants can offer guidance, suggestions, and feedback during the research process, acting as supportive companions in a student's academic journey. These AI tools create a more interactive and engaging student research and learning experience (Buruk, 2023).

AI-driven chatbots and virtual assistants have emerged as powerful tools that can significantly enhance research, particularly in data exploration and collection (Buruk, 2023). These intelligent conversational agents engage with users, streamline data collection, provide instant access to information, and offer valuable feedback and support (Strobl et al., 2019). Let's delve deeper into how students can leverage this technology effectively in their research endeavours, supported by real-world examples.

1. Data Collection Through Chatbots and Virtual Assistance

Collecting data is often a critical step in the research process. Still, engaging participants effectively and gathering high-quality information can be challenging. AI-driven chatbots and virtual assistants provide an innovative solution:

Conversational Surveys: Students can employ chatbots to conduct surveys conversationally. Unlike traditional static survey forms, chatbots can engage participants in interactive conversations, making the data collection process more engaging and user-friendly. For example, a psychology student researching stress levels among college students could deploy a chatbot to collect responses through a series of natural language questions, creating a more dynamic and personalized experience.

Interview Assistance: Chatbots can assist in conducting structured interviews. Students can program chatbots to ask standardized questions, record responses, and even follow up with probing questions based on participants' answers. This approach ensures consistency in data collection and eliminates the potential bias introduced by human interviewers. An educational researcher, for instance, might use a chatbot to interview teachers about their experiences with online teaching during the COVID-19 pandemic.

Data Validation: Virtual assistants can aid in data validation and quality control. They can prompt participants for clarification or additional information when ambiguous or incomplete responses occur.

For instance, in a medical research project, a virtual assistant could ask follow-up questions to ensure the accuracy of patient-reported symptoms.

2. Information Retrieval Through Chatbots and Virtual Assistance

In the research process, students often need quick access to relevant literature, research materials, or answers to specific queries. AI-driven chatbots and virtual assistants are excellent resources for information retrieval:

Literature Search: Virtual assistants can search academic databases and libraries to retrieve research papers, articles, and references based on students' requests (Buruk, 2023). For instance, a biology student exploring the effects of a specific enzyme might ask a virtual assistant to find recent research papers on the topic.

Citation Assistance: Chatbots can assist students in generating citations and references in various citation styles (e.g., APA, MLA). They can extract publication details from research papers and format them according to the student's chosen style, simplifying the citation process.

Project Guidance: Students often encounter challenges during the research process. Virtual assistants can guide by suggesting relevant research methodologies, statistical analysis techniques, or potential data sources (Zohery, 2023). For instance, a student working on a marketing research project could seek advice from a virtual assistant on the most suitable survey design.

3. Feedback and Support Through Chatbots and Virtual Assistance

The research journey can be complex and daunting, and students benefit greatly from guidance, suggestions, and feedback. AI-driven virtual assistants can offer invaluable support:

Research Plan Development: Virtual assistants can assist students in creating structured research plans. They can help students define research objectives, develop hypotheses, and outline the steps required to conduct their studies. This guidance ensures that research projects are well-structured and aligned with academic standards.

Data Analysis Guidance: Chatbots can provide support in data analysis. Students can seek assistance with selecting appropriate statistical tests, interpreting results, and generating visualizations (Zohery, 2023). For example, a student in sociology could ask a chatbot for guidance on conducting regression analysis for their survey data.

Writing Assistance: Virtual assistants can aid students in writing by offering suggestions for improving clarity, coherence, and conciseness in their research papers (Chowdhury et al., 2023). They can highlight areas where revisions are needed and provide grammar and style recommendations(Golan et al., 2023). This support ensures that the final research output is of high quality.

Real-World Examples of AI-Driven Support

Grammarly: This AI-powered writing assistant helps students improve their writing skills by providing real-time grammar, style, and clarity feedback. Students widely use it to enhance the quality of research papers and essays.

Mendeley: This reference management tool utilizes AI to recommend relevant research papers and articles based on a user's reading habits and interests. It simplifies the process of discovering and organizing research materials.

IBM Watson Assistant: Watson Assistant is an AI-driven virtual assistant that can be customized to provide support in various domains, including research. Educational institutions have employed it to assist students with inquiries related to courses, libraries, and research resources.

In conclusion, AI-driven chatbots and virtual assistants have transformed the research landscape for students by facilitating data collection, streamlining information retrieval, and offering valuable guidance and support throughout the research process (Buruk, 2023). As these technologies evolve, students will increasingly rely on them to enhance their research capabilities and academic achievements.

4. Web Scraping Tools

Web scraping tools are AI-powered solutions that automate the process of extracting data from websites, databases, and social media platforms (Golan et al., 2023). For students, web scraping simplifies data collection by gathering information from online sources without manual intervention. This is invaluable for research or analysis projects where large volumes of data need to be collected. Tools like Beautiful Soup, Scrapy, and Puppeteer enable students to set up automated data extraction processes, saving time and ensuring data accuracy. Students can extract diverse data types, from news articles and social media mentions to product details on e-commerce websites. These web scraping tools empower students to efficiently collect and utilize data from online sources, enhancing the depth and scope of their research.

Web scraping tools have become indispensable for students engaged in various research endeavours. These tools empower students to automatically extract data from websites, databases, and social media platforms. In a research context, web scraping offers substantial advantages, allowing students to efficiently collect, analyze, and derive insights from diverse online sources. This comprehensive exploration will explore how web scraping tools enable students to enhance their data collection processes and achieve automation in their research activities.

Automation for Efficiency Offered by Web Scraping Tools

Automation is a crucial advantage of web scraping tools. Students can streamline the data collection process and save valuable time, especially when dealing with large volumes of data or frequent updates:

Beautiful Soup: Beautiful Soup is a Python library that simplifies web scraping. Students can write scripts to extract data from web pages with specific HTML structures. This tool automates navigating web pages, searching for desired elements, and extracting data, making it an excellent choice for beginners in web scraping.

Scrapy: Scrapy is a more advanced web scraping framework that provides a robust set of tools for data extraction. Students can define web scraping pipelines, manage multiple concurrent requests, and efficiently extract structured data from websites. Scrapy suits more complex web scraping projects and offers greater flexibility and customization options.

Let's explore some real-world examples where web scraping tools have been effectively utilized for research:

Political Science Research: A student researching political campaign strategies scraped campaign websites, news articles, and social media data to analyze candidate messaging, public sentiment, and the impact of social media on elections. The student efficiently gathered and analyzed vast amounts of election-related content by automating data collection.

Market Research: A business student interested in market trends scraped e-commerce websites to collect pricing data, product descriptions, and customer reviews for a competitive analysis project. Web scraping allowed the student to compile comprehensive datasets and identify pricing strategies and customer preferences.

Healthcare Analysis: A student studying healthcare trends and disease outbreaks utilized web scraping to gather data from health department websites, news sources, and social media. By automating data collection, the student tracked the spread of diseases, monitored public health responses, and conducted epidemiological research.

Academic Bibliometrics: Researchers and academic students employ web scraping to collect citation data from scholarly journals and conference proceedings. This data is used to analyze research trends, identify influential publications, and assess the impact of research papers in specific fields.

Challenges and Ethical Considerations in Web Scrapping

While web scraping tools offer numerous benefits, students should know the challenges and ethical considerations associated with their use. Firstly, ethical use is paramount. Students must ensure they scrape data from websites with permission and comply with legal and ethical guidelines. Some websites may have terms of service that prohibit web scraping, so students should exercise caution. Secondly, data quality can be a concern. The accuracy and reliability of scraped data may vary, requiring students to carefully validate and clean the collected data to minimize errors and inaccuracies.

Moreover, the frequency and volume of web scraping requests can pose challenges. Aggressive scraping practices can strain websites' servers and potentially disrupt their operations. Therefore, students should be mindful of the frequency and volume of their scraping activities to avoid causing any inconvenience.

Additionally, data privacy is a crucial consideration, especially when collecting data from social media platforms or websites containing user-generated content. Students should respect privacy regulations and refrain from collecting personally identifiable information without consent.

In conclusion, while web scraping tools are invaluable assets for students conducting research across diverse domains, using them responsibly and ethically is essential. By adhering to ethical principles, students can harness the power of web scraping to efficiently collect data, automate tasks, and gain valuable insights, enhancing the rigour of their research and contributing to advancements in their fields.

Free Web Scraping Tools

Beautiful Soup: Beautiful Soup is a popular Python library that is often used with other libraries like Requests. It provides a simple and intuitive way to parse HTML and XML documents, making it a favoured choice for those with basic Python programming skills. Its advantages include ease of use, flexibility, and suitability for small to medium-sized web scraping projects. However, it may not be as powerful as some paid alternatives, and more complex scraping tasks might require additional Python coding

Scrapy: Scrapy is an open-source web crawling framework for Python. It is well-suited for more extensive scraping tasks and can efficiently handle structured data collection from websites. Scrapy offers robust features for handling various data formats and provides scalability. However, it may have a steeper learning curve than Beautiful Soup, making it more suitable for users with some programming experience.

Figure 1.

Source:
https://www.mygreatlearning.com/academy/learn-for-free/courses/beautiful-soup

Figure 2.

Source: https://github.com/scrapy/scrapy

Paid Web Scraping Tools

Octoparse: Octoparse is a user-friendly web scraping tool offering free and paid plans. Its paid plans provide advanced features like scheduling, cloud extraction, and automatic IP rotation. The advantage of Octoparse lies in its ease of use, making it accessible to users with limited coding skills. Its intuitive visual interface allows users to build scraping tasks by simply pointing and clicking. However, its free plan has limitations on the number of pages that can be scraped, and it might need to be more suitable for large-scale projects.

Import.io: Import.io is a paid web scraping platform that offers a wide range of features for data extraction. It provides automated data extraction, integration with various databases, and the ability to schedule and automate scraping tasks. Import.io is suitable for more complex and extensive scraping requirements. Its primary advantage is its scalability and flexibility. However, its paid plans can be relatively expensive for students or researchers on a tight budget.

Figure 3.

Source:
https://pitchbook.com/profiles/company/230979-52

Sentiment Analysis APIs

Tools like the Google Cloud Natural Language API or IBM Watson Sentiment Analysis can quickly determine textual data's sentiment (positive, negative, or neutral).

Example: A PhD student researching social media responses to climate change policies can use sentiment analysis to gauge public sentiment and identify influential narratives.

Data Cleaning and Preprocessing Tools

Python libraries like pandas and sci-kit-learn offer functionalities for cleaning and preprocessing data, ensuring it's ready for analysis.

Example: A bachelor's student working on a survey-based research project can use these tools to remove outliers and missing values from the dataset before analysis.

Selecting the Right AI Method for Analysi

Choosing the appropriate AI method for qualitative analysis is critical. Standard methods include natural language processing (NLP) for textual data, machine learning for pattern recognition, and topic modelling for thematic analysis.

Example: An undergraduate student researching online gaming communities can employ topic modelling techniques like Latent Dirichlet Allocation (LDA) to uncover prevalent themes in user-generated content.

5. Computer Vision

Computer vision is a branch of AI that enables computers to interpret and understand visual information from images or videos. In other words, Computer vision, a branch of artificial intelligence (AI), has emerged as a transformative tool for students across diverse disciplines, enabling visual data processing, analysis, and comprehension through images. This technology offers students powerful capabilities for analyzing and interpreting visual data. Image analysis, a fundamental aspect of computer vision, allows students to process and analyze images or videos for research (Zohery, 2023). For example, in biology, computer vision can assist in identifying and classifying species based on images of organisms. Additionally, data extraction from images becomes possible with computer vision, allowing students to recognize and extract text or information from photographs, which can be particularly useful in fields like journalism or content analysis. Computer vision equips students with the ability to work with visual data in innovative ways, broadening the scope of their research possibilities.

In an academic context, computer vision offers students powerful capabilities, including image analysis and data extraction from images, fostering innovation and efficiency in their research endeavours.

Image Analysis

One of the critical applications of computer vision in academia is image analysis. Students can leverage this technology to extract valuable insights and information from images or videos, thus enhancing their research across various fields:

Biology and Ecology: In biology, students can employ computer vision to analyze images of organisms, plants, or wildlife. For instance, computer vision algorithms can be trained to identify and classify species based on images, enabling researchers to monitor biodiversity and track ecosystem changes. Conservationists can benefit from this technology by using image analysis to assess the population dynamics of endangered species.

Medicine and Healthcare: Computer vision has profound implications for the medical field. Students can use AI-powered image analysis to interpret medical images, such as X-rays, MRI scans, or histopathological slides (Delahanty et al., 2018; Kung et al., 2023). These tools assist in early disease detection, accurate diagnosis, and treatment planning (Garcia-Vidal et al., 2019). For instance, a medical student studying radiology can employ computer vision algorithms to identify abnormalities in medical images, supporting clinical decision-making (Oshiro et al., 2020).

Astronomy and Astrophysics: In astronomy, computer vision enables the analysis of celestial images and videos captured by telescopes and space probes. Students can apply computer vision techniques to identify celestial objects, track their movements, and analyze data from astronomical observations. This is vital for astronomical research, where the analysis of vast volumes of visual data is common.

Environmental Science: Students in environmental science can benefit from computer vision to monitor ecological changes. For instance, analyzing satellite images using computer vision algorithms can help track deforestation, land cover changes, or ice cap extent. This data is invaluable for understanding the impact of climate change on the environment.

Data Extraction From Images

Computer vision's ability to extract data from images opens up many possibilities for students conducting research across disciplines (Strobl et al., 2019). This capability facilitates data collection, analysis, and interpretation:

Text Recognition: AI-powered optical character recognition (OCR) technology is instrumental in helping students extract text from images. For instance, historical documents, handwritten notes, or archival materials can be digitized through text recognition. This allows historians, linguists, and researchers to preserve and analyse textual data that would otherwise be inaccessible.

Document Analysis: Document analysis is paramount in fields like law and social sciences. Computer vision can extract structured data from scanned documents, enabling students to efficiently process and analyze legal texts, surveys, or government reports. This technology streamlines data extraction, allowing researchers to focus on data interpretation and analysis.

Art and Cultural Heritage: Art history and cultural heritage studies benefit from computer vision's ability to analyze artwork. Students can use image analysis to identify styles, periods, or artists by examining the visual characteristics of paintings, sculptures, or artefacts. This contributes to a deeper understanding of cultural heritage and artistic movements.

Real-World Examples

Wildlife Conservation: Researchers in wildlife conservation have used computer vision to monitor and protect endangered species. For instance, camera traps equipped with computer vision technology can automatically identify and count individual animals in the wild. This data aids in population estimation and conservation efforts.

Medical Image Analysis: Computer vision algorithms are widely employed in medical image analysis (Delahanty et al., 2018). For instance, a group of medical students developed a tool that uses computer vision to detect diabetic retinopathy by analyzing retinal images. This innovation enables early diagnosis and intervention for diabetic patients.

Art Authentication: Art history students can employ computer vision to authenticate artworks. Algorithms can analyze brushstroke patterns, colour palettes, and other visual features to determine paintings' authenticity, helping combat art forgery.

Challenges and Considerations

While computer vision offers numerous advantages, students should be aware of challenges and ethical considerations:

1. Data Privacy

When working with images or videos containing individuals, data privacy emerges as a paramount concern for students conducting research. Safeguarding individuals' privacy rights and adhering to applicable regulations is imperative to ensure ethical data practices:

Informed consent stands as a cornerstone in research involving human subjects. Students must obtain explicit consent from individuals featured in images or videos, outlining the purpose of data collection, its intended use, and any associated risks or benefits. Consent forms should be comprehensive and transparent, ensuring individuals fully understand and consent to using their data in research.

Anonymization of data is a crucial step in protecting individuals' privacy. Students can anonymize or de-identify images or videos by removing or altering personally identifiable information (PII), preventing individuals from being identified. Rigorous application of anonymization techniques is essential to mitigate the risk of re-identification and ensure the anonymity of data subjects.

Data storage and security measures are paramount to safeguarding collected data. Students must implement robust encryption, access controls, and secure storage methods to prevent unauthorized access or data breaches. Adequate data protection measures are necessary to uphold data privacy and maintain individuals' trust in research practices.

Students can uphold individuals' privacy rights and ensure ethical conduct when working with images or videos in research by being vigilant in obtaining informed consent, rigorously anonymising data, and implementing robust data security measures. These practices demonstrate a commitment to ethical standards and foster trust and integrity in research.

2. Data Quality

The quality of input data significantly impacts the accuracy and reliability of computer vision results. Students should be mindful of data quality considerations:

Image Resolution: Images and videos used for analysis should have sufficient resolution and clarity. Low-quality or pixelated images can lead to inaccurate results, as computer vision algorithms may lose or misinterpret details.

Data Preprocessing: Preprocessing steps, such as noise reduction and image enhancement, may be necessary to improve data quality. Students should be prepared to apply appropriate preprocessing techniques to optimize data for analysis.

Dataset Bias: Dataset bias can affect the performance of computer vision models. Suppose the dataset used for training the model does not represent the target population or contains biases; the model's results may be skewed. Students should be cautious and transparent about dataset biases in their research.

3. Ethical Use

Ethical considerations are central when applying computer vision, particularly in domains where privacy and bias are prominent concerns:

Bias and Fairness: Students should know the potential for bias in computer vision systems. Biases can arise from imbalanced datasets or algorithmic decisions. Researchers must strive to mitigate bias by diversifying datasets, conducting fairness audits, and ensuring equitable representation.

Facial Recognition: Facial recognition technology raises ethical concerns due to its potential for privacy invasion and misuse. Students should approach facial recognition research cautiously and adhere to strict ethical guidelines. Considerations should include obtaining explicit consent for facial data collection and assessing the social and moral implications of the technology.

Transparency and Accountability: Students should be transparent about their research methodologies, including the algorithms and data sources used. Openly sharing research findings, methodologies, and limitations contributes to transparency and fosters accountability.

Responsible Deployment: Students should prioritise accountable and ethical use when deploying computer vision systems in real-world applications. This includes considering the technology's potential societal impacts, moral frameworks, and consequences. Ethical considerations should guide decision-making and deployment strategies.

In conclusion, computer vision is a transformative tool that empowers students to analyze images, extract data from visuals, and derive meaningful insights across various academic domains. This technology enhances the efficiency of research and enables students to explore new dimensions of data analysis and interpretation, fostering innovation and advancement in their respective fields of study.

While computer vision offers tremendous potential for research and innovation, it comes with significant responsibilities and ethical considerations. Students engaging in computer vision research must prioritize data privacy, data quality, and ethical use. These considerations are essential for complying with legal and moral standards and ensuring that computer vision technology's benefits are realized without causing harm or perpetuating bias. Ultimately, ethical and responsible research practices contribute to advancing knowledge while respecting individuals' rights and dignity (Fyfe, 2023).

4. Data Analytics Platforms

Data analytics platforms, enhanced by AI, provide students with advanced tools for exploring, visualizing, and analyzing data. AI-enhanced data analytics platforms such as Tableau and Power BI have revolutionized how students approach data exploration and visualization. These tools empower students across various academic disciplines to interact with data dynamically, uncover insights, and effectively communicate their research findings. This comprehensive exploration will explore how these platforms facilitate data visualization and exploration, offering students a powerful toolkit for their research endeavours.

Data Visualization

Data visualization is critical to data analysis and research, enabling students to represent complex datasets in a visual and understandable format. AI-enhanced platforms like Tableau and Power BI excel in this regard:

Interactive Visualizations: Tableau and Power BI offer various interactive visualization options, from bar charts and scatter plots to heat maps and treemaps. Students can choose the most suitable visualization type for their data and research goals. For example, a business student studying sales data can create interactive bar charts to visualize regional sales performance over time, allowing quick insights into trends and variations.

Dashboards: These platforms empower students to design interactive dashboards that consolidate multiple visualizations and data elements on a single screen. Dashboards serve as powerful tools for presenting research findings comprehensively. A public health student investigating disease outbreaks can develop a dashboard displaying maps, charts, and tables to illustrate the spread of the disease, its demographics, and affected regions.

Real-Time Updates: Tableau and Power BI can connect to live data sources, ensuring up-to-date visualisations and dashboards. Students engaged in dynamic research can create dashboards that automatically refresh with the latest data, keeping their analyses current. For instance, a finance student tracking stock market trends can build a real-time dashboard displaying stock prices, news feeds, and performance indicators.

Storytelling: These platforms facilitate data storytelling, allowing students to craft narratives around their data. They can guide viewers through research, highlighting key findings, trends, and insights. For instance, a sociology student studying demographic changes can use storytelling features to narrate the evolution of population demographics over the years, adding context and meaning to the data.

Integration: Tableau and Power BI seamlessly integrate with various data sources, including databases, spreadsheets, and cloud services. Students can connect to diverse data repositories, ensuring their research encompasses many data points. A student conducting market research can consolidate data from surveys, CRM systems, and social media into a unified visualization.

Data Exploration

Data exploration is a crucial phase of the research process, enabling students to delve into their datasets, identify patterns, and formulate hypotheses. AI-enhanced data analytics platforms offer robust capabilities for data exploration:

Data Manipulation: Tableau and Power BI provide students with intuitive data manipulation tools. Students can interactively filter, sort, and transform data, facilitating in-depth exploration. For instance, an environmental science student studying climate data can filter datasets by variables like temperature, precipitation, and location to examine specific trends.

Advanced Analytics: These platforms incorporate advanced analytical functions that allow students to perform calculations, statistical analyses, and predictive modelling. Students can test hypotheses, perform regression analysis, and generate forecasts within the platform. A psychology student investigating factors influencing student performance can employ statistical tools to analyze survey data and identify significant predictors.

Data Profiling: Tableau and Power BI offer data profiling capabilities that assist students in understanding their datasets better. Students can assess data quality, detect outliers, and identify missing values. Data profiling aids students in making informed decisions about data preparation and cleaning. For example, a marketing student can use data profiling to identify inconsistent customer data in a CRM database, facilitating data cleansing efforts.

Data Aggregation: These platforms support data aggregation and summarization, allowing students to condense large datasets into manageable insights. Aggregation functions can be applied to numerical data, enabling students to calculate totals, averages, or percentages. A public policy student analyzing government expenditure data can aggregate spending by department or category to assess budget allocations.

Geospatial Analysis: Tableau and Power BI include geospatial analysis features, enabling students to incorporate geographic data into their research. Geographical mapping, heat maps, and spatial analysis tools can be used to explore spatial patterns and correlations. For instance, an urban planning student can create maps to visualize city traffic patterns, population density, and land use.

Data Analysis

Statistical Analysis: Students can leverage these platforms to perform various statistical analyses. Whether they are conducting surveys, experiments, or working with large datasets, Tableau and Power BI provide tools to calculate descriptive statistics, test hypotheses, and identify correlations. For instance, a psychology student researching the relationship between study habits and academic performance can employ statistical tests within the platform to determine significant associations.

Predictive Modeling: Predictive modelling is a valuable feature of data analytics platforms. Students can build predictive models using machine learning algorithms integrated into these platforms. By training models on historical data, they can forecast future trends, make data-driven predictions, and optimize decision-making. For instance, an economics student studying stock market trends can develop predictive models based on historical market data to anticipate price fluctuations.

Insights Generation: These platforms facilitate the generation of actionable insights from data. Through interactive exploration and data manipulation, students can uncover patterns, anomalies, and trends that may take time to be apparent. Drilling down into data allows for a deeper understanding of research findings. For example, a sociology student analyzing survey responses can use data analytics to identify demographic segments with distinct preferences or behaviours.

Time-Series Analysis: Time-series analysis is crucial in various fields, such as finance, economics, and climate science. Students can use Tableau and Power BI to analyze time-dependent data, detect seasonality, and make forecasts. For instance, an environmental science student can explore historical climate data to identify long-term trends and predict future temperature fluctuations.

Data Presentation

Reporting: Tableau and Power BI offer robust reporting capabilities, allowing students to create comprehensive reports summarizing their research findings. These reports can include text, visualizations, and interactive elements, providing a holistic view of the research. Students can customize reports to meet the specific needs of their target audience. For example, a public health student investigating disease outbreaks can generate reports that include maps, charts, and statistical summaries, making the information accessible to policymakers.

Dashboard Creation: Besides traditional reports, these platforms enable students to design interactive dashboards. Dashboards consolidate multiple visualizations, data elements, and insights onto a single screen. This feature streamlines data communication and enhances the impact of research findings. Students can create dashboards that cater to diverse stakeholders, such as academic advisors, colleagues, or project collaborators. For example, a marketing student can develop a marketing campaign dashboard that displays key performance indicators, campaign metrics, and audience engagement data.

Data Storytelling: Effective data presentation involves storytelling. Tableau and Power BI offer storytelling features that enable students to craft narratives around their data. Students can highlight key insights, trends, and implications by guiding viewers through the research process. Storytelling makes research findings more relatable and engaging. A data science student exploring customer behaviour can use storytelling to convey how specific actions impact customer retention and sales.

Accessibility: These platforms provide accessibility features, ensuring that research findings can be easily understood by a broad audience, including those with diverse abilities. Students can create reports and dashboards compatible with screen readers, support keyboard navigation, and include alternative text for visual elements. Accessibility considerations ensure that research is inclusive and reaches a broad audience.

In conclusion, AI-enhanced data analytics platforms like Tableau and Power BI empower students with data exploration and visualization capabilities and advanced data analysis and presentation tools. These tools provide a dynamic data visualization and manipulation environment, enabling students to gain deeper insights from their datasets. Through real-world examples and practical applications, students can harness the full potential of these platforms to enhance their research and contribute to academic and professional fields. These platforms provide a comprehensive ecosystem for students to conduct research, derive insights, and communicate their findings with clarity and impact, contributing to academic excellence and informed decision-making.

5. Survey and Form Builders

I-powered survey and form builders have become indispensable tools for students engaged in research, surveys, and data collection. These platforms offer a range of features that simplify the entire data collection process, from designing customized surveys to analyzing and reporting the results. In this comprehensive exploration, we will delve into the capabilities of AI-powered survey and form builders, such as SurveyMonkey and Google Forms, and how they empower students to efficiently collect, analyze, and report data for their academic and research endeavours.

Custom Surveys

One of the primary advantages of AI-powered survey and form builders is their ability to facilitate the creation of custom surveys tailored to the unique requirements of students' research projects or academic assessments. These platforms offer several key benefits in this regard:

Pre-Designed Templates: Survey and form builders often provide a library of pre-designed survey templates covering various topics and purposes. Students can choose templates that closely align with their research objectives, saving time and effort in survey creation. For instance, a sociology student studying social attitudes can select a pre-designed template for attitude assessment and customize it to suit their research questions.

User-Friendly Interfaces: These platforms feature intuitive, user-friendly interfaces that make survey design accessible to students of all technical backgrounds. The drag-and-drop functionality and straightforward question formatting allow students to create complex surveys easily. An education student exploring teaching methods can use the user-friendly interface to design surveys that gather feedback from teachers and students.

Question Types: Survey and form builders offer various question types, including multiple-choice, open-text, Likert scale, and matrix questions. Students can choose the most suitable question types to gather diverse data types. For example, a marketing student conducting a product satisfaction survey can use a Likert scale question to gauge customer opinions on various product features.

Data Collection

AI-powered survey and form builders excel in automating the data collection process, simplifying the management of responses from participants:

Online Distribution: Students can efficiently distribute surveys to their target audience via email, social media, or embedded links on websites. These platforms enable students to reach a broad and geographically diverse audience. A healthcare student researching patient satisfaction can distribute surveys to patients through email, collect responses online, and track participation rates.

Response Management: Survey and form builders automatically collect and organize responses in a centralized database. This feature ensures students can efficiently manage and access all collected data in one location (Zohery, 2023). A psychology student investigating sleep patterns can rely on these platforms to compile and store survey responses for analysis.

Real-Time Tracking: Students can monitor survey participation and responses in real-time. These platforms provide analytics dashboards that display response rates and trends, allowing students to gauge the progress of their data collection efforts (Oshiro et al., 2020). For instance, a political science student studying voter preferences can track survey response rates leading to an election.

Data Analysis

While survey and form builders primarily focus on data collection, many of these platforms offer fundamental data analysis features that aid students in the initial stages of understanding their data:

Summary Statistics: These platforms generate summary statistics, including mean, median, mode, and standard deviation, to give students an overview of their data. This feature benefits students who need quick insights into their survey results. A business student investigating customer satisfaction can use summary statistics to assess satisfaction levels.

Data Visualization: Some survey and form builders include essential data visualization tools that allow students to create simple charts and graphs based on survey responses. Visualization aids in presenting data in a more understandable format. For example, a biology student studying species distribution can create a bar chart to visualize the frequency of species in different regions.

Reporting and Sharing

AI-powered survey and form builders facilitate the creation of reports and the sharing of survey data with others. These features enhance the overall value and impact of student research:

Report Generation: Students can use these platforms to generate reports that compile survey results, summaries, and visualizations into a structured format. Reports can include insights, observations, and conclusions drawn from the data. A social work student conducting a needs assessment survey can create a comprehensive report detailing community needs and recommendations for intervention.

Data Export: Survey and form builders often allow students to export survey data in various formats, such as Excel, CSV, or PDF. This flexibility enables students to work with the data in external analysis tools or share it with collaborators. For instance, a computer science student exploring user preferences can export survey data for further analysis using specialized software.

Sharing Options: Students can easily share surveys, reports, or data dashboards with peers, instructors, or project stakeholders. These platforms provide options for sharing via email, direct links, or embedded code on websites. A public policy student collaborating with fellow researchers can use these sharing features to distribute surveys and share research findings seamlessly.

In conclusion, AI-powered survey and form builders like SurveyMonkey and Google Forms have emerged as invaluable tools for students engaged in research, surveys, or data collection. These platforms simplify data collection, from survey design to response management, while providing basic data analysis capabilities (Chowdhury et al., 2023). Additionally, they enable students to generate reports, visualize data, and share findings effectively. As a result, students can focus more on deriving insights from their data and conducting meaningful research, ultimately contributing to academic excellence and informed decision-making across various academic disciplines.

CONCLUSION

In conclusion, integrating AI into qualitative research offers students and researchers at all academic levels a wealth of opportunities to enhance the efficiency and depth of their work. By utilizing AI tools for data collection, screening, and analysis, scholars can unlock deeper insights, streamline research processes, and significantly contribute to their respective fields. However, it is imperative to approach AI research with ethical considerations, ensuring that AI is leveraged responsibly and transparently. The future of qualitative research is undoubtedly intertwined with the power of AI, and as students and scholars, embracing these technologies can propel us to new heights of academic excellence.

REFERENCES

Buruk, O. (2023). Academic Writing with GPT-3.5 (ChatGPT): Reflections on Practices, Efficacy and Transparency. *ACM International Conference Proceeding Series, 3*, 144–153. 10.1145/3616961.3616992

Chowdhury, S., Dey, P., Joel-Edgar, S., Bhattacharya, S., Rodriguez-Espindola, O., Abadie, A., & Truong, L. (2023). Unlocking the value of artificial intelligence in human resource management through AI capability framework. *Human Resource Management Review, 33*(1), 100899. doi:10.1016/j.hrmr.2022.100899

Christou, P. (2023). How to Use Artificial Intelligence (AI) as a Resource, ow Methodological and Analysis Tool in Qualitative Research? *The Qualitative Report, 28*(7), 1968–1980. doi:10.46743/2160-3715/2023.6406

Delahanty, R. J., Kaufman, D., & Jones, S. S. (2018). Development and Evaluation of an Automated Machine Learning Algorithm for In-Hospital Mortality Risk Adjustment Among Critical Care Patients. *Critical Care Medicine*, *46*(6), E481–E488. doi:10.1097/CCM.0000000000003011 PMID:29419557

Fyfe, P. (2023). How to cheat on your final paper: Assigning AI for student writing. *AI & Society*, *38*(4), 1395–1405. doi:10.1007/s00146-022-01397-z

Garcia-Vidal, C., Sanjuan, G., Puerta-Alcalde, P., Moreno-García, E., & Soriano, A. (2019). Artificial intelligence to support clinical decision-making processes. In EBioMedicine (Vol. 46, pp. 27–29). doi:10.1016/j.ebiom.2019.07.019

Golan, R., Reddy, R., Muthigi, A., & Ramasamy, R. (2023). Artificial intelligence in academic writing: a paradigm-shifting technological advance. In Nature Reviews Urology (Vol. 20, Issue 6, pp. 327–328). doi:10.1038/s41585-023-00746-x

King, M. R. (2023). A Conversation on Artificial Intelligence, Chatbots, and Plagiarism in Higher Education. *Cellular and Molecular Bioengineering*, *16*(1), 1–2. doi:10.1007/s12195-022-00754-8 PMID:36660590

Kung, T. H., Cheatham, M., Medenilla, A., Sillos, C., De Leon, L., Elepaño, C., Madriaga, M., Aggabao, R., Diaz-Candido, G., Maningo, J., & Tseng, V. (2023). Performance of ChatGPT on USMLE: Potential for AI-assisted medical education using large language models. *PLOS Digital Health*, *2*(2), e0000198. doi:10.1371/journal.pdig.0000198 PMID:36812645

Oshiro, J., Caubet, S. L., Viola, K. E., & Huber, J. M. (2020). Going Beyond "Not Enough Time": Barriers to Preparing Manuscripts for Academic Medical Journals. *Teaching and Learning in Medicine*, *32*(1), 71–81. doi:10.1080/10401334.2019.1659144 PMID:31530189

Roe, J., Renandya, W. A., & Jacobs, G. M. (2023). A Review of AI-Powered Writing Tools and Their Implications for Academic Integrity in the Language Classroom. *Journal of English and Applied Linguistics*, *2*(1), 22–30. doi:10.59588/2961-3094.1035

Schmohl, T., Watanabe, A., Fröhlich, N., & Herzberg, D. (2020). How can Artificial Intelligence Improve the academic writing of students? *The Future of Education*, 12–14. https://thesiswriter.zhaw.ch/

Strobl, C., Ailhaud, E., Benetos, K., Devitt, A., Kruse, O., Proske, A., & Rapp, C. (2019). Digital support for academic writing: A review of technologies and pedagogies. *Computers & Education*, *131*, 33–48. doi:10.1016/j.compedu.2018.12.005

ZoheryM. (2023). ChatGPT in Academic Writing and Publishing_ A Comprehensive Guide 2023. *Artificial Intelligence in Academia, Research and Science: ChatGPT as a Case Study*, 10–61. doi:10.5281/zenodo.7803703

Chapter 9
AI Tools for Efficient Writing and Editing in Academic Research

M. Abinaya
https://orcid.org/0009-0000-4424-7812
SRM Institute of Science and Technology, India

G. Vadivu
https://orcid.org/0000-0003-4953-0566
SRM Institute of Science and Technology, India

ABSTRACT

Readers embark on a journey exploring AI's profound impact on content creation. It begins by tracing AI's evolution, underscoring its pivotal role in modern content production. The narrative delves deep into AI mechanisms, decoding algorithms, and the significance of natural language processing. It meticulously analyses AI tool classifications, emphasizing their benefits in content generation, writing style enhancement, and grammar checks. The chapter illuminates AI's role in boosting productivity and creativity, offering practical guidance on tool selection. Importantly, it stresses human proofreading's unique touch in the final editing phase. Anticipating future advancements, it envisions seamless integration of AI and human creativity in popular writing platforms.

1. INTRODUCTION

Artificial intelligence (AI) has undeniably emerged as an unstoppable power in our swiftly advancing technological environment, making a lasting impact on numerous aspects of our existence. In the domain of content creation, specifically in writing and editing, AI has transformed conventional methods, greatly improving the speed and effectiveness of the entire editing process. This chapter thoroughly explores the historical development of AI in this specific context, tracing its beginnings from basic grammar check-

DOI: 10.4018/979-8-3693-1798-3.ch009

ers to advanced language processing algorithms (Fitria, 2023). As a result, it provides a comprehensive overview of its evolution.

The exploration begins by conducting a comprehensive analysis of the early stages of AI in writing. Simple grammar checkers emerged as pioneering tools during this period, although their functionality was limited. Despite their limitations, these fundamental tools provided the basis for the creation of more complex applications. Gaining a comprehensive understanding of the difficulties encountered by AI developers in the early stages offers valuable perspectives on the initial obstacles that influenced the development of AI in the fields of writing and editing (Chen, 2023). With the advancement of technology, AI writing tools have undergone substantial changes, integrating complex algorithms and utilizing machine learning techniques. These advancements enabled intricate language processing, leading to revolutionary innovations in plagiarism detection, style recommendations, and proofreading.

The process of evolution did not reach its peak with writing; AI has smoothly incorporated itself into the editing process, bringing forth novel methods for detecting plagiarism, providing style suggestions, and conducting proofreading. By means of this integration, a novel epoch of editing suggestions has arisen, in which algorithms scrupulously evaluate context, tone, and style. This chapter thoroughly analyses these advanced algorithms, revealing the complexities of their operation and illuminating their significant influence on the editing process (Adams & Chuah, 2022). By understanding the intricacies of these algorithms, readers develop a deep comprehension of AI's abilities in editing written content, enabling them to use these tools efficiently and responsibly.

Nevertheless, in the midst of these notable advancements, ethical quandaries emerged. This section rigorously examines the ethical dilemmas that arise from the utilization of AI tools, encompassing concerns regarding algorithmic biases, data privacy, and the intricate equilibrium between automation and human creativity. Recognizing these difficulties is crucial for the responsible application of AI in the fields of writing and editing (Dergaa et al., 2023). This chapter prompts readers to carefully consider the ethical challenges associated with integrating AI into the creative process. It aims to cultivate a strong sense of ethical duty among both content creators and technologists.

In the end, this chapter offers a comprehensive examination of the historical advancement of AI in the fields of writing and editing, establishing a strong basis for further investigation into AI tools for producing impactful content. Equipped with this extensive understanding that includes historical background, technological progress, ethical concerns, and transformative effects, writers, editors, and content creators are enabled to utilize AI in a responsible manner, enhancing the quality and influence of their work in a world that is increasingly influenced by AI. Moreover, this chapter serves as a valuable reference for scholars and researchers, providing guidance for future advancements in the ever-evolving field of AI and written communication.

2. AI TOOLS FOR ACADEMIC RESEARCH AND WRITING

The incorporation of AI tools has become essential in the constantly changing field of academic research and writing, bringing about a new era of effectiveness, precision, and creativity (Marzuki et al., 2023). This section of the chapter provides a detailed examination of how AI tools can be practically used in academic research and writing. It not only explains the underlying technologies but also shows how authors and researchers can use these tools to significantly improve the quality and impact of their work.

2.1 Natural Language Processing (NLP) and AI Algorithms

Sophisticated algorithms and NLP methods are the core components of AI writing and editing tools. NLP algorithms, known for their exceptional capacity to interpret syntactic structures and semantic interpretations, serve as the foundation of AI tools. This exploration clarifies how these algorithms not only understand literal meanings but also analyse idiomatic expressions, subtle tones, and contextual details (Malik et al., 2022). By examining concrete instances and persuasive analyses, authors and scholars acquire invaluable knowledge about the practical implementation of NLP, enabling them to fully grasp the extent of AI's comprehension of human language.

2.2 Enhancing Grammar, Style, and Content: Improving Scholarly Work

Academic writers and researchers must prioritize precision and strict adherence to grammatical conventions without any room for compromise.

Grammar Checks for Accuracy and Consistency

AI-powered grammar checks have become indispensable tools in this endeavour. This section explores the intricacies of how AI tools thoroughly analyse academic papers, guaranteeing both flawless writing and strict adherence to complex grammar rules. Through the seamless integration of these grammar checks into their writing process, scholars can concentrate on expressing their ideas, assured that their work adheres to the utmost standards of linguistic precision (Bolt, 1992).

Style Refinement

Each academic discipline typically possesses its own distinct writing style and set of standards. AI algorithms are crucial in this particular context. They assess and skilfully align existing writing styles with the particular academic criteria or the preferences of the intended readership. This section demonstrates how AI enhances writing styles to ensure that scholarly work effectively connects with the intended audience, using a variety of examples. Researchers can optimize their writing by adopting AI-driven style enhancements, which allow them to customize their content with precision, resulting in improved readability and comprehension (Rouhiainen, 2018).

Enhancing Content

Clarity and coherence hold utmost importance in the domain of academic research. The AI content enhancement tools discussed in this section have demonstrated their ability to bring about significant changes. The analysts thoroughly examine written material, identifying repetitions, recommending the most appropriate word choices, and improving the overall logical flow. This segment effectively showcases the ways in which these tools enable scholars to enhance the persuasiveness of their arguments through practical demonstrations. Through the process of simplifying their narratives, researchers can enhance their academic papers, ensuring that they are both devoid of errors and captivatingly persuasive (Ng et al., 2022).

2.3 Effortless Integration

Comprehending the intricacies of AI tools is essential, but equally significant is their smooth incorporation into academic writing and research procedures. This section provides a plethora of pragmatic advice and optimal methodologies. Scholars are provided with comprehensive guidance, ranging from selecting the appropriate AI tool for specific writing requirements to accurately interpreting the suggestions given. Furthermore, the conversation explores the ethical implications, of promoting conscientious utilization of AI tools in academic settings (Weber & Huici, 2020). By adopting these understandings, writers and researchers can confidently navigate the AI field, utilizing its capacity to improve their scholarly pursuits while maintaining the utmost standards of academic honesty.

Essentially, this section acts as a guiding light, leading scholars through the complex landscape of AI-driven academic writing and research. By clarifying the technology, demonstrating practical uses, and providing practical advice, it enables researchers to both accept the future of scholarly communication and make valuable contributions to their fields, equipped with the transformative abilities of AI tools. In the ever-changing academic world, the combination of human intelligence and AI has the potential to redefine academic excellence, making scholarly pursuits more influential, accessible, and innovative than ever.

3. ADVANTAGES OF AI TOOLS FOR EDITING AND WRITING

The integration of AI tools in writing and editing has the potential to bring about significant transformation (Gilat & Cole, 2023). These tools offer unique advantages that redefine creative expression and scholarly communication in the constantly changing field. This section explores the diverse benefits of AI tools in the domains of writing and editing, revealing their significant influence on productivity, content quality, and the limitless realm of creativity.

3.1 Efficiency and Facilitating Creative Liberty

Transforming the Workflow

AI tools are emerging as innovative assistants, freeing writers and editors from burdensome and time-consuming manual tasks. The automation of grammar checking and basic editing has transformed what used to be a laborious and tedious task into a seamless process. This enables professionals to focus their energy on the creative aspects of content creation (Carbonell et al., 2018). This automation not only accelerates the editing process but also serves as a catalyst for generating ideas and developing stories.

Nurturing Profound Creativity

AI tools facilitate a more profound exploration of creativity by relieving professionals from the tedious responsibilities. Writers and editors have the ability to explore the complexities of storytelling, explore various writing techniques, and create narratives that deeply connect with readers. By ensuring meticulous handling of grammatical errors and basic editing concerns, creative individuals are able to explore unexplored areas, pushing the limits of traditional storytelling and academic discourse.

3.2 Enhancing Content Quality

Watchful Partners

AI tools surpass basic automation by serving as diligent collaborators, meticulously detecting errors, providing style recommendations, and ensuring unmatched coherence in content (Kuleto et al., 2021). The final outcome is refined, well-informed, and inherently accessible content for the reader. These tools ensure that the audience receives flawlessly crafted, error-free writing that adheres to the most stringent editorial standards, thanks to their thorough examination.

Significant Influence

The profound influence on the quality of content is apparent in each meticulously constructed sentence. AI tools optimise the utilisation of language, rectify grammatical subtleties, and augment the overall legibility. Equipped with these tools, writers and editors have the ability to create content that not only meets strict editorial standards but also strongly connects with readers, establishing a deep bond between the creator and the audience.

3.3 Exceptional Creativity and Innovation

Increasing Efficiency and Empowering Innovation

An important benefit of AI tools is their capacity to increase productivity while preserving creativity. By accelerating the editing process, these tools enable professionals to generate an abundance of top-notch content within tight deadlines. This newfound efficiency allows creative individuals to freely explore unexplored creative territories (Savaget et al., 2019). Writers have the ability to explore various genres, delve into intricate narratives, and create intellectually stimulating works. Editors have the ability to concentrate on refining manuscripts with accuracy and delicacy, guaranteeing that the fundamental nature of the author's voice is maintained while following the most elevated editorial criteria.

Fostering Creativity and Novelty

the automation of monotonous editing tasks serves as a catalyst for innovation. Writers and editors are urged to engage in unconventional writing techniques, delve into avant-garde storytelling methods, and put forward innovative ideas that question societal norms and conventional wisdom. AI tools alleviate creative professionals from the tedious tasks of editing, enabling them to generate and implement projects that were previously constrained by the restrictions of manual work.

the incorporation of AI tools in the fields of writing and editing goes beyond simple technological progress; it introduces a new era of artistic freedom and academic brilliance. Writers and editors, liberated from the limitations of manual editing, can achieve unparalleled levels of productivity and innovation. By adopting AI's support, these experts not only enhance their work process but also foster a culture of limitless imagination and revolutionary narrative, fundamentally transforming the field of writing and editing (Mazzone & Elgammal, 2019). The future of writing and editing looks extremely promising as the collaboration between human ingenuity and AI thrives. This partnership will bring together efficiency, quality, and unmatched creativity.

4. EXPLORE VARIOUS AI WRITING AND EDITING TOOLS

AI writing and editing tools have become essential allies for authors, editors, and businesses in the constantly changing world of digital content creation. This section thoroughly explores the wide range of these tools, each carefully designed to target specific aspects of text generation and improvement. By utilising advanced algorithms and machine learning, these tools have revolutionised the process of content creation, guaranteeing a balance of precision, innovation, and audience involvement.

Word and Grammar Checkers: Guardians of Linguistic Accuracy

Grammar and spell checkers serve as the unwavering protectors of linguistic precision, forming the fundamental cornerstone of AI writing and editing tools. Within the complex network of language, even a slight mistake can interrupt the coherence of communication. These checkers thoroughly examine each sentence, detecting and correcting any grammatical and spelling errors. They go beyond simple correction; their role is to safeguard the fundamental structure of language, guaranteeing that the information remains free of errors and linguistically flawless (Câmara Pereira, 2007). These tools are essential for authors and editors, as they carefully improve manuscripts and provide polished, error-free writing to their readers. The utilisation of these technologies ensures not only accuracy but also maintains the authenticity of the written content, cultivating a profound sense of confidence between authors and readers.

Tools for Style Suggestions: Creating Compelling Narratives

Style suggestion tools exemplify AI's profound comprehension of human expression. In the domain of literature, style encompasses more than mere aesthetics; it serves as the essence of storytelling. These tools go beyond the boundaries of grammar and explore the complexities of sentence structure, word selection, and tone. Through meticulous evaluation of writing styles, they offer authors invaluable insights and recommendations. These seemingly subtle suggestions have a profound impact (Razack et al., 2021). They enable authors to articulate their thoughts with sophistication and influence, bridging the divide between language and sentiment. Style suggestion tools not only streamline prose, but also enhance it by imbuing narratives with depth, resonance, and authenticity. Using these tools, authors acquire the skills to not only communicate information but also to elicit emotions, crafting narratives that are not simply read but deeply experienced, fostering a profound bond with the readers.

Content Creation Tools: The Catalysts of User Engagement

The field of creative automation has undergone a significant change with the introduction of AI-powered tools that generate content. These tools are not just creators; they are skilled architects of engagement, customizing content for specific platforms and audience preferences. Through the process of interpreting context, comprehending the complexities of audience behavior, and following platform-specific guidelines, these tools generate content that goes beyond mere relevance; it evokes a profound response (Liapis et al., 2013). Each piece, whether it be articles, blog posts, social media updates, or product descriptions, is carefully crafted to suit the specific requirements of its respective medium. This customization guarantees that the content not only integrates smoothly into its digital environment but also engages the audience, prompting reactions, discussions, and conversions.

Adopting these tools not only represents technological progress, but also indicates a fundamental change in how we produce, consume, and engage with content. AI tools serve as more than just collaborators for authors; they act as mentors, providing guidance in achieving linguistic excellence and emotional impact. Editors perceive these technologies as more than just assistants; they view them as curators who shape narratives that captivate the digital audience. For businesses, these tools serve as valuable assets that act as catalysts, driving their online presence to unprecedented levels of engagement and influence.

Within the realm of digital storytelling, AI writing and editing tools play a crucial role. They are not merely components, but rather the fundamental structure that combines accuracy, inventiveness, and captivation to form narratives that surpass the limitations of the screen. These narratives create immersive, influential, and long-lasting experiences. In the digital age, these tools serve as guides, shedding light on the way to a future where every word is not only written, but carefully constructed, not only read, but fully encountered, all due to the transformative capabilities of AI.

In today's content creation industry, where efficiency and accuracy are crucial, choosing the right AI writing and editing tools is a vital decision. This section is an essential guide that helps readers navigate the complex process of selecting the most suitable tools based on their specific requirements, financial limitations, and workflow dynamics. By considering crucial elements such as financial constraints, ensuring that the features of a product match the requirements, and implementing techniques to integrate the workflow, readers are equipped to make well-informed choices that improve the effectiveness and innovation of their writing processes.

5. CONSIDERATION OF BUDGET FACTORS:

Maximising Value While Adhering to Financial Constraints

In a world where resources are limited, the careful consideration of budgetary factors is crucial. This section thoroughly examines the cost-effectiveness of AI tools, providing a comprehensive analysis of both free and commercial solutions. Through comparing the distinctive characteristics and abilities, readers acquire a refined comprehension of the unique benefits provided by each alternative. While free solutions may be economically attractive, they may have restrictions when it comes to advanced features. Conversely, commercial solutions typically provide a wider range of features, which may justify their expense for professionals or businesses with particular requirements (Zhu et al., 2022). By clarifying these distinctions, readers are empowered to make calculated choices, guaranteeing that their investment in AI tools harmonises effortlessly with their financial limitations while optimising the value obtained from their selection.

Aligning Features With Requirements: Customising Solutions to Individual Needs

The essence of choosing suitable AI tools lies in the congruence of features with specific requirements. This segment emphasises the significance of self-awareness, urging readers to carefully assess their individual requirements and ambitions. AI technologies encompass a wide range of applications, including grammar and style checks as well as sophisticated algorithms for content generation. Gaining a comprehensive understanding of one's distinct needs is crucial. Grammar checks are essential for academic researchers, whereas content marketers prioritise the generation of creative content. This section empowers readers to make informed decisions based on their specific requirements by equipping them with the knowledge to evaluate the features offered by different AI tools. This alignment guarantees that the chosen tools not only fulfil their intended purpose, but also allow for expansion and development as the demands of writing inevitably shift in the course of time.

Workflow integration techniques refer to the methods used to improve efficiency by seamlessly integrating different processes. These techniques aim to streamline workflows and eliminate any unnecessary steps or bottlenecks. By integrating various systems and tools, organisations can optimise their operations and enhance overall productivity.

Integrating AI tools into current workflows is a revolutionary undertaking. This topic explores the intricacies of incorporating independent AI tools compared to those that are integrated into popular writing software. Standalone tools typically offer specific functionalities, whereas integrated solutions provide a smooth user experience within familiar platforms. Readers are provided with clear instructions on both approaches, enabling them to make decisions that align with their current work processes. Readers are empowered with insightful guidance to effectively integrate AI tools into their workflows, encompassing academic research, professional writing, and creative content creation. Through a comprehensive grasp of integration techniques, individuals can maximise their productivity, guaranteeing that AI technologies act as catalysts for heightened creativity and efficiency rather than disruptive factors.

Empowering Readers to Make Informed Decisions and Maximize Productivity and Creativity

To summarise, this section acts as a source of valuable information, guiding readers to make well-informed and strategic choices when choosing AI writing and editing tools. Through careful consideration of financial limitations, strategic alignment of features with personal needs, and adept mastery of workflow integration techniques, individuals transcend the role of mere technology consumers and instead assume the role of architects of their own writing processes. Equipped with this abundance of knowledge, individuals can effortlessly incorporate AI technologies into their artistic pursuits, enhancing their efficiency, nurturing their imagination, and guaranteeing that every written word is supported by the accuracy and effectiveness of state-of-the-art AI (Duan et al., 2019). This emerging collaboration between human intelligence and technological capability signifies a future in which writing transcends mere duty and becomes an artistic endeavor. Each piece of writing is envisioned as a work of exceptional skill, skilfully crafted through the harmonious fusion of human imagination and the revolutionary potential of AI.

6. SELECTING THE APPROPRIATE AI WRITING AND EDITING TOOLS

The strategic incorporation of AI tools represents a significant turning point in the constantly evolving field of writing and editing. This section acts as a guide, directing writers and editors on how to fully utilise AI tools while still maintaining the core aspects of human intuition and creativity (Elmawi, 2021). This section provides professionals with the necessary knowledge and skills to achieve exceptional editing by exploring the intricacies of using different tools, finding the right balance between human intuition and AI accuracy, and recognising the importance of human proofreading.

Using a Range of Tools for Thorough Editing

When it comes to editing, having both depth and breadth is equally important. It is crucial to employ a wide range of AI technologies, with each tool designed for specific aspects of grammar, style, and content coherence (Gevrey et al., 2003). By utilising a comprehensive editing approach that combines these tools, writers and editors guarantee a thorough analysis of their work. Specialised tools are capable of identifying subtle grammatical errors, improving writing styles, and enhancing the overall coherence of content. This comprehensive strategy ensures a meticulous editing process, in which minor imperfections and discrepancies are corrected, enhancing the text to a sophisticated and perfected condition. Expanding the application of AI tools not only improves the editing process but also promotes a culture of ongoing improvement, where every content piece is seen as a chance for refinement and enhancement.

Achieving a Balance Between Human and AI Editing

The combination of human intuition and AI precision is the foundation of effective editing. Although AI techniques are highly proficient at detecting technical flaws, human judgement is essential for maintaining the contextual relevance and organic progression of the content. This section emphasises the significance of achieving a careful equilibrium between the knowledge offered by AI tools and the nuanced comprehension brought by human editors. Excessive dependence on AI, although alluring due to its effectiveness, can jeopardise the personal connection that renders content relatable and captivating (Dong et al., 2020). By employing a well-balanced approach, authors and editors maintain the integrity and coherence of their work, guaranteeing that the end result deeply and significantly connects with the intended audience. The incorporation of human creativity and intuition enhances the content by imbuing it with depth and emotion, surpassing mere technical accuracy and embracing the artistic nature of storytelling.

Enhancing Quality to Unprecedented Levels

Human proof-readers are the ultimate guardians of quality and authenticity in the extensive process of editing. Their contribution, particularly during the concluding phases of editing, is of utmost importance. This section highlights the crucial role played by human proof-readers, particularly in the context of editing powered by AI (Haber & Schindler, 1981). Although AI possesses superior capabilities, human proof-readers provide an unparalleled layer of context and comprehension that machines may fail to recognize. They possess the ability to discern variations in tone, intention, and cultural subtleties, thereby adding a refined element that amplifies the attractiveness of the content to the target audience. Human proofreading extends beyond mere technical accuracy; it guarantees that the information is not only correct, but also appropriate in its context and emotionally impactful. Human proofreading plays a crucial role in maintaining a delicate equilibrium between technology and human involvement. It serves as the ultimate quality control mechanism, ensuring flawless, culturally attuned, and contextually suitable end results.

Mastering the utilization of AI tools goes beyond mere technical skill; it encompasses a comprehension of the intricate relationship between technology and humanity. By utilising AI tools' precision and retaining human intuition, writers and editors can access a realm of possibilities where each content piece becomes a flawless masterpiece, effortlessly combining technical accuracy with emotional impact. This proficiency elevates the process of editing from a simple technical duty to an artistic endeavour, wherein each word is carefully selected, every sentence transition smoothly, and every piece of content evolves into a captivating narrative that engages, educates, and evokes emotional responses from its audience. As professionals embrace the combination of human creativity and technological expertise, the future of editing looks extremely promising. This collaboration enhances the core of written communication to new and unparalleled levels.

The future of AI writing and editing tools holds a promise of unprecedented creativity, collaboration, and efficiency. As technology advances, these tools are set to become indispensable resources for authors and editors, reshaping the landscape of written communication. By emphasizing the importance of using a variety of tools and balancing human and AI editing, while acknowledging the indispensable nature of human proofreading, authors and editors are poised to make the most of AI tools while maintaining the integrity, coherence, and context of their work.

7. SHAPING THE FUTURE OF WRITING AND EDITING

Increased Creativity

Future AI writing tools are not mere assistants; they are catalysts for creativity. By offering fresh concepts and distinctive writing styles, these tools stimulate creativity in ways previously unexplored (Park, 2023). Authors, often bound by creative limitations, find in AI companions that encourage them to venture into uncharted territories of imagination. These tools become partners in ideation, helping authors break free from the confines of conventional thinking and produce content that is truly unique and captivating.

Real-Time Collaboration

The future heralds a new era of collaboration, where AI-driven writing tools facilitate real-time collaboration among writers. Imagine a scenario where authors collaborate on the same document, refining ideas, and shaping narratives in real-time. These tools not only enhance efficiency but also foster a sense of teamwork, where ideas seamlessly blend, and the document's tone and style remain consistent. This collaborative synergy ensures that diverse perspectives converge, resulting in content that is rich, nuanced, and multifaceted.

Multimodal Abilities

The future AI writing tools are not confined to text; they embrace multimodal capabilities, integrating text with photos, videos, and other media elements. This amalgamation empowers authors to create interactive and compelling content across various platforms. Whether it's crafting multimedia-rich articles, engaging social media posts, or immersive storytelling experiences, these tools enable seamless integration of diverse media, enhancing the overall impact of the content (Ippolito et al., 2022). The narrative becomes not just words on a page but a multimedia journey that captivates the audience's senses.

Personalized Writing Assistance

AI technologies of the future will offer personalized suggestions tailored to each user's tastes and writing routines. These tools will evolve alongside users, learning from their writing styles and preferences. The assistance provided will be finely tuned, enhancing users' abilities and refining their work over time. Imagine having an AI companion that understands your unique voice, suggests improvements in alignment with your style, and acts as a mentor, guiding your growth as a writer.

8. REDEFINING THE WRITING EXPERIENCE

Integration With Word Processors

The integration of AI writing helpers into well-known word processors like Google Docs and Microsoft Word ushers in a new era of seamless creation. Users no longer need additional applications; intelligent suggestions and grammar checks are seamlessly integrated within familiar interfaces. The barriers between writing and editing blur as AI becomes an integral part of the writing process, enhancing the user experience and elevating the quality of content produced.

Browser Extensions

AI writing tools, in the form of browser extensions, provide real-time editing and proofreading assistance while users create content online. From composing emails to crafting social media posts, these extensions ensure consistent and polished communication across digital platforms (Shringi, 2023). The instantaneous nature of these tools not only enhances the quality of online interactions but also boosts users' confidence, knowing that their digital presence is flawless and professional.

Mobile Apps

The future holds AI-powered mobile applications, transforming smartphones and tablets into portable writing studios. Users can create quality content while on the move, whether it's drafting business emails or weaving imaginative narratives. With intelligent writing support readily available at their fingertips, users can seamlessly transition between devices, ensuring their writing remains polished and impactful regardless of location or time constraints.

Integration in the Classroom

Educational platforms will harness AI writing capabilities to aid students and teachers in honing their writing skills. These tools become invaluable companions in the classroom, providing personalized guidance, identifying areas for improvement, and enhancing students' overall writing proficiency. By integrating AI tools into educational environments, future generations of writers are nurtured, ensuring they possess the skills and confidence to excel in the digital age (Kim et al., 2018).

the future of AI writing and editing tools holds a transformative potential that extends far beyond mere technological advancement. It embodies a vision where creativity knows no bounds, collaboration knows no barriers, and the art of writing is elevated to unprecedented heights. Authors and editors, armed with these advanced tools, find themselves on the cusp of a new era, where every keystroke is infused with the precision of AI and the depth of human creativity. As these technologies seamlessly integrate into common writing environments, the writing experience is redefined, becoming more intuitive, efficient, and impactful than ever before.

In this future, the distinction between human and AI editing blurs, and the writing process becomes a harmonious synergy between human intuition and technological prowess. With the collaborative assistance of AI, authors and editors navigate the complexities of language with finesse, producing content that is not just well-crafted but truly extraordinary. The future of AI writing and editing tools is not just a technological evolution; it is a revolution in the art of storytelling, where every word penned is a testament to the boundless possibilities of human creativity augmented by the transformative power of AI.

9. CASE STUDY

In the fast-paced world of digital marketing, where attention spans are short and competition is fierce, creating captivating and engaging content is key to grabbing the audience's attention. In this case study, we will delve into the real-world applications of AI writing and editing tools through the lens of XYZ Marketing Solutions, a digital marketing company tasked with promoting a cutting-edge smartphone. By examining their journey, we can understand the transformative power of AI-enhanced editing in the realm of content creation (Nair & Gupta, 2021).

9.1 The Challenge of Digital Marketing

In a landscape saturated with information, XYZ Marketing Solutions faced the challenge of introducing a new smartphone to the market. To capture the audience's interest and encourage pre-orders, they needed compelling blog pieces, enticing product descriptions, and attention-grabbing social media posts. This required not only creativity but also a deep understanding of consumer behaviour, market trends, and effective communication strategies.

9.2 A Game-Changer for Content Development

Recognizing the need for efficiency and precision, XYZ Marketing Solutions integrated cutting-edge AI-enhanced editing tools into their content creation process. These tools were not just sophisticated grammar checkers; they were powered by advanced algorithms that analysed vast amounts of data, including consumer behaviour and competitor content. Using natural language processing, these tools optimized headlines, refined product descriptions, and ensured the content resonated with the intended audience.

9.3 Transformative Impact of AI-Enhanced Editing

Increased Efficiency

By swiftly analysing extensive datasets, AI systems streamlined the research process. This freed up valuable time for content creators, allowing them to focus on generating innovative ideas and fostering creativity. Armed with data-backed insights, writers could channel their energy into crafting content that truly resonated with the audience.

Enhanced Engagement

AI tools delved into social media patterns, helping XYZ Marketing Solutions decipher the content types that resonated most with their audience. By understanding these dynamics, the marketing team produced content that was highly shareable, likeable, and comment-worthy. This heightened user engagement, creating a ripple effect as the content reached a wider audience organically.

Improved SEO

AI tools not only refined the content but also optimized it for search engines. The structured content, infused with pertinent keywords, climbed the search engine results pages (SERPs). This improvement in SEO boosted organic traffic to XYZ's website, ensuring that the smartphone launch garnered maximum online visibility.

Consistent Brand Voice

Maintaining a consistent brand voice across platforms is vital for building trust and brand loyalty. AI tools, by analysing past successful content, ensured that XYZ's brand voice remained unwavering. This consistency in style not only strengthened brand identity but also fostered trust among consumers, making them more receptive to the marketing message.

Compare and Contrast

To validate the impact of AI-enhanced editing, XYZ Marketing Solutions conducted A/B testing. Content edited with AI tools was published on one platform, while conventionally edited content was released on another. The results spoke volumes: user engagement, click-through rates, and conversion rates for the AI-enhanced content surpassed those of conventionally edited content. This clear contrast underscored the effectiveness of AI-enhanced editing in driving meaningful engagement and conversions.

The Synergy of Human Creativity and AI Precision

This case study illuminates the transformative potential of AI writing and editing tools in the realm of digital marketing. By intelligently incorporating AI algorithms into their content production process, XYZ Marketing Solutions not only saved time but also significantly amplified the impact of their marketing efforts. The findings underscore a crucial truth: the marriage of human creativity and AI precision is a powerful alliance. When AI tools are seamlessly integrated, they empower human creativity rather than overshadowing it. The result is content that not only meets technical standards but also resonates deeply with the audience, driving engagement, brand loyalty, and ultimately, business success.

In the competitive arena of digital marketing, where every click and interaction matter, embracing AI-enhanced editing isn't just a choice; it's a strategic imperative. As XYZ Marketing Solutions exemplifies, the future of marketing lies in the harmonious fusion of human ingenuity and technological prowess, where AI-enhanced editing tools serve as catalysts for creativity, ensuring that every piece of content tells a compelling story and leaves a lasting impression on the digital landscape (Van Esch & Stewart Black, 2021). With AI by their side, marketers can navigate the complexities of the digital world with confidence, delivering content that not only captures attention but also captivates hearts and minds, fostering meaningful connections with the audience in the ever-evolving digital realm.

10. CONCLUSION

Based on our extensive research into AI writing and editing tools, we have seen a major shift in written content production. We found a compelling narrative of human creativity and AI precision seamlessly integrated as we examined practical applications, weighing their benefits and drawbacks. In the future, AI technologies will accelerate writing and editing, revealing content's precision and efficacy. AI-powered content creation became synonymous with precision and speed. AI transformed written content in marketing and education, boosting its quality and impact. During this technological chaos, the human touch became more important. AI was good at improving language, but it couldn't capture cultural context or human emotions. The broad spectrum of human experiences allowed us to connect, empathize, and weave stories that stirred deep emotional responses in readers. our exploration shows that the future of writing relies on a symbiotic relationship between human brilliance and computational precision. This collaboration blends human creativity and AI accuracy like a symphony. AI provides valuable data, suggests improvements, and refines new ideas with its computational power. The human mind gives these words life by telling stories that captivate, inspire, and provoke thought. we enter a world where technology fosters creativity and expands human expression when we imagine this collaboration. This vast expanse where human creativity and AI peacefully coexist promises writing progress and a storytelling revolution. This partnership seamlessly blends technological innovation and human intuition.

REFERENCES

Adams, D., & Chuah, K. M. (2022). Artificial intelligence-based tools in research writing: current trends and future potentials. *Artificial Intelligence in Higher Education*, 169-184.

Bolt, P. (1992). An evaluation of grammar-checking programs as self-help learning aids for learners of English as a foreign language. *Computer Assisted Language Learning*, *5*(1-2), 49–91. doi:10.1080/0958822920050106

Câmara Pereira, F. (2007). *Creativity and artificial intelligence: a conceptual blending approach*. Mouton de Gruyter. doi:10.1515/9783110198560

Carbonell, P., Jervis, A. J., Robinson, C. J., Yan, C., Dunstan, M., Swainston, N., Vinaixa, M., Hollywood, K. A., Currin, A., Rattray, N. J. W., Taylor, S., Spiess, R., Sung, R., Williams, A. R., Fellows, D., Stanford, N. J., Mulherin, P., Le Feuvre, R., Barran, P., ... Scrutton, N. S. (2018). An automated Design-Build-Test-Learn pipeline for enhanced microbial production of fine chemicals. *Communications Biology*, *1*(1), 66. doi:10.1038/s42003-018-0076-9 PMID:30271948

Chen, T. J. (2023). ChatGPT and other artificial intelligence applications speed up scientific writing. *Journal of the Chinese Medical Association*, *86*(4), 351–353. doi:10.1097/JCMA.0000000000000900 PMID:36791246

Dergaa, I., Chamari, K., Zmijewski, P., & Saad, H. B. (2023). From human writing to artificial intelligence generated text: Examining the prospects and potential threats of ChatGPT in academic writing. *Biology of Sport*, *40*(2), 615–622. doi:10.5114/biolsport.2023.125623 PMID:37077800

Dong, Y., Hou, J., Zhang, N., & Zhang, M. (2020). Research on how human intelligence, consciousness, and cognitive computing affect the development of artificial intelligence. *Complexity*, *2020*, 1–10. doi:10.1155/2020/1680845

Duan, Y., Edwards, J. S., & Dwivedi, Y. K. (2019). Artificial intelligence for decision making in the era of Big Data–evolution, challenges and research agenda. *International Journal of Information Management*, *48*, 63–71. doi:10.1016/j.ijinfomgt.2019.01.021

Elmawi, E. E. (2021). *The Impact of Using Peer Editing as an Effective Feedback Tool on Developing Libyan EFL Students' Writing Performance*.

Fitria, T. N. (2023, March). Artificial intelligence (AI) technology in OpenAI ChatGPT application: A review of ChatGPT in writing English essay. In *ELT Forum. Journal of English Language Teaching*, *12*(1), 44–58.

Gevrey, M., Dimopoulos, I., & Lek, S. (2003). Review and comparison of methods to study the contribution of variables in artificial neural network models. *Ecological Modelling*, *160*(3), 249–264. doi:10.1016/S0304-3800(02)00257-0

Gilat, R., & Cole, B. J. (2023). How will artificial intelligence affect scientific writing, reviewing and editing? The future is here…. *Arthroscopy*, *39*(5), 1119–1120. doi:10.1016/j.arthro.2023.01.014 PMID:36774329

Haber, R. N., & Schindler, R. M. (1981). Error in proofreading: Evidence of syntactic control of letter processing? *Journal of Experimental Psychology. Human Perception and Performance*, *7*(3), 573–579. doi:10.1037/0096-1523.7.3.573

Ippolito, D., Yuan, A., Coenen, A., & Burnam, S. (2022). Creative writing with an ai-powered writing assistant: Perspectives from professional writers. *arXiv preprint arXiv:2211.05030.*

Kim, Y., Soyata, T., & Behnagh, R. F. (2018). Towards emotionally aware AI smart classroom: Current issues and directions for engineering and education. *IEEE Access : Practical Innovations, Open Solutions*, *6*, 5308–5331. doi:10.1109/ACCESS.2018.2791861

Kuleto, V., Ilić, M., Dumangiu, M., Ranković, M., Martins, O. M., Păun, D., & Mihoreanu, L. (2021). Exploring opportunities and challenges of artificial intelligence and machine learning in higher education institutions. *Sustainability (Basel)*, *13*(18), 10424. doi:10.3390/su131810424

Liapis, A., Yannakakis, G., & Togelius, J. (2013). Designer modeling for personalized game content creation tools. In *Proceedings of the AAAI Conference on Artificial Intelligence and Interactive Digital Entertainment* (Vol. 9, No. 2, pp. 11-16). Academic Press.

Malik, P., Mittal, V., Nautiyal, L., & Ram, M. (2022). NLP techniques, tools, and algorithms for data science. *Artificial Intelligence for Signal Processing and Wireless Communication*, *11*, 123–148. doi:10.1515/9783110734652-006

Marzuki, W., Widiati, U., Rusdin, D., Darwin, & Indrawati, I. (2023). The impact of AI writing tools on the content and organization of students' writing: EFL teachers' perspective. *Cogent Education*, *10*(2), 2236469. doi:10.1080/2331186X.2023.2236469

Mazzone, M., & Elgammal, A. (2019, February). Art, creativity, and the potential of artificial intelligence. In Arts (Vol. 8, No. 1, p. 26). MDPI. doi:10.3390/arts8010026

Nair, K., & Gupta, R. (2021). Application of AI technology in modern digital marketing environment. *World Journal of Entrepreneurship, Management and Sustainable Development*, *17*(3), 318–328. doi:10.1108/WJEMSD-08-2020-0099

Ng, D. T. K., Luo, W., Chan, H. M. Y., & Chu, S. K. W. (2022). Using digital story writing as a pedagogy to develop AI literacy among primary students. *Computers and Education: Artificial Intelligence*, *3*, 100054. doi:10.1016/j.caeai.2022.100054

Park, J. (2023). Artificial intelligence–assisted writing: A continuously evolving issue. *Science Editing*, *10*(2), 115–118. doi:10.6087/kcse.318

Razack, H. I. A., Mathew, S. T., Saad, F. F. A., & Alqahtani, S. A. (2021). Artificial intelligence-assisted tools for redefining the communication landscape of the scholarly world. *Science Editing*, *8*(2), 134–144. doi:10.6087/kcse.244

Rouhiainen, L. (2018). *Artificial Intelligence: 101 things you must know today about our future*. Lasse Rouhiainen.

Savaget, P., Chiarini, T., & Evans, S. (2019). Empowering political participation through artificial intelligence. *Science & Public Policy*, *46*(3), 369–380. doi:10.1093/scipol/scy064 PMID:33583994

Shringi, K. (2023). Matt Frisbie on Browser Extensions. *IEEE Software*, *40*(4), 118–120. doi:10.1109/MS.2023.3265374

Van Esch, P., & Stewart Black, J. (2021). Artificial intelligence (AI): Revolutionizing digital marketing. *Australasian Marketing Journal*, *29*(3), 199–203. doi:10.1177/18393349211037684

Weber, N., & Huici, F. (2020, May). SOL: effortless device support for AI frameworks without source code changes. In *2020 20th IEEE/ACM International Symposium on Cluster, Cloud and Internet Computing (CCGRID)* (pp. 736-743). IEEE. 10.1109/CCGrid49817.2020.00-16

Zhu, J., Zhang, J., & Feng, Y. (2022). Hard budget constraints and artificial intelligence technology. *Technological Forecasting and Social Change*, *183*, 121889. doi:10.1016/j.techfore.2022.121889

Chapter 10
Enlightening Cases:
Utilization of Exemplary AI-Enhanced Research Endeavors

Sucheta Agarwal
https://orcid.org/0000-0001-6525-3007
Institute of Business Management, GLA University, Mathura, India

Sachin Kumar Mangla
Jindal Global Business School, O.P. Jindal Global University, India

Veland Ramadani
Faculty of Business and Economics, South-East European University, North Macedonia

ABSTRACT

The aim is to showcase the remarkable achievements of AI-integrated research, illustrating the significant impact of AI has had across various industries and academia. The approach involves gathering case studies and conducting comprehensive analyses, with a specific emphasis on AI-enhanced research initiatives. The findings underscore the value of AI-based methods and tools in guiding research and industry-related tasks. Through the examination of AI-related case studies, academics and business professionals have been able to enhance productivity and organizational performance by effectively implementing AI. The originality of this study lies in its thorough examination of AI's role in research and industries, featuring numerous case examples from diverse disciplines. The integration of AI in industries has become the foundation for case studies and related content/cases used in academia to educate students. This comprehensive approach offers a fresh perspective on the innovation and significance of AI in research and practical applications. By presenting various scenarios, the chapter will explore the societal and practical implications of successful AI-integrated endeavors, emphasizing AI's ability to transform sectors, improve decision-making, and address complex challenges.

DOI: 10.4018/979-8-3693-1798-3.ch010

INTRODUCTION

Artificial intelligence (AI) research is expanding rapidly, bringing with it revolutionary changes (Adigwe et al. 2024; Yang et al., 2024). AI technologies are highly beneficial in exploring and gaining unprecedented insights into a variety of fields (Crompton & Burke, 2023; Hunt, 2014). One of the most intriguing aspects of AI research is the difficulty in precisely defining the technology. Undoubtedly, the "artificial" nature of AI arises from the way it is created—through human ingenuity and imagination rather than natural (especially biological or evolutionary) processes. Consequently, AI possesses a certain attribute (intelligence) as a result of a specific process (being created, designed, or generated in this manner). The field of study known as artificial intelligence (AI) investigates how to endow computers with the complexity to function intelligently across an expanding array of fields; it is distinct from psychology or sociology. Embracing the entirety of computer science's interests, including programming, logical formalisms, abstraction, and detail, AI prioritizes algorithms over behavioral data, synthesis over analysis, and engineering (doing) over science (knowing) (Kabudi et al., 2021).

The phrase "field of science and engineering concerned with the computational aspects of AI" refers to the comprehension of creating objects that exhibit intelligent behavior, as well as the broader concept of intelligent behavior (Hunt, 2014; Kabudi et al., 2021). Much of the work conducted in the modern era has been inspired by early studies on the mechanisms of the mind, laying the foundation for the evolution of modern logical reasoning (Boden, 2008). Since 1950, when Alan Turing first envisioned the fascinating notion of "thinking machines," research on AI has proliferated across numerous fields, generating a growing body of prior work (e.g., Kabudi et al., 2021; Kurzweil, 1985; Simmons & Chappell, 1988). Emerging technologies have also transformed the way teaching and learning are conducted in the educational system. With the advancement of AI technology, its educational applications are also expanding (Crompton & Burke, 2023). Offering personalized instruction, dynamic assessments, and meaningful engagement in online, mobile, or hybrid learning settings presents intriguing new opportunities. For instance, in response to teacher shortage, few countries have proposed to employing AI to replace certain roles with robots (Zhang & Aslan, 2021). Despite the expansion of AI in education, AIEd (artificial intelligence in education) innovations are still in the early stages of exploration and discussion. Additionally, there is limited collaboration with educational institutions on relevant interventions, such as AI-enabled adaptive systems (Kabudi et al., 2021).

Moreover, there is a notable disconnect between the technologies being utilized in actual classroom environments and those with real-world applications (Bates et al., 2020). AI has had a significant impact on individuals, businesses, and civilizations. It provides systematic reasoning capabilities based on inputs and learns through the differences in predicted results as it forecasts and adapts to changes in its ecosystem and the stimuli it receives from its surroundings. In the early days of AI, algorithms mainly focused on supervised and unsupervised learning, leveraging computational properties found in biological organisms and nature itself to address data-intensive challenges. The recent global adoption of technologies like ChatGPT, google bard, and Perplexity AI etc., demonstrates their diverse range of use cases, spanning from software development and testing to poetry, essays, business letters, and contracts (Rudolph et al., 2023). However, this widespread adoption has also raised new questions regarding the value of traditional human endeavors and concerns about the difficulty in distinguishing between human and AI authorship, particularly in academic and educational settings (Crompton & Burke, 2023; Stokel-Walker, 2023; Zhang & Aslan, 2021). These challenges stem from the broad spectrum of natural language processing (NLP) tasks that ChatGPT, google bard, and Perplexity AI is used for, which can yield both positive and negative outcomes, including text production, language translation, and question answering (Rudolph et al., 2023).

Objectives of the Study

This study elaborates on the significance of AI-enhanced research endeavors in the industrial-academic field by focusing on the following objectives:

1. Explore theoretical perspectives of AI-enhanced research endeavors.
2. Examine various cases of AI-enhanced research endeavors.
3. Assess the contribution of AI-enhanced research endeavors to industry and academia.

CONCEPTUAL BACKGROUND

The concept of artificial intelligence has long been a topic of discussion in the public sphere. Science fiction movies and debates often depict a scenario where intelligent computers eventually dominate the planet, subjecting humans to a subordinate existence under the rule of AI. While this portrayal may seem like a caricature of AI, the truth is that AI is already integrated into our daily lives, with many of us regularly utilizing technology. AI technology is no longer confined to the realm of speculation; rather, it has become an indispensable component of the business models of numerous organizations, including educational institutions (Bates et al., 2020; Crompton & Burke, 2023; Hunt, 2014). It is also a pivotal strategic element in the plans of various businesses, government agencies, non-governmental organizations, and educational sectors worldwide (Adigwe et al., 2024; Kabudi et al., 2021; Yang et al., 2024). The profound influence of AI has garnered considerable attention in academic circles, shifting the focus of current studies towards examining the impacts and consequences of the technology, rather than solely concentrating on its performance implications, as has been the primary research focus for many years ((Zhang & Aslan, 2021). The core concepts of non-human intelligence trained to execute specific tasks are encapsulated by the definitions of AI found in existing literature (Boden, 2008; Kurzweil, 1985; Rudolph et al., 2023; Stokel-Walker, 2023).

Russell and Norvig (2016) define AI as systems that replicate cognitive functions traditionally associated with human traits such as speech, learning, and problem-solving. Lu's work (2019) provides a nuanced and comprehensive description of AI, framing it as the ability to independently comprehend and learn from external inputs to achieve specific objectives through adaptive modification. Unlike human-level AI, which is more focused on cognition and has not yet fully replicated the complexities of human thought and emotion, the advent of big data has enabled algorithms to excel at specific tasks (such as autonomous scheduling, gaming, robotic vehicles, etc.) and apply AI in practical ways. The increasing capability of machines to perform various tasks is currently facilitated by AI, which is utilized by individuals and organizations at both local and large scales within the business and society. AI's capacity to surpass certain human limitations in cognition, creativity, and computational demands is opening up new avenues of application across various sectors including industry, finance, healthcare, marketing, and education (Lu, 2019; Stokel-Walker, 2023; Yang et al., 2024). This expansion significantly impacts productivity and performance. AI-enabled technologies are swiftly permeating organizations, revolutionizing fields once thought to be solely human domains, such as manufacturing and business (Adigwe et al., 2024; Bates et al, 2020). Machine intelligence is presently harnessed in autonomous vehicles, chatbots, autonomous planning and scheduling, gaming, medical diagnosis, translation, and even spam detection, owing to advancements in AI systems (Rudolph et al., 2023).

Expert forecasts outlined in Yang et al. (2024) suggest that by 2075, AI systems may surpass human capabilities in certain tasks. Additionally, some researchers express concerns about potential negative impacts on humanity if artificial intelligence progresses toward superintelligence (Chen & Lin, 2024; Lu, 2019). Currently, the general public lacks a comprehensive understanding of the ethical and financial implications of AI and big data, as well as their broader effects on human existence, culture, sustainability, and technological advancement.

Although the widespread adoption of AI is expected to lead to enhanced productivity, reliability, and efficiency across various global economic sectors, not everyone shares this optimistic outlook. Estimates regarding labor displacement indicate that by 2030, automation may affect up to one-third of current work activities (Poba-Nzaou et al., 2021). Research into the consequences of this significant shift has portrayed a picture of a changing labor market, predicting a transition of workers into more creative and analytical professions that support AI technology (Chen & Lin, 2024; Russell & Norvig, 2016). However, the question arises: Is this specific vision of the AI future applicable to both developed and developing economies worldwide? AI holds the potential to replace numerous repetitive and rule-based tasks, potentially leading to the loss of a substantial number of jobs in developing economies. While there is a risk of AI displacing millions of jobs in emerging economies, there are also advantages to concentrating AI in wealthy countries, where technology is likely to create new, higher-skilled professions (Poba-Nzaou et al., 2021). Researchers are actively investigating the social and economic dimensions of AI, along with its impact on individuals and society throughout its development (Adigwe et al., 2024; Kurzweil, 1985; Stokel-Walker, 2023). Consequently, it is evident that decisions must be made with a forward-looking perspective, acknowledging that there will likely be both winners and losers.

Therefore, earlier studies were utilized to assess the impact of AI on various sectors, including the research economy (Hunt, 2014; Simmons & Chappell, 1988; Yang et al., 2024). In the subsequent section, a more detailed examination of AI's impact, supported by notable case studies, is presented.

Exemplary Cases Related to AI Endeavors

This chapter explores the essence of this integration, showcasing real-world business scenarios where AI has enriched academia, fueled research endeavors, and yielded tangible outcomes for various sectors. It investigates into exemplary AI-driven initiatives in the realms of social and business management, emphasizing how researchers and educators leverage this transformative technology to tackle practical challenges and lay the groundwork for future achievements.

The case study approach is renowned for its ability to delve into phenomena in depth. However, what about examining pre-existing narratives? This method emphasizes both primary and secondary cases. Researchers utilize this approach to construct, assess, and interpret scenarios based on primary and secondary instances collected from professionals, academicians, and students. The primary objectives often include uncovering fresh perspectives, identifying trends across various scenarios, and assessing theoretical frameworks against prevalent narratives. The following are the secondary cases regarding the contribution of AI in various sectors, which were collected from articles, newspapers, or other secondary sources.

Case 1: Machine Learning in FMCG Industry

ITC, currently one of the largest Fast Moving Consumer Goods (FMCG) companies in India, holds a significant presence in almost every Indian household. With a portfolio comprising over 60 brands spanning various FMCG categories, the company directly impacts nearly 2 million retail outlets. Each day, it contends with competition from over a hundred firms. Challenges faced by ITC include issues such as improperly labeled data and recommendations that are difficult to interpret. To address these challenges, ITC has been investing in simplifying user experience (UX) training while ensuring continuous training of users. This approach aims to ensure that all stakeholders benefit from recommendations throughout the product life cycle. Additionally, efforts are directed towards enhancing the comprehensibility of the model and streamlining planning and execution processes.

Among the stakeholders are marketers, salespeople, and manufacturers, each playing a vital role in our operations. Mr. X, ITC's chief of sales analytics, humorously remarked on diverse product range, quipping, "we make everything." He elaborated on how the organization leverages machine learning and analytics to generate personalized recommendations addressing complex sales and distribution challenges. Emphasizing the algorithms' ability to complement rather than replace the sales representative, Mr. X highlighted their significance in the process. With over 30,000 salespeople dedicated to reaching and finalizing agreements with over 2 million stores in India, Mr. X encouraged everyone to embrace their inner salesperson.

"It's extremely challenging to keep track of which products to offer to each outlet and understand each outlet's preferences," he explained. ITC surpasses standard segmentation requirements by treating each outlet individually and embracing hyper-personalization (Naik, 2022). (The name is retained as Mr. X in this case to protect confidentiality).

This example illustrates how AI assists ITC in addressing challenges related to their respective roles. This case study serves as a valuable resource for researchers and academics seeking to understand or apply various topics in their studies.

Case Study 2: Flipkart's Enhanced Competitiveness Through Artificial Intelligence

Flipkart, a prominent online retailer, firmly believes that the future belongs to artificial intelligence (AI). Leveraging AI, Flipkart accurately identifies the rational and emotional factors that influence consumer purchasing decisions. In addition, Flipkart initiated the "AI For India" program last year, aiming to fully capitalize on the lucrative commercial opportunities arising from India's increasing smartphone penetration and Internet user base. Through AI For India, Flipkart intensifies its utilization of AI to automate backend processes, enhance user experience, and reinforce service differentiation. The cornerstone of success for an e-commerce business lies in its ability to deliver goods or services swiftly, efficiently, and cost-effectively. Flipkart is committed to leveraging AI through its AI For India program to enhance customer experience and address the unique inefficiencies prevalent in the Indian e-retail sector. These initiatives represent a fraction of the enhancements the company is implementing to attract the next 100 million customers. Recognizing the escalating competition from Amazon India, the domestic e-retailer is approaching this objective with utmost seriousness. Flipkart has been able to experiment with new strategies, streamline operations, and bolster data security more effectively, all thanks to its proprietary big data analytics platform. The company has curated a repertoire of at least forty insights for each of its expansive clientele exceeding 100 million, enabling in-depth analysis of consumer purchasing patterns, enhancement of brand recognition, and identification of fraudulent activities. These insights encompass a wide array of factors, ranging from preferred brands and transaction frequencies to GPS locations and browsing behavior. Flipkart harnesses the power of AI to deliver personalized search recommendations to its users. Recognizing the diverse customer base in India, the company employs photo recognition, a deep learning application, for catalogue search, product categorization, discovery, and recommendations. Through the integration of AI, Flipkart has revolutionized the landscape of affordable and convenient shopping, emerging as the frontrunner in India's e-commerce industry. With Walmart's acquisition, the company's technological and financial prowess is set to further amplify. The company's unwavering commitment to growth and expansion, underscored by its reliance on automation, bots, and AI as indispensable tools, is unlikely to waver (Das, 2018).

This case study significantly enriches the existing knowledge base on artificial intelligence in the marketplace, offering academics and researchers fresh insights into market-related phenomena. Moreover, it serves as an invaluable educational resource for scholars and students studying management, particularly those specializing in marketing. By examining this case, students can gain a deeper understanding of how businesses leverage AI-driven technology to enhance productivity, foster growth, and maintain competitiveness in dynamic market environments. Educators can also use this case to initiate discussions on the adoption of new technologies, strategic decision-making, and the implications of AI integration in contemporary business landscapes. In swift, this case study offers insightful perspectives and practical applications for both academia and industry.

Case 3: AI Enhancing Travel Experiences

Historically, customers have encountered frustrations when booking travel, grappling with the complexity of the process, the plethora of options, and the time-consuming searches involved. However, thanks to AI, online travel aggregators can now integrate features such as voice-assisted booking and automatically generated personalized itineraries, thereby enhancing efficiency and user-friendliness in the booking process. In May 2023, MakeMyTrip and Microsoft are set to launch voice-assisted booking services in Indian languages. The beta version of this integration is currently available in Hindi and English. This feature will enable users to customize holiday packages based on various factors such as occasion, budget, preferred activities, and travel dates, as well as assist with booking these packages. Additionally, it will offer personalized travel recommendations tailored to individual user preferences. According to Mr. Y, a senior manager, 'This initiative broadens access to the online travel ecosystem for every segment and demographic across the nation.' He added, 'It eliminates barriers related to language, literacy, and the ability to navigate complex app environments.' (The name is retained in this case as Mr. Y to protect confidentiality).

Airports have embraced the integration of AI technologies as well. According to a spokesperson from Mumbai's Chhatrapati Shivaji Maharaj International Airport (CSMIA) and other Adani-operated airports, various AI technologies, including generative models, will be implemented. These technologies will be utilized for purposes such as detecting foreign object debris on the runway, predicting footfall or passenger load at least four to twelve hours in advance, and other functionalities. Furthermore, Adani Airports has invested in a video analytics system powered by AI to aid in identifying travelers who may require additional assistance (Matta, 2023).

Researchers, academics, and managers often cite the aforementioned scenario as a prime example of how exemplary AI initiatives can surpass competitors and ultimately enhance customer satisfaction for businesses. Such instances serve as catalysts for exploring new avenues of inquiry into the application of AI in bolstering the health of the travel sector.

Case 4: AI Is Improving Efficiency in the Hospitality Industry

AI is revolutionizing guest interactions in hotels through personalized services. Many hoteliers are leveraging AI-powered chatbots and virtual assistants to provide instant responses to customer inquiries regarding facilities, local recommendations, and room availability. At selected hotels, guests can utilize features such as mobile keys to swiftly access their rooms upon check-in and communicate with hotel staff via chat from any location. Moreover, AI has facilitated the creation and distribution of advertisements without the need for complex creative teams, streamlining marketing initiatives. AI is perceived as a silent but efficient worker operating in the background to seamlessly manage all aspects of hotel operations (Matta, 2023).

When discussing the effectiveness and efficiency of managerial functions, scholars and management students may reference this case as a valuable illustration. While AI has alleviated the workload for personnel, it has also diminished the reliance on human labor. The positive and negative aspects of AI provide researchers with fresh perspectives to explore in this domain.

Case 5: SBI and Chatbot SIA

The State Bank of India, the largest public sector lender in India, has introduced Sia, an AI-powered chatbot, following in the footsteps of other private sector giants like HDFC and Yes Bank. Sia is programmed to address customer inquiries and offer information about SBI's wide range of products and services. The chatbot's design enables it to address user inquiries on various subjects, such as term deposits, auto loans, RDs, home loans, school loans, and personal loans. SBI's digital platforms, notably inTouch, are already leveraging AI and other technologies. Chatbots and similar workforce enablement technologies have proven effective for SBI, leading to enhanced productivity and quality of customer service staff. Millions of clients utilize a range of self-service options, including smartphone apps and SMS banking, which have been made accessible to them.

According to reports, the bank asserts that over 80% of SBI transactions are completed through non-branch channels, exclusively utilizing machines and without the involvement of SBI staff. Many private sector banks have already embraced chatbots and AI, with their utilization in banking steadily rising. Recently, HDFC introduced EVA, an AI-powered chatbot that utilizes AI to address client issues. Other notable examples include the Yes Pay bot from Yes Bank, KAI from Digi Bank, and software robotics from ICICI Bank, all of which leverage the latest advancements in AI technology (Deoras, 2017).

This above-mentioned case depicts the utilization of tool of AI in the improvement of efficiency and effectiveness in the process of the organization. This provides the great understanding to the researcher and management students belongs to certain specializations such as operational, information technology, banking and finance etc.

The primary studies have also been collected from various academicians, researchers, and students belonging to STEM fields to analyze AI endeavors more clearly. With the help of interviews, the following cases have been framed and are mentioned below:

Case 6: AI's Impact on Student Learning and Employment

AI has transformed many aspects of our daily lives, including education and employment. AI serves as a helpful tool for students, supporting them with various academic tasks. It can generate emails and essays on specified topics to assist students with their schoolwork. Furthermore, AI aids students in debugging code and comprehending complex topics, thereby improving their overall learning experience. Moreover, AI's capacity to interpret complex code into simpler language speeds up tasks, allowing students to easily complete complex assignments. The 24/7 availability of AI enhances student learning by providing continual assistance. However, AI's advancements have also led to significant changes in the job market. Machines equipped with AI capabilities are increasingly replacing human tasks, leading to concerns about job displacement. While AI presents remarkable potential for undertaking diverse tasks, it is imperative to harness this technology responsibly, ensuring its alignment with societal well-being.

This case study investigates how AI simplifies basic activities for students, reshapes the employment market, and emphasizes the significance of responsible AI use.

It highlights the transformative impact of AI on student learning and employment. While AI offers numerous benefits for students, it also poses challenges in the form of job market disruption. Therefore, it is crucial to leverage AI responsibly to maximize its benefits while mitigating its potential drawbacks.

Case 7: Directing the Benefits and Challenges of AI Implementation

AI is a powerful tool that can automate work, increase productivity, and streamline decision-making in various industries, including banking, manufacturing, healthcare, and transportation. However, alongside these advantages come significant challenges. AI systems may replace some human jobs, raising concerns about unemployment and workforce transitions and presenting a significant risk of job displacement. Furthermore, privacy issues and the accuracy of information are just two ethical issues surrounding AI that call for close examination and responsible development. The automation of repetitive work by AI presents issues for human employment, despite its promise for time-saving and efficiency improvements. This is especially true for individuals trained in skills that AI can now effectively complete. Additionally, serious privacy concerns arise from the gathering, storing, and use of personal data by AI systems.

This case examines the many facets of AI, exploring both its advantages and disadvantages. It highlights the intricate relationship between the benefits and drawbacks of AI. While AI has great potential to boost innovation and efficiency across industries, it also comes with ethical, societal, and financial challenges that must be carefully considered before implementation.

Case 8: Enhancing Education With Artificial Intelligence

AI has emerged as a disruptive technology in education that is fundamentally changing both the way knowledge is accessed and taught. Like a knowledgeable friend or colleague, AI is a versatile tool that offers quick access to a wide range of information on any subject. AI helps individuals in their search for knowledge by providing explanations and suggestions, akin to a book. Furthermore, AI broadens learning perspectives by generating ideas and promoting original thought through methods such as:

Author's query: Provide a Case-Based Question on Consumer Behavior

AI's Reaction: As a marketing manager for a prominent consumer electronics manufacturer, you've noticed a significant shift in customer behavior towards online shopping, particularly in light of the COVID-19 pandemic. Outline your strategy for understanding and adapting to these changes in consumer behavior. Discuss the research you would conduct to identify key variables—such as price sensitivity, convenience, and trust in online transactions—that influence consumers' decisions to shop online. Explain how you would utilize this insight into consumer behavior to tailor marketing campaigns specifically to their preferences and enhance their online shopping experience. Finally, analyze the opportunities and potential challenges associated with adapting to evolving consumer behavior in the digital era.

Author's query: Provide a Few Questions Regarding the Business Environment

AI's Reaction: What effects does the current state of the economy have on consumer purchasing behavior? What regulatory changes are anticipated in the sector, and what implications might they carry for business operations? How do emerging technologies influence the competitive landscape within the industry? What are the most recent consumer preference trends, and how are companies adapting to meet these demands?"

These AI-generated answers enable educators to assist students in comprehending difficult concepts and subjects more deeply. Although AI offers numerous advantages, its widespread use raises questions about dependency and its potential impact on traditional teaching techniques. The integration of AI in education has revolutionized teaching strategies and accessibility to content, presenting unprecedented opportunities for enhanced learning outcomes. While AI serves as a valuable tool for both educators and learners, it is crucial to exercise caution to prevent over-reliance on AI at the expense of traditional teaching methods. Educators can leverage AI to enrich learning experiences while preserving the inherent value of traditional teaching techniques by adopting a balanced approach and using it judiciously.

The above-mentioned case emphasizes the importance of striking a balance between the use of AI and conventional teaching methods, highlighting the enduring benefits of books in fostering writing and reading habits. It examines how AI can aid in teaching and learning, while also addressing any potential negative effects and its impact on traditional teaching methods.

Case 9: How AI Affects Research Dynamics

AI techniques are becoming increasingly common and valuable in modern research practices. These resources assist researchers in investigating a wide range of subjects and provide insightful recommendations when they encounter difficulties. Scholars often utilize AI to assist them in selecting thesis topics and subtopics, as well as in exploring the theoretical significance and explanation of their studies. The integration of AI into the research process raises concerns about the potential deterioration of human connection between supervisors and researchers, despite the convenience and efficiency of the technology. While AI tools such as literature review explorers facilitate rapid information retrieval, they may inadvertently impact researchers' comprehension and reading habits.

Researchers' cognitive capacities may be hampered by this reliance on AI, which may have an effect on their originality and creativity. Additionally, researchers can learn about new developments in any field from AI, such as

Author's Query: Provide Ideas for Sustainable Research Topics.

AI's Reaction: Evaluating the effects of green supply chain management practices on corporate sustainability performance; assessing the efficiency of sustainable packaging solutions in reducing environmental footprints; examining consumer perceptions and the adoption of eco-friendly products and services; analyzing the impact of sustainable agriculture practices on food security and environmental conservation; and investigating the financial and environmental benefits of integrating renewable energy sources in urban settings.

Author's Query: Please Recommend the Table of Contents for the Thesis Titled "Impulsive Buying Behavior Among Youth Towards E-Commerce"

AI's Reaction:

Table of Contents

Introduction

1.1 Background of the Study

1.2 Statement of the Problem

1.3 Objectives of the Study

1.4 Scope and Delimitations

1.5 Significance of the Study

1.6 Structure of the Thesis

Literature Review

2.1 Conceptual Framework of Impulse Buying

2.2 Factors Influencing Impulse Buying Behavior

2.3 The Rise of E-commerce and Its Impact on Consumer Behavior

2.4 Impulse Buying Behavior Among Youth

2.5 Theoretical Perspectives on Youth Impulse Buying in E-commerce

Research Methodology

3.1 Research Design

3.2 Population and Sample

3.3 Data Collection Methods

3.4 Data Analysis Techniques

Demographic Profile of Youth E-commerce Consumers

4.1 Age, Gender, and Socioeconomic Status

4.2 Online Shopping Habits

4.3 Frequency of E-commerce Purchases

Understanding Youth Impulse Buying Behavior in E-commerce

5.1 Psychological Triggers of Impulse Buying

5.2 Social Influences on Youth Impulse Buying

5.3 Technological Factors Affecting Impulse Buying

5.4 Comparison of Offline and Online Impulse Buying Behavior
Impulse Buying Strategies Employed by E-commerce Platforms
6.1 Design and User Interface Elements
6.2 Personalization and Recommendation Systems
6.3 Limited-Time Offers and Flash Sales
Implications of Youth Impulse Buying in E-commerce
7.1 Economic Impact
7.2 Social and Environmental Consequences
7.3 Challenges and Opportunities for E-commerce Businesses
Managing Youth Impulse Buying Behavior in E-commerce
8.1 Education and Awareness Programs
8.2 Regulatory Measures
8.3 Ethical Considerations for E-commerce Platforms
Conclusion
9.1 Summary of Findings
9.2 Contributions to Knowledge
9.3 Recommendations for Future Research
References
Appendices"

AI generated the aforementioned responses, and it has been noted how insightful the explanations are. It is crucial for researchers to consider the potential effects on cognitive capacities and human interaction when integrating AI into their research procedures. Through a well-balanced strategy and a focus on meaningful collaboration, researchers can harness the advantages of AI without sacrificing the fundamental components of human creativity and innovation in their work.

This narrative underscores the importance of researchers finding a balance between utilizing AI tools and preserving human involvement throughout the study process. While AI offers clear advantages in terms of accessibility and efficiency, researchers must still maintain their capacity for critical thinking and cultivate meaningful relationships with their supervisors. Researchers may take advantage of AI's benefits while maintaining the importance of human creativity and innovation in their work by striking the correct equilibrium.

These are just a few examples of innovative cases utilizing AI that are currently being implemented across various domains. These cases highlight the vast potential of AI to tackle real-world problems, generate valuable data insights, and foster innovation across multiple industries. As AI evolves, its integration into academic and industrial research offers the potential to steer businesses towards a more prosperous, equitable, and sustainable future.

Valuable Insights

The power of AI is driving a transformative journey in the business landscape. Industry and academia can seize new opportunities, overcome challenging obstacles, and derive new lessons for success in the global economy by embracing AI-enhanced research activities. To fully leverage AI for the benefit of business, academia, and society at large, it will be imperative to cultivate a collaborative ecosystem involving academia, government, and business. AI technology is advancing swiftly, and it is expected to play a bigger role in industry and education in the near future. AI technologies hold great promise for increasing access to learning opportunities, scaling up individually customized learning experiences, and optimizing methods and strategies for desired learning outcomes in various sectors.

AI is both a way of thinking and a method. The integration of AI requires critical awareness of AI ethics in industry and academia, as well as transdisciplinary and multidisciplinary teamwork in long-term, intensive research. Educators and industry professionals will be able to apply new teaching and learning methodologies, along with more helpful suggestions and examples, as research related to AI grows. Despite doubts, fears, or mistrust, AI continues to open up new possibilities for technological and educational advancements. The integration of AI has both exciting and potentially hazardous consequences for a range of industries. AI holds great promise for startups as it can accelerate innovation, streamline operations, and improve hyper-personalized user experiences.

However, it becomes crucial to address ethical dilemmas and concerns regarding data privacy. As AI has the potential to enhance productivity, forecast market trends, and streamline procedures in well-established businesses, it also has the potential to disrupt jobs and require worker reskilling. AI's capacity to analyze extensive medical datasets holds promise for advancements in diagnosis and treatment, particularly in sectors like healthcare, despite concerns about algorithmic bias and the exploitation of sensitive data. Ultimately, the implications of AI are as diverse as the companies that employ it, necessitating a thorough evaluation of both its immense promise and intrinsic hazards. The possibilities are vast, especially since industry adoption of AI is still in its infancy. Consequently, it would be intriguing for businesses and academic organizations to research the various effects of AI in numerous contexts.

ACKNOWLEDGMENT

The authors would like to acknowledge the use of AI for enhancing language and correcting grammatical errors in the present study.

REFERENCES

Adigwe, C. S., Olaniyi, O. O., Olabanji, S. O., Okunleye, O. J., Mayeke, N. R., & Ajayi, S. A. (2024). Forecasting the Future: The Interplay of Artificial Intelligence, Innovation, and Competitiveness and its Effect on the Global Economy. *Asian Journal of Economics. Business and Accounting*, *24*(4), 126–146.

Bates, T., Cobo, C., Mariño, O., & Wheeler, S. (2020). Can artificial intelligence transform higher education? *International Journal of Educational Technology in Higher Education*, *17*(42), 1–12.

Boden, M. A. (2008). *Mind as machine: A history of cognitive science*. Oxford University Press.

Chen, J. J., & Lin, J. C. (2024). Artificial intelligence as a double-edged sword: Wielding the POWER principles to maximize its positive effects and minimize its negative effects. *Contemporary Issues in Early Childhood*, *25*(1), 146–153. doi:10.1177/14639491231169813

Crompton, H., & Burke, D. (2023). Artificial intelligence in higher education: The state of the field. *International Journal of Educational Technology in Higher Education*, *20*(22), 1–22. doi:10.1186/s41239-023-00392-8

Das, A. K. (2018). How Flipkart is Using Artificial Intelligence to Stay Ahead of Competition. Available at: https://hiredigital.com/blog/how-flipkart-is-using-artificial-intelligence

Deoras, S. (2017). SBI Introduces Its Own Chatbot SIA, To Address Customer Queries. Available at: https://analyticsindiamag.com/sbi-introduces-chatbot-sia-address-customer-queries/

Hunt, E. B. (2014). *Artificial intelligence*. Academic Press.

Kabudi, T., Pappas, I., & Olsen, D. H. (2021). AI-enabled adaptive learning systems: A systematic mapping of the literature. *Computers and Education: Artificial Intelligence*, *2*(1), 1–12. doi:10.1016/j.caeai.2021.100017

Kurzweil, R. (1985). What Is Artificial Intelligence Anyway? As the techniques of computing grow more sophisticated, machines are beginning to appear intelligent—But can they actually think? *American Scientist*, *73*(3), 258–264.

Lu, Y. (2019). Artificial intelligence: A survey on evolution, models, applications and future trends. *Journal of Management Analytics*, *6*(1), 1–29. doi:10.1080/23270012.2019.1570365

Matta, A. (2023) How AI in travel and hospitality is enhancing experiences and optimising operations. Available at https: //www.forbesindia.com/article/take-one-big-story-of-the-day/how-ai-in-travel-and-hospitality-is-enhancing-experiences-and-optimising-operations/87027/1

Naik, A. R. (2022). How ITC is Using Machine Learning. Available at: https://analyticsindiamag.com/how-itc-is-using-machine-learning/

Poba-Nzaou, P., Galani, M., Uwizeyemungu, S., & Ceric, A. (2021). The impacts of artificial intelligence (AI) on jobs: An industry perspective. *Strategic HR Review*, *20*(2), 60–65. doi:10.1108/SHR-01-2021-0003

Rudolph, J., Tan, S., & Tan, S. (2023). War of the chatbots: Bard, Bing Chat, ChatGPT, Ernie and beyond. The new AI gold rush and its impact on higher education. *Journal of Applied Learning and Teaching*, *6*(1), 364–389.

Russell, S. J., & Norvig, P. (2016). *Artificial intelligence: a modern approach*. Pearson.

Simmons, A. B., & Chappell, S. G. (1988). Artificial intelligence-definition and practice. *IEEE Journal of Oceanic Engineering*, *13*(2), 14–42. doi:10.1109/48.551

Stokel-Walker, C. (2023). What is the future of artificial intelligence? *New Scientist*, *258*(3439), 1–9. doi:10.1016/S0262-4079(23)00886-2

Yang, D., Zhao, W. G., Du, J., & Yang, Y. (2024). Approaching Artificial Intelligence in business and economics research: A bibliometric panorama (1966–2020). *Technology Analysis and Strategic Management*, *36*(3), 563–578. doi:10.1080/09537325.2022.2043268

Zhang, K., & Aslan, A. B. (2021). AI technologies for education: Recent research & future directions. *Computers and Education: Artificial Intelligence*, *2*(1), 1–11. doi:10.1016/j.caeai.2021.100025

Chapter 11
The Researcher's Sidekick: Unleashing ChatGPT's Potential in Academic Research

Minisha Gupta
https://orcid.org/0000-0002-9422-6267
Quality Cognition Private Limited, India

Preeti Bhaskar
https://orcid.org/0000-0002-1957-8035
University of Technology and Applied Sciences, Oman

ABSTRACT

This research aims to delves into the perspectives of researchers in unleashing ChatGPT's potential in academic research. The researchers are encouraged to extensively discuss their perspectives on perceived benefits, limitations of ChatGPT in academic research, as well as share insights into potential strategies for enhancing ChatGPT's effectiveness in academic research. The study uses interpretative phenomenological analysis (IPA) as the research methodological framework to gain insights into the perspectives of researchers, aligning with the objectives of the study. The study was carried out in the Uttarakhand region of India. Semi-structured in-depth interviews were carried out to collect data from the researchers. The authors(s) always maintained respect, privacy concerns, and a non-judgmental outlook towards the research participant during sample selection and interview. Semi-structured in-depth interviews were carried out to collect data from the researchers.

INTRODUCTION

In the era of digitalization and technological advancements, a new dimension of communication and information exchange has emerged in the form of ChatGPT. Apart from merely answering user questions, it acts as a conversational partner with its groundbreaking language model. ChatGPT possesses exceptional proficiency in natural language processing and conversation, offering users a revolutionary tool for interaction. ChatGPT represents a significant advancement in human-computer interaction,

DOI: 10.4018/979-8-3693-1798-3.ch011

providing academics with a versatile tool that enhances productivity, creativity, and innovation in academic pursuits. This platform transcends the limitations of individual research tools like Grammarly, Zotero, and Mendeley. Instead, it amalgamates the functionalities of these tools, providing academics and researchers with a unified platform to efficiently complete their academic assignments. ChatGPT disseminates knowledge about research and academia, simplifying various tasks and responsibilities for academicians, including writing research papers, preparing lecture notes, crafting PowerPoint slides, developing question papers, and other academic endeavors.

With its ability to recognize and produce easily understandable outputs across different academic fields, ChatGPT has gained recognition and importance among academicians. Its straightforward interaction process has made it an invaluable asset for academics, aiding their growth in both scholarship and research. Moreover, it fosters creativity and innovation among academicians by enabling them to devise new teaching strategies and methods, as well as develop AI-based simulation exercises to enhance student learning.

ChatGPT serves as more than just an AI tool for assisting academicians, researchers, and scholars in writing or enhancing their research articles (Huang & Tan, 2023). It expedites the process of completing research papers by suggesting systematic organization and structuring of manuscripts. Moreover, ChatGPT delves into previous research reviews, enhancing researchers' efficiency. Crafting conceptual or theoretical research papers typically demands substantial time investment, yet ChatGPT streamlines this process by automatically generating usable data and information for scientists, researchers, or academicians to incorporate into their work. This processed information significantly aids in the creation of academic or research papers. Researchers can also utilize ChatGPT to implement formatting and proofreading techniques, thereby elevating the quality of their research papers. Consequently, ChatGPT saves considerable time, energy, and resources for research professionals. Furthermore, with ChatGPT's data management capabilities, researchers can identify relevant information and conduct further analysis with ease. Its fast and user-friendly interface enhances the efficiency of research scientists in paper writing, making ChatGPT a widely recognized and esteemed AI tool among research and academic publishers.

Prior to the advent of ChatGPT, researchers had access to various other AI tools such as Mendeley (a reference manager), Google Scholar (for searching research papers), Scopus, Zotero, Ideascape, and more. These tools primarily relied on traditional machine learning (ML) algorithms, which processed structured data to develop models and information (Tyagi & Chahal, 2022). Over time, these AI tools evolved, with newer models of AI, including federated learning and ML algorithms, being adopted and implemented by companies (Li et al., 2020a; Li et al., 2020b).

To comprehensively investigate both the positive and negative aspects of ChatGPT and its increasing significance in research, the authors have undertaken a study. This chapter aims to delve into the perspectives of researchers in unleashing ChatGPT's potential in academic research. The chapter is structured in a systematic format. The next section will unravel the research work explaining the emergence and impact of ChatGPT in academic research, followed by research methodology, findings, discussion, and conclusion of the research.

LITERATURE REVIEW

The advent of ChatGPT, an advanced language model developed by OpenAI, has sparked considerable interest among scholars and researchers seeking innovative ways to harness artificial intelligence (AI) for academic endeavors. OpenAI introduced ChatGPT in November 2022 (Huang & Tan, 2023). This language-based AI tool is built on a deep neural network (DNN) architecture known as the transformer model, which employs the process of self-attention to identify the importance of each segment of input data by weighing them differently. The transformer model is adept at selecting from vast text databases to understand context and meaning by tracing relationships in sequential data, encompassing all input it receives.

After completing its pre-trained phase, ChatGPT processes input data and responds to users' queries or doubts. It represents an updated and improved iteration of Chatbot, leveraging the Generative Pre-Trained Transformer to generate responses from stored database information and employing Natural Language Processing (NLP) techniques. NLP, a field of AI, utilizes algorithms to analyze and interpret human language (King, 2022; Radford et al., 2018; Manning & Schutze, 1999). When a question is posed or text is inputted, ChatGPT generates an output based on its understanding of the input and inherent patterns. These responses can take various forms, ranging from providing detailed information on specific topics to offering concise answers or even crafting detailed essays, all while maintaining proper communication patterns (Balel, 2023).

ChatGPT's versatility extends beyond generating output in various formats; it also performs a multitude of tasks on behalf of academicians and researchers. These tasks include writing sections of research papers, crafting introductions or literature review sections, proofreading documents, analyzing data, preparing conclusions or implications based on submitted data, and enhancing the language of written drafts. ChatGPT's popularity stems from its wide-ranging applications, which encompass automatically creating content, translating documents, and editing and proofreading documents (Golan et al., 2023; Kurian et al., 2023; Hammad, 2023; Zheng & Zhan, 2023).

The proficiency of ChatGPT in understanding and generating output in natural human language has become its primary focus point for academicians and researchers. This capability has rendered ChatGPT a valuable tool across various disciplines (Brown et al., 2020). It aids researchers in compiling their literature reviews, analyzing their data, formulating hypotheses, and framing the findings and conclusions of their research studies. By leveraging ChatGPT's language processing abilities, academicians can streamline and enhance various aspects of their research processes, ultimately contributing to more efficient and insightful research studies.

Proficiency of ChatGPT in understanding and generation of output in natural human language has become its main focus point for academicians and researchers. This ability of ChatGPT has made it a valuable tool for academicians among different disciplines. It helps researchers in compiling their literature reviews, analysing their data, formulating hypothesis, framing findings and conclusion of their research studies.

Furthermore, with the advent of ChatGPT, researchers can anticipate more collaborative research endeavors, as it facilitates real-time integration and knowledge sharing among researchers. This fosters the synchronization of data and information from diverse perspectives, which is crucial for collaborative research in interdisciplinary fields. Moreover, ChatGPT enables a detailed understanding and framing of complex research objectives or questions. In addition to the aforementioned features, ChatGPT also serves as a virtual assistant for researchers and academicians (Ramesh et al., 2022). Through its virtual assistant feature, it empowers academicians to search for relevant literature for their research papers. ChatGPT aids in managing citations and references, and it assists in developing proposals or various sections of research papers that may typically pose challenges. It enhances researchers' thought processes by suggesting and sharing new avenues of knowledge, thereby unleashing their creativity. By automating certain tasks, ChatGPT allows academicians to focus more on complex tasks, thereby increasing their creativity and productivity. This integration of ChatGPT into the research process not only streamlines workflows but also enhances collaboration and innovation within the academic community.

ChatGPT proves invaluable for both academicians and students alike. In instances of complex issues or projects, students can receive immediate results and feedback from ChatGPT, enhancing their learning experience. It fosters classroom interactions between teachers and students, promotes interactive learning, and transforms traditional learning cultures into advanced and intelligent processes (Liu et al., 2020). ChatGPT supports personalized learning by providing students with immediate feedback, thereby serving as both a research and learning tool for both academicians and students.

However, despite its benefits, concerns arise regarding the generalized nature of ChatGPT's answers, which may lead to biased and unethical outcomes. This stems from ChatGPT's retrieval of information from diverse databases, raising questions about the reliability and validity of the information it provides (Bender & Friedman, 2018). Hence, it becomes imperative to recognize and address biases inherent in the information received from ChatGPT, ensuring fair and unbiased outcomes that can be utilized in research endeavors. By acknowledging and mitigating these biases, ChatGPT can continue to serve as a valuable tool in academia, promoting equitable and ethical research practices.

The literature on ChatGPT's utilization in academic learning and research demonstrates a significant paradigm shift among scholars and their approach to research work. From facilitating natural language understanding to fostering collaborative research endeavors, this AI model's applications are diverse and promising. While ChatGPT proves to be a useful and beneficial research tool for researchers and academicians, it also comes with certain limitations.

One major concern revolves around the generalizability of responses and the potential for biased and unethical results. Scholars have noted instances where responses from ChatGPT lack accuracy and reliability, posing challenges for researchers and academicians (Wallace et al., 2019). Furthermore, there are occasions where ChatGPT provides misleading and inaccurate information, impacting the overall results and potentially limiting its usage by prospective and forward-thinking users. Hence, there is a pressing need for detailed research to fully unleash the potential of ChatGPT among academicians. Addressing concerns such as response generalizability, bias, ethical considerations, accuracy, and reliability will be essential in maximizing the benefits of ChatGPT while mitigating its limitations. Through thorough investigation and refinement, ChatGPT can continue to evolve as a valuable and trustworthy tool in academic research and learning environments.

This research-based chapter is dedicated to exploring both the advantages and limitations of ChatGPT in research work among academicians. By thoroughly investigating these aspects, the aim is to provide researchers with insights into optimizing the utilization of ChatGPT while addressing ethical concerns and reliability issues inherent in its usage. Understanding these challenges is paramount for ensuring the quality and integrity of research outcomes. Through this exploration, we strive to bridge the gap between AI-based intuitive models like ChatGPT and the research community, thereby facilitating a more seamless integration of such tools into the research process. Ultimately, this endeavor seeks to enhance the efficiency and effectiveness of research methodologies while promoting ethical practices in academic endeavors.

METHODOLOGY

In this research, Interpretative Phenomenological Analysis (IPA) methodological framework has been used to gain insights into the perspectives of researchers in unleashing ChatGPT's potential in academic research. IPA method is utilized to explore individuals' subjective experiences and how they derive meaning from them (Smith & Nizza, 2022; Creswell, 2013) It delves into understanding how people interpret their lived experiences, emotions, thoughts, and actions within specific contexts (Eatough & Smith, 2017; Alase, 2017). The analysis, often performed on a small participant sample, emphasizes grasping unique perspectives and meanings attributed by individuals to their experiences (Smith and Osborn, 2008; Chiu & Quayle, 2022). In this study, researchers were encouraged to extensively discuss their perspectives on benefits and limitations of ChatGPT in academic research

Sampling

The study was carried out in the Uttarakhand region of India. The region consists of one central university, eleven state universities, three deemed universities, and seventeen private universities. To ensure diversity, we approached 10 researchers from each university who were using ChatGPT for academic research. Initially, 96 researchers expressed interest and agreed to interviews. All participants provided written consent and ethics forms following Creswell (2013). Despite planning to include all agreed participants, the study concluded after interviews with 56 researchers as no new information emerged. Consequently, the final sample was limited to 56 researchers, reaching the saturation point of data.

Data Collection

Semi-structured in-depth interviews were carried out to collect data from the researchers. The authors(s) always maintained respect, privacy concerns, and a non-judgmental outlook towards the research participant during sample selection and interview. The wording of the interview questions was way probing and open-ended to make participant express their live experience on selected research phenomenon. At the beginning of the interview, the researcher(s) encouraged the discussion by asking some of the following questions:

- In your opinion, what are the benefits of using ChatGPT in academic research?
- How has ChatGPT influenced or enhanced your research process?
- What challenges or limitations have you encountered while using ChatGPT for academic research?
- Are there specific aspects of the research process where ChatGPT has been less effective?
- What factors motivate you to use ChatGPT for academic research? Is it primarily for time-saving, idea generation, or content drafting? Please elaborate on your motivations
- Are there any factors that inhibit you from utilizing ChatGPT to its full potential in your academic research?
- Are there technical challenges or barriers to integrating ChatGPT into your existing research workflow that act as inhibitors?

- Are there functionalities or improvements you would like to see in future versions of ChatGPT to better meet the specific needs of academic researchers?
- Do you think providing customizable prompt templates tailored for different stages of academic research (e.g., literature review, methodology) would enhance the usability of ChatGPT?

The validity and reliability of the interview questions were confirmed by 16 researchers. Following researchers' recommendations, modifications were incorporated into the interview questions. The revised versions were then presented to assess the construct's validity with a different set of 8 researchers who were not initially involved in the validity and reliability assessment. Consideration for the convenience of research participants was given, with interviews conducted both face-to-face and online (utilizing platforms like MS Teams, Google Meet, and Zoom). On average, each participant underwent interviews lasting between 50 and 120 minutes.

Data Analysis

IPA employs an inductive approach to data analysis, involving researchers immersing themselves in participants' narratives to identify recurring themes and construct an interpretative framework. The process includes stages such as sample selection, data collection through in-depth interviews, transcription, and rigorous analysis. Researchers follow a four-step method outlined by Smith and Osborn (2003) and Moustakas (1994) for coding, pattern identification, and theme development, capturing the essence of participants' experiences.

FINDINGS AND DISCUSSION

The findings reveal the perspectives of researcher's in unleashing ChatGPT's potential in academic research. Through IPA analysis, the study has identified "super-ordinate themes" and "sub-themes" highlighting benefits and limitations of ChatGPT for academic research. The analysis revealed three themes under the benefits of ChatGPT for academic research. These include knowledge augmentation, time-saving and increase research yield. On the other hand, limitation also included include accuracy and reliability, ethical considerations and limited features.

Benefits of ChatGPT in Academic Research

Increase Research Yield

ChatGPT is a crucial tool for improving research productivity as it helps organize research articles and improves linguistic coherence. Because of its capacity to create outlines and recommend logical sequences for various sections of a paper, it greatly streamlines the research process. The latest researchers validate similar conclusions, noting that ChatGPT has the capability to generate credible research ideas, conduct literature reviews, and offer suggestions (Dowling and Lucey, 2023). Moreover, Alshater, (2023) contended that AI tools like ChatGPT could assist researchers in analysing and interpreting data, as well as in devising innovative research scenarios and generating findings. Furthermore, ChatGPT's capacity to increase overall coherence, suggest vocabulary additions, and modify sentences makes research articles more eloquent and captivating in terms of language. This contributes to improving the content's readability and clarity, which enhances the impact and manner ideas are presented in research work. Huang & Tan, (2023) and Kim (2023) highlighted ChatGPT ability to assess and recommend enhancements in grammar, sentence structure, and editing with exceptional performance. ChatGPT supportive communication and subsequent corrections, have been highlighted by Haleem et al., (2023).

"ChatGPT makes research work far simpler by assisting in creating the structure of the research paper. It has been very helpful because of its capacity to create outlines, recommend the correct sequence for information presentation, and provide suggestions on how to organize various sections, such as the introduction, methods, findings, and discussion." (Respondents-36).

"ChatGPT provides remarkably coherent and refined language. It helps me to increase my vocabulary, polish my sentences, and make sure my work is coherent throughout. The tool helps in refine my writing and makes it more compelling as well as concise. Its recommendations for language usage and sentence construction have greatly improved the readability and clarity of my research papers, which ultimately contributed to a more persuasive presentation of my opinions." (Respondents-3).

Knowledge Augmentation

ChatGPT has transformed research approaches by providing instant access to a vast repository of information for all discipline (Aithal & Aithal, 2023). Researchers can easily access a vast array of information on many subjects, staying updated on the latest developments across different research fields. This skill fosters creative linkages across several disciplines, advancing interdisciplinary viewpoints that go across established disciplinary boundaries. Because ChatGPT facilitates a more integrated knowledge across many areas, it hence contributes to increasing the depth and range of research endeavours. Rice and colleagues (2023) suggested that ChatGPT could be effectively utilized to drive advancements in technology and diverse fields of study.

"ChatGPT has been a really helpful tool for me in my research activities, offering immediate access to a vast amount of data and information a plethora of sources. It's like having a library at my fingertips, which allows me to delve deeply into a variety of subjects and remain up to date on the most recent advancements across multiple research domains." (Respondents-11).

"My multidisciplinary research efforts have benefited significantly from it. It facilitates a comprehensive approach to my research by combining concepts from various disciplines easily. I have been able to make linkages between several disciplines because of this ability, which has encouraged innovative cross-disciplinary viewpoints and provided doors to novel concepts." (Respondents-23).

Time-Saving

ChatGPT proves to be a useful time-saving tool for researchers, especially during the initial stages of their research work. Its prompt responses effectively accelerate the collection of information, supporting the development of several research paper sections. Furthermore, ChatGPT acts as a collaborative researcher, offering insights and refining ideas. Aithal and Aithal (2023) discovered that AI-driven GPTs are anticipated to complement conventional libraries by offering tailored information assistance. This accelerates conversations, encouraging creativity ultimately optimizing the overall research exploration process in short time The findings of the present research have been supported by contemporary scholars. Kalla and Smith, (2023) argued that integrating ChatGPT into the educational landscape could lead to a significant reduction in user workload and save time.

"In my experience, ChatGPT has been a huge help in cutting down on time spent on initial research. Its capacity to quickly assemble data, produce concise summaries, and respond quickly to certain inquiries has significantly accelerated the gathering of initial data. This time-saving aspect is particularly beneficial when I need to write introduction section of the research paper. It enables me to quickly examine the subjects from a variety of perspectives." (Respondents-46).

"Without a doubt, adding ChatGPT to brainstorming sessions promotes creativity and also saves time significantly. As a collaborative partner, ChatGPT quickly adds concepts, ideas, and creative ideas, which accelerates our brainstorming session. Its rapid information processing speeds up discussions encourages novel concepts, and increases research potential in a short amount of period." (Respondents-15).

Limitations of ChatGPT in Academic Research

Accuracy and Reliability

One major limitation of ChatGPT-generated information is its accuracy, which means that careful fact-checking and cross-referencing with credible sources are important. Despite having an extensive amount of information, ChatGPT occasionally offers incorrect incomplete, or obsolete information. Hariri (2023) suggests that ChatGPT adeptness at generating text resembling human writing could lead to its misuse in disseminating false. Researchers continue to be cautious for outdated information which necessitates careful verification to ensure research accuracy and reliability. As a result, researchers consistently engage in extensive fact-checking to validate findings before incorporating them into their research work. information and creating inaccurate content. Moreover, due to the absence of human supervision and fact verification, ChatGPT might generate inaccurate results (Fuchs, 2023; Stokel-Walker and Van Noorden, 2023; Shahriyar and Hayawi, 2023). In a recent discussion, Yu (2023) emphasized how the combination of human capabilities with technology creates a synergy, resulting in increased efficiency and ultimately offering a competitive advantage to users.

"Even though it provides a wealth of information, fact-checking and critical analysis are necessary. There are times when the ChatGPT may offer incorrect partial, or out-of-date information. Because of this, researchers must cross-reference data with reliable sources to ensure the accuracy of the information being examined." (Respondents-19).

"As a researcher, my focus is always making sure that the information provided by ChatGPT is accurate. For example, the ChatGPT may provide inconsistent or obsolete details when examining previous data; hence, careful cross-referencing and verification are necessary to ensure the accuracy of my research." (Respondents-23).

Ethical Considerations

The ethical concerns related to ChatGPT are about the possible bias that exists in its content, which may pose a challenge for impartiality and fairness of data and information. As the ChatGPT learns from datasets likely to contain errors, it is at risk of repeating them in its outputs. To identify and address potential bias that might influence their work, researchers shall carefully examine and verify content produced by ChatGPT. The objective is to ensure that the information derived from ChatGPT is reliable and impartial, so as to preserve the integrity of the research process. Alshater (2023) raised concerns regarding the research output produced by ChatGPT, highlighting its susceptibility to factors like data quality and diversity, ethical considerations, and its limited capability to provide substantial insights.

"The potential for bias in the produced information is the main ethical concern when using ChatGPT. Large datasets are used to train ChatGPT, and if these datasets include biases, ChatGPT may unintentionally reinforce or reflect such biases in its results. Such bias could impact the information's objectivity and integrity. To identify and minimize any biases that can affect their study, researchers must be vigilant, closely examining, and confirming the ChatGPT generated information." (Respondents-34)

"In my experience, the ethical implications of biases within ChatGPT generated content are evident, especially when delving into societal or cultural topics. ChatGPT may unintentionally reinforce preconceptions or stereotypes that come from biased datasets. For example, in my research on social issues, I have come across situations where the ChatGPT outputs unintentionally reflect societal biases. This has forced me to rigorously evaluate and correct any biases in the material before using it in my research." (Respondents-17).

Limited Features

Researchers encounter limitations due to the limited customization options available for tailoring ChatGPT to meet specific research requirements. Despite its wide variety of characteristics, ChatGPT's generic methodology could not accurately meet the particular requirements of every research project, particularly ones with extremely specific objectives. Therefore, to guarantee accurate integration into their research initiatives, researchers dedicating their attention to such specialist disciplines must refine or analyze information provided by ChatGPT. The findings are confirmed by Roumeliotis & Tselikas (2023), concluded that ChatGPT is limited to providing general knowledge on the selected subject matter and cannot provide an exhaustive analysis.

"In order to meet the particular research requirements, there are limited customisation options available in ChatGPT. While the model offers a broad range of capabilities, it might not cater precisely to the unique demands of every research project. The general approach of the ChatGPT require further efforts to adapt and improve its results." (Respondents-38).

"In my own research, I've encountered difficulties in integrating ChatGPT with the specialized vocabulary for specific subjects. For instance, in molecular biology research, ChatGPT's couldn't understand the terminology and jargon and generated wrong output. This means that further work must be done to

clarify or analyze the information that ChatGPT generates so that it may be precisely integrated into my specialized research projects." (Respondents-2).

CONCLUSION

ChatGPT has become an invaluable resource for academic research because of its many features, which greatly improve and revolutionize the field of academic research. Researchers are now able to instantly access a vast reservoir of information because of its unparalleled capacity for knowledge augmentation, which transforms their ability to delve deeply into a variety of subjects and keep up to date on cutting-edge developments across a wide range of areas. The ChatGPT tool's ability to seamlessly integrate insights from many different subjects promotes interdisciplinary approaches, which in turn fosters creative linkages between disciplines and breaks down traditional boundaries of research. Consequently, ChatGPT expands the scope and depth of study, facilitating a more comprehensive knowledge across various discipline. Additionally, ChatGPT is an invaluable time-saver during the preliminary research phase, expediting the collection of information as well as assisting in creating the structure of the research papers' various sections. Its collaborative features additionally assist speed up conversations, encourage creative thinking, and broaden the scope of research within a limited timeframe. Rapid information processing stimulates creative thinking, broadens viewpoints, and enhances the entire process of exploring investigation. Furthermore, ChatGPT greatly improves research productivity by organizing articles and improving linguistic coherence. It improves research works' readability, clarity, and overall effect through the creation of outlines, logical sequence suggestions, and language refinement. ChatGPT makes a significant contribution to producing research papers that are more coherent and captivating by assisting with paper structuring and language clarity.

While ChatGPT has made significant progress in changing academic research landscape, its application is not without limitations. The main concerns are the accuracy and reliability which, because of the potential for incorrect or incomplete information, require thorough fact checking and verification by the researchers. Ethical considerations related to potential bias embedded in ChatGPT generated content also pose a problem of impartiality and fairness. In addition, the tool's restricted customization options provide constraints, particularly concerning highly specialized research requirements. Although ChatGPT has many features, its generalized approach might not be able to fully address the specific demands of each research project. As a result, researchers would need to put in additional effort to modify or enhance ChatGPT's outputs to meet their specific requirements. While ChatGPT's contributions are significant in terms of accelerating up research processes, it is still essential to maintain the reliability and credibility of academic research.

Practical Implications

This study contributes to the understanding of ChatGPT's benefits and limitations for academic research. The study intends to provide significant insight into how ChatGPT is being utilized in real academic settings by studying researchers' perspectives. These insights help higher education institutions, policymakers and ChatGPT service providers in refining and improving the ChatGPT's effectiveness to better align with the specific needs of researchers. These valuable insights have the potential to serve as a scope for higher education institutions, policymakers, and ChatGPT service providers, directing them in their efforts to enhance ChatGPT's effectiveness for academic research.

Research Limitations

In the qualitative study, perceptions and experiences of researchers' was captured within the specified timeframe. In the future, conducting longitudinal research becomes essential to gain insights on how perceptions and experiences have changed over period of time among the researchers towards ChatGPT for academic research. It's important to note that our study exclusively focuses on researchers in India. While this focus allows for an in-depth exploration of the experiences within this context, it also brings about a limitation. The experiences and viewpoints of researchers in India might not be fully representative of the diverse experiences of researchers in other countries. As academic and research practices can vary significantly across regions, a broader international perspective would provide a more comprehensive understanding of how ChatGPT is perceived and utilized in academic research globally.

ACKNOWLEDGMENT

We would like to thank the authors and reviewers of the book and members of publishing house to provide us this opportunity to present our work. This research received no specific grant from any funding agency in the public, commercial, or not-for-profit sectors.

REFERENCES

Aithal, S., & Aithal, P. S. (2023). Effects of AI-Based ChatGPT on Higher Education Libraries. *International Journal of Management, Technology, and Social Sciences*, *8*(2), 95–108. doi:10.47992/IJMTS.2581.6012.0272

Alase, A. (2017). The interpretative phenomenological analysis (IPA): A guide to a good qualitative research approach. *International Journal of Education and Literacy Studies*, *5*(2), 9–19. doi:10.7575/aiac.ijels.v.5n.2p.9

AlshaterM. (2022, December 26). Exploring the role of artificial intelligence in enhancing academic performance: A case study of ChatGPT. doi:10.2139/ssrn.4312358

Balel, Y. (2023). The Role of Artificial Intelligence in Academic Paper Writing and Its Potential as a Co-Author. *European Journal of Therapeutics*, *29*(4), 984–985. doi:10.58600/eurjther1691

Bender, E. M., & Friedman, B. (2018). Data statements for natural language processing: Toward mitigating system bias and enabling better science. *Transactions of the Association for Computational Linguistics*, *6*, 587–604. doi:10.1162/tacl_a_00041

Brown, T., Mann, B., Ryder, N., Subbiah, M., Kaplan, J. D., Dhariwal, P., ... Amodei, D. (2020). Language models are few-shot learners. *Advances in Neural Information Processing Systems*, *33*, 1877–1901.

Chiu, J., & Quayle, E. (2022). Understanding online grooming: An interpretative phenomenological analysis of adolescents' offline meetings with adult perpetrators. *Child Abuse & Neglect, 128*, 105600. doi:10.1016/j.chiabu.2022.105600 PMID:35338948

Creswell, J. W., & Poth, C. N. (2016). *Qualitative inquiry and research design: Choosing among five approaches*. Sage publications.

Dowling, M., & Lucey, B. (2023). ChatGPT for (finance) research: The Bananarama conjecture. *Finance Research Letters*, *53*, 103662. doi:10.1016/j.frl.2023.103662

Eatough, V., & Smith, J. A. (2017). Interpretative phenomenological analysis. The Sage handbook of qualitative research in psychology, 193-209.

Fuchs, K. (2023, May). Exploring the opportunities and challenges of NLP models in higher education: Is ChatGPT a blessing or a curse? *Frontiers in Education*, *8*, 1166682. doi:10.3389/feduc.2023.1166682

Golan, R., Reddy, R., Muthigi, A., & Ramasamy, R. (2023). Artificial intelligence in academic writing: A paradigm-shifting technological advance. *Nature Reviews. Urology*, *20*(6), 1–2. doi:10.1038/s41585-023-00746-x PMID:36829078

. Haleem, A., Javaid, M., & Singh, R. P. (2022). An era of ChatGPT as a significant futuristic support tool: A study on features, abilities, and challenges. *BenchCouncil transactions on benchmarks, standards and evaluations, 2*(4), 100089.

Hammad, M. (2023). The impact of artificial intelligence (AI) Programs on writing scientific research. *Annals of Biomedical Engineering*, *51*(3), 459–460. doi:10.1007/s10439-023-03140-1 PMID:36637603

Hariri, W. (2023). Unlocking the Potential of ChatGPT: A Comprehensive Exploration of its Applications. *Technology*, *15*(2), 16.

Hristovski, D., Rindflesch, T., & Peterlin, B. (2013). Using literature-based discovery to identify novel therapeutic approaches. *Cardiovascular & Hematological Agents in Medicinal Chemistry (Formerly Current Medicinal Chemistry-Cardiovascular & Hematological Agents), 11*(1), 14-24.

Huang, J., & Tan, M. (2023). The role of ChatGPT in scientific communication: Writing better scientific review articles. *American Journal of Cancer Research*, *13*(4), 1148. PMID:37168339

Kalla, D., & Smith, N. (2023). Study and Analysis of ChatGPT and its Impact on Different Fields of Study. *International Journal of Innovative Science and Research Technology*, *8*(3).

Kim, S. G. (2023). Using ChatGPT for language editing in scientific articles. *Maxillofacial Plastic and Reconstructive Surgery*, *45*(1), 13. doi:10.1186/s40902-023-00381-x PMID:36882591

Kurian, N., Cherian, J. M., Sudharson, N. A., Varghese, K. G., & Wadhwa, S. (2023). AI is now everywhere. *British Dental Journal*, *234*(2), 72–72. doi:10.1038/s41415-023-5461-1 PMID:36707552

Kushwaha, A. K., & Kar, A. K. (2021). MarkBot – A Language Model-Driven Chatbot for Interactive Marketing in Post-Modern World. *Information Systems Frontiers*. Advance online publication. doi:10.1007/s10796-021-10184-y

Li, J., Larsen, K., & Abbasi, A. (2020a). TheoryOn: A design framework and system for unlocking behavioral knowledge through ontology learning. *Management Information Systems Quarterly*, *44*(4), 1733–1772. doi:10.25300/MISQ/2020/15323

Li, T., Sahu, A. K., Talwalkar, A., & Smith, V. (2020b). Federated learning: Challenges, methods, and future directions. *IEEE Signal Processing Magazine*, *37*(3), 50–60. doi:10.1109/MSP.2020.2975749

Liu, Y., Han, T., Ma, S., Zhang, J., Yang, Y., Tian, J., He, H., Li, A., He, M., Liu, Z., Wu, Z., Zhao, L., Zhu, D., Li, X., Qiang, N., Shen, D., Liu, T., & Ge, B. (2023). Summary of chatgpt-related research and perspective towards the future of large language models. *Meta-Radiology*, *1*(2), 100017. doi:10.1016/j.metrad.2023.100017

Manning, C. D., & Schütze, H. (1999). Lexical acquisition. *Foundations of statistical natural language processing, 999*, 296-305.

Moustakas, C. (1994). *Phenomenological research methods*. Sage Publications. doi:10.4135/9781412995658

Radford, A., Narasimhan, K., Salimans, T., & Sutskever, I. (2018). Improving language understanding by generative pre-training. Academic Press.

Radford, A., Wu, J., Child, R., Luan, D., Amodei, D., & Sutskever, I. (2019). Language models are unsupervised multitask learners. *OpenAI blog, 1*(8), 9.

Ramesh, T. R., Lilhore, U. K., Poongodi, M., Simaiya, S., Kaur, A., & Hamdi, M. (2022). Predictive analysis of heart diseases with machine learning approaches. *Malaysian Journal of Computer Science*, 132–148.

Rice, S., Crouse, S. R., Winter, S. R., & Rice, C. (2023). The advantages and limitations of using ChatGPT to enhance technological research. *Technology in Society*, 102426.

Roumeliotis, K. I., & Tselikas, N. D. (2023). ChatGPT and Open-AI Models: A Preliminary Review. *Future Internet*, *15*(6), 192. doi:10.3390/fi15060192

Shahriar, S., & Hayawi, K. (2023). Let's have a chat! A Conversation with ChatGPT: Technology, Applications, and Limitations. *arXiv preprint arXiv:2302.13817.*

Smith, J. A., & Nizza, I. E. (2022). *Essentials of interpretative phenomenological analysis.* American Psychological Association. doi:10.1037/0000259-000

Smith, J. A., & Osborn, M. (2003). Interpretative Phenomenological Analysis. *Qualitative Psychology.*

Stokel-Walker, C., & Van Noorden, R. (2023). What ChatGPT and generative AI mean for science. *Nature*, *614*(7947), 214–216. doi:10.1038/d41586-023-00340-6 PMID:36747115

TajikE.TajikF. (2023). A comprehensive Examination of the potential application of ChatGPT in Higher Education Institutions. TechRxiv. *Preprint*, 1-10.

Tyagi, A. K., & Chahal, P. (2022). Artificial intelligence and machine learning algorithms. In Research Anthology on Machine Learning Techniques, Methods, and Applications (pp. 421-446). IGI Global. doi:10.4018/978-1-6684-6291-1.ch024

Uc-Cetina, V., Navarro-Guerrero, N., Martin-Gonzalez, A., Weber, C., & Wermter, S. (2022). Survey on reinforcement learning for language processing. *Artificial Intelligence Review*, 1–33. doi:10.1007/s10462-022-10205-5

Van De Schoot, R., De Bruin, J., Schram, R., Zahedi, P., De Boer, J., Weijdema, F., Kramer, B., Huijts, M., Hoogerwerf, M., Ferdinands, G., Harkema, A., Willemsen, J., Ma, Y., Fang, Q., Hindriks, S., Tummers, L., & Oberski, D. L. (2021). An open source machine learning framework for efficient and transparent systematic reviews. *Nature Machine Intelligence*, *3*(2), 125–133. doi:10.1038/s42256-020-00287-7

Wallace, E., Feng, S., Kandpal, N., Gardner, M., & Singh, S. (2019). Universal adversarial triggers for attacking and analyzing NLP. *arXiv preprint arXiv:1908.07125*. doi:10.18653/v1/D19-1221

Yu, H., & Guo, Y. (2023, June). Generative artificial intelligence empowers educational reform: Current status, issues, and prospects. *Frontiers in Education*, *8*, 1183162. doi:10.3389/feduc.2023.1183162

Zheng, H., & Zhan, H. (2023). ChatGPT in scientific writing: A cautionary tale. *The American Journal of Medicine*, *136*(8), 725–726.e6. doi:10.1016/j.amjmed.2023.02.011 PMID:36906169

Chapter 12
Transformative Horizons: Exploring ChatGPT's Impact on Scientific Research

Ankita Pathak
Institute of Business Management, GLA University, Mathura, India

Sunil Mishra
https://orcid.org/0000-0002-5915-9038
Medi-Caps University, India

Majdi Anwar Quttainah
https://orcid.org/0000-0002-6280-1060
Kuwait University, Kuwait

ABSTRACT

ChatGPT has played a revolutionary role in the field of scientific research. The usage of ChatGPT has contributed to the advancement of knowledge in numerous fields. The first section of the chapter explains the fundamental ideas of ChatGPT, emphasizing its contextual awareness and natural language processing powers. In addition, ChatGPT's incorporation into scientific research represents a paradigm change by providing faster data processing, simplified literature reviews, and creative hypothesis formulation. The benefits are evident in its ability to enhance efficiency, foster interdisciplinary collaboration, and democratize access to scientific knowledge. However, challenges include ethical considerations, biases in training dataset, and the imperative of ensuring model transparency. Striking a balance between ChatGPT's capabilities and addressing these limitations is crucial for realizing its full potential as a transformative force in advancing scientific inquiry.

1. INTRODUCTION

Round the clock, the field of artificial intelligence has evidenced a remarkable transformation, with the emergence of advanced language models. It has reshaped the way we interact with and extract knowledge from vast data repositories. Among these transformative innovations, ChatGPT stands out as a leading

DOI: 10.4018/979-8-3693-1798-3.ch012

contender, which offers a unique and powerful tool for engaging in natural language conversations with AI. Beyond its widespread adoption in various sectors, ChatGPT has been making significant inroads into the scientific community, where its applications are catalyzing breakthroughs, streamlining research processes, and expanding the boundaries of human knowledge.

The scientific community has traditionally been driven by rigorous experimentation, extensive literature review, and collaborative discourse among researchers. While these foundations remain essential, the integration of ChatGPT has introduced a new dimension to scientific inquiry. This language model, powered by deep learning is trained on a diverse corpus of text, which possesses the capacity to understand, generate, and discuss scientific concepts across a wide spectrum of disciplines. The model of GPT models are designed purposely to generate coherent natural language text that follows human-like patterns. They are capable of generating phrases, paragraphs and even complete papers.

GPT models is superior from their other competitor model like bard, Openi Ai. The model of Chatgpt has undergo a two-step training process: pre-training and fine-tuning. The GPT model is exposed to enormous volumes of text data, including web pages, links, document set and books, without proper controlled in preparatory phase. Through this process, the model learns to anticipate the next sequential word in a text sequence according to the context provided by preceding words. This pre-training step is crucial for language modeling as it helps the model to grasp language patterns, syntax, grammar, and semantics by analyzing extensive text data set. Utilizing a smaller labeled dataset after the pre-training phase allows the model to be fine-tuned for a specific downstream task. The system weights and biases can better coincide with the desired goal through the process of fine-tuning. This combination of pre-training and fine-tuning empowers GPT models to generate coherent, contextually appropriate text aligned with specific tasks, making them versatile tools for various natural language processing activities.

Researchers are using ChatGPT to speed up the process of finding and sharing information. ChatGPT functions as a virtual collaborator that offer immediate insights into intricate research inquiries, propose theories, and even help with paper preparation. Beyond simple automation, it plays a more significant role in accelerating scientific advancement by fostering a dynamic interaction between human knowledge and machine intelligence. ChatGPT's impact on research goes beyond the research assistance. Additionally, it has made scientific information more accessible to everybody. Through natural language dialogue, ChatGPT helps the general public to understand difficult scientific ideas and encourage a culture of scientific literacy and interest. ChatGPT is transforming scientific communication in various ways like information sharing, research collaboration as well as investigation.

Furthermore, ChatGPT's influence extends beyond its utility as a research assistant. It has also become a hub for scientific discourse and collaboration. Online forums, discussion boards, and social media platforms increasingly feature conversations driven by ChatGPT, where scientists and enthusiasts engage in debates, share knowledge, and brainstorm ideas. This open and accessible avenue for scientific dialogue has the potential to foster innovation by bringing together diverse perspectives and expertise from around the world.

The adaptability of ChatGPT across various scientific domains is a testament to its versatility. From biology to astrophysics, from climate science to quantum computing, ChatGPT demonstrates its ability to comprehend intricate theories and offer insights that complement the work of domain-specific experts. This adaptability has positioned ChatGPT as a powerful tool for interdisciplinary research, where the boundaries between fields blur, leading to unexpected connections and novel discoveries.

Moreover, the growth of ChatGPT in the scientific community has sparked discussions about the ethical use of AI in research. Questions surrounding transparency, bias, and responsible AI deployment are at the forefront of these conversations. Researchers and institutions are actively working to ensure that ChatGPT and similar models are used ethically and responsibly, mitigating potential risks and biases that may arise during scientific interactions.

The explanation discusses about how ChatGPT is changing research in the future, revolutionising information exchange, and reshaping scientific inquiry. The role of AI in research will change as it develops its area and our research will highlight the exciting opportunities and obligations that come with this game-changing technology.

2. GROWTH OF CHATGPT IN SCIENTIFIC COMMUNITY

In recent years, there has been an increasing prevalence of integrating chatbots and artificial intelligence (AI) into research and teaching. The machine learning and natural language processing techniques allows Chatbots to act as automated conversational agents. It can mimic like human interaction. But there are also moral issues that need to be addressed with the expansion of use of chatbots and AI in a variety of fields . The objective of study is to examine the moral dilemmas raised by the use of AI and chatbots in research, and it can be overcome and reduce the misuse.

The Chatgpt functions as a research assistant which provide essential help to researchers and ensuring the smooth execution of research projects. According to (Stevano & Deane 2022), chatgpt as a research assistant's fulfil the responsibilities of carrying out, and analysing research initiatives as well as creating research papers and presentations for the research proposal. According to (Johnson & Harris 2023), research assistants is involved in various research related activities such as gathering and analysing data and preparing manuscripts. ChatGPT help researchers with their academic writing by offering writing support and advice on grammar, tone, and style. It can also support in checking sentence formation and offer rapid access to pertinent data and information as per the requirement of the user. ChatGPT can automate time-consuming jobs like formatting and data input. The time saving feature of chatgpt allow researchers to concentrate on more complex activities like analysis and interpretation. It is important to consider that Chatgpt acts as helping hand. ChatGPT can help in writing process, but ultimately human researchers are responsible for the content in academic papers. Chatgpt create research questions and hypotheses, plan and carry out investigations and gather, examine, and analyse data. A researcher summarises their findings and publishes them in scholarly journals or other publications. The primary goals is to use research to expand the knowledge and benefit society.

Development of ChatGPT from its earliest iterations to its present form has transformed it into a vital resource for pushing scientific advancement. It is leaving a substantial mark across several areas such as data manipulation, concept creation, and collaborative endeavours. With the continued advancement of AI technology, it is expected that subsequent advancements and discoveries will have a dramatic impact on the future direction of scientific research. Over the last several years, the scientific and academic communities have placed a high priority on the investigation and promotion of ChatGPT.

3. APPLICATION OF CHATGPT IN SCIENTIFIC RESEARCH

ChatGPT has emerged as a powerful tool with diverse applications in scientific research, revolutionizing the way researchers approach various tasks. One notable application is the assistance in scientific paper

Figure 1. Shows the various application of AI in various activities

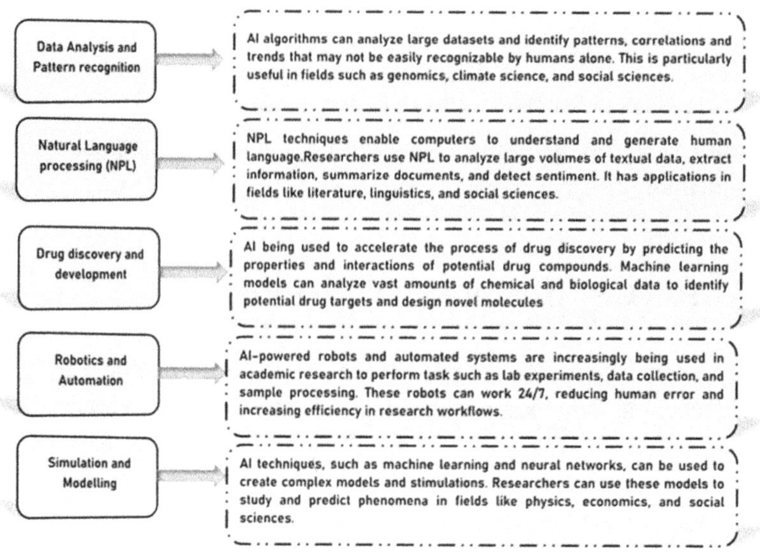

writing. Websites like I Love PhD provide step-by-step guides on how to leverage ChatGPT for crafting high-quality scientific research papers, making the writing process more accessible and efficient. The versatility of ChatGPT extends to aiding researchers in brainstorming, generating outlines, and even providing subject-specific commands for different sections of a paper, including introduction, methods, results, and discussion.

Humans being used to carry out the duties of the research assistant but advancement in technology has made AI systems like chatbots to function as research assistants. Chatbots with AI capabilities can be an excellent helper to academic research. Chatbots is regarded as effective instruments for gathering and analysing vast volumes of data quickly and effectively. It gives researchers the quick, clear, consisted data to the researcher for further analysis. AI research assistants are always around the clock with the infinite capacity to generate the output, in contrast to human research assistants. As chatbots are available around-the-clock, researchers can use them to obtain information and gather data whenever and wherever required. It provide individualised services. Chatbots have the ability to tailor their knowledge to the preferences of the researcher, which results in customised research experience. Chatbots can help to reduce the subjectivity and prejudice that human research assistants may bring into the study process. chatgpt could produce better-quality data by utilising artificial intelligence. It lower the possibility of human error and provide consistent and accurate information. Automation is an important characteristic of AI systems. Repetitive and time-consuming chores can be automated by chatbots, and liberating up academician to concentrate on more intricate and significant areas of their research. Researchers can identify relevant papers and publications more rapidly, if a chatbot are trained to offer quick access to research databases. Chatbot can help team member by automatically giving them updates and reminder related to their upcoming deadline. Researchers may save up time and concentrate on more intricate, creative parts of their work by automating some research chores. Researchers' disparities may be lessened with the use of chatbots. Researchers often struggle to find funding for their work and faces difficult to hire research assistants in industrialised nations. The use of chatbots can result in more effective teamwork which leads to higher-caliber findings. These chatbots provide assistance but cannot take the place of the researcher's as it is a crucial job. Similar to human research assistants, these chatbots also require constant, attentive monitoring to prevent derivations.

Furthermore, researchers can use ChatGPT for collaborative research endeavours. The model excels in conversation-based tasks, fostering improved contextual understanding and coherent response generation, thus enhancing collaboration and discussions among researchers. The benefits of ChatGPT in scientific research extend to increased productivity. Chatgpt also reduces the time spent on editing work. Researchers can focus more on generating content and improving the quality of their research. Additionally, ChatGPT proves valuable in the scientific writing process by expediting the generation of content, and providing researchers more time for critical thinking and analysis.

Ethical considerations are paramount in the use of ChatGPT in research, as highlighted in a study. The findings emphasize the significant potential of ChatGPT-3 when used wisely and ethically in scientific and academic settings. It also showcase the importance of responsible AI utilization in the research domain (Qasem, 2023). ChatGPT has become an invaluable asset in scientific research, offering support in various aspects, from writing research papers and facilitating collaboration to enhancing productivity. Researchers can harness the capabilities of ChatGPT to streamline their workflow, thereby contributing to advancements in the scientific landscape.

The capacity to manage and analyse enormous amounts of data is vital in scientific investigations. Salvagno et al. (2023) stated that ChatGPT has served an important part in changing the methods by which investigators engage and analyse this data. The following are the application of chatgpt in research.

- **Data Extraction From Scientific Literature Using Natural Language Processing**

One of the significant applications of ChatGPT in scientific research lies in automating the literature review process. One of the major use of ChatGPT in data processing is the retrieval of pertinent knowledge from scientific studies. According to Chen (2023), ChatGPT's natural language processing algorithms enable quick identify and extract important data points, conclusions, and synopses from scientific publications. Researchers can quickly gather and compile data from several sources because to this flexibility. This minimizes the time required for manual literature reviews. Moreover, it increases the study process's effectiveness. According to Van Dis et al. (2023), ChatGPT can identify patterns, movements, and relationships in data and give researchers a clear and comprehensive understanding of their findings. The ability to accurately and quickly extract complex data is extremely valuable for researchers who wish to derive significant conclusions and gain advantageous understanding from their findings. Researchers may easily extract relevant data from large records of academic papers by utilizing the language model's natural language processing capabilities (Zhang & Wang, 2021). Through the use of ChatGPT, researchers can accelerate the preliminary phases of their work by saving time and money on information retrieval.

- **Automated Detection of Data Trends and Movements**

ChatGPT has a great capacity to detect trends and patterns in large datasets, which make it a very effective property. Using machine learning, ChatGPT can find linkages, deviations, and other pertinent relationships within data. It provides researchers with useful data that might not be obvious through analysis by hand. Such automatic pattern recognition is a useful tool for academics, which allow them to discover new connections, propose new theories, and encourage scientific creativity. The researchers who are at the early stage in the ideation and conceptualization stages, ChatGPT is an invaluable resource. Researchers can explore and enhance their ideas through interactive talks with the model and yield insights and views that might not have been noticed earlier (Radford et al., 2019). The collaborative method fosters creativity and helps to provide original research questions and directions.

- **Forecasting and Predictive Modelling**

Predictive modelling and forecasting are two of ChatGPT's data processing and analysis applications. ChatGPT provides the capability to predict future changes and occurrences through the analysis of past data and the discovery of underlying patterns. According to Kim (2023), the ability to foresee is very useful in a variety of scientific fields, such as economics, epidemiological research, and weather science. The exact prediction is critical in directing evidence-based decision-making. Applications of ChatGPT for data processing and analysis have the potential to significantly increase the efficiency and productivity of scientific research. Chatgpt can help investigators to find emerging theories, uncover hidden insights, and propel scientific progress by assisting them in retrieving, combining, and understanding data. With the development of AI technology, it is feasible to predict the development of more-powerful tools, which leads to important developments in the field of data processing and analysis.

- **Generation and Validation of Hypotheses**

ChatGPT has played an important role in assisting investigators in the formation of new research enquiries and hypotheses, in addition to its engagement in data analysis and processing. Salah et al. (2023) stated that ChatGPT supports researchers in generating innovative research queries and conjectures. ChatGPT possesses the capability to scrutinize extensive volumes of scientific literature, thereby pinpointing trends, patterns, and recurrent motifs. ChatGPT's language generating features have been used to help scholars write and edit publications. According to Brown et al. (2020), academics can utilise this approach to compose sections of papers, enhance linguistic coherence, and obtain real-time comments for improving overall writing quality. This collaborative writing method guarantees a polished final result while expediting the development of manuscripts.

- **Suggestions for Prospective Research Directions Based on Current Research**

ChatGPT is skilled in sifting a large body of academic research to discover Patterns, designs, and reoccurring It will suggest possible research areas for researchers to pursue. It can offer prospective study topics to scholars to examine by swiftly analysing enormous amounts of data, ultimately uncovering hidden relationships and generating fresh ideas that might otherwise be neglected. ChatGPT can help to predict future research trends by evaluating the body of existing literature and interacting with scholars. According to Smith et al. (2022), this tool facilitates proactive planning and positioning in quickly changing scientific settings.

- **Identifying Knowledge Gaps and Inconsistencies**

ChatGPT is capable of detecting gaps and irregularities information by contrasting and comparing data from several research. ChatGPT can direct investigators in the direction of enquiries that require additional review by emphasising on the areas of uncertainty or discrepancy. ChatGPT can notify researchers about issues that need more research by pointing up areas of uncertainty or divergence, and gain advance scientific understanding on the topics.

- **Creating Novel Concepts and Thoughts Through Problem-Solving Creativity**

ChatGPT excels in innovative problem-solving, produce novel ideas and concepts that have the ability to stimulate novel theories in addition to its function. ChatGPT can provide novel answers to challenging scientific issues, and encourage researchers to consider unconventional perspectives and question conventional thinking. According to Green et al. (2023), this promotes the integration of diverse views and encourages to build a holistic approach to problem-solving. Research partnerships across cultures can be facilitated by ChatGPT's language translation capabilities. Chatgpt made possible for researchers with diverse linguistic backgrounds to interact easily, and overcome linguistic obstacles and promote an international flow of ideas (Radford et al., 2019).

- **Providing Assistance With Hypothesis Validation and Testing**

Investigators must rigorously evaluate and appraise the idea which lead to creation of a hypothesis through experiments and comprehensive analysis. ChatGPT can help in:

❖ developing appropriate designs for experiments and procedures.

❖ recognising possible confounding variables and the causes of bias which may have an influence on experiment outcomes.

❖ suggesting statistical tests and methods of analysis for interpretation of data

❖ developing alternative causes or projections can be empirically evaluated in contrast to the initially proposed theory. ChatGPT can play an important role in guaranteeing the robustness and legitimacy of academic results.

- **Enhancing Collaboration and Communication**

Communication and teamwork are essential elements of successful scientific endeavours. It investigates how ChatGPT helps to improve the sharing of thoughts and data among the scientific community. This includes:

❖ Facilitate the investigator by linking them with appropriate specialists and resources.
❖ Using natural language processing to improve interaction among experts and non-experts.
❖ Assist with the creation of grant submissions, research articles, and conference presentations.
❖ The importance of successful communication and collaboration in scientific endeavours cannot be emphasised. ChatGPT shows potential in facilitating the movement of thoughts and data within the scientific arena. It includes exchanges between investigators and the general public, due to its natural language processing skills.

One of the most difficult issues in scientific study is successfully communicating complicated concepts to those who lack specialised knowledge. ChatGPT's ability to distil scientific subject matter into easily understandable responses. It can improve interactions between politicians, researchers, business partners, and other stakeholders. Effective interaction is essential for developing ties between academics and other fields, which encourage trust among participants in research, and guide choices based on their interest area. ChatGPT can assist researchers in gaining Grant Proposals for Research Papers and Conference Presentations. Grant submissions, research articles, and conference presentations require a significant amount of work from researchers. ChatGPT can help in these endeavours by:

❖ Producing document outlines based on input or specified criteria.
❖ Making recommendations to improve the language, framework, and readability of written content.
❖ Creating visualizations like charts and graphs will improve the presentation of study findings.

Effective cross-cultural communication is essential in today's global scientific research environment. ChatGPT's multilingual content generation capabilities and real-time translation abilities can benefit academics worldwide. It collaborates and share knowledge more effectively. ChatGPT facilitates the growth of a more cohesive international scientific community by removing language barriers. ChatGPT applications will bring interaction and collaboration which will reshape the scientists engage and distribute knowledge. ChatGPT utilises AI's superiority to speed communication processes and foster collaboration which will foster innovation and drive scientific achievement. ChatGPT can be used for collaboration with various researcher of different country and region. ChatGPT can serve as a mediator in interdisciplinary projects, promote communication and share information amongst specialists in various domains.

- **Creating Interesting and Relevant Educational Resources**

ChatGPT may be used to develop informative and accessible instructional resources for a variety of audiences in addition to explaining complicated subjects. ChatGPT can help to make scientific education more accessible and interesting by creating information targeted to diverse age groups, educational levels, and interests. ChatGPT has created the following teaching materials:

❖ Games and interactive quizzes that evaluate and enhance scientific knowledge
❖ Personalised plans for instruction as well as instructional modules for teachers
❖ Science-related information, articles, and visualizations to pique your interest.
❖ Promoting Public Participation in Scientific Discussions and Achievements

ChatGPT can also help to increase public participation in scientific discussions and discoveries. It synthesis the most current study findings and presenting them in an approachable manner, it enables people to stay informed about scientific advancements and participate in discussions about emerging technology, moral dilemmas, and their consequences. ChatGPT can also act as an internet-based science communicator, answering enquiries and dispelling myths about many scientific issues.

- **Customised Education and Coaching**

ChatGPT has the potential to revolutionise scientific education by providing students with personalised experiences of learning. ChatGPT can alter its explanations and problem-solving procedures to optimise understanding as well as retention by identifying one's style of learning, strengths, and limitations. This personalised technique to education can help learners to narrow educational gaps and achieve in their scientific endeavours. ChatGPT's impact goes beyond the scientific field, as it has helped to encourage public involvement and improve science education. ChatGPT has been used to increase public knowledge and understanding of science, as well as its potential to revolutionise science education. ChatGPT application have enormous promise for increasing scientific knowledge, engagement, and interest among the general population. ChatGPT is positioned to play a critical role in motivating the coming generations of researchers and promoting a more educated society by harnessing the potential of AI to make science more accessible.

- **Research Planning and Study Design**

Machine learning techniques are used in AI-powered experimental design tools to optimise various parameters. Researchers can save time and effort when designing studies by automating experimental design processes. This allow researchers to devote more time to data interpretation and analysis. These AI technologies can lower R&D expenses and human mistake rates. Researcher-created models must account for a wide variety of characteristics and variables in order to properly employ AI techniques for experimental design model creation. Researchers are able to create study designs that optimise their efficacy by feeding particular criteria into these models.

- **Assistance Artificial Intelligence in Data Analysis**

Data analysis tools driven by artificial intelligence (AI) have revolutionised the field. The older approaches depended on human procedures which have restricted processing capabilities. These tools analyse, extract, and find patterns in large datasets using machine learning methods. The usage of AI will speed up research output production, cut down on expenses and time, and improve efficiency. Researchers must specify their project's goals and the precise insights and results to obtain from the study in order to employ AI techniques for data analysis efficiently. Additionally, they have to collect pertinent data and make sure it is clean, organised, and appropriate for analysis. Ultimately, it is crucial that the researchers ascertain which AI tools and algorithms are most suited for the objectives of their investigation.

- **Usage of Artificial Intelligence for Peer Review Assistance**

The amount of submissions for peer review is always increasing. Millions of working hours can be saved and academic output could be boosted by cutting down the review time. With the help of AI-powered peer review tools, a semi-automated peer review system can be developed that would identify contentious or low-quality research. While AI is not currently capable of doing peer review, it can be successfully integrated into the process with the right AI technologies. It offers advice on where to publish an article and how to do preliminary quality control on submitted articles.

- **Automated Code Generation for Computational Research**

ChatGPT can help with normal programming jobs, code snippet generation, and coding advice in computational research. The development of algorithms and models is expedited by this application, particularly in domains where coding is essential to the research process (Zhang & Wang, 2021).

4. CHALLENGES

In the past few years, integrating artificial intelligence and natural language processing tools into scientific research has opened new horizons and possibilities for researchers across diverse disciplines. Among these revolutionary technologies, ChatGPT has shown promise in scientific research because to its advanced language creation capabilities. Its potential to assist researchers in data analysis, hypothesis generation, and communication within and beyond the scientific community has been widely acknowledged.

The most important issues is the possibility of bias present in AI training data, which could distort the finding of the study and negatively impact community. Furthermore, AI frequently produces inaccurate, erroneous, or irrelevant conclusions since it lacks the advanced knowledge of human researchers. The limitation of AI is its incapacity to understand context and complexity, which are essential components in research study fields. This shortcoming causes mistakes and incorrect data interpretations. Moreover, AI frequently lacks the analytical and creative skills that human researchers possess, which limits the scope of study and restricts the possibility of ground-breaking findings. The lack of empathy in AI systems is important concern as it ignores behavioural and emotional aspects which is essential to many different disciplines of study. As a result, participants, and research community would raise the validity of study and findings produced by AI. It would diminish their significance and reliability.

It is critical to recognise the concern that have been expressed related to the inappropriate usage of chatbots in investigations. It is necessary to take steps to reduce the misuse in research related activity. The results that chatbots provide frequently require human analysis and interpretation in order to make them relevant and useful. Furthermore, the application of chatgpt in the research must to be transparent and open. Chatbots can be trained on biased datasets, which might lead to biased outcomes. Researchers need to be careful with the data used by the programmer for training the chatbots as it will reduce the chances of generating inappropriate data. It is critical that researchers and their human counterparts employ strategies for identifying and reducing bias in the results generated by these AI systems. Finally, it is legally necessary to establish clear regulations that control the application of chatbots to research, and also ensure proper, responsible and ethical use. Researchers can create best practices of integrating chatbots into research methodologies by working with experts in the field of artificial intelligence and ethics. It is important for the public to be aware of the potential risks associated with the usage of AI based chatgpt application. Researchers have an ethical responsibility to consider the implications of using chatbots in their work and make sure that their use does not violate participant rights or cause harm to research communities.

However, as with any powerful tool, ChatGPT is not without its unique set of challenges when applied in the context of scientific research. These challenges extend beyond technical limitations and encompass ethical, methodological, and practical considerations that necessitate careful deliberation.

- **Reliability and Accuracy**

Although ChatGPT has shown remarkable ability to produce text that closely mimics human conversation, there could be times when it produces false or misleading data. Verifying the authenticity, precision, and reliability of AI-generated data is essential to preserve the integrity of scientific research. A notable obstacle is the possible absence of domain-specific knowledge in ChatGPT. Scientific research frequently uses technical and intricate language, that models have a comprehensive understanding of the field. ChatGPT could find it difficult to deliver accurate and contextually relevant information without refined domain-specific expertise (Smith et al., 2021).

- **Prejudices in AI Models**

The ChatGPT relies on vast amounts of textual data for its learning process, and if there is bias in the data, it will provide biased outcomes. The AI model some time unintentionally propagate these preconceptions, which will have an impact on scientific research going forward. It might be difficult for ChatGPT to understand scientific material since it is full of unclear terminology and notions. When presented with unclear scientific terminology, the model may misinterpret or deliver false information, which would impair its trustworthiness in research applications (Jones & Brown, 2022).

• **An Excessive Reliance on AI**

ChatGPT progress, can make researchers excessive dependent upon the AI tools, which might lead to a loss in investigators' capacity for thinking critically and autonomous problem-solving. Within the scientific community, analytical thinking and autonomous problem solving are used. Though ChatGPT exhibits the capability to produce text of exceptional quality, it is not resilient to producing poor or improper replies. Maintaining a consistent standard of high-quality text from ChatGPT necessitates continual supervision, training, and improvement in research.

• **Biasness in the Dataset**

The effectiveness is impacted by the caliber and variety of the data received for training. When the training data contains biases, it can result in models that are themselves biased, potentially causing adverse ramifications in sectors like healthcare, criminal justice medical services, law enforcement, and employment. Strict source verification is necessary for scientific study. Misinformation might spread as a result of ChatGPT's incapacity to assess the validity of its training data. This calls into question the reliability of the model in a research setting (Miller, 2020).

• **Generalization**

The training of ChatGPT often involves the utilization of large datasets, which can give rise to problems related to overfitting and the model's adaptability to new or unanticipated data. To improve ChatGPT's generalization capabilities, there is a need to explore and implement novel training methodologies and strategies. Scientific researchers need explanations for replies generated by models as there is biasness in the data. Researchers' capacity to comprehend, verify, and expand upon the data supplied by the model can be hindered by a lack of openness in the decision-making process (Li & Gupta, 2021).

• **Explainability**

ChatGPT is an intricate model that presents challenges when it comes to interpretation and elucidation. The complexity make it more difficult to understand how the model makes decisions and identify any potential biases or errors. It's possible that ChatGPT won't be able to fully comprehend scientific talks, which might result in misconceptions or incorrect interpretations of complex scientific concepts. The contextual constraints of the model can make it more difficult for it to produce pertinent and correct answers in intricate scientific discussions (Johnson & White, 2023). ChatGPT have the capacity to produce intricate outputs that are not invariably straightforward to grasp or elucidate. The openness of these models, which sheds light on their reasoning methods and provides insights into their underlying mechanisms. It may boost confidence and allow users to make more accurate choices based on the derived material.

• **Energy Consumption and Security Concern**

ChatGPT models' size and complexity, required a large amount of processing power which puts adverse effect on the environment. ChatGPT has the capacity to produce risky material like as violence and fake news. Precautions and actions must be taken to prevent the development of such content.

• **Real-Time Responsiveness**

ChatGPT has the ability of creating real-time text, while some time response times may occasionally be slowed. It may be utilized for a variety of applications by improving the pace, responsiveness, quickness of ChatGPT.

• **Cultural and Linguistic Bias**

AI tool, ChatGPT has cultural and language biases for some traditional societies, which can end up in incomplete or unsuitable replies. To correct these biases, more diverse training databases is needed to consider different cultures and languages.

• **Domain-Specific Knowledge Adaptation**

Even though ChatGPT has a wide knowledge and understanding of many areas, it lacks the deep domain- particular expertise requirement for certain applications. It is critical to develop ways for effectively adjusting and refining AI language models to fit certain domains, sectors in order to completely unleash their powers. ChatGPT may provide rational and contextually acceptable responses, but it may fail to absorb complicated information or maintain consistency across long conversations. It need to boost the model's ability to distinguish and keep context in extended text sequences.

5. ETHICAL CONSIDERATIONS

Artificial intelligence (AI) systems offer numerous benefits in the field of research, but many voices warn against use of chatgpt due to a number of ethical concerns. There are serious ethical concerns about data security, privacy, and participant exploitation that arise when AI is used in research The application of chatpgt in research needs to be carefully managed by human specialists in order to minimise ethical issues and preserve the integrity of research findings.

There are a number of ethical issues with using chatbots in research, including data privacy, bias in data, accuracy accountability, lack of openness, and abuse possibilities. Large volumes of personal data are collected and stored by chatbots, which raise the issue related to data security and privacy. Furthermore, biases and inaccuracies in the data used to train chatbots also impact on the accuracy of their replies. Once more, the validity and reliability of study findings is impacted by the lack of clarity over the data. There is no clear accountability on the correctness of the data produced by chatgpt. There are questions regarding the openness and accountability of the results produced by chatgpts as researcher relay on the content generated. Researcher use the same work in the background, which create challenge for the researcher to evident the content. Ultimately, chatgpt is the potential tool for social manipulation and exploitation, and the decisions they produce may be biased against or detrimental to particular groups. For instance, chatbot responses to frequently asked queries concerning political disputes have the potential to skew public perception. programmers and developers can instruct chatbots to respond to public inquiries about the Russian/Ukrainian war in a way that furthers their own political agenda by teaching them to give either favourable or negative replies. The possibility of misusing chatbots is seen to be the most hazardous and damaging. Chatbots can generate the abused content in many ways that are harmful to people and communities. These include disseminating false information, swaying public opinion, taking advantage of weaker segments of the population, fostering prejudice and discrimination, and impairing the validity of research. The biasness in training of the chatbots would lead to disseminate propaganda and false information, which might negatively affect public opinion and decision-making. Chatbots can offer inaccurate or misleading information to the elderly or those with low levels of computer literacy. For a deeper understanding of the potential misuse of chatbots in research and public policy, here are few instances. If a Chatbots are trained on a biased dataset then it will diagnose the illness incorrectly and can recommend harmful therapy, which affect the health of the patience. In academic research also chatbots can provide biased or erroneous results that might spread incorrect or misleading information.

Figure 2. Shows the ethical challenges

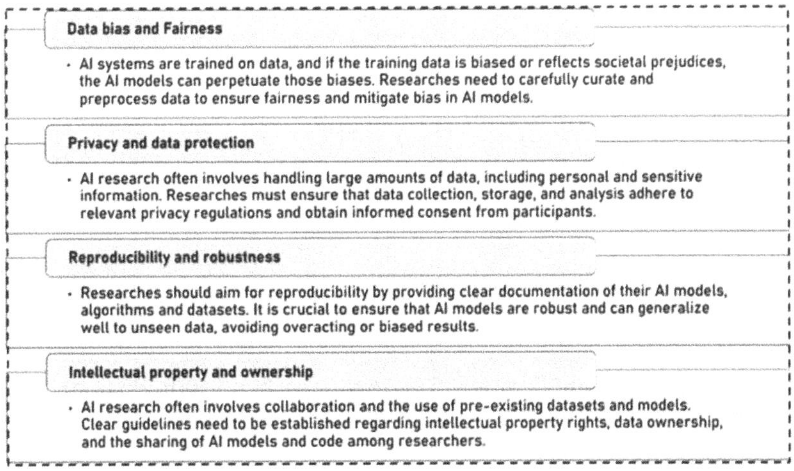

The bias training of the would lead to unreliable findings in a social science study. As a result, we must be extremely aware of these shortcomings, particularly with relation to the ethical issues.

Moral deliberations regarding the utilization of ChatGPT in scientific investigation includes.

- **Data Confidentiality and Security**

AI is being utilised more and more in data analysis and processing. According to Liebrenz et al. (2023) Data security and privacy have grown its importance. The preservation of confidential details and ethical handling of data are still critical. It has access to an extensive repository of user information, which gives rise to apprehensions regarding privacy and safeguarding data. It is crucial to establish guidelines and legal frameworks to guarantee the protection of user data and its responsible utilization. ChatGPT may be utilised for handling confidential data such as medical records, financial information, and private communications. As a result, it is critical to protect the safety and privacy of sensitive information.

- **Authorship and Intellectual Property**

It play a role in generating research concepts, suppositions, and even written materials, leading to inquiries regarding intellectual property entitlements and the assignment of authorship.

- **Accountability and Transparency**

Ali and Djalilian (2023) stated that it is critical to promote openness in AI-backed research and assume responsibilities for the outputs in order to establish confidence among both members of academia and the general public. ChatGPT is becoming increasingly prominent and prevalent. It is critical to identify the persons or entities accountable for the model's actions and choices. It entails answering issues concerning data ownership utilized in ChatGPT training and determining accountability for the models generated outputs. Its use may have detrimental repercussions.

- **Prejudice and Equity**

It exhibit prejudice if trained on biased datasets, possibly resulting to unfair outcomes, particularly in areas like as work, health care, and the judiciary.

- **Misuse and Abuse**

It may be used for creating false identities, spreading fake news, and providing false information. It is important to tackle these obstacles and guarantee that ChatGPT is employed suitably and morally. According to Mhlanga (2023) advanced language models, such as ChatGPT, can be used for improper purposes such as spam production, disseminating misleading information, creating deep fake material, or engaging in online harassment. Implementing measures like filtering content, authentication of users, and regular monitoring can help to reduce the possibility of harmful operations.

- **Openness and Explanation**

Crawford et al. (2023) stated that ChatGPT is a complex and sophisticated model prototype that can be difficult to understand and describe. As a result, it is necessary to maintain accessibility and explain ability of the model particularly in fields where its assessments may have significant effects for both individuals and society as a whole.

- **Misinformation and Autonomy**

ChatGPT can produce inaccurate or deceptive information, which can have significant consequences, particularly in medical and healthcare, education, and politics. It has the ability to impact human behaviour and decisions. It calls into question personal liberty and self-government.

- **Interactions Resembling Human Behaviour**

Marchandot et al. (2023) stated that ChatGPT language can strongly mimic human-authored writing but it raises problems regarding ethical considerations associated with the user interaction

- **Discrimination and Bias**

Khlaif (2023) stated that ChatGPT undergoes training on enormous datasets that may contain prejudices, preconceived notions, and discriminatory language. This unintentional learning might result in impolite or stereotype-reinforcing responses. Improving the accuracy of training data, improving the model's design, and encouraging fairness will decrease prejudiced outputs

- **Ethical Problems**

In order to solve ethical problems, programmers, investigators, and the larger AI community must adopt a proactive approach. They need to collaborate recognize, comprehend and address possible challenges. It may ensure that ChatGPT are created and utilised properly, which maximise the benefits and eliminate difficulties.

6. CONTROVERSIAL STORIES

Certain author like Listverse (2023), Parikh et al. (2023) have come up with the controversial stories which put the light on the usage of ChatGPT and their issues.

i. The sci-fi magazine Clarkes World faced a deluge of story submissions generated by AI, with many suspected to be created using ChatGPT. Consequently, the magazine stopped accepting new entries due to the sheer volume of subpar machine-generated content.

ii. In the realm of education, ChatGPT has stirred controversy as college students have used it to craft essays, causing concerns among educators who find it challenging to discern AI-generated work. As AI advances in sophistication, detecting AI-generated content becomes progressively difficult, prompting inquiries about academic honesty.

7. FUTURE PROSPECTS

In light of these obstacles and ethical issues, ChatGPT has considerable promise for revolutionising scientific research. Several upcoming possibilities include:

- **Improved AI Models**

As artificial intelligence (AI) technology progresses, it is expected to see improved and more reliable models in the future. Such models have the ability to eliminate prejudices, increase contextual knowledge, and give researchers with even more essential assistance.

- **Cross-Disciplinary Research**

McGee (2023) found that ChatGPT has a capacity to handle and combine data from several fields. It has the ability to enable revolutionary transdisciplinary research. It opens up fresh views and discoveries.

- **Democratizing Scientific Research**

ChatGPT, plays a significant role in democratising scientific enquiry. It make complicated scientific ideas more understandable and make the research easier. It enables a broad variety of people to engage in the scientific process to contribute to the growth of our knowledge.

- **Enhanced Language Comprehension**

Aljanabi (2023) stated that GPT can presently create high-quality text, and advancements in language comprehension may enable even more intricate and advanced apps in the future.

- **Personalisation**

ChatGPT can provide tailored responses depending on user data, and in near future improvements can lead to even more customised and tailored interactions. Current advances may enable ChatGPT to support a broader variety of languages with improved comprehension and producing capabilities. In terms of linguistic diversity, ChatGPT can already produce text in a number of dialects.

- **Applications in Real Time**

Real-time text production is currently possible using ChatGPT, but future developments could make real-time text generating software even quicker and more responsive.

- **Integration With Other Technologies**

Ollivier et al. (2023) found that ChatGPT currently has the ability to work with various technologies, including Chabot's and virtual assistants. Future improvements, may bring much more smooth and engaging interactions across a variety of platforms and devices.

- **Improved Grasp of Situational Context**

Improved responses could result from improvements in ChatGPT's capacity to comprehend the context of a discussion or text. It will be more accurate as well as more relevant.

- **Enhanced Capacity to Manage Feelings**

Lecler et al. (2023) stated that the capacity of ChatGPT to identify and respond to emotions may be improved, which might result in more individualised and empathic interactions.

- **Collaboration With Human Experts**

It is possible for ChatGPT to develop its ability for identifying and responding to emotions. It leads to interactions that are both more sympathetic and catered to specific requirements.

- **Enhanced Creativity**

Anderson et al. (2023) in research stated that ChatGPT might be taught to compose artistic material like poetry, music lyrics, and tales.

- **Ongoing Acquisition of Knowledge**

Through its interactions with users, ChatGPT has the ability to learn, and enhance both its capabilities and replies over time.

- **Specialized Field Models**

As the need for specific knowledge grows across a range of sectors, it is expected that the development of AI language models will increase. It will be modified for specific industries, such as science, law, finance, and medical. Because of these specialist models, users in these areas may obtain information that is more accurate, relevant, and comprehensive.

- **Enhanced Comprehension Within Context**

Baidoo-Anu and Owusu Ansah (2023) stated that ChatGPT has ability to grasp the context and provide is to scientists. It is anticipated that these upgraded models would be better able to comprehend and recall context in lengthier text sequences, resulting in more logical and trustworthy talks even during prolonged exchanges.

- **Enhanced Precautions for Safety and Security Will Grow Increasingly Indispensable**

It is anticipated that researchers and developers will place a high premium on installing safeguards and monitoring mechanisms to guarantee the appropriate and moral use of AI models and to lessen the likelihood of negative exploitation.

8. CONCLUSION

Incorporation of ChatGPT's into scientific research has opened up a new world of opportunities with substantial advantages and complex difficulties. ChatGPT has shown to be an effective tool for data analysis, literature reviews, and developing hypotheses. Its capacity to comprehend and produce writing which is similar to person has speed up the process of research. It allows scientists to analyse large, and complicated datasets to extract valuable information from large dataset in short period of time. The study showed that ChatGPT can serve as a strong support for research and instructional activities. Researcher describe ChatGPT as an innovative technology possessing immense potential to transform a multitude of areas within research and education. Academics see ChatGPT as a potent instrument that can produce writing that resembles that of a person. This feature of chatgpt is appreciated which has advantageous effects on research projects. ChatGPT can speed up information access. It also help with language understanding, and support literature reviews, which will greatly benefit scientific investigation in learning processes. ChatGPT is expected to be a useful tool in the field of academic research, especially when it comes to finding and evaluating relevant material for the subjects. Furthermore, its capacity to provide language support such as mistake detection and translation assistance which helps the researcher in exploring multilingual literature. This feature is consistent with other study highlighting the usefulness of ChatGPT for literature reviews. Moreover, scholars view ChatGPT as a teaching tool in addition to a research tool. It can improve instructional strategies and promote the spread of knowledge by making sources and information easier to access. As a result, academics view ChatGPT as a tool that may improve productivity and professional efficiency by saving time. According to Dergaa et al.,2022 the innovative qualities of ChatGPT can encourage scholars to pursue new lines of inquiry, and allow them to stay up to date with the quickly changing field of study. From this perspective, ChatGPT's idea generating function is considered as a feature that enhances the calibre and productivity of research. It acts as a spark for the creation of new ideas and fields of study. However, the results also brought to light to ethical dilemmas that academics faced with relation to ChatGPT. The problems of plagiarism and the spread of false material will major concern in the use of chatgpt in academic research.

Language barriers have been eliminated, which foster interdisciplinary collaborations, and communication between academics with different backgrounds. Chatgpt has been made easier for the various academicians. Usage of Chatgpt in educational contexts has also expanded, and has improved scientific knowledge accessibility and encouraging participatory learning. Although ChatGPT might improve research, it is important to remember that idea formation still requires human judgement and interpretation. ChatGPT is considered a useful tool for academic writing, it cannot be considered for writing full papers on its own. It highlights the need of human thinking and interpretation in academic writing.

Although ChatGPT is regarded as a revolutionary tool that might completely change the way of academics research yet the academic circles need to focus on limits and ethical consequences. It is imperative to recognise the inherent constraints associated with the use of ChatGPT in scientific research. The model's reliance on pre-existing data introduces the risk of perpetuating biases present in the training data, necessitating careful consideration of ethical implications. Additionally, the challenge of ensuring transparency and interpretability remains a pertinent concern, especially when the black-box nature of deep learning models may hinder the understanding of decision-making processes.

Despite these limitations, the benefits outweigh the challenges, and the responsible integration of ChatGPT into scientific research holds immense promise. As we move forward, it is imperative to address ethical considerations, refine model capabilities, and foster a collaborative environment that encourages the responsible use of AI technologies. ChatGPT's is the potential tool for expanding scientific understanding and pushing the envelope of discovery in the dynamic field of research.. In future research, researchers might create scales using the theoretical framework. The strategy enables the implementation of more comprehensive research with bigger cohorts and quantitative methodologies. Interviewing people from different age groups and/or culturally varied communities can also improve the inclusiveness of research. However, as ChatGPT is still in its early stages, further research need to be done by means of ongoing observations or repeated studies. Further research should examine the effectiveness of artificial intelligence (AI) methods like ChatGPT for efficiently analysing large datasets and investigate related benefits, challenges, and implications for academic fields.

REFERENCES

Advanced Science News. (2023). Science Articles. https://www.advancedsciencenews.com/where-and-how-should-ChatGPT-be-used-in-the-scientific-literature/

Agility Portal. (2023). Collaboration with Researcher. https://agilityportal.io/blog/streamlining-communication-and-collaboration-with-ChatGPT-and-intranet-portals/

Ali, M. J., & Djalilian, A. (2023, March). Readership awareness series–paper 4: Chatbots and ChatGPT-ethical considerations in scientific publications. In *Seminars in ophthalmology* (pp. 1–2). Taylor & Francis.

Aljanabi, M. (2023). ChatGPT: Future directions and open possibilities. Mesopotamian journal of Cybersecurity, 2023, 16-17.

Anderson, N., Belavy, D. L., Perle, S. M., Hendricks, S., Hespanhol, L., Verhagen, E., & Memon, A. R. (2023). AI did not write this manuscript, or did it? Can we trick the AI text detector into generated texts? The potential future of ChatGPT and AI in Sports & Exercise Medicine manuscript generation. *BMJ Open Sport & Exercise Medicine*, *9*(1), e001568. doi:10.1136/bmjsem-2023-001568 PMID:36816423

Baidoo-AnuD.Owusu AnsahL. Education in the Era of Generative Artificial Intelligence (AI): Understanding the Potential Benefits of ChatGPT in Promoting Teaching and Learning (January 25, 2023). Available at SSRN 4337484. doi:10.2139/ssrn.4337484

Bayesian Spectacles. (2023). Testing Hypothesis. https://www.bayesianspectacles.org/redefine-statistical-significance-xx-a-chat-on-p-values-with-ChatGPT/

Chen, T. J. (2023). ChatGPT and other artificial intelligence applications speed up scientific writing. *Journal of the Chinese Medical Association*, *86*(4), 351–353. doi:10.1097/JCMA.0000000000000900 PMID:36791246

Crawford, J., Cowling, M., & Allen, K. A. (2023). Leadership is needed for ethical ChatGPT: Character, assessment, and learning using artificial intelligence (AI). Journal of University Teaching & Learning Practice, 20(3), 2.

Cyfirma. (2023). Challenges. https://www.cyfirma.com/outofband/ChatGPT-ai-in-security-testing-opportunities-and-challenges/

Discourse (2023, March). Hypothesis. https://discourse.datamethods.org/t/accuracy-of-ChatGPT-on-statistical-methods/6402

Green, M. (2023). Ethical Considerations and Bias Mitigation in the Use of ChatGPT for Scientific Research. Ethics in AI Conference Proceedings, 45-58.

KhlaifZ. N. (2023). Ethical Concerns about Using AI-Generated Text in Scientific Research. Available at SSRN 4387984. doi:10.2139/ssrn.4387984

Kim, S. G. (2023). Using ChatGPT for language editing in scientific articles. *Maxillofacial Plastic and Reconstructive Surgery*, *45*(1), 13. doi:10.1186/s40902-023-00381-x PMID:36882591

Lecler, A., Duron, L., & Soyer, P. (2023). Revolutionizing radiology with GPT-based models: Current applications, future possibilities and limitations of ChatGPT. *Diagnostic and Interventional Imaging*, *104*(6), 269–274. doi:10.1016/j.diii.2023.02.003 PMID:36858933

Liebrenz, M., Schleifer, R., Buadze, A., Bhugra, D., & Smith, A. (2023). Generating scholarly content with ChatGPT: Ethical challenges for medical publishing. *The Lancet. Digital Health*, *5*(3), e105–e106. doi:10.1016/S2589-7500(23)00019-5 PMID:36754725

Listverse (2023, March 22). Controversies. https://listverse.com/2023/03/22/ten-controversial-news-stories-surrounding-ChatGPT/

Make Use Of. (2023). Key Challenges. https://www.makeuseof.com/openai-ChatGPT-biggest-probelms/

Marchandot, B., Matsushita, K., Carmona, A., Trimaille, A., & Morel, O. (2023). ChatGPT: The next frontier in academic writing for cardiologists or a pandora's box of ethical dilemmas. *European Heart Journal Open*, *3*(2), oead007. doi:10.1093/ehjopen/oead007 PMID:36915398

McGee, R. W. (2023). Is ChatGPT biased against conservatives? an empirical study. An Empirical Study.

Mhlanga, D. (2023). Open AI in education, the responsible and ethical use of ChatGPT towards lifelong learning. Education, the Responsible and Ethical Use of ChatGPT Towards Lifelong Learning.

Ollivier, M., Pareek, A., Dahmen, J., Kayaalp, M. E., Winkler, P. W., Hirschmann, M. T., & Karlsson, J. (2023). A deeper dive into ChatGPT: History, use and future perspectives for orthopaedic research. *Knee Surgery, Sports Traumatology, Arthroscopy : Official Journal of the ESSKA*, *31*(4), 1190–1192. doi:10.1007/s00167-023-07372-5 PMID:36894785

Parikh, P. M., Shah, D. M., & Parikh, K. P. (2023). Judge Juan Manuel Padilla Garcia, ChatGPT, and a controversial medicolegal milestone. *Indian Journal of Medical Sciences*, *75*(1), 3–8. doi:10.25259/IJMS_31_2023

Qasem, F. (2023). ChatGPT in scientific and academic research: Future fears and reassurances. *Library Hi Tech News*, *40*(3), 30–32. doi:10.1108/LHTN-03-2023-0043

Radford, A. (2019). Language Models are Few-Shot Learners. arXiv preprint arXiv:1905.08144

SalahM.AlhalbusiH.IsmailM. M.AbdelfattahF. (2023). Chatting with ChatGPT: Decoding the mind of Chatbot users and unveiling the intricate connections between user perception, trust and stereotype perception on self-esteem and psychological well-being. Research Square, 1-26. doi:10.21203/rs.3.rs-2610655/v2

Salvagno, M., Taccone, F. S., & Gerli, A. G. (2023). Can artificial intelligence help for scientific writing? *Critical Care*, *27*(1), 1–5. PMID:36597110

SEO AI. (2023). Multilingual. https://seo.ai/blog/how-many-languages-does-ChatGPT-support/

Smith, J. (2022). Knowledge Synthesis with ChatGPT: Connecting Diverse Perspectives in Scientific Research. *Journal of AI Research*, *15*(2), 123–145.

TS2 Space. (2023). Collaboration. https://ts2.space/en/collaborative-ai-ChatGPT-5s-role-in-facilitating-remote-work-and-team-communication

The Ticker. (2023). Public Outreach. https://theticker.org/9831/opinions/ChatGPT-will-benefit-the-public-if-regulated/

Van Dis, E. A., Bollen, J., Zuidema, W., van Rooij, R., & Bockting, C. L. (2023). ChatGPT: Five priorities for research. *Nature*, *614*(7947), 224–226. doi:10.1038/d41586-023-00288-7 PMID:36737653

Zhang, Y., & Wang, X. (2021). Leveraging ChatGPT for Automated Literature Review. *Proceedings of the International Conference on Artificial Intelligence*.

Chapter 13 Navigating the Ethical Landscape: AI's Impact on Academic Research and Integrity

Shivam Bhardwaj
https://orcid.org/0000-0001-5327-7802
Institute of Business Management, GLA University, Mathura, India

Vivek Agrawal
https://orcid.org/0000-0001-7665-7103
Institute of Business Management, GLA University, Mathura, India

Mayank Sharma
Technische Hochschule, Rosenheim, Germany

Sucheta Agarwal
Institute of Business Management, GLA University, Mathura, India

Jitendra Kumar Dixit
Institute of Business Management, GLA University, Mathura, India

Ankit Saxena
Institute of Business Management, GLA University, Mathura, India

ABSTRACT

This research delves into the complex and multifaceted relationship between artificial intelligence (AI) and ethical considerations in academic research. Using literature review and interview method, it highlights the immense potential of AI to streamline research processes and warns against potential pitfalls like data privacy breaches, algorithmic biases, and loss of research autonomy. The study emphasizes the crucial role of researchers in ensuring data integrity, maintaining research reproducibility, mitigating bias, and using AI responsibly. It advocates for robust data governance, open-source practices, and interdisciplinary collaboration to navigate the ethical landscape of AI-powered research. Recognizing the limitations of its scope and the dynamic nature of AI and ethical considerations, the research calls for continuous learning, adaptation, and development of ethical frameworks to ensure the responsible and ethical integration of AI in academic endeavors.

DOI: 10.4018/979-8-3693-1798-3.ch013

1. INTRODUCTION

"Success in creating AI would be the biggest event in human history. Unfortunately, it might also be the last unless we learn how to avoid the risks." — Stephen Hawking

The term "artificial intelligence (AI)" came into discussion during the Dartmouth Conference in 1956, a landmark gathering featuring influential figures like John McCarthy, Marvin Minsky, Allen Newell, and Herbert A. Simon, who convened to explore the possibilities of developing machines capable of exhibiting intelligence (Russel and Norvig, 2010). According to the IEEE Guide for Terms and Concepts in Intelligent Process Automation (2017), AI encompasses cognitive automation, machine learning, reasoning, hypothesis generation and analysis, natural language processing, and intentional algorithm mutation. Aggarwal (2018) characterizes AI as a broad concept that includes analytical methodologies like machine learning, neural networks, and deep learning techniques. AI, within the realm of computer science, aims to simulate intelligent behavior in computers, potentially enhancing human capabilities and enabling tasks typically associated with intelligent individuals (Baker and Smith, 2019; Naqvi, 2020).

The integration of AI into academic research represents a paradigm shift in knowledge production. With its ability to analyze large datasets and discern complex patterns, AI has revolutionized various research fields, overcoming barriers faced by researchers lacking extensive proficiency (Akgun and Greenhow, 2022; Remian, 2019). The adoption of AI technologies has propelled interdisciplinary collaboration, leveraging robust computational power and technological advancements to enhance research procedures' effectiveness and security. Natural Language Processing (NLP) methodologies, for instance, have significantly influenced literature reviews, sentiment analysis, and linguistic studies, while predictive modeling across disciplines has led to the development of insightful predictive models.

The profound implications of AI's integration into academic research cannot be overstated. While it offers unprecedented opportunities for innovation and discovery, it also presents ethical challenges that must be navigated with care. As AI becomes increasingly pervasive in scholarly investigation, it becomes imperative to critically examine its impact on academic integrity and ensure that ethical principles guide its application. Thus, this chapter explores the ethical landscape of AI's impact on academic research, aiming to elucidate the complexities involved and provide guidance for maintaining integrity in this rapidly evolving domain.

2. EMERGENCE OF THE CONCEPT

The academic trajectory of AI spans decades marked by breakthroughs, paradigm shifts, and technological advancements. Originating in the mid-20th century, scholars-initiated investigations into computers matching human intelligence. The 1950s and 1960s saw a focus on symbolic AI, emphasizing symbol manipulation to replicate human cognitive processes (Inozemtsev et al., 2017). Pioneering programs like the Logic Theorist and the General Problem Solver laid the groundwork for rule-based systems, coinciding with the establishment of dedicated AI research labs and departments (Collinsworth and Benjamin, 2022; Natale and Ballatore, 2020). The "AI winter" of the 1970s and 1980s dampened enthusiasm, attributed to unmet expectations and limited computing power. However, this period also spurred critical reflections on AI's limitations and potential, leading to renewed focus and innovation. The mid-1980s witnessed a resurgence with advances in machine learning, particularly the development of the backpropagation algorithm (Pietikäinen and Silven, 2022; Yao et al., 2017). This breakthrough enabled more efficient training of artificial neural networks, laying the foundation for modern deep learning techniques. The late 20th century saw a notable transition towards machine learning dominance within the AI research landscape. Researchers increasingly focused on developing algorithms capable of learning from data and improving performance iteratively. Academic institutions played a pivotal role in driving these advancements, contributing to the development of support vector machines, reinforcement learning algorithms, and the widespread utilization of neural networks in various domains such as image recognition and natural language processing.

The 21st century witnessed a remarkable expansion and diversification of AI within academia. Advancements in computational capabilities, fueled by Moore's Law and the advent of specialized hardware like graphics processing units (GPUs), facilitated the training of larger and more complex models. Extensive datasets became increasingly available, thanks to the proliferation of digital technologies and the rise of big data. Deep learning techniques, particularly convolutional neural networks and recurrent neural networks revolutionized fields like computer vision and sequential data processing.

Multidisciplinary collaborations further broadened AI applications, incorporating insights from fields such as robotics, natural language processing, computer vision, and reinforcement learning (Cantú-Ortiz et al., 2020; Dwivedi et al., 2021). These collaborations facilitated the development of AI-powered systems capable of autonomous decision-making, language understanding, and perception. However, with the rapid proliferation of AI technologies, ethical considerations have come to the forefront. Concerns regarding bias in AI algorithms, data privacy, and responsible technology use pose significant challenges to the field's advancement (Hasan, 2021; Hsu, 2023). Biases present in training data can propagate through AI systems, leading to unfair outcomes and reinforcing societal inequalities. Moreover, the ethical implications of AI's increasing autonomy and decision-making capabilities raise complex questions about accountability and transparency (MIjwil et al., 2023). The future of AI research lies in addressing these ethical challenges through concerted efforts in hardware development, algorithmic advancements, and interdisciplinary collaborations (Kamila, 2023; Miao et al., 2021). Innovations in AI hardware, such as neuromorphic computing and quantum computing, hold promise for overcoming existing limitations and enabling more efficient and ethical AI systems. Algorithmic advancements, including techniques for bias mitigation and interpretability, are essential for ensuring AI systems' fairness and transparency. Interdisciplinary partnerships between AI researchers, ethicists, policymakers, and other stakeholders are crucial for developing frameworks and guidelines that promote responsible AI development and deployment.

3. INTEGRATION OF AI IN ACADEMIC RESEARCH

The dynamics of the academic research field are changing dramatically, thanks to Artificial Intelligence (AI). Everyone from the World Economic Forum to the academic fraternity themselves agrees it's a big deal. Sure, some people worry about machines making research decisions, but AI can be a huge helper. Imagine a tool that can help with writing research papers, finding new ideas to study, and even analyzing giant piles of scientific data. That's what AI can do! It's like having a super-powered research assistant that can spot hidden patterns humans might miss (Chen et al., 2020; Chen et al., 2022; Jarrah et al., 2023). This lets researchers ask even better questions and make even cooler discoveries. AI is also a whiz at crunching numbers. It can handle mountains of data, finding trends and connections a human researcher might overlook. This isn't just helpful, it can lead to breakthroughs in all sorts of fields (Rosyanafi et al., 2023). Not only does AI make research faster, but it can lead to breakthroughs in fields as diverse as social sciences, medicine, astronomy, and materials science etc. Collaboration is another area where AI is making waves. New AI-powered tools can scan through vast libraries of scientific papers in seconds, saving researchers countless hours (Bueno, 2020; Oravec, 2023). These tools also make it easier for researchers to share ideas and work together. The more researchers can collaborate, the faster research moves forward! In complex research, AI extends its support in analyzing data to make predictions (Illia, 2023; Khlaif et al., 2023). These predictions help researchers make better decisions and get even closer to those "aha!" moments. The impact of AI extends beyond the research lab. In the classroom, AI-driven platforms are personalizing learning experiences for each student. These platforms undertake a myriad of tasks, including title generation, paper structuring, content generation, and plagiarism verification, thereby empowering educators and learners alike (Johnson et al., 2024; Smith et al., 2023; Soubhari et al., 2023). By harnessing the capabilities of AI, educators can deliver tailored instruction and feedback, optimizing learning outcomes and fostering a deeper understanding of complex concepts.

Overall, AI is making research faster, smarter, and more collaborative. It's a powerful tool that can help researchers make amazing discoveries. But with any big change, there are things to consider. The next section will talk about some of the challenges of using AI in research and how to make sure it's done responsibly.

4. ETHICAL CONCERNS WITH THE INTEGRATION OF AI INTO ACADEMIC RESEARCH

Artificial intelligence (AI) is revolutionizing research, accelerating discovery, and fostering collaboration on complex problems. However, this exciting potential comes with ethical considerations that demand attention (Francke and Bennett, 2019; Michel-Villarreal, 2023). One major concern is bias (Ray 2023; Sutherland-Smith, 2008). AI algorithms learn from the data they're trained on, and if that data is biased, the results can be discriminatory. This can happen in a few ways. For instance, if certain groups are missing from the data, the AI's conclusions may not apply to everyone, potentially harming underrepresented populations. Similarly, AI used for tasks like grant review or paper selection could perpetuate existing biases in academia, disadvantaging certain research areas or academics. Even researchers themselves can introduce bias when designing AI models by choosing biased data or analysis methods (Moya et al., 2023). Data privacy and security are also crucial issues (Abd-Elaal, 2019; Michel-Villarreal, 2023). AI research often involves vast amounts of sensitive data, raising concerns about data breaches and unauthorized access. Even anonymized data can potentially be re-identified with advanced techniques. Researchers need to ensure participants understand how their data will be used and have explicitly consented to its use in AI research(Dergaa et al., 2023). The use of AI in research also presents challenges to academic integrity and reproducibility (Bin-Nashwan et al., 2023; Singh and Singh, 2023). The complexity of some AI models makes it difficult to understand how they reach conclusions, hindering the ability to verify and replicate research findings. Another question arises: when AI significantly contributes to research outputs, who gets credit? How should authorship be assigned? Finally, there's the risk of AI misuse – tools could be exploited to fabricate data, manipulate results, or plagiarize work (Perkins, 2023). Beyond these immediate concerns, the broader societal impact of AI in research needs consideration. AI automation could lead to job losses in certain scientific fields, requiring workforce retraining. If not

Table 1. AI tools assisting in academic research (Source: Created by authors)

Task	Tool	Description
Literature Review	Scilit	Summarizes research papers, identifies key findings and trends, and generates bibliographies.
	Elicit	Answers research questions using its knowledge base of scholarly articles, provides citations and summarizes key points.
	Scholarcy	Analyzes research papers and identifies related articles, helps find gaps in the literature.
	Consensus	Uses natural language processing to analyze research papers and provide consensus on key arguments and findings.
	PaperPal	Summarizes research papers and extracts key information, helping researchers quickly grasp the main points.
Writing & Editing	ChatGPT	AI tool for content generation
	Bard	AI tool for content generation
	QuillBot	Paraphrases sentences and rephrases text, helps improve clarity and avoid plagiarism.
	Grammarly	Checks for grammar, spelling, and plagiarism, improves overall writing quality.
	ProWritingAid	Offers comprehensive grammar and style checks, suggests edits for clarity and conciseness.
	Hemingway Editor	Highlights overly complex sentences and suggests improvements for readability.
	Writesonic	Generates different creative text formats of text content, including poems, code, scripts, musical pieces, emails, letters, etc.
Citation & Reference Management	Mendeley	Organizes and manages research papers, generates bibliographies in different citation styles.
	Zotero	Open-source reference management tool that allows users to organize, annotate, and share research papers.
	EndNote	Popular reference management tool that integrates with various academic databases.
	Cite This For Me	Generates citations in different citation styles, helps avoid plagiarism.

developed and implemented inclusively, AI-driven research could further disadvantage marginalized communities. AI-generated research results could also be manipulated and spread as misinformation, eroding public trust in science (Cotton et al., 2024). Overreliance on AI for research tasks could even hinder human efforts in exploration, writing, and analysis.

Addressing these ethical challenges mandates proactive measures on the part of researchers, academic institutions, and policymakers (Susilawati et al., 2022). This includes advocating for transparency and accountability in AI-driven research practices, fortifying data governance frameworks to safeguard privacy and confidentiality, fostering diversity and inclusivity in research methodologies, and promoting interdisciplinary collaboration to navigate complex ethical dilemmas (Cotton et al., 2023). To navigate these challenges adeptly, the academic community must foster a culture of ethical awareness, accountability, and continual learning. Robust training programs, workshops, and institutional policies can equip researchers with the requisite ethical acumen to navigate complex ethical landscapes effectively.

5. IMPORTANCE OF ETHICAL CONSIDERATIONS IN MAINTAINING ACADEMIC INTEGRITY

Science is getting a major upgrade with Artificial Intelligence (AI) on the scene. It's like having a superpowered research assistant who can tackle everything from writing papers to brainstorming new ideas and analyzing mountains of data. But with any powerful tool, there are things to keep in mind, especially when it comes to ethics and making sure research is done honestly. The integration of Artificial

Intelligence (AI) into academic research presents both exciting possibilities and significant challenges in upholding ethical research practices and academic integrity. While AI offers a powerful toolkit for researchers, its responsible use necessitates careful consideration of ethical principles. An ethical issue refers to any situation that could potentially undermine the respect for a socially legitimate moral value (Swisher, 2022). The inclusion of ethical issues is of utmost importance in upholding the principles of academic integrity, as they play a significant role in enhancing the credibility, reliability, and excellence of scholarly investigations.

Central to ethical research with AI remains the well-being of research participants. Informed consent is paramount, ensuring participants understand the potential involvement of AI in data collection or analysis (Ghotbi, 2023; Odrakiewicz, 2022). Researchers must also be vigilant about algorithmic bias – AI systems trained on biased data can perpetuate those biases in research outcomes. Mitigating such bias requires careful selection of data and rigorous analysis methods. Transparency is even more critical with AI. Traditional reporting practices may not adequately explain AI's role in research. Researchers must disclose how AI was used, including its limitations and potential biases (Eatson, 2023; Liu et al, 2023). This fosters trust within the academic community and allows for critical evaluation of AI-driven findings.

Academic integrity is also challenged by AI's capabilities (Yeo, 2023). The ease with which AI can generate text raises concerns about plagiarism. Researchers must ensure the responsible use of AI tools, employing them for tasks like reference management or initial drafts, not to replace their critical thinking and writing (Mohammadkarimi, 2023). Fabrication of data, a serious breach of integrity, can also be disguised by AI's data manipulation capabilities (Rane et al., 2023). Researchers must prioritize data provenance and maintain clear audit trails to ensure the trustworthiness of their findings. The legal landscape surrounding AI in research is still evolving (Jeyaraman et al., 2023). Researchers must stay informed about relevant regulations to ensure participant privacy and data security. Universities also have a role to play in developing policies and guidelines for the ethical use of AI in research.

In the age of AI-powered research, maintaining ethical practices and academic integrity is crucial. Fostering a culture of ethical awareness, promoting transparency, and prioritizing responsible AI use can enable the academic community to harness AI's power for groundbreaking discoveries while upholding high academic integrity standards. This approach contributes to the advancement of knowledge and society's betterment.

6. AN EXPERIMENT WITH AI FOR ETHICAL CONSIDERATION: THE INTERVIEW OF CHATGPT

As AI tools increasingly permeate academia, experiments like interviewing ChatGPT offer insights into AI's role in research. In this study, ChatGPT (Version 3.5) was interviewed to explore its perspective on academic research activities. The researcher initiated a series of questions using prompts, capturing ChatGPT's responses for analysis.

A series of questions using prompts was initiated by the researcher and the responses received were captured (QUESTION & RESPONSE 1-14) which are mentioned below:

Figure 1. Question & Response 1

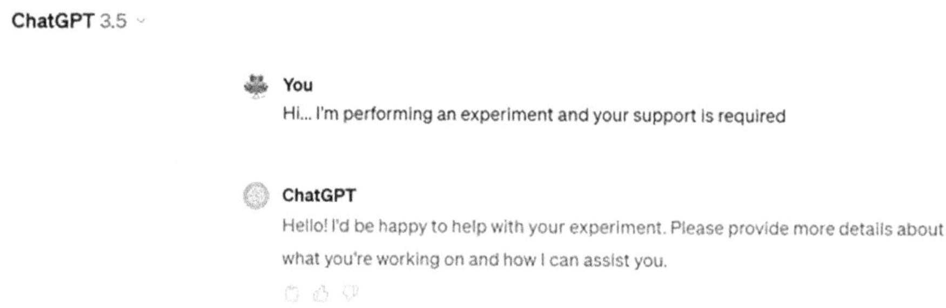

7. KEY TAKEAWAYS

Through the above interview, several key themes emerged, shedding light on the potential benefits and challenges associated with integrating AI assistance into the research process. The AI content generator (ChatGPT 3.5) showcased a diverse range of capabilities aimed at assisting academic researchers in various aspects of their work, including information retrieval, summarization of research papers, literature review assistance, idea generation, data analysis, writing assistance, coding support, grammar and style checking, and conceptual clarifications. This comprehensive suite of tools provides researchers with valuable support, enabling them to efficiently gather information, synthesize complex concepts, and enhance the quality of their academic output. However, despite its impressive capabilities, the AI content generator(ChatGPT 3.5) also presented several limitations and considerations that researchers must take into account. Notably, the AI lacks access to real-time information, may exhibit biases based on its training data, cannot conduct original research, and raises ethical concerns regarding academic integrity and plagiarism. Researchers must approach the use of AI assistance with caution, verifying information independently and ensuring compliance with ethical standards and institutional policies. Achieving a balance between leveraging AI assistance and upholding academic integrity emerged as a key challenge for researchers. While AI tools offer efficiency and accessibility, researchers must exercise caution to ensure that their use of AI assistance aligns with ethical standards and academic integrity principles. Collaboration between human researchers and AI tools was identified as a promising approach, enabling researchers to maximize the benefits of AI assistance while leveraging their expertise and judgment.

Artificial intelligence (AI) is the science and engineering of creating intelligent systems, that mimic human intelligence. It includes expert systems, machine learning, natural language processing, speech recognition, and machine vision. AI has revolutionized creative jobs like academic writing, computing, and arts, making it a disruptive breakthrough while improving human performance. In academic settings, the preservation of integrity stands as the bedrock upon which scholarly pursuits are built. Integrity encompasses a spectrum of values including honesty, trust, fairness, respect, and responsibility. It is incumbent upon individuals within academic communities to uphold these ethical principles diligently, thereby ensuring the foundation of scholarly integrity remains steadfast. At the heart of academic integrity lies the ethical imperative to credit original work and properly cite sources. Adherence to established guidelines is paramount in this endeavor, as it not only acknowledges the contributions of others but also upholds the principles of fairness and respect within scholarly discourse. However, the integration of AI tools in academic research introduces new dimensions to the discourse on academic integrity. While these tools offer unprecedented efficiency and accuracy in data analysis, they also present ethical challenges. For instance, the use of AI for automated content generation raises questions about the authenticity and attribution of research outputs. Ensuring transparency and accountability in the utilization of AI tools becomes crucial to upholding academic integrity in the digital age.

Nevertheless, the scope of ethical considerations extends beyond mere rule adherence. It necessitates a deeper commitment to transparency and accountability. By embracing these principles, academic integrity becomes more than a set of regulations; it becomes a cornerstone of trust among peers, facilitating the free exchange of knowledge and ideas within scholarly communities. The breach of ethical standards, such as plagiarism, cheating, or data falsification, poses a significant threat to the integrity of academic pursuits, especially in the context of AI utilization. Such breaches not only compromise individual credibility but also undermine the trust and credibility of the entire academic institution. To safeguard academic integrity amidst the utilization of AI tools, it is imperative to employ strategies that foster a culture of honesty and ethical conduct. Proper citation techniques play a crucial role in this regard, ensuring that credit is given where it is due and scholarly contributions are duly acknowledged. Additionally, effective time management skills mitigate the last-minute pressures that may tempt individuals towards dishonest behavior. Yet, beyond individual actions, building a culture of honesty requires concerted efforts to promote open communication about ethical dilemmas arising from AI integration. Providing resources for students and faculty to navigate academic challenges ethically in the context of AI utilization fosters a community where ethical considerations are actively discussed and upheld.

Ultimately, upholding academic integrity is not merely a regulatory requirement; it is a fundamental commitment to preserving the integrity of scholarly pursuits, even as technology evolves. By adhering to ethical principles, fostering a culture of honesty, and promoting transparency and accountability in the utilization of AI tools, educational institutions can cultivate an environment of trust and excellence that underpins the pursuit of knowledge and innovation in the digital era.

REFERENCES

Abd-Elaal, E. S., Gamage, S. H., & Mills, J. E. (2019, January). Artificial intelligence is a tool for cheating academic integrity. In *30th Annual Conference for the Australasian Association for Engineering Education (AAEE 2019): Educators becoming agents of change: Innovate, integrate, motivate* (pp. 397-403). Academic Press.

Aggarwal, C. C. (2018). Neural networks and deep learning. Springer, 10(978), 3.

Akgun, S., & Greenhow, C. (2022). Artificial Intelligence (AI) in Education: Addressing Societal and Ethical Challenges in K-12 Settings. In *Proceedings of the 16th International Conference of the Learning Sciences-ICLS 2022*. International Society of the Learning Sciences.

Baker, T., & Smith, L. (2019). Educ-AI-tion rebooted? Exploring the future of artificial intelligence in schools and colleges. Retrieved from Nesta Foundation website: https://media.nesta.org.uk/documents/Future_of_AI_and_education_v5_WEB.pdf

Bin-Nashwan, S. A., Sadallah, M., & Bouteraa, M. (2023). Use of ChatGPT in academia: Academic integrity hangs in the balance. *Technology in Society*, *75*, 102370. doi:10.1016/j.techsoc.2023.102370

Bueno, D. C. (2020). Preventing Plagiarism towards Nurturing Research Integrity: A Descriptive-Mapping Review. *Online Submission, 3*, 15–30.

Cantú-Ortiz, F. J., Galeano Sánchez, N., Garrido, L., Terashima-Marin, H., & Brena, R. F. (2020). An artificial intelligence educational strategy for the digital transformation. *International Journal on Interactive Design and Manufacturing, 14*(4), 1195–1209. doi:10.1007/s12008-020-00702-8

Chen, L., Chen, P., & Lin, Z. (2020). Artificial intelligence in education: A review. *IEEE Access : Practical Innovations, Open Solutions, 8*, 75264–75278. doi:10.1109/ACCESS.2020.2988510

Chen, X., Zou, D., Xie, H., Cheng, G., & Liu, C. (2022). Two decades of artificial intelligence in education. *Journal of Educational Technology & Society, 25*(1), 28–47.

Collinsworth, A., & Benjamin, D. (2022). Uses of Artificial Intelligence in Healthcare: A Structured Literature Review. *Bridging Human Intelligence and Artificial Intelligence*, 339-353.

Cotton, D. R., Cotton, P. A., & Shipway, J. R. (2023). Chatting and cheating: Ensuring academic integrity in the era of ChatGPT. *Innovations in Education and Teaching International*, 1–12.

Dergaa, I., Chamari, K., Zmijewski, P., & Saad, H. B. (2023). From human writing to artificial intelligence generated text: Examining the prospects and potential threats of ChatGPT in academic writing. *Biology of Sport, 40*(2), 615–622. doi:10.5114/biolsport.2023.125623 PMID:37077800

Dwivedi, Y. K., Hughes, L., Ismagilova, E., Aarts, G., Coombs, C., Crick, T., Duan, Y., Dwivedi, R., Edwards, J., Eirug, A., Galanos, V., Ilavarasan, P. V., Janssen, M., Jones, P., Kar, A. K., Kizgin, H., Kronemann, B., Lal, B., Lucini, B., ... Williams, M. D. (2021). Artificial Intelligence (AI): Multidisciplinary perspectives on emerging challenges, opportunities, and agenda for research, practice and policy. *International Journal of Information Management, 57*, 101994. doi:10.1016/j.ijinfomgt.2019.08.002

Francke, E., & Bennett, A. (2019, October). The potential influence of artificial intelligence on plagiarism: A higher education perspective. In *European Conference on the Impact of Artificial Intelligence and Robotics (ECIAIR 2019)* (pp. 131-140). Academic Press.

Ghotbi, N. (2023). Ethics of Artificial Intelligence in Academic Research and Education. In *Handbook of Academic Integrity* (pp. 1355–1366). Springer International Publishing. doi:10.1007/978-3-031-54144-5_143

Hasan, A. R. (2021). Artificial Intelligence (AI) in accounting & auditing: A Literature review. *Open Journal of Business and Management, 10*(1), 440–465. doi:10.4236/ojbm.2022.101026

Hsu, H. P. (2023). Can Generative Artificial Intelligence Write an Academic Journal Article? Opportunities, Challenges, and Implications. *Irish Journal of Technology Enhanced Learning, 7*(2), 158–171. doi:10.22554/ijtel.v7i2.152

IEEE Corporate Advisory Group (CAG). (2016). IEEE guide for terms and concepts in intelligent process automation. The Institute of Electrical and Electronics Engineers Standards Association. https://ieeexplore.ieee.org/iel7/8070669/8070670/08070671.pdf

Illia, L., Colleoni, E., & Zyglidopoulos, S. (2023). Ethical implications of text generation in the age of artificial intelligence. *Business Ethics, the Environment & Responsibility*, *32*(1), 201–210. doi:10.1111/beer.12479

Inozemtsev, V., Ivleva, M., & Ivlev, V. (2017, June). Artificial intelligence and the problem of computer representation of knowledge. In *2nd International Conference on Contemporary Education, Social Sciences and Humanities (ICCESSH 2017)* (pp. 1151-1157). Atlantis Press. 10.2991/iccessh-17.2017.268

Jarrah, A. M., Wardat, Y., & Fidalgo, P. (2023). Using ChatGPT in academic writing is (not) a form of plagiarism: What does the literature say. *Online Journal of Communication and Media Technologies*, *13*(4), e202346. doi:10.30935/ojcmt/13572

Jeyaraman, M., Ramasubramanian, S., Balaji, S., Jeyaraman, N., Nallakumarasamy, A., & Sharma, S. (2023). ChatGPT in action: Harnessing artificial intelligence potential and addressing ethical challenges in medicine, education, and scientific research. *World Journal of Methodology*, *13*(4), 170–178. doi:10.5662/wjm.v13.i4.170 PMID:37771867

Kamila, M. K., & Jasrotia, S. S. (2023). Ethical issues in the development of artificial intelligence: recognizing the risks. *International Journal of Ethics and Systems*.

Khlaif, Z. N., Mousa, A., Hattab, M. K., Itmazi, J., Hassan, A. A., Sanmugam, M., & Ayyoub, A. (2023). The Potential and Concerns of Using AI in Scientific Research: ChatGPT Performance Evaluation. *JMIR Medical Education*, *9*, e47049. doi:10.2196/47049 PMID:37707884

Liu, H., Azam, M., Bin Naeem, S., & Faiola, A. (2023). An overview of the capabilities of ChatGPT for medical writing and its implications for academic integrity. *Health Information and Libraries Journal*, *40*(4), 440–446. doi:10.1111/hir.12509 PMID:37806782

Miao, F., Holmes, W., Huang, R., & Zhang, H. (2021). *AI and education: A guidance for policymakers*. UNESCO Publishing.

Michel-Villarreal, R., Vilalta-Perdomo, E., Salinas-Navarro, D. E., Thierry-Aguilera, R., & Gerardou, F. S. (2023). Challenges and opportunities of Generative AI for higher education as explained by ChatGPT. *Education Sciences*, *13*(9), 856. doi:10.3390/educsci13090856

Mijwil, M. M., Hiran, K. K., Doshi, R., Dadhich, M., Al-Mistarehi, A. H., & Bala, I. (2023). ChatGPT and the future of academic integrity in the artificial intelligence era: A new frontier. *Al-Salam Journal for Engineering and Technology*, *2*(2), 116–127. doi:10.55145/ajest.2023.02.02.015

Mohammadkarimi, E. (2023). Teachers' reflections on academic dishonesty in EFL students' writings in the era of artificial intelligence. *Journal of Applied Learning and Teaching*, *6*(2).

Moor, J. (2006). The Dartmouth College artificial intelligence conference: The next fifty years. *AI Magazine*, *27*(4), 87–87.

Morrison, F. M. M., Rezaei, N., Arero, A. G., Graklanov, V., Iritsyan, S., Ivanovska, M., Makuku, R., Marquez, L. P., Minakova, K., Mmema, L. P., Rzymski, P., & Zavolodko, G. (2023). Maintaining scientific integrity and high research standards against the backdrop of rising artificial intelligence use across fields. *Journal of Medical Artificial Intelligence*, *6*, 6. doi:10.21037/jmai-23-63

Moya, B., Eaton, S. E., Pethrick, H., Hayden, K. A., Brennan, R., Wiens, J., ... Lesage, J. (2023). Academic integrity and artificial intelligence in higher education contexts: A rapid scoping review protocol. *Canadian Perspectives on Academic Integrity*, *5*(2), 59–75.

Naqvi, Z. (2020). Artificial intelligence, copyright, and copyright infringement. *Marq. Intell. Prop. L. Rev.*, *24*, 15.

Natale, S., & Ballatore, A. (2020). Imagining the thinking machine: Technological myths and the rise of artificial intelligence. *Convergence (London)*, *26*(1), 3–18. doi:10.1177/1354856517715164

Odrakiewicz, P., Orlykovskyi, M., & Gaylord, M. (2022). Integrity, Sustainability, And Intellectual Capital Challenges in Management Education in The Era of Artificial Intelligence. *Mest Journal, 10*(1).

Oravec, J. A. (2023). Artificial Intelligence Implications for Academic Cheating: Expanding the Dimensions of Responsible Human-AI Collaboration with ChatGPT. *Journal of Interactive Learning Research*, *34*(2), 213–237.

Perkins, M. (2023). Academic Integrity considerations of AI Large Language Models in the post-pandemic era: ChatGPT and beyond. *Journal of University Teaching & Learning Practice, 20*(2), 07.

Pietikäinen, M., & Silven, O. (2022). Challenges of Artificial Intelligence—From Machine Learning and Computer Vision to Emotional Intelligence. *arXiv preprint arXiv:2201.01466.*

Rane, N. L., Choudhary, S. P., Tawde, A., & Rane, J. (2023). ChatGPT is not capable of serving as an author: Ethical concerns and challenges of large language models in education. *International Research Journal of Modernization in Engineering Technology and Science*, *5*(10), 851–874.

Ray, P. P. (2023). ChatGPT: A comprehensive review on background, applications, key challenges, bias, ethics, limitations and future scope. *Internet of Things and Cyber-Physical Systems.*

Remian, D. (2019). Augmenting education: ethical considerations for incorporating artificial intelligence in education. Academic Press.

Rosyanafi, R. J., Lestari, G. D., Susilo, H., Nusantara, W., & Nuraini, F. (2023). The dark side of innovation: Understanding research misconduct with chat gpt in nonformal education studies at universitas negeri surabaya. *Jurnal Review Pendidikan Dasar: Jurnal Kajian Pendidikan dan Hasil Penelitian,* *9*(3), 220-228.

Singh, H., & Singh, A. (2023). ChatGPT: Systematic review, applications, and agenda for multidisciplinary research. *Journal of Chinese Economic and Business Studies*, *21*(2), 193–212. doi:10.1080/14765284.2023.2210482

Soubhari, T., Nanda, S. S., Lone, T. A., & Beegam, P. S. (2023). Digital hacks, creativity shacks, and academic menace: The ai effect. In *Sustainable Development Goal Advancement Through Digital Innovation in the Service Sector* (pp. 208–232). IGI Global. doi:10.4018/979-8-3693-0650-5.ch014

Susilawati, E., Lubis, H., Kesuma, S., Pratama, K., & Khaira, I. (2022). The Mediating Role of Moral Self-Regulations between Automated Essay Scoring Adoption, Students' Character and Academic Integrity among Indonesian Higher Education Sector. *Eurasian Journal of Educational Research*, *102*(102), 54–71.

Sutherland-Smith, W. (2008). *Plagiarism, the Internet, and student learning: Improving academic integrity*. Routledge. doi:10.4324/9780203928370

Swisher, K. (2022). The Right to (Human) Counsel: Real Responsibility for Artificial Intelligence. *South Carolina Law Review*, *74*, 823.

Yao, X., Zhou, J., Zhang, J., & Boër, C. R. (2017, September). From intelligent manufacturing to smart manufacturing for industry 4.0 driven by next generation artificial intelligence and further on. In *2017 5th international conference on enterprise systems (ES)* (pp. 311-318). IEEE.

Yeo, M. A. (2023). Academic integrity in the age of Artificial Intelligence (AI) authoring apps. *TESOL Journal*, *14*(3), 716. doi:10.1002/tesj.716

Chapter 14
AI in Research:
Challenges and Future Directions

Shalini Srivastava
Global Banking School, UK

Ankita Bajpai
SRM University, India

Olabode Gbobaniyi
https://orcid.org/0000-0002-0722-0335
Global Banking School, UK

ABSTRACT

The three-level model of learning provides a useful entry point for understanding artificial intelligence and its potential impact on human activities. When AI entered social practices at the level of operations, it augmented and complemented activities, thus increasing the efficiency and effectiveness of the way things were done. Likewise, at the level of acts, AI has replaced, substituted, and automated acts that were previously done by humans. Thus, the integration of AI into the realm of research has ushered in a transformative era of data-driven discovery and innovation. AI in research not only spans diverse fields, from enhancing data analysis to aiding decision-making processes, but more importantly, it has become a dynamic field with significant potential and challenges. The purpose of this chapter is to explore its challenges and future directions.

1. INTRODUCTION

In the ever-evolving landscape of research, Artificial Intelligence (AI) has emerged as a potent and disruptive force, reshaping the methodologies and outcomes across diverse fields (Van Roy, et al., 2021). The rapid advancements in AI technologies have had a profound impact on research in all areas of human society including the economy, politics, science, and education (Flasiński, 2016). Furthermore, with the potential to automate many tasks that currently require human intervention, AI has attracted considerable

DOI: 10.4018/979-8-3693-1798-3.ch014

interest in research from a variety of fields. However, harnessing this technology effectively, ethically, and equitably remains a challenge (Zlateva, et al., 2024). With the rapid integration of AI into various aspects of research, its infiltration into mainstream education seems imminent (Topol, 2019; Civaner, et al., 2022). This intersection has sparked intense discussions and conjectures about the future of AI in research and education, revolving around its potential uses and limitations. As a result, the integration of such a transformative technology into existing educational practices demands an informed, considerate approach. It necessitates not only an understanding of the capabilities and limitations of AI but also a forward-thinking blueprint for researchers and educators (Savage, 2022). This chapter aims to offer a comprehensive overview of the potential opportunities and challenges that AI presents for research and general education.

The current excitement about AI in research has continued to lead to a technology push, where AI is viewed as a solution to a wide variety of problems. It is probably fair to say that the potential and challenges of AI in research are still not adequately understood. AI can be understood as a general-purpose technology, and it can be applied in research in many ways, such as:

1. **Data Processing and Analysis:** AI's ability to learn, process, and analyse data quickly and efficiently has been a game-changer for researchers. It not only allows for gained insights into solving many distinct problems ranging from classification and regression to clustering but also the identification of patterns, trends, and correlations that might be challenging for humans to discern in vast amounts of data (Adadi & Berrada, 2018). Additionally, AI's unparalleled computational capability to extract information from high-dimensional data such as unstructured data, has been identified to help unlock the value of data, free up high-value work, and enhance predictive capabilities for decision-making (Eggers, et al., 2017).
2. **Automation of Repetitive Tasks**: AI can automate mundane and repetitive tasks, freeing up researchers' time to focus on more complex and creative aspects of their work. This includes tasks like data cleaning, literature reviews, and even some elements of experimental design. For instance, in healthcare-related research, AI's use of its conventional machine learning (ML) models is being used for analysing structured information while its conventional natural language processing (NLP) approaches are being used to analyse unstructured information in electronic health records of patients (Wang & Preininger, 2019).
3. **Enhanced Decision Making:** Machine learning algorithms can aid researchers in making informed decisions by providing insights based on data analysis. This is particularly beneficial in fields where data are abundant, such as genomics or climate science (McClure, et al., 2020).
4. **Scientific Discovery:** AI can contribute to scientific discovery by identifying new patterns or relationships in data that might be overlooked by traditional methods. It can help generate hypotheses and guide researchers towards promising areas of investigation (McClure, et al., 2020).
5. **Predictive Modeling:** AI models can be employed to create predictive models in various scientific domains. This is particularly valuable for fields like medicine, where predicting disease outcomes or drug responses can significantly impact patient care and treatment strategies. For instance, after the outbreak of the COVID-19 pandemic, AI's algorithmic system was applied in Qatar to predict the impact of the lockdown policy on COVID-19 cases assisting in the formulation of a social restriction policy (Wynants, et al., 2020). Likewise, AI's ML predictions on social service demands have been developed and used to optimize the allocation of limited social resources in many countries such as the US, Sweden, Norway, and Denmark. For instance, AI's ML model of

homeless family shelter entry and length of stay was developed at New York University to study the likelihood of re-entry and the probability of a homeless family becoming a long-term stayer. The result of this model helps shelters in the US to understand the demand for the number of beds at any given time, so they can plan more efficient resource allocation based on predicted demand (Hong et al.,2018).

6. **Collaboration and Interdisciplinary Research:** AI facilitates collaboration between researchers from different disciplines. The interdisciplinary nature of AI research encourages scientists, computer scientists, and engineers to work together, fostering a holistic approach to problem-solving (Topol, 2019).
7. **Ethical Considerations:** As with any technology, ethical considerations are crucial. Researchers must be mindful of potential biases in AI algorithms, data privacy issues, and the responsible use of AI in research. Transparent and ethical AI practices are essential for maintaining trust in the scientific community (Yu, et al., 2018).
8. **Human-AI Collaboration:** The most effective use of AI in research often involves a symbiotic relationship between AI systems and human researchers. While AI can process data and perform certain tasks at incredible speeds, human researchers bring creativity, critical thinking, and a nuanced understanding of context to the table (Hajkowicz, et al., 2022).
9. **Education and Skill Development:** The integration of AI in academia necessitates researchers acquiring new skills. Educational programs should be developed to equip researchers with the knowledge and expertise needed to effectively utilize AI tools in their work (Nolan, 2024).

1.1 The Impact of AI on Research Methodologies and Practices

1- Breaking Down Language Barriers: AI, particularly Language Models like Large Language Models (LLMs), has indeed played a pivotal role in breaking down language barriers (Hajkowicz, et al., 2022). Translation services powered by AI have facilitated communication and collaboration among researchers from diverse linguistic backgrounds. This is essential for fostering international cooperation in research endeavours (Letham, et al., 2015).

2- Enhancing Quality of Collaborative Research Papers: The language capabilities of AI extend beyond translation. LLMs can assist non-native English speakers in writing and structuring their research papers. This contributes to the overall quality of collaborative research publications by ensuring clarity and coherence in the written content (Chubb, et al., 2021).

3- Accelerated Data Analysis: AI's ability to handle large datasets efficiently is a transformative aspect of its impact. Researchers can leverage AI-powered tools and algorithms for rapid data analysis, allowing them to uncover patterns, trends, and insights in a fraction of the time it might take through traditional methods.

4- Handling Unstructured Data: Many AI models, especially those based on Machine Learning (ML), excel at processing unstructured data. This is particularly relevant in research where data may come in various formats and structures. AI can automate the handling of such unstructured data, making it more accessible and usable for analysis (Castagno & Khalifa, 2020).

5- Efficient Application to Collect Data: AI streamlines the data processing pipeline by efficiently applying sophisticated ML models to collected data. This bypasses tedious and time-consuming manual processing steps, allowing researchers to focus on the interpretation of results and the formulation of insights (Ramarao-Mine, et al., 2022).

6- **Complex Computation and Learning:** AI is capable of handling complex computations that were once impractical for researchers to perform manually. Additionally, machine learning models can learn from the data they are trained on, adapting, and improving over time. This iterative learning process is invaluable for refining models and enhancing their predictive capabilities (Hajkowicz, et al., 2022).
7- **Facilitating Future Improvement:** The iterative nature of AI learning means that as more data becomes available, models can continuously improve. This has significant implications for the advancement of research over time. The ability of AI systems to adapt and evolve based on new information contributes to the dynamic and progressive nature of scientific inquiry (McClure, et al., 2020).

2. CURRENT APPLICATIONS OF AI IN RESEARCH

Currently, AI advancements make it able to keep track of multiple uncertainties that accumulate through extensive research pipelines. One benefit of this is to make data acquisition more efficient by prioritising data gathering where there is uncertainty (Nolan, 2024). For instance, Alibaba, the world's largest e-commerce platform, as it sells more than Amazon and eBay combined uses AI as an integral part of its daily operations and is used to predict what customers might buy. Using natural language processing (NLP), the company automatically generates product descriptions for the website. Another way Alibaba uses AI is in its City Brain project to create smart cities. The project uses artificial intelligence algorithms to help reduce traffic congestion by tracking every vehicle in the city. In addition, through its cloud computing division Alibaba Cloud, Alibaba helps farmers monitor crops to improve yields and reduce costs through artificial intelligence (Jiang, et al., 2021). Additionally, like Alibaba, Amazon uses AI in its operations by sending customers messages about items they may like buying based on their previous interests. The AI algorithms of these retail giants collect a lot of data about their customer's buying habits and use such data to predict what they need even before they need it through predictive analytics.

Most recently, at a time when many brick-and-mortar stores are struggling to figure out how to stay relevant, Amazon, the US's largest online retailer is offering a new convenience store concept called Amazon Go. Unlike other companies, registration at the checkout is not necessary. The stores have artificial intelligence technology that tracks which items the customer picks, tracks, and automatically charges for those items through the Amazon Go app on your phone. Since there is no cash register, customers take their bags to fill, and cameras follow their every move to identify and bill each bagged item (Jiang, et al., 2021).

Indicated below are some points to further help our understanding of the current application of AI in research:

1- **Gathering and Collecting Data:** AI can be employed to gather data from various sources such as websites, social media platforms, academic journals, and more. This automated data collection process is particularly valuable when dealing with large volumes of information (Littman, et al., 2022).
2- **Processing and Cleaning Data:** Once the data is collected, AI algorithms can assist in processing and cleaning it. This involves organizing, structuring, and standardizing the data to make it ready for analysis. Automated data cleaning helps ensure accuracy and consistency (Nicholson & Slonim, 2022).

3- **Pattern Recognition and Analysis:** AI algorithms, especially those based on machine learning, excel at identifying patterns and trends within datasets. In content research, this could involve analysing user behaviour, identifying popular topics, or understanding audience preferences based on engagement data (Haenlein & Kaplan, 2019).
4- **Insights Generation:** The goal of AI-powered data mining and analysis is to generate meaningful insights. By processing vast amounts of data quickly, AI can uncover hidden correlations and provide valuable information that might not be immediately apparent through manual analysis (Littman, et al., 2022).
5- **Content Strategy Optimization:** The insights gained from AI-driven analysis can inform content strategy. For example, understanding which topics are trending or resonating with the audience can help content creators tailor their materials to better meet the needs and interests of their target audience (Littman, et al., 2022).
6- **Personalization and Recommendations:** AI can enhance content personalization by analysing user preferences and behaviours. This enables the delivery of more relevant and engaging content to individual users (Liu, et al., 2021). Recommendation systems, common in platforms like Netflix and Amazon, are a practical application of this concept.
7- **Efficiency and Scalability:** The automated nature of AI-powered data mining and analysis significantly improves efficiency and scalability. Tasks that would be time-consuming for humans, such as sifting through large datasets, can be accomplished rapidly, allowing researchers and content creators to focus on higher-level tasks (Haenlein & Kaplan, 2019).
8- **Challenges and Ethical Consideration:** It's important to note the challenges associated with AI-powered data analysis, such as potential biases in algorithms, the need for careful interpretation of results, and ethical considerations related to data privacy. Researchers and content creators must be vigilant in addressing these issues (Baruffaldi, et al., 2020).

3. CHALLENGES POSED BY AI IN RESEARCH: THE RISE OF ETHICAL EXPECTATIONS AND REGULATIONS

Although the application of AI has increased tremendously due to its numerous benefits and its ability to collate, analyse, and save time on large data, there are several challenges posed by the adoption of AI for research, including discrimination, fairness, bias, ethics, explainability, transparency, accountability, privacy, safety, and reliability (Hajkowicz, et al., 2022; Pi, 2021). The increasing use of AI in research has generated concerns about ethics and ensuring that AI solutions perform as intended (Schiff, et al., 2021). AI ethics is concerned with the important question of how researchers should behave to minimise ethical harm that can arise, either from unethical designs, inappropriate applications, or misuse (Yu, et al., 2018). Furthermore, AI use in research is based on its learning algorithms and its use of historical data, thus, making it only to see the world as a repetition of the past.

3.1 Discrimination, Fairness, Bias, Reliability, Privacy, and Safety

Despite AI's numerous benefits, there is ample evidence of discrimination, intentional or unintentional, against certain individuals or groups. AI systems should respect human rights, diversity, and the autonomy of individuals. For instance, Amazon created an AI recruiting tool to rank candidates and make hiring decisions, which has been identified to discriminate against based on the candidate's racial background. Additionally, for technical jobs such as software engineers, the AI tool was also found to automatically ignore women's CVs, eliminating women's chance to get such jobs (Kodiyan, 2019). The literature indicates that the root of this form of prejudice lies in the way traditional gender ideology and latent discrimination are captured in the data from which the algorithm learns (Leavy et al., 2020).

On fairness and/or bias, AI systems should be inclusive, and accessible, and should not involve or result in unfair discrimination against individuals, communities, or groups. However, AI's algorithm design does not automatically produce a biased result, but it has been identified that in cases of bias, the algorithms inherit existing bias from historical data that contains remnants of bias from human decision-making and culture (Pi, 2021). In the case of Amazon, it was identified that the significant component of data that was utilised to train the AI recruiting system was the CVs of mostly male employees. This resulted in gender inequality and bias based on the natural reflection of existing male dominance in the workplace as the AI algorithm had studied the trend and continually sustained it. Another example of the ethical implication based on bias was that of the US investigative journalism organisation ProPublica, which found COMPAS, a machine learning-based software deployed in the US to assess the probability of a criminal defendant re-offending, to be strongly biased against black Americans. The COMPAS system was more likely to incorrectly predict that black defendants would re-offend, while simultaneously, and incorrectly, predicting the opposite in the case of white defendants (ProPublica, 2016). Similarly, an Amazon self-learning tool used to judge jobseekers was found to significantly favour men, ranking them highly compared to women based on male characteristics (Dastin, 2018). Therefore, based on these real-world incidents, it can be argued that data-driven decision-making is not free from existing, real-world biases. However, researchers must be aware that if the decisions made by AI will have a large-scale and profound impact on various aspects of society and individuals, the components for data inputs must be as fair as possible. This is because if the data components are developed with awareness, the AI algorithms can inherit or even exacerbate historical inequities underlying the input data (Pi, 2021). Hence, it is essential to put algorithm design and the quality of input data under scrutiny, to prevent unfair, biased, and discriminatory algorithmic decisions. Additionally, AI systems should not only reliably operate under their intended purpose, but they must also respect and uphold privacy rights and data protection and ensure the security of data. An example of a regulation towards this was the European Union's general data protection regulation (GDPR) includes articles limiting the use of automated decision systems including requirements related to privacy, safety, explainability and contestability.

3.2 Explainability, Accountability, and Transparency

Another fundamental aspect of fairness is the provision of reasoning for the decisions made by algorithms. Researchers must ensure that transparency is of crucial importance, with participants being provided with explanations and access to information about the procedures and data they are being collected from them or how the impact of the research results will affect them (Scantamburlo, 2019). Transparency of the decision-making process towards research and the use of AI is the mechanism that will facilitate accountability as it allows the tracking of the entire procedure, as well as the detection of responsibilities when any form of failure occurs (Diakopoulos, 2016). However, due to AI's lack of simplicity and observable analyses, it is challenging for researchers and decision-makers to ensure explainability, transparency, and accountability when it comes to its results and decisions (Angelov, et al., 2021; Sanderson, et al.,

2022). An example provided by Yu, et al. (2018) indicated that teachers from a Houston school prevailed in a lawsuit with their schools over an algorithmic performance evaluation system, where those who received a positive rating won praise, and those who received a negative rating were terminated. Based on this, some teachers in the school believed that the system penalized them unfairly, however, they had no way of knowing for certain, since the firm that developed the software, the SAS Institute considered its algorithm a trade secret and refused to reveal its workings. In court, a federal judge determined that the program had violated the teachers' civil rights because they have the right to know the reason behind the decisions that affect his/her career, even if they are made by a computer. This example is a good illustration of the problems faced by using AI's ML, where users have no way of knowing the reasons the algorithm made its decisions and who to blame when the decisions are undesirable (Yu, et al., 2018). As a result, there must be a requirement for explainability and transparency of the AI's algorithms to ensure their accountability. Based on this, this chapter aligns with Pi's definition of explainability "as the ability of algorithmic systems to present an understandable post-hoc explanation in various ways such as natural language explanations, visual explanations, and explanations by example, for the causes of their decisions (2021). Once the reasoning behind the AI's decisions is revealed to users, participants, or policymakers, it is left for them to decide whether to adopt these decisions leaving them to be held accountable for the behavior and the potential impacts of AI decisions (Bieker et al., 2016). This is also because users are often unable to describe in detail how the decision comes about, or on which aspects of the data the decision was based (Adadi and Berrada, 2018).

Additionally, available knowledge indicates that AI algorithms with higher prediction accuracy, usually take the unexplainable form to understand and discover the subtle correlation between the input variables (Letham et al., 2015). This opaque nature of AI algorithms makes communication between machine learning experts, policymakers, and other domain specialists difficult (Letham et al., 2015). Improving the explainability of machine learning will provide more transparency into how decisions are reached, enabling decision-makers and citizens to track and understand the whole process of decision-making, and eventually upgrade the accountability of the algorithmic decision-making system (Pi, 2021). For instance, on 31 March 2021, it was indicated that the five main financial regulators in the US issued an information request to financial institutions to provide detailed information on their use of AI and machine learning. They indicated the information provided will be to help ensure 'compliance with applicable laws and regulations' (US Treasury, 2021). Likewise, on 21 April 2021, the European Union was indicated to propose the first legal framework on AI which includes fines of up to 6% of company revenue for non-compliance (European Commission, 2021).

4. PROMOTING AI USE IN RESEARCH

The challenges described above are interspersed with each other which further exacerbates the unreliability and undesirability of AI algorithms in certain sectors. However, the consistent advancement in AI makes it to be recognized as one of the most powerful agents of change, while its algorithmic ability to adapt, self-correct, and learn, makes it to be on the verge of surpassing the limits of human intelligence (Barrett, 2023). Additionally, scholars have pointed out that AI has grown in such a way that it is being taken up in every domain and stage of research, from hypothesis generation to experiment design, monitoring, and simulation, all the way to scientific publication and communication. As a result, it is argued that in the future, AI may optimise many research workflows end-to-end – from data collection to final statistical analysis. However, as discussed in *subsection 3.2*, the inability to interpret and explain AI algorithms is a growing concern for its usage even though not all forms of AI lack interpretability, with tools such as decision trees or reserve engineering offering some insight into AI logic (Barrett, 2023). For instance, it was discovered that an AI predictive policing algorithm platform, PredPol, with the capability to help the policing resource allocation towards future crime risk prediction, improperly linked black people to greater suspicion of having committed crimes thereby leading to more arrests (Selbst, 2017). However, due to the complexity of PredPol's algorithm, it was unclear how the PredPol's decision was made to detect its bias. As argued by Perry, et al., if police officers do not understand the prediction bases of the software, there is an increased likelihood of not accepting its predictions, thus, hampering the effectiveness of the predictive analytic tools (2013). This may explain the reason why of 70 police agencies surveyed in the US, only 70 per cent of them used predictive tools, while 22 per cent of the agencies surveyed used or relied on the decisions of the AI tool (Perry et al., 2013).

Studies have continued to describe why interpretation and explanation pose conceptual challenges, even if AI could explain its logic. As research and science continue to evolve, some topics may become so intellectually demanding that no one can understand them except for a few specialists (i.e., the mathematics of string theory) (Chubb, et al., 2022; Nolan, 2024). However, if AI algorithms were to discover such knowledge, it is unclear what their explanation for human scientists would look like. Similarly, translating into human-digestible form what an AI algorithm has learnt in a hugely dimensional data space may yield hard-to-understand lines of reasoning, even if individual parts of the argument are clear. In some cases, explanations need to be illustrated by images. However, Barrett points out that while image recognition applications have progressed, it is challenging for AI algorithms to construct images to assist with explanation (2023). Therefore, to promote the use of AI in taking a significant role in the research and decision-making processes, there is a need for researchers and developers to address some of the fundamental issues discussed above. Presented and discussed below are some directions that future research can explore to ensure an explainable, transparent, accountable, and prevalent use of AI in research.

4.1 User-Centered Explainable AI

Although there continue to be several advances in the use of AI in research in many fields, its full potential is yet to be realized. This according to the literature is due to its opaqueness and required and desired accountability in some fields of research and decision-making processes (Wanner, et al., 2020). In addressing the issues of AI's opacity, explainable artificial intelligence (XAI) was initiated and promoted to "enable human users to understand, appropriately trust, and effectively manage the emerging generation of artificially intelligent partners" (Gunning, 2017). The literature indicates that XAI is ultimately a human-computer interaction (HCI) interface between the researcher/user and the AI that shifts towards a more interpretable understanding of AI analytics and processes. HCI allows for ease in interpreting the reasons behind AI predictions and can transform a non-transparent model or prediction into one that is transparent and trustworthy (Angelov, et al., 2021; Ribeiro, 2016). To ensure and promote AI's interpretability, scholars have proposed two forms of interpretability; *global interpretability* i.e., "the understanding of the whole analytic and process of the trained model" and *local interpretability* i.e., the understanding of the effects of a trained model on a particular input and its corresponding outcome (Friedler, et al. 2019). As a result, an applicable way to classify AI interpretability is to divide its users based on their level of knowledge in AI analytics and processes in terms of technical and non-technical users (Wanner et al., 2020). However, research has shown that most HCI of XAI focuses primarily on providing "technical" interpretations to technical users, to enable them to debug or improve the algorithm's performance, leaving out interpretations to non-technical AI end users (Pi, 2021).

The review of recent literature suggests an increasing awareness of interpretations and explanations of AI predictions needed by different users (Angelov, et al., 2021). This is based on the notion that while technical users or analysts may find themselves interested in the internal workings of the prediction estimators, non-technical users or decision-makers will be more interested in the key details or data points that led to the prediction (Ehsan, et al., 2021; Liao, 2020; Pi, 2021). Therefore, user-centered XAI should be used to provide a certain level of transparency for all users to reduce the notion of bias and discriminatory predictions.

4.2 Algorithmic Impact Assessment (AIA)

Knowledge in the field of AI indicates that a poorly designed and unregulated algorithm has potential adverse and far-reaching effects on users. As a result, research bodies and governmental authorities across the world have increasingly advocated practical frameworks to assess AI's algorithmic systems (Moss, et al., 2020; Ribera & Lapedriza, 2019). To anticipate and mitigate the negative consequences of algorithmic decision-making, the AIA was proposed towards four goals, including, providing the public with information about the systems that decide their fate, granting meaningful access for external researchers to review and audit the systems, developing the expertise of public agencies to assess the performance and impact of automated decision systems, and strengthening due process by offering the public the opportunity to engage with the AIA process before, during, and after the assessment (Ribera & Lapedriza, 2019).

The AIA requires a self-assessment of algorithmic systems within public agencies to assess potential impacts on fairness, justice, bias, and other harms and to make mitigation plans (Ribera & Lapedriza, 2019). To complement the insufficient internal self-assessment, AIA also emphasizes the establishment of regularly conducted external researcher review processes (Moss, et al., 2020). Furthermore, AIA emphasizes the combined participation of public authorities, domain experts, and the public because algorithmic decision-making processes can be extremely intricate, and challenges such as bias and systematic error cannot be easily identified by singular entities (Pi, 2021). As a result, continuous external expert analyses are recommended at both group and interdisciplinary levels (Moss, et al., 2020). The AIA framework also recommends a public disclosure of the purpose, scope, intended use, and self-assessment process of the algorithmic system, these must be done in addition to ensuring adherence to the associated policies at the start of the assessment process, to collect early external feedback and where necessary adjust the assessment for the most pertinent public concerns (Koene, et al., 2019). For instance, The Canadian Government requires a questionnaire-style impact analysis to ensure that its agencies use AI's ML algorithms compatible with their core administrative law principles such as transparency, accountability, legality, and procedural fairness (Kuziemski, 2020). Likewise, the US Congress proposed "The Algorithmic Accountability Act of 2019" which requires companies to perform impact assessments of automated decision systems and evaluate their impact on accuracy, fairness, bias, discrimination, privacy, and security (MacCarthy, 2019).

4.3 Transformation Towards AI-Powered Culture

The COVID-19 pandemic has shown the critical role that AI plays in facilitating rapid policy decisions based on real-time data analytics and prediction (Ramarao-Milne, et al., 2022). However, not all sectors of global economies are openly receptive to embracing AI, with some indicating the lack of capacity as a reason for their hesitance (OECD, 2021). While multiple private and public sector organizations have reeled up efforts to embrace and prioritize the use of AI through different approaches including changes to organizational culture, implementation of new regulatory frameworks, and the development of new individual capacities, it has been argued that the easiest start for the transformation and adoption towards an AI-powered culture is for governments through education *"using the three tiers of education"* or social development and infrastructure sectors to establish training projects and opportunities, that can either be financed wholly or partly through them or in collaboration with private sector organizations (Fountaine, 2019). Developing such training projects can improve the public perception, knowledge, skills, and attitudes towards AI.

5. FUTURE DEVELOPMENT PATHWAYS

Here, we review the developmental pathways for AI in research.

1. Researchers and research organisations seeking to uplift AI capability must make decisions about hardware, software, and computational infrastructure upgrades, including access to cloud computing services. Available knowledge indicates that tools have improved substantially over recent years, and they are likely in that trajectory in the future (Davies, et al., 2021). However, there are many unknowns about quantum computing; it could potentially lead to a step change and paradigm shift in AI resulting in substantially elevated capability. Quantum computing services are already available to AI developers and researchers may need to factor this into their longer-term AI capability development strategies (Kusters, et al., 2020).
2. For researchers and research organizations to achieve competitive differentiation and enhanced problem-solving abilities with AI will be determined by the quality of their datasets. Vast volumes of publicly available data will have to remain for AI development. For instance, the CSIRO team used machine learning to identify COVID-19 virus mutations with a likely impact on disease severity (Ramarao-Milne, et al., 2022). This was indicated to be done on only 0.3% of the available viral data points due to a lack of patient information for the rest (Bauer, et al., 2021). This demonstrates the rate-changing potential for high-quality datasets with the need for increased investments in high-quality data that will be fit-for-purpose, provenance assured, validated, up-to-date, and ethically obtained. This, further means that researchers and research organisations seeking to upgrade AI capability will need to become adept at acquiring, storing, protecting, and recording metadata (Kiron, 2017).
3. Research organizations will need strategies for talent acquisition and retention, given the strong demand for AI skills. These organizations will need to offer competitive remuneration packages to attract and retain skilled AI workers. The feasibility of talent acquisition and retention will need consideration by research organisations while making decisions about whether to grow certain types of AI capabilities (Hajkowicz, et al., 2016) Additionally, there is the likelihood of increased

awareness and expansion of the number of education and training courses available to researchers or scientists seeking to upgrade their AI capabilities (Toney & Flagg, 2020).

4. The ability to capture the value of human-AI collaboration rests upon buy-in from the research and scientific community and several factors influence this. Hajkowicz, et al. indicated that trust is one of them, particularly in non-data science domains, which relates to AI literacy (2022). Research has shown that while professionals with a background in computer science and programming are more supportive of the development of AI (Zhang & Dafoe, 2019), there are still significant limitations around the level of AI awareness and understanding across many research and science sectors (Gillespie, et al., 2021). As a result, examining and improving the AI literacy of the population will help science and research organisations build an understanding and acceptance of AI (Gillespie, et al., 2021; Zhang & Dafoe, 2019). To maximise the complementary strengths of human scientists and AI systems, AI applications need to be designed and evaluated with the human scientist workflow in mind.
5. In their literature, Hajkowicz, et al. indicated that many research organizations acknowledge the lack of gender and ethnic/cultural diversity in AI and STEM workforces as a challenge they are working to address (2022). Improving workforce diversity will be an important developmental pathway for AI capability uplift in research and within research organisations.
6. The implication arising from an AI development pathway regarding its ethics performance bar is likely to be higher and more tightly regulated in the future. With increased societal awareness about issues and expectations, many current voluntary principles and guidelines are likely to become laws in the future (Hajkowicz, et al., 2016; Kusters, et al., 2020).

6. CONCLUSION

The uptake of AI technologies within science and research domains holds the promise of productivity improvement. This is much needed as the global science sector is amid an ongoing productivity slump where more research effort is being invested to achieve the same (or fewer) outcomes. The science productivity slump is causing a broader productivity slump across most industries and economies. As a general-purpose technology, AI provides a promising stimulus to improve productivity in all domains of science and research and all industries in general. Better still, is the available evidence from research case studies that AI is improving the efficiency and effectiveness of science that enables discoveries to happen faster, safer, and at minimal cost. Accelerating the productivity of research could be the most economically and socially valuable of all the uses of artificial intelligence (AI). While AI is penetrating all domains and stages of science, its full potential is said to be far from realised. Therefore, it is imperative that research organizations, policymakers, and actors across research systems can do much more to accelerate, upgrade, and deepen the uptake of AI in science, magnifying its positive contributions to research. This will not only require education, training, and upgrades of both hardware and software technological components but also ensure the development and application of AI is ethically sound and responds appropriately to societal expectations, regulations, and legislation.

Though the future remains of positive trajectory for AI, the notion that AI will be doing research by itself seems unlikely. This is because scientific research not only requires creativity and judgement, it also requires logic and communication skills which lie beyond the reach of AI capabilities in the current and foreseeable future. This, however, emphasizes the importance of harmonious collaboration between human scientists and powerful AI systems to achieve better and more advanced outcomes.

The authors therefore conclude that the strategic integration of AI into academic research has the potential to reshape the scientific landscape. Researchers who embrace this technology with a thoughtful approach, understanding its capabilities and limitations, stand to benefit significantly in terms of efficiency, discovery, and the advancement of knowledge. the multidisciplinary impact of AI in research extends beyond just data analysis. It encompasses language support, collaboration enhancement, and the efficient handling of diverse data types, ultimately contributing to the acceleration of scientific discovery and the improvement of research quality on a global scale. We can say that AI-powered data mining and analysis play a crucial role in content research by automating the process of gathering, processing, and extracting valuable insights from large datasets. This, in turn, empowers content creators and strategists to make informed decisions and optimize their approach based on data-driven findings.

REFERENCES

Adadi, A., & Berrada, M. (2018). Peeking inside the black box: A survey on explainable artificial intelligence (XAI). *IEEE Access : Practical Innovations, Open Solutions*, *6*, 52138–52160. doi:10.1109/ACCESS.2018.2870052

Angelov, P. P., Soares, E. A., Jiang, R., Arnold, N. I., & Atkinson, P. M. (2021). Explainable artificial intelligence: An analytical review. *Wiley Interdisciplinary Reviews. Data Mining and Knowledge Discovery*, *11*(5), e1424. doi:10.1002/widm.1424

Barrett, G. (2023). Artificial intelligence for science in Africa. Academic Press.

Baruffaldi, S., van Beuzekom, B., Dernis, H., Harhoff, D., Rao, N., Rosenfeld, D., & Squicciarini, M. (2020). Identifying and measuring developments in artificial intelligence: Making the impossible possible. Academic Press.

Bauer, D. C., Metke-Jimenez, A., Maurer-Stroh, S., Tiruvayipati, S., Wilson, L. O., Jain, Y., Perrin, A., Ebrill, K., Hansen, D. P., & Vasan, S. S. (2021). Interoperable medical data: The missing link for understanding COVID-19. *Transboundary and Emerging Diseases*, *68*(4), 1753–1760. doi:10.1111/tbed.13892 PMID:33095970

Bieker, F., Friedewald, M., Hansen, M., Obersteller, H., & Rost, M. (2016). A process for data protection impact assessment under the European general data protection regulation. *Privacy Technologies and Policy: 4th Annual Privacy Forum, APF 2016, Frankfurt/Main, Germany, September 7-8, 2016 Proceedings*, *4*, 21–37.

Castagno, S., & Khalifa, M. (2020). Perceptions of artificial intelligence among healthcare staff: A qualitative survey study. *Frontiers in Artificial Intelligence*, *3*, 578983. doi:10.3389/frai.2020.578983 PMID:33733219

Chubb, J., Cowling, P., & Reed, D. (2022). Speeding up to keep up: Exploring the use of AI in the research process. *AI & Society*, *37*(4), 1439–1457. doi:10.1007/s00146-021-01259-0 PMID:34667374

Civaner, M. M., Uncu, Y., Bulut, F., Chalil, E. G., & Tatli, A. (2022). Artificial intelligence in medical education: A cross-sectional needs assessment. *BMC Medical Education*, *22*(1), 772. doi:10.1186/s12909-022-03852-3 PMID:36352431

Davies, A., Veličković, P., Buesing, L., Blackwell, S., Zheng, D., Tomašev, N., Tanburn, R., Battaglia, P., Blundell, C., Juhász, A., Lackenby, M., Williamson, G., Hassabis, D., & Kohli, P. (2021). Advancing mathematics by guiding human intuition with AI. *Nature*, *600*(7887), 70–74. doi:10.1038/s41586-021-04086-x PMID:34853458

Diakopoulos, N. (2016). Accountability in algorithmic decision making. *Communications of the ACM*, *59*(2), 56–62. doi:10.1145/2844110

Eggers, W. D., Schatsky, D., & Viechnicki, P. (2017). AI-augmented government. Using cognitive technologies to redesign public sector work. *Deloitte Center for Government Insights*, *1*, 24.

Ehsan, U., Liao, Q. V., Muller, M., Riedl, M. O., & Weisz, J. D. (2021, May). Expanding explainability: Towards social transparency in AI systems. In *Proceedings of the 2021 CHI conference on human factors in computing systems* (pp. 1-19). 10.1145/3411764.3445188

European Commission. (2021). Proposal for a Regulation laying down harmonised rules on artificial intelligence. European Commission.

Flasiński, M. (2016). *Introduction to artificial intelligence*. Springer. doi:10.1007/978-3-319-40022-8

Fountaine, T., McCarthy, B., & Saleh, T. (2019). Building the AI-powered organization. *Harvard Business Review*, *97*(4), 62–73.

Friedler, S. A., Scheidegger, C., Venkatasubramanian, S., Choudhary, S., Hamilton, E. P., & Roth, D. (2019, January). A comparative study of fairness-enhancing interventions in machine learning. In *Proceedings of the conference on fairness, accountability, and transparency* (pp. 329-338). 10.1145/3287560.3287589

Gunning, D., Stefik, M., Choi, J., Miller, T., Stumpf, S., & Yang, G. Z. (2019). XAI—Explainable artificial intelligence. *Science Robotics*, *4*(37), eaay7120. doi:10.1126/scirobotics.aay7120 PMID:33137719

Haenlein, M., & Kaplan, A. (2019). A brief history of artificial intelligence: On the past, present, and future of artificial intelligence. *California Management Review*, *61*(4), 5–14. doi:10.1177/0008125619864925

Hajkowicz, S., Naughtin, C., Sanderson, C., Schleiger, E., Karimi, S., Bratanova, A., & Bednarz, T. (2022). Artificial intelligence for science–Adoption trends and future development pathways. Academic Press.

Hajkowicz, S., Reeson, A., Rudd, L., Bratanova, A., Hodgers, L., Mason, C., & Boughen, N. (2016). Tomorrow's digitally enabled workforce: Megatrends and scenarios for jobs and employment in Australia over the coming twenty years. Academic Press.

Hong, B., Malik, A., Lundquist, J., Bellach, I., & Kontokosta, C. E. (2018). Applications of machine learning methods to predict readmission and length-of-stay for homeless families: The case of win shelters in New York City. *Journal of Technology in Human Services*, *36*(1), 89–104. doi:10.1080/15228835.2017.1418703

Jiang, J. A., Wade, K., Fiesler, C., & Brubaker, J. R. (2021). Supporting serendipity: Opportunities and challenges for Human-AI Collaboration in qualitative analysis. *Proceedings of the ACM on Human-Computer Interaction, 5*(CSCW1), 1-23. 10.1145/3449168

Kiron, D. (2017). Lessons from becoming a data-driven organization. *MIT Sloan Management Review, 58*(2).

Kodiyan, A. A. (2019). An overview of ethical issues in using AI systems in hiring with a case study of Amazon's AI-based hiring tool. *Researchgate Preprint*, 1-19.

Koene, A., Clifton, C., Hatada, Y., Webb, H., & Richardson, R. (2019). A governance framework for algorithmic accountability and transparency. Academic Press.

Kusters, R., Misevic, D., Berry, H., Cully, A., Le Cunff, Y., Dandoy, L., Díaz-Rodríguez, N., Ficher, M., Grizou, J., Othmani, A., Palpanas, T., Komorowski, M., Loiseau, P., Moulin Frier, C., Nanini, S., Quercia, D., Sebag, M., Soulié Fogelman, F., Taleb, S., ... Wehbi, F. (2020). Interdisciplinary research in artificial intelligence: Challenges and opportunities. *Frontiers in Big Data, 3*, 577974. doi:10.3389/fdata.2020.577974 PMID:33693418

Kuziemski, M., & Misuraca, G. (2020). AI governance in the public sector: Three tales from the frontiers of automated decision-making in democratic settings. *Telecommunications Policy, 44*(6), 101976. doi:10.1016/j.telpol.2020.101976 PMID:32313360

Leavy, S., Meaney, G., Wade, K., & Greene, D. (2020). Mitigating gender bias in machine learning data sets. *Bias and Social Aspects in Search and Recommendation: First International Workshop, BIAS 2020, Lisbon, Portugal, April 14 Proceedings, 1*, 12–26.

Letham, B., Rudin, C., McCormick, T. H., & Madigan, D. (2015). Interpretable classifiers using rules and Bayesian analysis: Building a better stroke prediction model. Academic Press.

Liao, Q. V., Gruen, D., & Miller, S. (2020, April). Questioning the AI: informing design practices for explainable AI user experiences. In *Proceedings of the 2020 CHI conference on human factors in computing systems* (pp. 1-15). 10.1145/3313831.3376590

Littman, M. L., Ajunwa, I., Berger, G., Boutilier, C., Currie, M., Doshi-Velez, F., . . . Walsh, T. (2022). Gathering strength, gathering storms: The one-hundred-year study on artificial intelligence (AI100) 2021 study panel report. *arXiv preprint arXiv:2210.15767.*

Liu, N., Shapira, P., & Yue, X. (2021). Tracking developments in artificial intelligence research: Constructing and applying a new search strategy. *Scientometrics, 126*(4), 3153–3192. doi:10.1007/s11192-021-03868-4 PMID:34720254

MacCarthyM. (2019). An examination of the Algorithmic Accountability Act of 2019. *Available at* SSRN 3615731. doi:10.2139/ssrn.3615731

McClure, E. C., Sievers, M., Brown, C. J., Buelow, C. A., Ditria, E. M., Hayes, M. A., Pearson, R. M., Tulloch, V. J. D., Unsworth, R. K. F., & Connolly, R. M. (2020). Artificial intelligence meets citizen science to supercharge ecological monitoring. *Patterns (New York, N.Y.), 1*(7), 100109. doi:10.1016/j.patter.2020.100109 PMID:33205139

Moss, E., Watkins, E. A., Metcalf, J., & Elish, M. C. (2020, April). Governing with algorithmic impact assessments: six observations. In *Watkins, Elizabeth and Moss, Emanuel and Metcalf, Jacob and Singh, Ranjit and Elish, Madeleine Clare, Governing Algorithmic Systems with Impact Assessments: Six Observations (May 14, 2021). AAAI/ACM Conference on Artificial Intelligence, Ethics, and Society (AIES).* 10.2139/ssrn.3584818

Nicholson, K., & Slonim, A. (Eds.). (2022). *Artificial intelligence: your questions answered.* Australian Strategic Policy Institute.

Nolan, A. (2024). Artificial intelligence in science: Challenges, opportunities, and the future of research. Academic Press.

OECD. (2021). Database of national AI policies. Organisation for Economic Cooperation and Development, Artificial Intelligence Policy Observatory. OECD.

Perry, W. L., McInnis, B., Price, C. C., Smith, S. C., & Hollywood, J. S. (2013). Findings for Practitioners, Developers, and Policymakers. *In Predictive Policing: The Role of Crime Forecasting in Law Enforcement Operations*, 115-38. Available at https://www.jstor.org/stable/10.7249/j.ctt4cgdcz.13

Pi, Y. (2021). Machine learning in governments: Benefits, challenges, and future directions. *JeDEM-eJournal of eDemocracy and Open Government, 13*(1), 203-219.

Ramarao-Milne, P., Jain, Y., Sng, L. M., Hosking, B., Lee, C., Bayat, A., Kuiper, M., Wilson, L. O. W., Twine, N. A., & Bauer, D. C. (2022). Data-driven platform for identifying variants of interest in the COVID-19 virus. *Computational and Structural Biotechnology Journal, 20*, 2942–2950. doi:10.1016/j.csbj.2022.06.005 PMID:35677774

Ribeiro, M. T., Singh, S., & Guestrin, C. (2016, August). " Why should I trust you?" Explaining the predictions of any classifier. In *Proceedings of the 22nd ACM SIGKDD international conference on knowledge discovery and data mining* (pp. 1135-1144). 10.1145/2939672.2939778

Ribera, M., & Lapedriza, A. (2019, March). Can we do better explanations? A proposal of user-centered explainable AI. *CEUR Workshop Proceedings.*

Sanderson, C., Douglas, D., Lu, Q., Schleiger, E., Whittle, J., Lacey, J., Newnham, G., Hajkowicz, S., Robinson, C., & Hansen, D. (2023). AI ethics principles in practice: Perspectives of designers and developers. *IEEE Transactions on Technology and Society, 4*(2), 171–187. doi:10.1109/TTS.2023.3257303

Savage, N. (2022). Breaking into the black box of artificial intelligence. Academic Press.

Scantamburlo, T., Charlesworth, A., & Cristianini, N. (2018). Machine decisions and human consequences. *arXiv preprint arXiv:1811.06747.*

Schiff, D., Borenstein, J., Biddle, J., & Laas, K. (2021). AI ethics in the public, private, and NGO sectors: A review of a global document collection. *IEEE Transactions on Technology and Society, 2*(1), 31–42. doi:10.1109/TTS.2021.3052127

Selbst, A. D. (2017). Disparate impact in big data policing. *Ga. L. Rev., 52*, 109.

Toney, A., & Flagg, M. (2020). *US Demand for AI-Related Talent. Center for Security and Emerging Technology*. CSET. doi:10.51593/20200027

Topol, E. J. (2019). High-performance medicine: The convergence of human and artificial intelligence. *Nature Medicine*, *25*(1), 44–56. doi:10.1038/s41591-018-0300-7 PMID:30617339

US Treasury. (2021). *Request for Information and Comment on Financial Institutions' Use of Artificial Intelligence, Including Machine Learning*. Department of the Treasury, United States Government.

Van Roy, V., Rossetti, F., Perset, K., & Galindo-Romero, L. (2021). *AI watch-national strategies on artificial intelligence: A European perspective* (No. JRC122684). Joint Research Centre (Seville site).

Wang, F., & Preininger, A. (2019). AI in health: state of the art, challenges, and future directions. *Yearbook of medical informatics, 28*(01), 16-26.

Wanner, J., Herm, L. V., & Janiesch, C. (2020). How much is the black box? The value of explainability in machine learning models. Academic Press.

Wynants, L., Van Calster, B., Collins, G. S., Riley, R. D., Heinze, G., Schuit, E., Albu, E., Arshi, B., Bellou, V., Bonten, M. M. J., Dahly, D. L., Damen, J. A., Debray, T. P. A., de Jong, V. M. T., De Vos, M., Dhiman, P., Ensor, J., Gao, S., Haller, M. C., ... van Smeden, M. (2020). Prediction models for diagnosis and prognosis of COVID-19: Systematic review and critical appraisal. *BMJ (Clinical Research Ed.)*, 369. doi:10.1136/bmj.m1328 PMID:32265220

Yu, H., Shen, Z., Miao, C., Leung, C., Lesser, V. R., & Yang, Q. (2018). Building ethics into artificial intelligence. *arXiv preprint arXiv:1812.02953*. doi:10.24963/ijcai.2018/779

ZhangB.DafoeA. (2019). Artificial intelligence: American attitudes and trends. *Available at* SSRN 3312874.

Zlateva, P., Steshina, L., Petukhov, I., & Velev, D. (2024). A Conceptual Framework for Solving Ethical Issues in Generative Artificial Intelligence. In Electronics, Communications and Networks (pp. 110-119). IOS Press. doi:10.3233/FAIA231182

Chapter 15
Future Trends in AI and Academic Research Writing

Rupayan Roy
National Institute of Fashion Technology, India

R. Ashmika
https://orcid.org/0009-0006-9802-5290
National Institute of Fashion Technology, India

Apromita Chakraborty
National Institute of Fashion Technology, India

Iqra Sharafat
National Institute of Fashion Technology, India

ABSTRACT

This comprehensive exploration of the intersection between artificial intelligence (AI) and academic research writing unveils a transformative landscape that promises to redefine scholarly communication. AI-driven tools and applications are revolutionizing various stages of the research writing process, from content generation and literature review to peer review and publication. The chapter provides an overview of key takeaways, challenges, and possibilities in the realm of AI-enhanced research writing.

1 INTRODUCTION

The realm of academic research and scholarly writing has undergone a profound transformation in recent years, thanks to the integration of Artificial Intelligence (AI) technologies. From aiding researchers in drafting error-free manuscripts to revolutionizing the way literature is reviewed and synthesized, AI has become an invaluable ally in the academic world (*Savage & Vogel, 2013*). In this chapter, we will embark on a journey through the rapidly evolving landscape of AI in academic research writing. We will explore the current state of AI tools and their applications, as well as the ongoing and far-reaching impact of AI on schoVoglarly communication. AI's role as a writing assistant has significantly evolved.

DOI: 10.4018/979-8-3693-1798-3.ch015

Figure 1. Reference management (Reference Management, 2023)

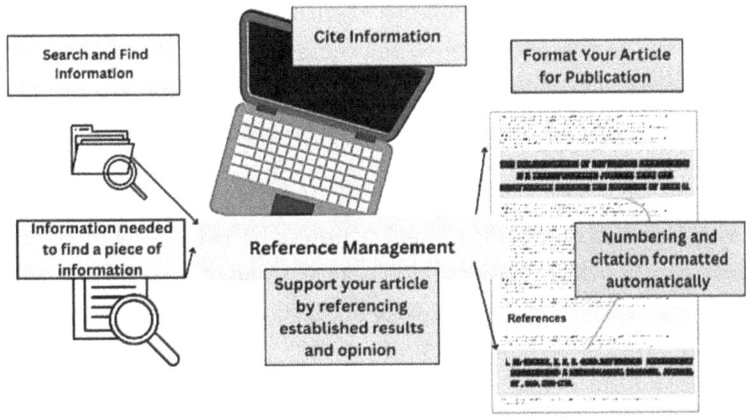

Gone are the days when it was primarily used for spell-checking and basic grammar correction *(Reguig & Mouffok, 2023)*. Modern AI writing assistants, such as Grammarly, ProWritingAid, and others, have raised the bar. They now offer advanced features like style analysis, tone detection, and even suggestions for clarity and conciseness. These tools have become indispensable companions for academics seeking to polish their writing and ensure that their ideas are communicated with precision *(Alharbi, 2023)*.

One of the most exciting developments in AI's role in academic research writing is its ability to generate content. AI algorithms, particularly those based on deep learning and natural language processing, have made remarkable strides in generating human-like text. Researchers can now leverage AI to assist in drafting research papers, abstracts, and even summaries. These tools not only save time but also offer valuable insights into structuring and presenting information effectively *(Lund et al., 2023)*. Maintaining proper citation and reference formats is a meticulous and time-consuming task in academic writing. AI tools have stepped in to simplify this process as shown in Figure 1. By recognizing patterns and contextual cues, AI can automatically format citations and references according to various citation styles, such as APA, MLA, or Chicago *(Sikarskie, 2020)*. This not only reduces the risk of citation errors but also allows researchers to focus more on the substance of their work.

Collaboration among researchers, often spanning geographical boundaries, is a hallmark of modern academic research. AI is making this collaboration more efficient and productive. Collaboration platforms and virtual research assistants powered by AI facilitate seamless communication, document sharing, and real-time collaboration on research projects. These tools enable researchers to work together more effectively, transcending time and space constraints *(Khang et al., 2023)*. AI has brought about a significant transformation in the way scholars conduct literature reviews. Traditionally, this process involved manual searching, reading, and synthesizing vast volumes of academic literature. AI-driven tools now assist researchers in sifting through extensive databases, identifying relevant papers, and even summarizing key findings *(Ahmad et al., 2023)*. This acceleration of the literature review process not only saves time but also enhances the comprehensiveness and accuracy of reviews. Peer review is the cornerstone of academic publishing, ensuring the quality and credibility of scholarly work. AI is augmenting the peer review process by assisting reviewers in identifying potential issues, such as plagiarism, statistical errors, or ethical concerns. AI-driven peer review systems analyze manuscripts and provide reviewers with insights, helping them make more informed judgments. Moreover, AI can be used to identify potential biases in reviews, contributing to fairer evaluations *(Yigitcanlar et al., 2020).*

Scholarly publishing platforms are evolving to incorporate AI-driven features that benefit both authors and readers. These platforms can suggest suitable journals for manuscript submission based on content and target audience. They can also provide dynamic, interactive publications that include multimedia elements and real-time updates. AI is ushering in a new era of scholarly communication, making research findings more accessible and engaging *(Pavlik, 2023).* In an increasingly globalized academic landscape, language barriers can hinder the dissemination of knowledge. AI-powered language translation tools bridge these gaps, allowing researchers to access and share research in multiple languages. This not only enhances the reach of academic work but also promotes cross-cultural collaboration and understanding *(Liao et al., 2023).*

AI has already made a significant impact on academic research writing, enhancing efficiency, improving the quality of output, and transforming scholarly communication. However, this is just the beginning. The following sections of this chapter will delve deeper into these trends, exploring the exciting possibilities that lie ahead and the ethical considerations that accompany this technological evolution. We will examine the potential for AI to revolutionize literature review processes, offer insights into the ethical considerations, and discuss strategies for preparing researchers for an AI-augmented future. Through this exploration, we aim to equip academics with the knowledge and tools needed to navigate the evolving landscape of AI in academic research writing.

2. AI-POWERED CONTENT GENERATION

In the ever-evolving landscape of academic research writing, Artificial Intelligence (AI) has emerged as a formidable force, revolutionizing various facets of the process. Among its many applications, AI-powered content generation stands out as a particularly transformative development *(Burlacu, 2023).* This section explores the capabilities and implications of AI in content creation, delving into three key aspects: automated content creation beyond text generation, AI-generated figures, tables, and visualizations, and the potential for personalized AI-generated content tailored to individual researchers.

2.1 Automated Content Creation: Beyond Text Generation

Traditionally, researchers have spent countless hours laboring over the composition of academic papers, reports, and summaries. The writing process often involves meticulous attention to detail, adherence to specific formatting guidelines, and the synthesis of complex information *(Joyner et al., 2018).* AI, equipped with natural language processing capabilities, has stepped in to alleviate some of this burden. AI-driven content generation tools have evolved beyond basic text generation. They can now produce coherent and contextually relevant content for a variety of purposes. For instance, AI can assist in drafting abstracts, introductions, and conclusions that capture the essence of a research paper. It can also be employed to generate content for research proposals, project summaries, and even press releases *(Dwivedi et al. 2023).* This expanded scope of AI-powered content creation not only saves researchers valuable time but also ensures consistency in tone and style throughout various sections of a document.

Furthermore, AI can facilitate content translation between languages, enabling researchers to reach a broader audience. This is especially valuable in the globalized academic world, where language barriers can limit the dissemination of knowledge. AI-driven translation tools can accurately translate research findings, making them accessible to non-native speakers and readers worldwide.

2.2 AI-Generated Figures, Tables, and Visualizations

In academic research, the presentation of data through figures, tables, and visualizations plays a critical role in conveying complex information concisely *(Dhoni, 2023)*. AI is making significant strides in automating the generation of these elements, further streamlining the research writing process. AI-driven software can analyze datasets and convert them into visually appealing figures and tables. These tools can identify trends, correlations, and patterns in data and represent them graphically. Researchers can then integrate these AI-generated visuals seamlessly into their papers, eliminating the need for manual chart creation and data formatting *(Wang et al., 2023)*. Moreover, AI is capable of creating custom visualizations tailored to specific research needs. Whether it's generating heatmaps, network diagrams, or interactive graphs, AI empowers researchers to present their findings in innovative ways. This not only enhances the visual appeal of research papers but also aids in conveying complex data more effectively to readers *(Gao, 2022)*.

2.3 Personalized AI-Generated Content for Researchers

As AI technologies continue to advance, the potential for personalized AI-generated content tailored to individual researchers is on the horizon. This marks a significant shift in how academics approach content creation and information dissemination.

Imagine an AI system that not only assists in drafting research papers but also understands a researcher's unique writing style, preferences, and areas of expertise *(Jiang et al., 2021)*. Such a system could generate content that aligns seamlessly with the researcher's existing body of work, ensuring consistency and coherence throughout their publications. Researchers would benefit from AI-generated content that feels like an extension of their own voice and knowledge. Additionally, AI can aid researchers in curating personalized summaries and briefings. For example, an AI assistant could scan newly published papers, extract key insights, and generate tailored summaries based on a researcher's specific interests *(Panda et al., 2019)*. This personalized approach to content generation saves researchers time and keeps them informed about the latest developments in their field.

The AI-powered content generation is reshaping academic research writing by extending beyond text generation to encompass figures, tables, visualizations, and even personalized content. Researchers are now equipped with powerful tools that not only expedite the writing process but also enhance the quality and impact of their work *(Bean & Melzer, 2021)*. As AI technologies continue to advance, the possibilities for content generation are boundless, promising a future where researchers can focus more on their core ideas and discoveries while AI handles the intricacies of content creation. However, as we embrace these advancements, it is essential to remain mindful of ethical considerations and ensure that AI augments, rather than replaces, the unique creativity and expertise of researchers.

Figure 2. AI writing assistant (Pepper, 2023)

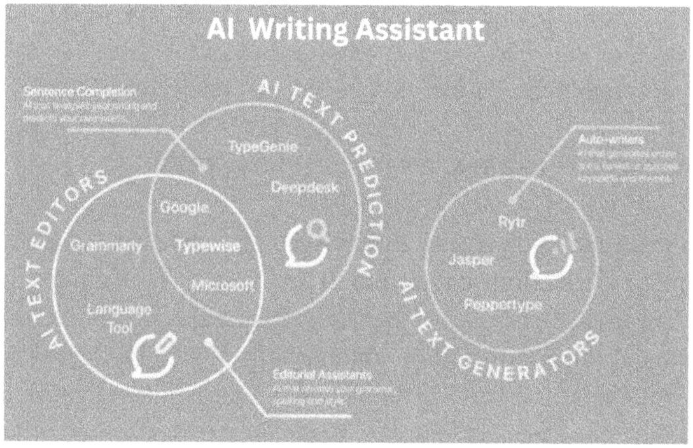

3. ENHANCED COLLABORATION WITH AI

In the realm of academic research, collaboration has long been a driving force behind ground breaking discoveries and innovative insights. The advent of Artificial Intelligence (AI) has ushered in a new era of collaboration, enhancing the way researchers work together *(Kooli, 2023)*. This section explores three key aspects of enhanced collaboration with AI: collaborative AI writing assistants, AI-enabled virtual research partners, and the facilitation of multilingual collaboration through AI.

3.1 Collaborative AI Writing Assistants

Collaboration in academic research often involves multiple authors working on the same document, which can lead to challenges in maintaining consistency, coherence, and formatting. Collaborative AI writing assistants have emerged to address these challenges, providing a collaborative environment where researchers can co-create and edit documents seamlessly *(Malik et al., 2023)*. These AI-powered platforms offer features like real-time collaborative writing, version control, and suggestions for maintaining a consistent writing style as depicted in Figure 2. They ensure that all collaborators are on the same page, literally and figuratively, as they work together on research papers, reports, and proposals. Whether researchers are in the same room or continents apart, collaborative AI writing assistants bridge the gap, enabling efficient teamwork. Moreover, these AI tools can provide in-context suggestions and recommendations, making it easier for authors to refine their writing *(Javaid et al., 2023)*.

They catch grammar and style issues, suggest alternative phrases, and even offer insights into improving readability. This real-time assistance not only enhances the quality of the written content but also expedites the editing process, allowing researchers to focus more on the substance of their work.

3.2 AI-Enabled Virtual Research Partners

Imagine having a virtual research partner who can assist you in every stage of your research project, from idea conception to data analysis and manuscript preparation. AI-enabled virtual research partners

Figure 3. Data analysis and result interpretation (Checco et al., 2021)

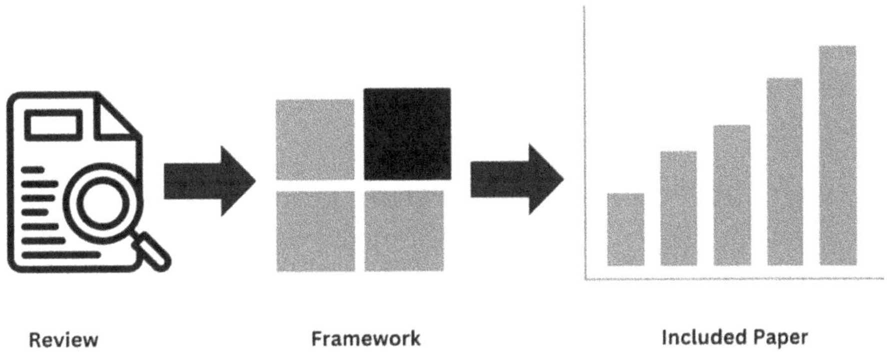

are becoming increasingly sophisticated, offering researchers valuable support and insights throughout their projects *(Spring, 2022)*. The Figure 2 illustrate a model of the data analysis and result interpretation.

At the early stages of research, AI-powered tools can assist in brainstorming research ideas by analyzing existing literature, identifying research gaps, and suggesting potential research questions. They can help researchers optimize their research designs, ensuring that experiments and data collection methods are well-planned and efficient. During data analysis, AI-driven algorithms can assist in the interpretation of results. These virtual research partners can identify trends, correlations, and outliers in datasets, helping researchers draw meaningful conclusions from their data *(Zehir et al., 2020)*. They can even suggest statistical tests and methodologies to ensure robust analysis. When it comes to writing research papers, virtual research partners can assist in drafting sections, generating figures and tables, and ensuring proper citation formatting. They become invaluable collaborators in the research process, enhancing productivity and the overall quality of research output.

3.3 Multilingual Collaboration Through AI

In an increasingly globalized academic landscape, collaboration often spans across language barriers. Researchers from different linguistic backgrounds may encounter challenges in communicating and collaborating effectively. AI, with its language translation capabilities, is breaking down these barriers and enabling multilingual collaboration. AI-driven translation tools can instantly translate text from one language to another, facilitating communication among researchers who speak different languages *(Uekusa, 2022)*. This is particularly beneficial for international collaborations, where team members may not share a common native language. Researchers can now collaborate seamlessly, exchange ideas, and work on shared documents without language becoming a hindrance. Furthermore, AI can assist in maintaining the accuracy and context of translations. These tools go beyond literal translation and consider the nuances and cultural context of languages. As a result, the quality of communication is improved, and misunderstandings are minimized *(BENBADA & BENAOUDA, 2023)*.

In summary, AI is ushering in a new era of enhanced collaboration in academic research. Collaborative AI writing assistants ensure consistent and efficient co-authorship, AI-enabled virtual research partners offer valuable insights and support throughout research projects, and AI-driven language translation tools facilitate multilingual collaboration. As researchers continue to collaborate on a global scale, AI serves as an invaluable ally, bridging gaps, streamlining processes, and enhancing the quality of collaborative research endeavors. Nevertheless, it is essential to balance the advantages of AI with ethical considerations and ensure that AI remains a tool that complements human ingenuity and creativity in the pursuit of knowledge.

4. AI FOR LITERATURE REVIEW AND KNOWLEDGE SYNTHESIS

Literature review, a crucial component of academic research, serves as the foundation for building knowledge and informing research directions. However, the ever-expanding volume of academic literature can make the process of identifying relevant sources, summarizing key findings, and synthesizing knowledge a daunting task. Artificial Intelligence (AI) has emerged as a powerful ally in this endeavor, offering innovative solutions to streamline literature review and knowledge synthesis *(Ali et al., 2023)*. In this section, we will explore three key aspects of AI in literature review and knowledge synthesis: intelligent literature search and retrieval, automated literature review summaries, and AI-driven concept mapping and relationship discovery.

4.1 Intelligent Literature Search and Retrieval

Efficient and comprehensive literature search is the first critical step in any research project. AI technologies have revolutionized this process by providing intelligent search and retrieval capabilities that go beyond keyword matching. AI-powered literature search engines use natural language processing algorithms to understand the context and intent of researchers' queries *(Caldarini et al., 2022)*. These systems can identify synonyms, related terms, and even infer the researcher's research goals, ensuring that the search results are highly relevant. Additionally, they can sift through vast databases of academic literature, including journals, conference proceedings, and preprints, to retrieve the most up-to-date and pertinent sources. Moreover, AI can assist researchers in filtering and categorizing search results based on parameters such as publication date, source credibility, and relevance *(Boella et al., 2016)*. This streamlines the process of identifying the most suitable sources for inclusion in the literature review. AI-driven literature search and retrieval not only save researchers valuable time but also enhance the quality and comprehensiveness of the literature review, ensuring that no relevant sources are overlooked.

4.2 Automated Literature Review Summaries

Once researchers have gathered a substantial collection of academic papers, the next challenge is to extract and synthesize relevant information from these sources. AI-powered automated literature review summaries provide an effective solution to this problem *(Alshami et al., 2023)*. These AI tools can analyze the content of multiple papers simultaneously, extracting key insights, findings, and themes. They can generate concise summaries that capture the essence of each paper, including the research question, methodology, results, and conclusions. These automated summaries save researchers hours of painstaking manual reading and summarization. Furthermore, AI can help researchers identify patterns and trends across a set of papers, offering a holistic view of the literature. By analyzing the summaries of multiple papers, researchers can gain a better understanding of the state of the field, identify gaps in existing knowledge, and refine their research questions. Automated literature review summaries not only expedite the knowledge synthesis process but also improve the accuracy and consistency of the summaries, reducing the risk of overlooking critical information.

4.3 AI-Driven Concept Mapping and Relationship Discovery

Understanding the connections and relationships between concepts, theories, and findings is fundamental to knowledge synthesis. AI-driven concept mapping and relationship discovery tools assist researchers in visualizing and navigating the intricate web of academic knowledge *(Cope et al., 2021)*. These AI systems can analyze the content of academic papers to identify key concepts and their interrelationships. They can generate visual concept maps that illustrate how different ideas and theories are connected. Researchers can use these maps to explore the conceptual landscape of their research field, identify emerging trends, and uncover hidden relationships between seemingly disparate topics. AI-driven relationship discovery goes beyond surface-level connections *(Hwang et al., 2020)*. It can uncover subtle relationships, such as causal links or correlations, between concepts, enabling researchers to gain deeper insights into the subject matter.

Moreover, these tools can facilitate the organization of literature review sections in research papers. By automatically generating structured summaries and concept maps, AI streamlines the process of synthesizing and presenting knowledge in a coherent and visually appealing manner *(Huang et al., 2023)*. In the end, AI is transforming the landscape of literature review and knowledge synthesis in academic research. Intelligent literature search and retrieval tools help researchers find the most relevant sources efficiently, automated literature review summaries expedite the process of extracting and summarizing information, and AI-driven concept mapping and relationship discovery enhance researchers' ability to navigate and synthesize complex knowledge. As the volume of academic literature continues to grow, AI remains a vital asset for researchers seeking to harness the power of knowledge synthesis in their academic pursuits. However, it is essential to strike a balance between AI automation and human expertise to ensure that the synthesis process remains informed by critical thinking and domain knowledge.

5. AI-DRIVEN PEER REVIEW AND EVALUATION

Peer review is the cornerstone of academic publishing, ensuring the quality, credibility, and integrity of scholarly work. However, the traditional peer review process has its challenges, including the potential for bias and the time-consuming nature of manual evaluation *(Schintler et al., 2023)*. Artificial Intelligence (AI) is transforming peer review and evaluation by providing innovative solutions to enhance the rigor and fairness of the process as shown in Figure 4.

In this section, we will explore three key aspects of AI-driven peer review and evaluation: AI-powered peer review assistance, predictive analytics for journal selection, and the role of AI in eliminating bias in peer review.

5.1 AI-Powered Peer Review Assistance

Peer reviewers play a crucial role in evaluating the quality and validity of research submissions. However, the peer review process can be demanding, and reviewers may encounter challenges such as identifying potential ethical issues, evaluating statistical methodology, and ensuring that the manuscript complies

Figure 4. AI-assisted peer review (Van der Velden et al., 2022)

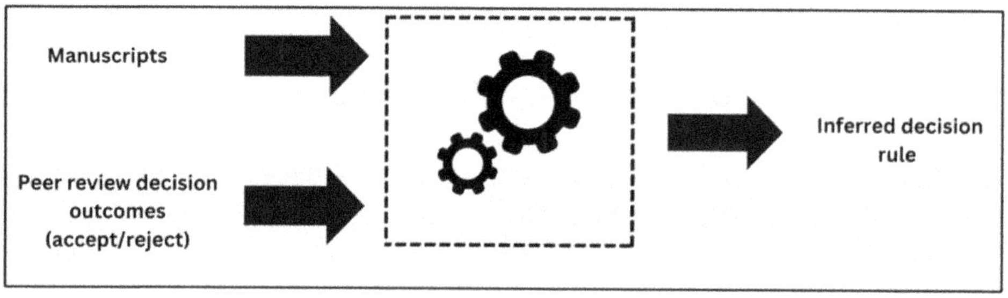

with journal-specific guidelines. AI-powered peer review assistance tools are designed to support reviewers in their assessments *(Checco et al., 2021)*. These tools analyse manuscripts using natural language processing (NLP) and machine learning algorithms to provide reviewers with valuable insights. They can flag potential ethical concerns, identify statistical errors, and highlight areas where the manuscript may not adhere to journal formatting requirements. Furthermore, AI can assist reviewers in assessing the overall quality and novelty of a submission by comparing it to existing literature. By analyzing the references and content of the manuscript, AI can help reviewers gauge the significance of the research and its contribution to the field. AI-powered peer review assistance not only enhances the efficiency of the review process but also ensures a more comprehensive and standardized evaluation, reducing the likelihood of overlooking critical issues.

5.2 Predictive Analytics for Journal Selection

Choosing the most appropriate journal for manuscript submission is a critical decision for researchers. It involves considering factors such as the journal's scope, target audience, impact factor, and acceptance rates. AI-driven predictive analytics are revolutionizing this aspect of the publishing process by providing researchers with data-driven recommendations for journal selection.

AI algorithms analyze the content of a manuscript, considering factors such as the research topic, keywords, and citations, to suggest suitable journals for submission *(Silva et al., 2015)*. These suggestions are based on historical data, including acceptance rates, review times, and the publication history of similar articles. By leveraging predictive analytics, researchers can make more informed decisions about where to submit their work, increasing the likelihood of acceptance and publication. This not only saves researchers time but also optimizes the dissemination of research findings to the most relevant audience.

5.3 Unbiased Evaluation and Elimination of Bias in Peer Review

One of the longstanding challenges in peer review is the potential for bias, whether based on factors like author demographics, institutional affiliations, or geographical locations. Bias can lead to unfair evaluations and hinder the diversity and inclusivity of academic publishing. AI offers a means to mitigate bias in peer review. By anonymizing manuscript submissions and concealing author identities, AI ensures that reviewers focus solely on the content and quality of the research *(Ramchandran et al., 2017)*. This blind review process eliminates potential bias associated with author demographics or affiliations. Furthermore, AI-driven algorithms can assess the consistency and fairness of reviewer evaluations. They can detect outliers and discrepancies in scores and comments, flagging potential instances of bias. Journal editors can then review these cases and take corrective actions to ensure unbiased evaluations. Moreover, AI can assist in diversifying the pool of peer reviewers. By analysing the expertise and research interests of potential reviewers, AI can suggest a more diverse group of experts, reducing the likelihood of bias based on reviewer demographics.

In short, AI-driven peer review and evaluation are reshaping the academic publishing landscape by enhancing the efficiency, fairness, and rigor of the peer review process. AI-powered peer review assistance aids reviewers in conducting thorough and standardized evaluations, predictive analytics assist researchers in selecting the most suitable journals, and AI plays a crucial role in eliminating bias by anonymizing submissions and diversifying the pool of reviewers. As AI continues to advance, it holds the potential to further improve the transparency and quality of peer review, contributing to the integrity of scholarly communication. However, it is essential to strike a balance between automation and human expertise to ensure that AI supports, rather than replaces, the essential role of peer reviewers and editors in maintaining academic rigor.

6. ETHICAL CONSIDERATIONS AND AI

As Artificial Intelligence (AI) continues to transform various aspects of academic research, it brings with it a set of ethical considerations that demand careful attention *(Luckin & Holmes, 2016)*. Maintaining research integrity and ethical standards is paramount in the scholarly world, and the integration of AI introduces both opportunities and challenges in this regard. In this section, we will explore three key aspects of ethical considerations and AI: addressing plagiarism and ethical writing, ensuring fair and ethical use of AI in research, and the role of AI in research integrity monitoring.

6.1 Addressing Plagiarism and Ethical Writing

One of the foremost ethical concerns in academic research is plagiarism—the unauthorized use or appropriation of someone else's work or ideas. While AI has the potential to assist researchers in various aspects of writing, it also introduces the risk of unintentional plagiarism if not used judiciously *(Ifelebuegu et al., 2023)*. AI-powered writing assistants, which offer suggestions for grammar, style, and content, must be used with caution. Researchers should ensure that any text generated or revised with the help of AI tools complies with ethical writing standards. Figure 5 demonstrates the process for AI driven plagiarism detection. This includes proper citation and attribution of sources, as well as originality in presenting ideas. To address this concern, researchers should be educated about the ethical use of AI tools and the importance of verifying the originality of their work. Institutions and journals can also provide guidelines on how to use AI writing assistants while maintaining ethical writing practices *(Jarrah et al., 2023)*.

Moreover, AI can play a role in detecting plagiarism by comparing a manuscript's content with a vast database of existing academic literature. AI-driven plagiarism detection tools are becoming increasingly sophisticated in identifying similarities between submitted work and existing publications. These tools help institutions and publishers maintain the integrity of research by identifying potential cases of misconduct.

Figure 5. AI-driven plagiarism detection (How to Copy..,, 2022)

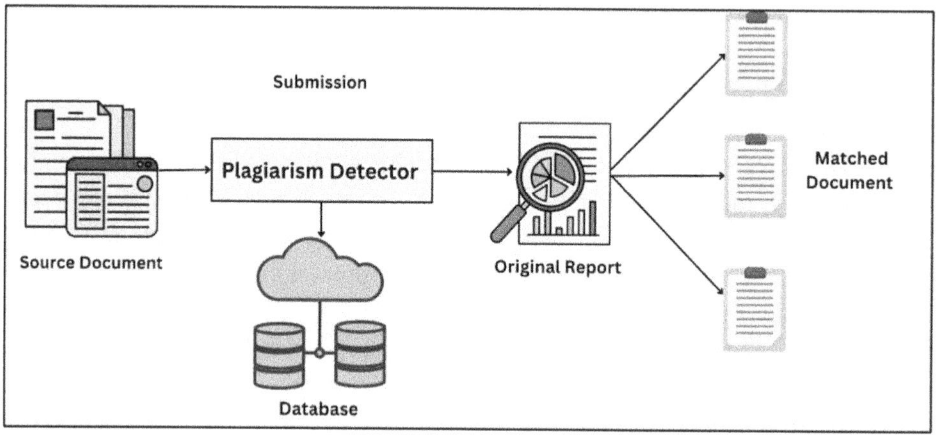

6.2 Ensuring Fair and Ethical Use of AI in Research

The ethical use of AI in research extends beyond writing assistance to encompass various aspects of the research process, from data collection and analysis to decision-making. Researchers must exercise ethical judgment and transparency when implementing AI technologies. In data-driven research, for instance, AI algorithms may be used to process and analyze large datasets *(Spring, 2022)*. Ethical considerations include obtaining informed consent from participants, protecting the privacy of individuals, and ensuring that data is used only for the intended research purposes. Additionally, AI algorithms used in research should be transparent and explainable. Researchers should be able to understand how AI arrived at certain conclusions or recommendations. Transparency is crucial for accountability and the reproducibility of research findings. Fairness and bias in AI systems are also ethical concerns. AI algorithms can inadvertently perpetuate biases present in training data, potentially leading to unfair or discriminatory outcomes *(Wang et al., 2023)*. Researchers must take measures to mitigate bias and ensure that AI-driven research is conducted impartially and equitably.

6.3 AI-Driven Research Integrity Monitoring

As research processes become increasingly automated and reliant on AI, the need for effective research integrity monitoring grows. Ensuring that AI-generated results are accurate and trustworthy is paramount for maintaining the credibility of research findings *(Ollivier et al., 2023)*. AI can be employed to monitor research integrity by conducting automated checks and audits of research processes. For example, AI can verify the consistency and accuracy of data collection and analysis methods, flagging any discrepancies or irregularities. Furthermore, AI-driven systems can help identify potential research misconduct, such as data fabrication or manipulation. By analyzing patterns in data and detecting anomalies, AI can assist in uncovering research fraud and ensuring the validity of research outcomes. Research integrity monitoring with AI extends to the peer review process as well. AI algorithms can assist in detecting irregularities or potential conflicts of interest among reviewers, contributing to a fair and impartial peer review process *(Checco et al., 2021)*.

At the end, ethical considerations are at the forefront of the integration of AI in academic research. Researchers must navigate the ethical use of AI in writing, data-driven research, and decision-making processes. Institutions, journals, and researchers themselves have a shared responsibility to educate, guide, and enforce ethical standards in AI-driven research. Additionally, AI-driven research integrity monitoring ensures that the ethical principles of transparency, fairness, and accuracy are upheld throughout the research lifecycle. As AI continues to evolve and play an increasingly central role in research, ethical considerations will remain a critical focal point, requiring ongoing vigilance and adaptation to ensure the integrity of scholarly work.

7. AI-ENHANCED RESEARCH PUBLISHING

The world of research publishing is undergoing a profound transformation with the integration of Artificial Intelligence (AI). AI technologies are revolutionizing various facets of the publication process, enhancing efficiency, accessibility, and the overall quality of academic dissemination *(Lund et al., 2023).* In this section, we will explore three key aspects of AI-enhanced research publishing: AI-powered journal suggestion systems, dynamic and interactive AI-enhanced publications, and AI-driven automated citation and reference formatting.

7.1 AI-Powered Journal Suggestion Systems

Selecting the right journal for manuscript submission is a critical decision for researchers. It involves considering factors such as the journal's scope, target audience, impact factor, and acceptance rates. AI-powered journal suggestion systems have emerged as invaluable tools to assist researchers in making informed choices *(Rusmiyanto et al., 2023).* These AI algorithms analyze the content of a manuscript, considering elements like research topics, keywords, and citations. Based on this analysis and historical data about the acceptance rates and publication history of similar articles, AI can suggest a list of journals that are most suitable for the submission. By leveraging AI-driven journal suggestion systems, researchers save time and increase the chances of their work being accepted *(Javaid et al., 2022).* This not only streamlines the publication process but also optimizes the dissemination of research findings to the most relevant audience.

7.2 Dynamic and Interactive AI-Enhanced Publications

Traditional research publications, typically in the form of static PDF documents, have limitations when it comes to conveying complex ideas and findings effectively. AI is changing this by enabling dynamic and interactive publications that offer readers a more engaging and informative experience *(Luckin & Holmes, 2016).* AI-powered tools can transform research papers into multimedia-rich, interactive documents. For instance, embedded videos, animations, and simulations can help explain complex concepts and experimental setups more effectively than text alone. Readers can interact with data visualizations, exploring research findings in an intuitive and engaging manner. Furthermore, AI can enhance the accessibility of research publications by providing features like text-to-speech functionality, language translation, and customizable reading layouts *(Zdravkova, 2022).* This ensures that research is accessible to a broader and more diverse audience, including individuals with disabilities and those who prefer different languages. Dynamic and interactive AI-enhanced publications not only improve the comprehension and engagement of readers but also facilitate knowledge dissemination and collaboration in a digital age.

7.3 AI-Driven Automated Citation and Reference Formatting

Proper citation and reference formatting is a meticulous and time-consuming task in academic writing. Errors in this aspect can lead to rejection by journals or difficulties in manuscript preparation. AI-driven automated citation and reference formatting tools are streamlining this process, ensuring accuracy and adherence to various citation styles *(Alshami et al., 2023).* AI algorithms can analyze a manuscript's content, identify cited sources, and automatically generate formatted citations and references according to the chosen citation style, such as APA, MLA, or Chicago. This eliminates the need for authors to manually format references, reducing the risk of citation errors. Additionally, AI can assist in updating citations and references as new research is published. Automated systems can track changes in the citation landscape, ensuring that publications remain up-to-date and in compliance with evolving citation guidelines *(Razack et al., 2023).* By automating citation and reference formatting, AI not only enhances the efficiency of the publication process but also reduces the burden on authors and editors, allowing them to focus more on the substance of their research.

In short, AI is ushering in a new era of research publishing that is characterized by efficiency, engagement, and accuracy. AI-powered journal suggestion systems aid researchers in selecting the most suitable publication venues, dynamic and interactive publications enhance the dissemination of research findings, and AI-driven automated citation and reference formatting tools ensure the precision of citations and references. These advancements not only benefit researchers but also readers and the academic community at large, making research more accessible and engaging. As AI technologies continue to evolve, the possibilities for enhancing research publishing are limitless, promising an even more dynamic and efficient future for scholarly communication *(DeCostanza et al., 2018).* However, it is crucial to strike a balance between innovation and tradition, ensuring that the core principles of rigorous academic research and ethical publishing are upheld in this AI-enhanced landscape.

8. CHALLENGES AND CONCERNS

As Artificial Intelligence (AI) continues to weave its way into the fabric of academic research and writing, it brings with it a host of challenges and concerns that researchers, institutions, and publishers must navigate. While AI offers significant benefits, such as improved efficiency and quality, it also raises important questions regarding privacy, dependency, and ethics *(Ray, 2023).* In this section, we will explore three key challenges and concerns associated with AI in academic research and writing: privacy and data security, AI tool dependency and skill gaps, and the ethical implications of AI-generated content.

8.1 Privacy and Data Security in AI-Enhanced Writing

The integration of AI into research writing processes involves the use of data, both personal and research-related. Researchers often share their manuscripts, research notes, and other sensitive information with AI-powered writing assistants, tools, and platforms *(Mondal et al., 2023).* This raises concerns about the privacy and security of this data. Privacy Concerns: When researchers use AI writing assistants,

Figure 6. Challenges and concerns in AI-enhanced writing (Li et al., 2020)

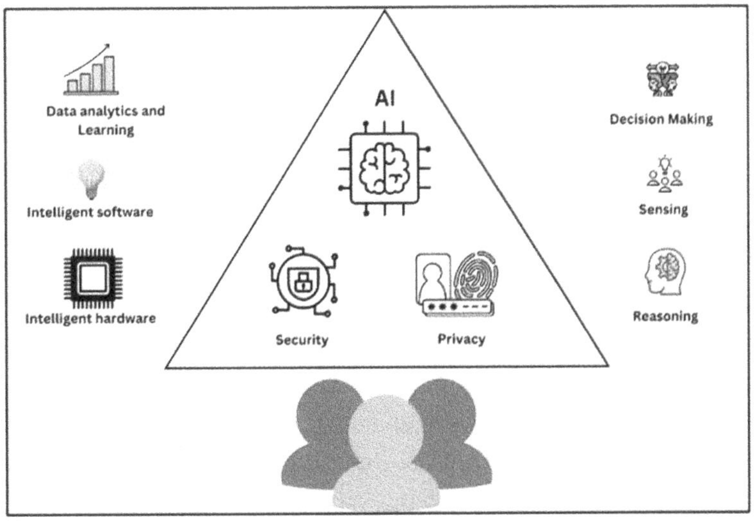

they may inadvertently disclose sensitive or proprietary research information. Figure 6 represented the different challenges and concerns related to AI assisted writing. Researchers must trust that the AI tools they use will respect their privacy and confidentiality. However, there is always a risk of data breaches or unauthorized access to research content.

Data Security: The storage and transmission of research data to AI tools need to meet robust security standards. Researchers, institutions, and tool providers must ensure that data is encrypted, protected from cyber threats, and compliant with data protection regulations such as GDPR or HIPAA *(ABIO, 2023).*

Ethical Use of Data: AI tools should be transparent about how they use and store data. Researchers should be aware of how their data is utilized by AI platforms, and any data usage should align with ethical standards *(Singh et al., 2020).*

Addressing privacy and data security concerns requires close collaboration between researchers, AI tool providers, and institutions to establish clear guidelines, ensure secure data handling practices, and uphold the ethical use of data in AI-enhanced research writing.

8.2 AI Tool Dependency and Skill Gaps

While AI tools offer significant assistance in academic research writing, there is a growing concern about researchers becoming overly dependent on these tools. This dependency raises several challenges:

Loss of Core Skills: Researchers may become reliant on AI for tasks like grammar and style correction, potentially leading to a decline in their own writing and editing skills. This could hinder their ability to produce high-quality academic work independently (*Elavarasi & Dhanalakshmi, 2022).*

Skill Gaps: There is a risk of skill gaps emerging within the research community. Not all researchers may have access to or proficiency with AI tools, potentially exacerbating disparities in research quality and *accessibility* (*Elavarasi & Dhanalakshmi, 2022).*

Over-Reliance on AI Recommendations: Researchers may unquestioningly accept AI-generated suggestions without critical evaluation. This can lead to the propagation of incorrect information or ideas, undermining the integrity of research *(Gaube et al., 2021).*

Reduced Creativity: Overdependence on AI may stifle researchers' creativity and originality. The reliance on AI-generated content might hinder the development of unique research perspectives and ideas *(Gaube et al., 2021).*

To address these challenges, institutions and researchers should promote a balanced approach to AI tool usage. Researchers should continue to cultivate their writing and research skills while harnessing AI as a supportive tool rather than a replacement. Moreover, institutions can offer training and resources to help researchers use AI tools effectively while maintaining a strong foundation in traditional research and writing skills.

8.3 Ethical Implications of AI-Generated Content

The rise of AI-generated content introduces ethical considerations that need careful examination:

Authorship and Attribution: Determining authorship and appropriate attribution for AI-generated content can be complex. Researchers should clearly indicate when AI tools have been used in their work and how they have contributed to the research process *(Partadiredja et al., 2020).*

Plagiarism and Originality: AI-generated content may inadvertently overlap with existing literature, potentially raising concerns about plagiarism. Researchers must ensure that AI-generated content is original and properly cited *(Partadiredja et al.,2020).*

Bias and Fairness: AI algorithms can inherit biases present in training data, potentially leading to biased or unfair content generation. Researchers should be vigilant in identifying and addressing bias in AI-generated content *(Liang et al ., 2023).*

Transparency: The transparency of AI-generated content is crucial. Researchers should be able to explain how AI tools have been used and how they have influenced the research process *(Liang et al., 2023).*

As AI-generated content becomes more prevalent in academic research writing, it is essential for researchers to uphold ethical standards, transparency, and integrity in their work. Institutions and publishers should provide guidelines and resources to help researchers navigate the ethical implications of AI-driven research and writing.

In the end, while AI offers significant advantages in academic research and writing, it also presents challenges and concerns that must be addressed to ensure responsible and ethical AI integration. Privacy and data security, preventing over-reliance on AI, and maintaining ethical standards in AI-generated content are all vital aspects of this ongoing dialogue. By approaching these challenges proactively and collaboratively, the research community can harness the potential of AI while preserving the integrity of scholarly work.

9. PREPARING RESEARCHERS FOR AN AI-ENHANCED FUTURE

The rapid integration of Artificial Intelligence (AI) into academic research and writing processes is reshaping the landscape of scholarly work. To thrive in this AI-enhanced future, researchers must acquire AI literacy and adapt their strategies to leverage the benefits of AI while upholding research integrity *(Wang et al.,2023).* In this section, we will explore three key aspects of preparing researchers for an AI-enhanced future: AI literacy and training for academics, strategies for adapting to AI-driven research writing, and integrating AI into research curriculum.

9.1 AI Literacy and Training for Academics

AI literacy is becoming an essential skill for researchers in various fields. Understanding AI concepts, capabilities, and limitations empowers researchers to harness AI's potential effectively. Here are key considerations for AI literacy and training:

AI Fundamentals: Researchers should receive training in AI fundamentals, including machine learning, natural language processing, and computer vision. This knowledge equips them with a foundational understanding of AI technologies *(Cox et al.,2019).*

Tool Proficiency: Training programs should focus on specific AI tools relevant to research writing, such as AI-powered writing assistants, citation formatting tools, and literature review aids. Researchers should learn how to use these tools effectively and ethically.

Ethical AI Usage: Ethical considerations should be integrated into AI training. Researchers should understand the ethical implications of using AI tools, including plagiarism prevention and bias mitigation*(Chan & C. K. Y., 2023).*

Privacy and Data Security: Training should cover privacy and data security best practices, especially when researchers share sensitive data with AI tools. Researchers must be aware of how data is handled and protected *(Chan & C.K.Y., 2023).*

Continuous Learning: AI is a rapidly evolving field. Researchers should engage in continuous learning to stay updated on AI advancements and their potential applications in research *(Chan & C. K. Y., 2023).*Institutions and academic organizations should prioritize AI literacy by offering training programs, workshops, and resources to help researchers develop AI competencies.

9.2 Strategies for Adapting to AI-Driven Research Writing

As AI becomes increasingly integrated into research writing processes, researchers must adapt their strategies to leverage AI effectively. Here are strategies for adapting to AI-driven research writing:

Augmentation, Not Replacement: Researchers should view AI as a tool for augmentation rather than a replacement for their skills. While AI can assist with grammar, style, and formatting, researchers should maintain their critical thinking and writing skills *(Shrivastava, 2023).*

Human-AI Collaboration: Researchers should embrace collaboration with AI tools. They can use AI to expedite tasks like proofreading and citation formatting, allowing them to focus more on research content and creativity *(Järvelä et al., 2023).*

Review AI Suggestions: Researchers should critically review AI-generated suggestions and recommendations. They should not blindly accept AI-generated content but ensure that it aligns with the research's goals and maintains ethical standards.

Ethical Awareness: Researchers should be vigilant about ethical considerations, especially when using AI for content generation. They should ensure that AI-generated content is original, properly attributed, and free from bias.

Balanced Workflow: Researchers should strike a balance between AI-assisted tasks and human-authored content. Maintaining control over the research narrative and maintaining an original voice is essential.

Continuous Improvement: Researchers should actively seek feedback from peers, mentors, or collaborators to improve their AI-enhanced writing skills. They should embrace a growth mindset and see AI as a tool for enhancing their research capabilities *(Ashktorab et al., 2020).*

9.3 Integrating AI Into Research Curriculum

To prepare the next generation of researchers for an AI-enhanced future, educational institutions should integrate AI into research curriculum. Here's how:

AI Modules: Develop dedicated AI modules or courses that introduce students to AI fundamentals and applications in research. These courses can cover AI writing tools, data analysis, and ethical considerations *(Sabuncuoglu,, 2020).*

Hands-On Experience: Provide students with hands-on experience using AI tools for research writing. Encourage them to apply AI techniques to their own research projects.

Interdisciplinary Collaboration: Promote interdisciplinary collaboration between AI experts and researchers in various fields. Encourage students to work on collaborative projects that leverage AI technologies *(Sabuncuoglu, 2020).*

Ethics Education: Incorporate ethics education into AI-related courses, emphasizing responsible AI usage, privacy, and bias mitigation.

Research AI: Encourage students to explore AI research topics related to their fields of study. AI can be a valuable tool for solving complex research problems.

Mentorship: Foster mentorship programs where experienced researchers guide students in navigating the integration of AI into research.

By integrating AI into research curriculum, educational institutions prepare students to leverage AI as a powerful tool in their research endeavours, fostering innovation and excellence. Preparing researchers for an AI-enhanced future requires a multifaceted approach that includes AI literacy and training, adaptation strategies, and curriculum integration. Researchers must acquire AI competencies, adapt their writing strategies, and maintain ethical awareness. Educational institutions play a pivotal role in equipping researchers and students with the skills and knowledge needed to navigate the evolving landscape of AI-enhanced research and writing successfully. As AI continues to advance, researchers who embrace AI literacy and incorporate AI into their research processes will be well-positioned to excel in academia and contribute to the advancement of knowledge.

10. CONCLUSION

In the rapidly evolving landscape of academic research and writing, Artificial Intelligence (AI) has emerged as a transformative force, offering researchers powerful tools to enhance efficiency, quality, and accessibility. Throughout this exploration of AI's role in research writing, we have delved into a multitude of facets, from AI-powered content generation to peer review assistance, and ethical considerations. As we draw this discourse to a close, let's summarize key takeaways and cast our gaze toward the future of AI and research writing. Throughout this journey, we've witnessed the profound impact of AI on the research writing process. AI-powered tools assist researchers in myriad ways, from grammar correction and citation formatting to literature review and content generation. They augment the capabilities of researchers, streamlining processes and improving the overall quality of academic output. Key takeaways include the crucial importance of AI literacy and training for researchers, the necessity of maintaining a balance between AI-assisted tasks and human expertise, and the ongoing significance of ethical considerations in AI integration into research writing. Looking ahead, the possibilities for AI and research writing are expansive. As AI algorithms continue to advance, we can anticipate enhanced collaboration and knowledge synthesis, the evolution of dynamic and interactive publications, and AI-driven research integrity monitoring to ensure the accuracy and trustworthiness of research outcomes. As we navigate this AI-enhanced future, it is imperative that researchers, institutions, and the academic community at large embrace a forward-looking perspective. AI is not a replacement for human creativity, critical thinking, or ethical judgment; rather, it is a powerful tool that can amplify these qualities. Researchers should remain adaptable, continually enhancing their AI literacy and seeking opportunities to integrate AI into their research processes while preserving their distinct voices and originality. Institutions should prioritize AI literacy and provide resources and support to facilitate the responsible and effective use of AI in research writing. Ethical considerations should continue to guide AI integration, ensuring that AI-enhanced research upholds the highest standards of integrity and fairness. In conclusion, the fusion of AI and research writing represents a dynamic and promising frontier. Embracing AI as a collaborator and tool for augmentation, rather than a replacement, will empower researchers to tackle complex challenges, broaden the horizons of knowledge, and usher in a new era of academic excellence. The future of research writing is a blend of human ingenuity and AI-powered innovation, where the possibilities are limitless, and the pursuit of knowledge knows no bounds.

REFERENCES

Abio, B. (2023). Is the world ready for ai-powered therapy? *Nature*, 617.

Ahmad, M., Abbas, S., Fatima, A., Ghazal, T. M., Alharbi, M., Khan, M. A., & Elmitwally, N. S. (2023). AI-Driven livestock identification and insurance management system. *Egyptian Informatics Journal*, *24*(3), 100390. doi:10.1016/j.eij.2023.100390

Albahri, A. S., Duhaim, A. M., Fadhel, M. A., Alnoor, A., Baqer, N. S., Alzubaidi, L., Albahri, O. S., Alamoodi, A. H., Bai, J., Salhi, A., Santamaría, J., Ouyang, C., Gupta, A., Gu, Y., & Deveci, M. (2023). A systematic review of trustworthy and explainable artificial intelligence in healthcare: Assessment of quality, bias risk, and data fusion. *Information Fusion*, *96*, 156–191. doi:10.1016/j.inffus.2023.03.008

Alharbi, W. (2023). AI in the Foreign Language Classroom: A Pedagogical Overview of Automated Writing Assistance Tools. *Education Research International*, *2023*, 2023. doi:10.1155/2023/4253331

Ali, O., Abdelbaki, W., Shrestha, A., Elbasi, E., Alryalat, M. A. A., & Dwivedi, Y. K. (2023). A systematic literature review of artificial intelligence in the healthcare sector: Benefits, challenges, methodologies, and functionalities. *Journal of Innovation & Knowledge*, *8*(1), 100333. doi:10.1016/j.jik.2023.100333

Alshami, A., Elsayed, M., Ali, E., Eltoukhy, A. E., & Zayed, T. (2023). Harnessing the Power of ChatGPT for Automating Systematic Review Process: Methodology, Case Study, Limitations, and Future Directions. *Systems*, *11*(7), 351. doi:10.3390/systems11070351

Ashktorab, Z., Liao, Q. V., Dugan, C., Johnson, J., Pan, Q., Zhang, W., ... Campbell, M. (2020). Human-ai collaboration in a cooperative game setting: Measuring social perception and outcomes. *Proceedings of the ACM on Human-Computer Interaction, 4*(CSCW2), 1-20. 10.1145/3415167

Bean, J. C., & Melzer, D. (2021). *Engaging ideas: The professor's guide to integrating writing, critical thinking, and active learning in the classroom*. John Wiley & Sons.

Benbada, M. L., & Benaouda, N. (2023). *Investigation of the Role of Artificial Intelligence in Developing Machine Translation Quality. Case Study: Reverso Context and Google Translate translations of Expressive and Descriptive Texts. Language Combination: Arabic-English/English-Arabic*(Doctoral dissertation, Faculty of Letters and Languages-Department of English).

Boella, G., Caro, L. D., Humphreys, L., Robaldo, L., Rossi, P., & van der Torre, L. (2016). Eunomos, a legal document and knowledge management system for the web to provide relevant, reliable and up-to-date information on the law. *Artificial Intelligence and Law*, *24*(3), 245–283. doi:10.1007/s10506-016-9184-3

Burlacu, C. (2023). *The Impact Of Ai-Powered Content Generation On Customer Experience* (Bachelor's thesis, University of Twente).

Caldarini, G., Jaf, S., & McGarry, K. (2022). A literature survey of recent advances in chatbots. *Information (Basel)*, *13*(1), 41. doi:10.3390/info13010041

Chan, C. K. Y. (2023). A comprehensive AI policy education framework for university teaching and learning. *International Journal of Educational Technology in Higher Education*, *20*(1), 1–25. doi:10.1186/s41239-023-00408-3

Checco, A., Bracciale, L., Loreti, P., Pinfield, S., & Bianchi, G. (2021). AI-assisted peer review. *Humanities & Social Sciences Communications*, *8*(1), 1–11. doi:10.1057/s41599-020-00703-8 PMID:38617731

Cope, B., Kalantzis, M., & Searsmith, D. (2021). Artificial intelligence for education: Knowledge and its assessment in AI-enabled learning ecologies. *Educational Philosophy and Theory*, *53*(12), 1229–1245. doi:10.1080/00131857.2020.1728732

Cox, A. M., Pinfield, S., & Rutter, S. (2019). The intelligent library: Thought leaders' views on the likely impact of artificial intelligence on academic libraries. *Library Hi Tech*, *37*(3), 418–435. doi:10.1108/LHT-08-2018-0105

DeCostanza, A. H., Marathe, A. R., Bohannon, A., Evans, A. W., Palazzolo, E. T., Metcalfe, J. S., & McDowell, K. (2018). *Enhancing human-agent teaming with individualized, adaptive technologies: A discussion of critical scientific questions*. US Army Research Laboratory Aberdeen Proving Ground United States.

Dhoni, P. (2023). *Exploring the Synergy between Generative AI*. Data and Analytics in the Modern Age.

Dwivedi, Y. K., Kshetri, N., Hughes, L., Slade, E. L., Jeyaraj, A., Kar, A. K., Baabdullah, A. M., Koohang, A., Raghavan, V., Ahuja, M., Albanna, H., Albashrawi, M. A., Al-Busaidi, A. S., Balakrishnan, J., Barlette, Y., Basu, S., Bose, I., Brooks, L., Buhalis, D., ... Wright, R. (2023). "So what if ChatGPT wrote it?" Multidisciplinary perspectives on opportunities, challenges and implications of generative conversational AI for research, practice and policy. *International Journal of Information Management*, *71*, 102642. doi:10.1016/j.ijinfomgt.2023.102642

Elavarasi, R., & Dhanalakshmi, P. (2022). Theoretical framework of employee skill gap analysis and its effects in organisation. *Business Environment and Technological Innovation-Emerging Trends-volume, II*, 75.

Gao, B. (2022). Research and implementation of intelligent evaluation system of teaching quality in universities based on artificial intelligence neural network model. *Mathematical Problems in Engineering, 2022*, 1–10. doi:10.1155/2022/5448359

Gaube, S., Suresh, H., Raue, M., Merritt, A., Berkowitz, S. J., Lermer, E., Coughlin, J. F., Guttag, J. V., Colak, E., & Ghassemi, M. (2021). Do as AI say: Susceptibility in deployment of clinical decision-aids. *NPJ Digital Medicine*, *4*(1), 31. doi:10.1038/s41746-021-00385-9 PMID:33608629

How to Copy and Paste Without Plagiarizing In 2022. (2022, October 18). Retrieved from Opportunities. http://opportunities. alumdev.columbia.edu/how-to-copy-an-essay-without-plagiarizing.php

Huang, Y., Lv, S., Tseng, K. K., Tseng, P. J., Xie, X., & Lin, R. F. Y. (2023). Recent advances in artificial intelligence for video production system. *Enterprise Information Systems*, *17*(11), 2246188. doi:10.1080/17517575.2023.2246188

Hwang, G. J., Xie, H., Wah, B. W., & Gašević, D. (2020). Vision, challenges, roles and research issues of Artificial Intelligence in Education. *Computers and Education: Artificial Intelligence*, *1*, 100001. doi:10.1016/j.caeai.2020.100001

Ifelebuegu, A. O., Kulume, P., & Cherukut, P. (2023). Chatbots and AI in Education (AIEd) tools: The good, the bad, and the ugly. *Journal of Applied Learning and Teaching*, *6*(2).

Jarrah, A. M., Wardat, Y., & Fidalgo, P. (2023). Using ChatGPT in academic writing is (not) a form of plagiarism: What does the literature say. *Online Journal of Communication and Media Technologies*, *13*(4), e202346. doi:10.30935/ojcmt/13572

Järvelä, S., Nguyen, A., & Hadwin, A. (2023). Human and artificial intelligence collaboration for socially shared regulation in learning. *British Journal of Educational Technology*, *54*(5), 1057–1076. doi:10.1111/bjet.13325

Javaid, M., Haleem, A., Singh, R. P., Khan, S., & Khan, I. H. (2023). Unlocking the opportunities through ChatGPT Tool towards ameliorating the education system. *BenchCouncil Transactions on Benchmarks. Standards and Evaluations*, *3*(2), 100115.

Javaid, M., Haleem, A., Singh, R. P., Suman, R., & Rab, S. (2022). Significance of machine learning in healthcare: Features, pillars and applications. *International Journal of Intelligent Networks*, *3*, 58–73. doi:10.1016/j.ijin.2022.05.002

Jiang, J. A., Wade, K., Fiesler, C., & Brubaker, J. R. (2021). Supporting serendipity: Opportunities and challenges for Human-AI Collaboration in qualitative analysis. *Proceedings of the ACM on Human-Computer Interaction, 5*(CSCW1), 1-23. 10.1145/3449168

Joyner, R. L., Rouse, W. A., & Glatthorn, A. A. (2018). *Writing the winning thesis or dissertation: A step-by-step guide*. Corwin Press.

Khang, A., Shah, V., & Rani, S. (Eds.). (2023). *Handbook of Research on AI-Based Technologies and Applications in the Era of the Metaverse*. IGI Global. doi:10.4018/978-1-6684-8851-5

Kooli, C. (2023). Chatbots in education and research: A critical examination of ethical implications and solutions. *Sustainability (Basel)*, *15*(7), 5614. doi:10.3390/su15075614

Li, Z., Sharma, V., & Mohanty, S. P. (2020). Preserving data privacy via federated learning: Challenges and solutions. *IEEE Consumer Electronics Magazine*, *9*(3), 8–16. doi:10.1109/MCE.2019.2959108

Liang, W., Yuksekgonul, M., Mao, Y., Wu, E., & Zou, J. (2023). GPT detectors are biased against non-native English writers. *arXiv preprint arXiv:2304.02819.*

Liao, Q. V., Subramonyam, H., Wang, J., & Wortman Vaughan, J. (2023, April). Designerly understanding: Information needs for model transparency to support design ideation for AI-powered user experience. In *Proceedings of the 2023 CHI conference on human factors in computing systems* (pp. 1-21). 10.1145/3544548.3580652

Luckin, R., & Holmes, W. (2016). Intelligence unleashed: An argument for AI in education. Academic Press.

Lund, B. D., Wang, T., Mannuru, N. R., Nie, B., Shimray, S., & Wang, Z. (2023). ChatGPT and a new academic reality: Artificial Intelligence-written research papers and the ethics of the large language models in scholarly publishing. *Journal of the Association for Information Science and Technology*, *74*(5), 570–581. doi:10.1002/asi.24750

Malik, A., Budhwar, P., & Mohan, H., & NR, S. (2023). Employee experience–the missing link for engaging employees: Insights from an MNE's AI-based HR ecosystem. *Human Resource Management*, *62*(1), 97–115. doi:10.1002/hrm.22133

Module: Reference Management. (2023). Retrieved from eqpoint.info: http://eqpoint.info/Reference_Management/Reference_Management_Overview.pdf

Mohammed, L. T., AlHabshy, A. A., & ElDahshan, K. A. (2022, June). Big data visualization: A survey. In *2022 International Congress on Human-Computer Interaction, Optimization and Robotic Applications (HORA)* (pp. 1-12). IEEE.

Mondal, S., Das, S., & Vrana, V. G. (2023). How to bell the cat? A theoretical review of generative artificial intelligence towards digital disruption in all walks of life. *Technologies*, *11*(2), 44. doi:10.3390/technologies11020044

Ollivier, M., Pareek, A., Dahmen, J., Kayaalp, M. E., Winkler, P. W., Hirschmann, M. T., & Karlsson, J. (2023). A deeper dive into ChatGPT: History, use and future perspectives for orthopaedic research. *Knee Surgery, Sports Traumatology, Arthroscopy : Official Journal of the ESSKA*, *31*(4), 1190–1192. doi:10.1007/s00167-023-07372-5 PMID:36894785

Panda, G., Upadhyay, A. K., & Khandelwal, K. (2019). Artificial intelligence: A strategic disruption in public relations. *Journal of Creative Communications*, *14*(3), 196–213. doi:10.1177/0973258619866585

Partadiredja, R. A., Serrano, C. E., & Ljubenkov, D. (2020, November). AI or human: the socio-ethical implications of AI-generated media content. In *2020 13th CMI Conference on Cybersecurity and Privacy (CMI)-Digital Transformation-Potentials and Challenges (51275)* (pp. 1-6). IEEE. 10.1109/CMI51275.2020.9322673

Pavlik, J. V. (2023). Collaborating with ChatGPT: Considering the implications of generative artificial intelligence for journalism and media education. *Journalism & Mass Communication Educator, 78*(1), 84–93. doi:10.1177/10776958221149577

Pepper, T. (2023, April 25). *A Beginner's Guide to Working With An AI Writing Assistant.* Retrieved from peppercontent.io: https://www.Peppercontent .io/blog/a-beginners-guide-to-working-with-an-ai-writing-assistant/

Ramachandran, L., Gehringer, E. F., & Yadav, R. K. (2017). Automated assessment of the quality of peer reviews using natural language processing techniques. *International Journal of Artificial Intelligence in Education, 27*(3), 534–581. doi:10.1007/s40593-016-0132-x

Ray, P. P. (2023). ChatGPT: A comprehensive review on background, applications, key challenges, bias, ethics, limitations and future scope. *Internet of Things and Cyber-Physical Systems.*

Razack, H. I. A., Mathew, S. T., Saad, F. F. A., & Alqahtani, S. A. (2021). Artificial intelligence-assisted tools for redefining the communication landscape of the scholarly world. *Science Editing, 8*(2), 134-144.

Reguig, Y., & Mouffok, A. I. (2023). *Comparative Analysis of Current Word Processing Applications That Use Artificial Intelligence Case of Study: The Use of Grammarly and Quillbot Amongst Third Year BA Students at Ibn Khaldoun University of Tiaret* (Doctoral dissertation, Université IBN KHALDOUN-Tiaret).

Rusmiyanto, R., Huriati, N., Fitriani, N., Tyas, N. K., Rofi'i, A., & Sari, M. N. (2023). The Role of Artificial Intelligence (AI) In Developing English Language Learner's Communication Skills. *Journal of Education, 6*(1), 750–757.

Sabuncuoglu, A. (2020, June). Designing one year curriculum to teach artificial intelligence for middle school. In *Proceedings of the 2020 ACM conference on innovation and technology in computer science education* (pp. 96-102). 10.1145/3341525.3387364

Savage, T. M., & Vogel, K. E. (2013). *An introduction to digital multimedia.* Jones & Bartlett Publishers.

Schintler, L. A., McNeely, C. L., & Witte, J. (2023). A Critical Examination of the Ethics of AI-Mediated Peer Review. *arXiv preprint arXiv:2309.12356.*

ShrivastavaV. (2023). Skilled Resilience: Revitalizing Asian American and Pacific Islander Entrepreneurship Through AI-Driven Social Media Marketing Techniques. *Available at* SSRN 4507541. doi:10.2139/ssrn.4507541

Sikarskie, A. (2020). *Digital research methods in fashion and textile studies.* Bloomsbury Publishing.

Silva, T., Ma, J., Yang, C., & Liang, H. (2015). A profile-boosted research analytics framework to recommend journals for manuscripts. *Journal of the Association for Information Science and Technology, 66*(1), 180–200. doi:10.1002/asi.23150

Singh, R. P., Hom, G. L., Abramoff, M. D., Campbell, J. P., & Chiang, M. F. (2020). Current challenges and barriers to real-world artificial intelligence adoption for the healthcare system, provider, and the patient. *Translational Vision Science & Technology, 9*(2), 45–45. doi:10.1167/tvst.9.2.45 PMID:32879755

Spring, M., Faulconbridge, J., & Sarwar, A. (2022). How information technology automates and augments processes: Insights from Artificial-Intelligence-based systems in professional service operations. *Journal of Operations Management, 68*(6-7), 592–618. doi:10.1002/joom.1215

Uekusa, S. (2022). Overcoming disaster linguicism: Using autoethnography during the COVID-19 pandemic in Denmark to explore how community translators can provide multilingual disaster communication. *Journal of Applied Communication Research, 50*(6), 673–690. doi:10.1080/00909882.2022.2141067

Van der Velden, B. H., Kuijf, H. J., Gilhuijs, K. G., & Viergever, M. A. (2022). Explainable artificial intelligence (XAI) in deep learning-based medical image analysis. *Medical Image Analysis, 79*, 102470. doi:10.1016/j.media.2022.102470 PMID:35576821

Wang, C., Liu, S., Yang, H., Guo, J., Wu, Y., & Liu, J. (2023). Ethical Considerations of Using ChatGPT in Health Care. *Journal of Medical Internet Research, 25*, e48009. doi:10.2196/48009 PMID:37566454

Wang, F., Liu, X., Liu, O., Neshati, A., Ma, T., Zhu, M., & Zhao, J. (2023, April). Slide4N: Creating Presentation Slides from Computational Notebooks with Human-AI Collaboration. In *Proceedings of the 2023 CHI Conference on Human Factors in Computing Systems* (pp. 1-18). 10.1145/3544548.3580753

Wang, X., Li, L., Tan, S. C., Yang, L., & Lei, J. (2023). Preparing for AI-enhanced education: Conceptualizing and empirically examining teachers' AI readiness. *Computers in Human Behavior, 146*, 107798. doi:10.1016/j.chb.2023.107798

Yigitcanlar, T., Desouza, K. C., Butler, L., & Roozkhosh, F. (2020). Contributions and risks of artificial intelligence (AI) in building smarter cities: Insights from a systematic review of the literature. *Energies, 13*(6), 1473. doi:10.3390/en13061473

Zdravkova, K. (2022). The potential of artificial intelligence for assistive technology in education. In Handbook on Intelligent Techniques in the Educational Process: Vol 1 Recent Advances and Case Studies (pp. 61-85). Cham: Springer International Publishing. doi:10.1007/978-3-031-04662-9_4

Zehir, C., Karaboğa, T., & Başar, D. (2020). The transformation of human resource management and its impact on overall business performance: big data analytics and AI technologies in strategic HRM. *Digital Business Strategies in Blockchain Ecosystems: Transformational Design and Future of Global Business*, 265-279.

Compilation of References

Haleem, A., Javaid, M., & Singh, R. P. (2022). An era of ChatGPT as a significant futuristic support tool: A study on features, abilities, and challenges. *BenchCouncil transactions on benchmarks, standards and evaluations, 2*(4), 100089.

Abd-Elaal, E. S., Gamage, S. H., & Mills, J. E. (2019, January). Artificial intelligence is a tool for cheating academic integrity. In *30th Annual Conference for the Australasian Association for Engineering Education (AAEE 2019): Educators becoming agents of change: Innovate, integrate, motivate* (pp. 397-403). Academic Press.

Abd-Elsalam, K. A., & Abdel-Momen, S. M. (2023). Artificial Intelligence's Development and Challenges in Scientific Writing. *Egyptian Journal of Agricultural Research, 101*(3), 714–717. doi:10.21608/ejar.2023.220363.1414

Abio, B. (2023). Is the world ready for ai-powered therapy? *Nature*, 617.

Abramova, I. E., Ananyina, A. V. (2010). Modernization of the language teaching system at the university. *Higher education in Russia,* (8-9), 93-98.

Adadi, A., & Berrada, M. (2018). Peeking inside the black box: A survey on explainable artificial intelligence (XAI). *IEEE Access : Practical Innovations, Open Solutions*, *6*, 52138–52160. doi:10.1109/ACCESS.2018.2870052

Adams, D., & Chuah, K. M. (2022). Artificial intelligence-based tools in research writing: current trends and future potentials. *Artificial Intelligence in Higher Education*, 169-184.

Adams, D., & Chuah, K. M. (2022). Artificial intelligence-based tools in research writing: Current trends and future potentials. *Artificial intelligence in higher education*, 169-184.

Adigwe, C. S., Olaniyi, O. O., Olabanji, S. O., Okunleye, O. J., Mayeke, N. R., & Ajayi, S. A. (2024). Forecasting the Future: The Interplay of Artificial Intelligence, Innovation, and Competitiveness and its Effect on the Global Economy. *Asian Journal of Economics. Business and Accounting*, *24*(4), 126–146.

Advanced Grammar Checker for Academic & Professional Writing - TRINKA. (2021, July 24). https://www.trinka.ai/

Advanced Science News. (2023). Science Articles. https://www.advancedsciencenews.com/where-and-how-should-ChatGPT-be-used-in-the-scientific-literature/

Aggarwal, C. C. (2018). Neural networks and deep learning. Springer, 10(978), 3.

Agility Portal. (2023). Collaboration with Researcher. https://agilityportal.io/blog/streamlining-communication-and-collaboration-with-ChatGPT-and-intranet-portals/

Ahmad, M., Abbas, S., Fatima, A., Ghazal, T. M., Alharbi, M., Khan, M. A., & Elmitwally, N. S. (2023). AI-Driven livestock identification and insurance management system. *Egyptian Informatics Journal*, *24*(3), 100390. doi:10.1016/j.eij.2023.100390

Ahmad, S. F., Alam, M. M., Rahmat, M. K., Mubarik, M. S., & Hyder, S. I. (2022). Academic and administrative role of artificial intelligence in education. *Sustainability (Basel)*, *14*(3), 1101. doi:10.3390/su14031101

AI for Research - scite.ai. (n.d.-c). scite.ai. https://scite.ai/

Aithal, S., & Aithal, P. S. (2023). Effects of AI-Based ChatGPT on Higher Education Libraries. *International Journal of Management, Technology, and Social Sciences*, *8*(2), 95–108. doi:10.47992/IJMTS.2581.6012.0272

Akgun, S., & Greenhow, C. (2022). Artificial Intelligence (AI) in Education: Addressing Societal and Ethical Challenges in K-12 Settings. In *Proceedings of the 16th International Conference of the Learning Sciences-ICLS 2022*. International Society of the Learning Sciences.

Alase, A. (2017). The interpretative phenomenological analysis (IPA): A guide to a good qualitative research approach. *International Journal of Education and Literacy Studies*, *5*(2), 9–19. doi:10.7575/aiac.ijels.v.5n.2p.9

Albahri, A. S., Duhaim, A. M., Fadhel, M. A., Alnoor, A., Baqer, N. S., Alzubaidi, L., Albahri, O. S., Alamoodi, A. H., Bai, J., Salhi, A., Santamaría, J., Ouyang, C., Gupta, A., Gu, Y., & Deveci, M. (2023). A systematic review of trustworthy and explainable artificial intelligence in healthcare: Assessment of quality, bias risk, and data fusion. *Information Fusion*, *96*, 156–191. doi:10.1016/j.inffus.2023.03.008

Alharbi, W. (2023). AI in the Foreign Language Classroom: A Pedagogical Overview of Automated Writing Assistance Tools. *Education Research International*, *2023*, 2023. doi:10.1155/2023/4253331

Ali, M. J., & Djalilian, A. (2023, March). Readership awareness series–paper 4: Chatbots and ChatGPT-ethical considerations in scientific publications. In *Seminars in ophthalmology* (pp. 1–2). Taylor & Francis.

Ali, O., Abdelbaki, W., Shrestha, A., Elbasi, E., Alryalat, M. A. A., & Dwivedi, Y. K. (2023). A systematic literature review of artificial intelligence in the healthcare sector: Benefits, challenges, methodologies, and functionalities. *Journal of Innovation & Knowledge*, *8*(1), 100333. doi:10.1016/j.jik.2023.100333

Aljanabi, M. (2023). ChatGPT: Future directions and open possibilities. Mesopotamian journal of Cybersecurity, 2023, 16-17.

Al-Sarayrah, W., Al-Aiad, A., Habes, M., Elareshi, M., & Salloum, S. A. (2021, March). Improving the deaf and hard of hearing internet accessibility: JSL, text-into-sign language translator for Arabic. In *International Conference on Advanced Machine Learning Technologies and Applications* (pp. 456-468). Cham: Springer International Publishing. 10.1007/978-3-030-69717-4_43

Alshami, A., Elsayed, M., Ali, E., Eltoukhy, A. E., & Zayed, T. (2023). Harnessing the Power of ChatGPT for Automating Systematic Review Process: Methodology, Case Study, Limitations, and Future Directions. *Systems*, *11*(7), 351. doi:10.3390/systems11070351

AlshaterM. (2022, December 26). Exploring the role of artificial intelligence in enhancing academic performance: A case study of ChatGPT. doi:10.2139/ssrn.4312358

Altmäe, S., Sola-Leyva, A., & Salumets, A. (2023). Artificial intelligence in scientific writing: A friend or a foe? *Reproductive Biomedicine Online*, *47*(1), 3–9. doi:10.1016/j.rbmo.2023.04.009 PMID:37142479

Anderson, N., Belavy, D. L., Perle, S. M., Hendricks, S., Hespanhol, L., Verhagen, E., & Memon, A. R. (2023). AI did not write this manuscript, or did it? Can we trick the AI text detector into generated texts? The potential future of ChatGPT and AI in Sports & Exercise Medicine manuscript generation. *BMJ Open Sport & Exercise Medicine*, *9*(1), e001568. doi:10.1136/bmjsem-2023-001568 PMID:36816423

Angelov, P. P., Soares, E. A., Jiang, R., Arnold, N. I., & Atkinson, P. M. (2021). Explainable artificial intelligence: An analytical review. *Wiley Interdisciplinary Reviews. Data Mining and Knowledge Discovery*, *11*(5), e1424. doi:10.1002/widm.1424

Ang, T. L., Choolani, M., See, K. C., & Poh, K. K. (2023). The rise of artificial intelligence: Addressing the impact of large language models such as ChatGPT on scientific publications. *Singapore Medical Journal*, *64*(4), 219. doi:10.4103/singaporemedj.SMJ-2023-055 PMID:37006087

Ashktorab, Z., Liao, Q. V., Dugan, C., Johnson, J., Pan, Q., Zhang, W., ... Campbell, M. (2020). Human-ai collaboration in a cooperative game setting: Measuring social perception and outcomes. *Proceedings of the ACM on Human-Computer Interaction, 4*(CSCW2), 1-20. 10.1145/3415167

Baidoo-AnuD.Owusu AnsahL. Education in the Era of Generative Artificial Intelligence (AI): Understanding the Potential Benefits of ChatGPT in Promoting Teaching and Learning (January 25, 2023). Available at SSRN 4337484. doi:10.2139/ssrn.4337484

Baker, T., & Smith, L. (2019). Educ-AI-tion rebooted? Exploring the future of artificial intelligence in schools and colleges. Retrieved from Nesta Foundation website: https://media.nesta.org.uk/documents/Future_of_AI_and_education_v5_WEB.pdf

Balel, Y. (2023). The Role of Artificial Intelligence in Academic Paper Writing and Its Potential as a Co-Author. *European Journal of Therapeutics*, *29*(4), 984–985. doi:10.58600/eurjther1691

Balik, N. R., & Shmyger, H. P. (2023). Implementation of artificial intelligence in education through the use of ChatGPT. *Current aspects of the development of STEAM education in the conditions of European integration: a collection of materials of the International Scientific and Practical Internet Conference*, 147-149.

Barney, J. B. (2020). Contributing to theory: Opportunities and challenges. *AMS Review*, *10*(1), 49–55. doi:10.1007/s13162-020-00163-y

Barrett, G. (2023). Artificial intelligence for science in Africa. Academic Press.

Barth, T. J., & Arnold, E. (1999). Artificial intelligence and administrative discretion: Implications for public administration. *American Review of Public Administration*, *29*(4), 332–351. doi:10.1177/02750749922064463

Baruffaldi, S., van Beuzekom, B., Dernis, H., Harhoff, D., Rao, N., Rosenfeld, D., & Squicciarini, M. (2020). Identifying and measuring developments in artificial intelligence: Making the impossible possible. Academic Press.

Bates, T., Cobo, C., Mariño, O., & Wheeler, S. (2020). Can artificial intelligence transform higher education? *International Journal of Educational Technology in Higher Education*, *17*(42), 1–12.

Battina, D. S. (2016). AI-Augmented Automation for DevOps, a Model-Based Framework for Continuous Development in Cyber-Physical Systems. *International Journal of Creative Research Thoughts (IJCRT).*

Bauer, D. C., Metke-Jimenez, A., Maurer-Stroh, S., Tiruvayipati, S., Wilson, L. O., Jain, Y., Perrin, A., Ebrill, K., Hansen, D. P., & Vasan, S. S. (2021). Interoperable medical data: The missing link for understanding COVID-19. *Transboundary and Emerging Diseases*, *68*(4), 1753–1760. doi:10.1111/tbed.13892 PMID:33095970

Bayesian Spectacles. (2023). Testing Hypothesis. https://www.bayesianspectacles.org/redefine-statistical-significance-xx-a-chat-on-p-values-with-ChatGPT/

Bazanova, E. M. (2016). Scientific publication: write in English or translate? *Science editor and publisher*, 1(1-4), 17-24.

Bean, J. C., & Melzer, D. (2021). *Engaging ideas: The professor's guide to integrating writing, critical thinking, and active learning in the classroom*. John Wiley & Sons.

Benbada, M. L., & Benaouda, N. (2023). *Investigation of the Role of Artificial Intelligence in Developing Machine Translation Quality. Case Study: Reverso Context and Google Translate translations of Expressive and Descriptive Texts. Language Combination: Arabic-English/English-Arabic*(Doctoral dissertation, Faculty of Letters and Languages-Department of English).

Bender, E. M., & Friedman, B. (2018). Data statements for natural language processing: Toward mitigating system bias and enabling better science. *Transactions of the Association for Computational Linguistics*, *6*, 587–604. doi:10.1162/tacl_a_00041

Benedetto, L., Cremonesi, P., & Parenti, M. (2019). A virtual teaching assistant for personalized learning. *arXiv preprint arXiv:1902.09289.*

Bergen, K. J., Johnson, P. A., de Hoop, M. V., & Beroza, G. C. (2019). Machine learning for data-driven discovery in solid Earth geoscience. *Science*, *363*(6433), eaau0323. doi:10.1126/science.aau0323 PMID:30898903

Bieker, F., Friedewald, M., Hansen, M., Obersteller, H., & Rost, M. (2016). A process for data protection impact assessment under the European general data protection regulation. *Privacy Technologies and Policy: 4th Annual Privacy Forum, APF 2016, Frankfurt/Main, Germany, September 7-8, 2016 Proceedings*, *4*, 21–37.

Big Encyclopedic Dictionary. (1991). *Soviet encyclopedia* (Vol. 1). Author.

Bin-Nashwan, S. A., Sadallah, M., & Bouteraa, M. (2023). Use of ChatGPT in academia: Academic integrity hangs in the balance. *Technology in Society*, *75*, 102370. doi:10.1016/j.techsoc.2023.102370

Bissoto, A., Valle, E., & Avila, S. (2021). Gan-based data augmentation and anonymization for skin-lesion analysis: A critical review. In *Proceedings of the IEEE/CVF conference on computer vision and pattern recognition* (pp. 1847-1856). 10.1109/CVPRW53098.2021.00204

Blaizot, A., Veettil, S. P., Saidoung, P., Moreno-García, C., Wiratunga, N., Aceves-Martins, M., Lai, N., & Chaiyakunapruk, N. (2022). Using artificial intelligence methods for systematic review in health sciences: A systematic review. *Research Synthesis Methods*, *13*(3), 353–362. doi:10.1002/jrsm.1553 PMID:35174972

Boden, M. A. (2008). *Mind as machine: A history of cognitive science*. Oxford University Press.

Boella, G., Caro, L. D., Humphreys, L., Robaldo, L., Rossi, P., & van der Torre, L. (2016). Eunomos, a legal document and knowledge management system for the web to provide relevant, reliable and up-to-date information on the law. *Artificial Intelligence and Law*, *24*(3), 245–283. doi:10.1007/s10506-016-9184-3

Bolt, P. (1992). An evaluation of grammar-checking programs as self-help learning aids for learners of English as a foreign language. *Computer Assisted Language Learning*, *5*(1-2), 49–91. doi:10.1080/0958822920050106

Boote, D. N., & Beile, P. (2005). Scholars before researchers: On the centrality of the dissertation literature review in research preparation. *Educational researcher, 34*(6), 3-15.

Borboni, A., Reddy, K. V. V., Elamvazuthi, I., AL-Quraishi, M. S., Natarajan, E., & Azhar Ali, S. S. (2023). The Expanding Role of Artificial Intelligence in Collaborative Robots for Industrial Applications: A Systematic Review of Recent Works. *Machines*, *11*(1), 111. doi:10.3390/machines11010111

Borges, A. F. S., Laurindo, F. J. B., Spínola, M. M., Gonçalves, R. F., & Mattos, C. A. (2021). The strategic use of artificial intelligence in the digital era: Systematic literature review and future research directions. *International Journal of Information Management*, *1*(April), 102225. Advance online publication. doi:10.1016/j.ijinfomgt.2020.102225

Brody, S. (2021). Scite. *Journal of the Medical Library Association: JMLA*, *109*(4), 707. doi:10.5195/jmla.2021.1331 PMID:34858110

Brown, T., Mann, B., Ryder, N., Subbiah, M., Kaplan, J. D., Dhariwal, P., ... Amodei, D. (2020). Language models are few-shot learners. *Advances in Neural Information Processing Systems*, *33*, 1877–1901.

Bueno, D. C. (2020). Preventing Plagiarism towards Nurturing Research Integrity: A Descriptive-Mapping Review. *Online Submission*, *3*, 15–30.

Burlacu, C. (2023). *The Impact Of Ai-Powered Content Generation On Customer Experience* (Bachelor's thesis, University of Twente).

Buruk, O. (2023). Academic Writing with GPT-3.5 (ChatGPT): Reflections on Practices, Efficacy and Transparency. *ACM International Conference Proceeding Series*, 3, 144–153. 10.1145/3616961.3616992

Busch, P. A., & Hausvik, G. I. (2023). Too Good to Be True? An Empirical Study of ChatGPT Capabilities for Academic Writing and Implications for Academic Misconduct.

Cain, W. (2023, March). GPTeammate: A design fiction on the use of variants of the GPT language model as cognitive partners for active learning in higher education. In *Society for Information Technology & Teacher Education International Conference* (pp. 1293-1298). Association for the Advancement of Computing in Education (AACE).

Caldarini, G., Jaf, S., & McGarry, K. (2022). A literature survey of recent advances in chatbots. *Information (Basel)*, *13*(1), 41. doi:10.3390/info13010041

Callahan, J. L. (2014). Writing literature reviews: A reprise and update. *Human Resource Development Review*, *13*(3), 271–275. doi:10.1177/1534484314536705

Câmara Pereira, F. (2007). *Creativity and artificial intelligence: a conceptual blending approach*. Mouton de Gruyter. doi:10.1515/9783110198560

Campbell, J. P., Daft, R. L., & Hulin, C. (1982). What to Study: Generating and Developing Research Questions. *Sage (Atlanta, Ga.)*.

Cantú-Ortiz, F. J., Galeano Sánchez, N., Garrido, L., Terashima-Marin, H., & Brena, R. F. (2020). An artificial intelligence educational strategy for the digital transformation. *International Journal on Interactive Design and Manufacturing*, *14*(4), 1195–1209. doi:10.1007/s12008-020-00702-8

Carbonell, P., Jervis, A. J., Robinson, C. J., Yan, C., Dunstan, M., Swainston, N., Vinaixa, M., Hollywood, K. A., Currin, A., Rattray, N. J. W., Taylor, S., Spiess, R., Sung, R., Williams, A. R., Fellows, D., Stanford, N. J., Mulherin, P., Le Feuvre, R., Barran, P., ... Scrutton, N. S. (2018). An automated Design-Build-Test-Learn pipeline for enhanced microbial production of fine chemicals. *Communications Biology*, *1*(1), 66. doi:10.1038/s42003-018-0076-9 PMID:30271948

Carneiro, A. S. R. (2022). Following the path of otherwise: Subalternized subjects, academic writing and the political power of discomfort. *Journal of Multicultural Discourses*, *17*(2), 138–157. doi:10.1080/17447143.2022.2113886

Castagno, S., & Khalifa, M. (2020). Perceptions of artificial intelligence among healthcare staff: A qualitative survey study. *Frontiers in Artificial Intelligence*, *3*, 578983. doi:10.3389/frai.2020.578983 PMID:33733219

Chan, C. K. Y. (2023). A comprehensive AI policy education framework for university teaching and learning. *International Journal of Educational Technology in Higher Education*, *20*(1), 1–25. doi:10.1186/s41239-023-00408-3

Chaplai, I. V., & Lebedeva, N. A. (2018). Realization of UNESCO goals for sustainable government management in Ukraine (preservation of land ecosystems – reserve "Askania-Nova"). PR and mass media in Kazakhstan: collection of scientific works. – PR and mass media in Kazakhstan: scientific work set / comp. and Ch. ed. L.S. Akhmetova, 44-53.

Checco, A., Bracciale, L., Loreti, P., Pinfield, S., & Bianchi, G. (2021). AI-assisted peer review. *Humanities & Social Sciences Communications*, *8*(1), 1–11. doi:10.1057/s41599-020-00703-8 PMID:38617731

Chen, J. J., & Lin, J. C. (2024). Artificial intelligence as a double-edged sword: Wielding the POWER principles to maximize its positive effects and minimize its negative effects. *Contemporary Issues in Early Childhood*, *25*(1), 146–153. doi:10.1177/14639491231169813

Chen, L., Chen, P., & Lin, Z. (2020). Artificial intelligence in education: A review. *IEEE Access : Practical Innovations, Open Solutions*, *8*, 75264–75278. doi:10.1109/ACCESS.2020.2988510

Chen, T. J. (2023). ChatGPT and other artificial intelligence applications speed up scientific writing. *Journal of the Chinese Medical Association*, *86*(4), 351–353. doi:10.1097/JCMA.0000000000000900 PMID:36791246

Chen, X., Zou, D., Xie, H., Cheng, G., & Liu, C. (2022). Two decades of artificial intelligence in education. *Journal of Educational Technology & Society*, *25*(1), 28–47.

Chiu, J., & Quayle, E. (2022). Understanding online grooming: An interpretative phenomenological analysis of adolescents' offline meetings with adult perpetrators. *Child Abuse & Neglect*, *128*, 105600. doi:10.1016/j.chiabu.2022.105600 PMID:35338948

Chiu, T. K., Xia, Q., Zhou, X., Chai, C. S., & Cheng, M. (2023). Systematic literature review on opportunities, challenges, and future research recommendations of artificial intelligence in education. *Computers and Education: Artificial Intelligence*, *4*, 100118. doi:10.1016/j.caeai.2022.100118

Chowdhury, S., Dey, P., Joel-Edgar, S., Bhattacharya, S., Rodriguez-Espindola, O., Abadie, A., & Truong, L. (2023). Unlocking the value of artificial intelligence in human resource management through AI capability framework. *Human Resource Management Review*, *33*(1), 100899. doi:10.1016/j.hrmr.2022.100899

Christou, P. (2023). How to Use Artificial Intelligence (AI) as a Resource, ow Methodological and Analysis Tool in Qualitative Research? *The Qualitative Report*, *28*(7), 1968–1980. doi:10.46743/2160-3715/2023.6406

Chubb, J., Cowling, P., & Reed, D. (2022). Speeding up to keep up: Exploring the use of AI in the research process. *AI & Society*, *37*(4), 1439–1457. doi:10.1007/s00146-021-01259-0 PMID:34667374

Civaner, M. M., Uncu, Y., Bulut, F., Chalil, E. G., & Tatli, A. (2022). Artificial intelligence in medical education: A cross-sectional needs assessment. *BMC Medical Education*, *22*(1), 772. doi:10.1186/s12909-022-03852-3 PMID:36352431

Collins, J. A., & Fauser, B. C. (2005). Balancing the strengths of systematic and narrative reviews. *Human Reproduction Update*, *11*(2), 103–104. doi:10.1093/humupd/dmh058 PMID:15618290

Collinsworth, A., & Benjamin, D. (2022). Uses of Artificial Intelligence in Healthcare: A Structured Literature Review. *Bridging Human Intelligence and Artificial Intelligence*, 339-353.

Cope, B., Kalantzis, M., & Searsmith, D. (2021). Artificial intelligence for education: Knowledge and its assessment in AI-enabled learning ecologies. *Educational Philosophy and Theory*, *53*(12), 1229–1245. doi:10.1080/00131857.2020.1728732

Corcoles, A. D., Kandala, A., Javadi-Abhari, A., McClure, D. T., Cross, A. W., Temme, K., Nation, P. D., Steffen, M., & Gambetta, J. M. (2020). Challenges and opportunities of near-term quantum computing systems. *Proceedings of the IEEE*, *108*(8), 1338–1352. doi:10.1109/JPROC.2019.2954005

Cotton, D. R., Cotton, P. A., & Shipway, J. R. (2023). Chatting and cheating: Ensuring academic integrity in the era of ChatGPT. *Innovations in Education and Teaching International*, 1–12.

Cox, A. M., Pinfield, S., & Rutter, S. (2019). The intelligent library: Thought leaders' views on the likely impact of artificial intelligence on academic libraries. *Library Hi Tech*, *37*(3), 418–435. doi:10.1108/LHT-08-2018-0105

Crawford, J., Cowling, M., & Allen, K. A. (2023). Leadership is needed for ethical ChatGPT: Character, assessment, and learning using artificial intelligence (AI). Journal of University Teaching & Learning Practice, 20(3), 2.

Creswell, J. W., & Poth, C. N. (2016). *Qualitative inquiry and research design: Choosing among five approaches*. Sage publications.

Crompton, H., & Burke, D. (2023). Artificial intelligence in higher education: The state of the field. *International Journal of Educational Technology in Higher Education*, *20*(22), 1–22. doi:10.1186/s41239-023-00392-8

Cui, Z., Jing, X., Zhao, P., Zhang, W., & Chen, J. (2021). A new subspace clustering strategy for AI-based data analysis in IoT system. *IEEE Internet of Things Journal*, *8*(16), 12540–12549. doi:10.1109/JIOT.2021.3056578

Curry, N., Kasparkova, A., Ganobcsik-Williams, L., & Gustafsson, M. (2023). Thinking outside the academic writing box. *Journal of Academic Writing*, *13*(1), ii–v. doi:10.18552/joaw.v10i1.968

Curtis, N. (2023). To ChatGPT or not to ChatGPT? The impact of artificial intelligence on academic publishing. *The Pediatric Infectious Disease Journal*, *42*(4), 275. doi:10.1097/INF.0000000000003852 PMID:36757192

Cyfirma. (2023). Challenges. https://www.cyfirma.com/outofband/ChatGPT-ai-in-security-testing-opportunities-and-challenges/

Das, A. K. (2018). How Flipkart is Using Artificial Intelligence to Stay Ahead of Competition. Available at: https://hiredigital.com/blog/how-flipkart-is-using-artificial-intelligence

Daubner, S. C., Gutierrez, V., & Rodriguez, M. (2018). Introducing Students to Biochemistry Through An Inquiry-Based Curriculum Documented Using Electronic Notebooks on SciNote. *The FASEB Journal*, *32*(S1), 663–667. doi:10.1096/fasebj.2018.32.1_supplement.663.7

Davies, A., Veličković, P., Buesing, L., Blackwell, S., Zheng, D., Tomašev, N., Tanburn, R., Battaglia, P., Blundell, C., Juhász, A., Lackenby, M., Williamson, G., Hassabis, D., & Kohli, P. (2021). Advancing mathematics by guiding human intuition with AI. *Nature*, *600*(7887), 70–74. doi:10.1038/s41586-021-04086-x PMID:34853458

De Vaujany, F. X., Mitev, N. N., Smith, M., & Walsh, I. (2014). Renewing Literature Reviews in MIS Research? A Critical Realist Approach. *A Critical Realist Approach.*

DeCostanza, A. H., Marathe, A. R., Bohannon, A., Evans, A. W., Palazzolo, E. T., Metcalfe, J. S., & McDowell, K. (2018). *Enhancing human-agent teaming with individualized, adaptive technologies: A discussion of critical scientific questions*. US Army Research Laboratory Aberdeen Proving Ground United States.

Delahanty, R. J., Kaufman, D., & Jones, S. S. (2018). Development and Evaluation of an Automated Machine Learning Algorithm for In-Hospital Mortality Risk Adjustment Among Critical Care Patients. *Critical Care Medicine*, *46*(6), E481–E488. doi:10.1097/CCM.0000000000003011 PMID:29419557

Deoras, S. (2017). SBI Introduces Its Own Chatbot SIA, To Address Customer Queries. Available at: https://analyticsindiamag.com/sbi-introduces-chatbot-sia-address-customer-queries/

Dergaa, I., Chamari, K., Zmijewski, P., & Saad, H. B. (2023). From human writing to artificial intelligence generated text: Examining the prospects and potential threats of ChatGPT in academic writing. *Biology of Sport*, *40*(2), 615–622. doi:10.5114/biolsport.2023.125623 PMID:37077800

DeYoung, J., Jain, S., Rajani, N. F., Lehman, E., Xiong, C., Socher, R., & Wallace, B. C. (2019). ERASER: A benchmark to evaluate rationalized NLP models. *arXiv preprint arXiv:1911.03429*

Dhoni, P. (2023). *Exploring the Synergy between Generative AI.* Data and Analytics in the Modern Age.

Diakopoulos, N. (2016). Accountability in algorithmic decision making. *Communications of the ACM*, *59*(2), 56–62. doi:10.1145/2844110

Discourse (2023, March). Hypothesis. https://discourse.datamethods.org/t/accuracy-of-ChatGPT-on-statistical-methods/6402

Dong, Y., Hou, J., Zhang, N., & Zhang, M. (2020). Research on how human intelligence, consciousness, and cognitive computing affect the development of artificial intelligence. *Complexity*, *2020*, 1–10. doi:10.1155/2020/1680845

Dönmez, İ., Sahin, I., & Gülen, S. (2023). Conducting academic research with the ai interface chatgpt: Challenges and opportunities. *Journal of STEAM Education, 6*(2), 101-118.

Doody, O., & Bailey, M. E. (2016). Setting a research question, aim and objective. *Nurse Researcher*, *23*(4), 19–23. doi:10.7748/nr.23.4.19.s5 PMID:26997231

Dowling, M., & Lucey, B. (2023). ChatGPT for (finance) research: The Bananarama conjecture. *Finance Research Letters*, *53*, 103662. doi:10.1016/j.frl.2023.103662

Duan, Y., Edwards, J. S., & Dwivedi, Y. K. (2019). Artificial intelligence for decision making in the era of Big Data–evolution, challenges and research agenda. *International Journal of Information Management*, *48*, 63–71. doi:10.1016/j.ijinfomgt.2019.01.021

Dubose, J., & Marshall, D. (2023). AI in academic writing: Tool or invader. *Public Services Quarterly*, *19*(2), 125–130. doi:10.1080/15228959.2023.2185338

Duerr, S., & Gloor, P. A. (2021). Persuasive Natural Language Generation—A Literature Review. *arXiv preprint arXiv:2101.05786.*

Duymaz, Y. K., & Tekin, A. M. (2024). Harnessing artificial intelligence in academic writing: Potential, ethics, and responsible use. *European Journal of Therapeutics*, *30*(1), 87–88. doi:10.58600/eurjther1755

Dwivedi, Y. K., Sharma, A., Rana, N. P., Giannakis, M., Goel, P., & Dutot, V. (2023). Evolution of artificial intelligence research in Technological Forecasting and Social Change: Research topics, trends, and future directions, *Technological Forecasting and Social Change*, 192. https://www.sciencedirect.com/science/article/pii/S0040162523002640 doi:10.1016/j.techfore.2023.122579

Dwivedi, Y. K., Hughes, L., Ismagilova, E., Aarts, G., Coombs, C., Crick, T., Duan, Y., Dwivedi, R., Edwards, J., Eirug, A., Galanos, V., Ilavarasan, P. V., Janssen, M., Jones, P., Kar, A. K., Kizgin, H., Kronemann, B., Lal, B., Lucini, B., ... Williams, M. D. (2021). Artificial Intelligence (AI): Multidisciplinary perspectives on emerging challenges, opportunities, and agenda for research, practice and policy. *International Journal of Information Management*, *57*, 101994. doi:10.1016/j.ijinfomgt.2019.08.002

Dwivedi, Y. K., Kshetri, N., Hughes, L., Slade, E. L., Jeyaraj, A., Kar, A. K., Baabdullah, A. M., Koohang, A., Raghavan, V., Ahuja, M., Albanna, H., Albashrawi, M. A., Al-Busaidi, A. S., Balakrishnan, J., Barlette, Y., Basu, S., Bose, I., Brooks, L., Buhalis, D., ... Wright, R. (2023). "So what if ChatGPT wrote it?" Multidisciplinary perspectives on opportunities, challenges and implications of generative conversational AI for research, practice and policy. *International Journal of Information Management*, *71*, 102642. doi:10.1016/j.ijinfomgt.2023.102642

Eatough, V., & Smith, J. A. (2017). Interpretative phenomenological analysis. The Sage handbook of qualitative research in psychology, 193-209.

Eggers, W. D., Schatsky, D., & Viechnicki, P. (2017). AI-augmented government. Using cognitive technologies to redesign public sector work. *Deloitte Center for Government Insights*, *1*, 24.

Ehsan, U., Liao, Q. V., Muller, M., Riedl, M. O., & Weisz, J. D. (2021, May). Expanding explainability: Towards social transparency in AI systems. In *Proceedings of the 2021 CHI conference on human factors in computing systems* (pp. 1-19). 10.1145/3411764.3445188

Elavarasi, R., & Dhanalakshmi, P. (2022). Theoretical framework of employee skill gap analysis and its effects in organisation. *Business Environment and Technological Innovation-Emerging Trends-volume*, *II*, 75.

Elish, M. C., & Boyd, D. (2018). Situating methods in the magic of Big Data and AI. *Communication Monographs*, *85*(1), 57–80. doi:10.1080/03637751.2017.1375130

Elmawi, E. E. (2021). *The Impact of Using Peer Editing as an Effective Feedback Tool on Developing Libyan EFL Students' Writing Performance*.

Emiratli, A., Marchuk, M., & Osadcha, K. (2017). The problem of formation of academic writing skills among future programmers. *Ukrainian Journal of Educational Studies and Information Technology*, (3), 25–30.

Engstrom, D. F., Ho, D. E., Sharkey, C. M., & Cuéllar, M. F. (2020). Government by algorithm: Artificial intelligence in federal administrative agencies. *NYU School of Law*, Public Law Research Paper, (20-54).

Erickson, L. B., Young, J. R., & Pinnegar, S. (2011). Endnote. *Studying Teacher Education*, *7*(2), 215–216. doi:10.1080/17425964.2011.591192

European Commission. (2021). Proposal for a Regulation laying down harmonised rules on artificial intelligence. European Commission.

Exner-Stöhr, M., Kopp, A., Kühne-Hellmessen, L., Oldach, L., Roth, D., & Zimmermann, A. (2017). *The potential of Artificial Intelligence in academic research at a Digital University*. Gesellschaft für Informatik.

Fahd, K., & Miah, S. J. (2023). Designing and Evaluating a Big Data Analytics Approach for predicting students' success factors. *Journal of Big Data*, *10*(1), 159. doi:10.1186/s40537-023-00835-z

Feng, S. Y., Gangal, V., Wei, J., Chandar, S., Vosoughi, S., Mitamura, T., & Hovy, E. (2021). A survey of data augmentation approaches for NLP. *arXiv preprint arXiv:2105.03075*. doi:10.18653/v1/2021.findings-acl.84

Filipenko, L. V., Dumanskyi, O. V., & Kozak, O. V. (2023). Academic integrity in the scientific and educational environment of educational institutions of Ukraine: a view through the prism of the presence of artificial intelligence. *Academic visions*, (19). 120-130.

Fink, A. (2019). *Conducting research literature reviews: From the internet to paper*. Sage publications.

Fitria, T. N. (2023, March). Artificial intelligence (AI) technology in OpenAI ChatGPT application: A review of ChatGPT in writing English essay. In *ELT Forum. Journal of English Language Teaching*, *12*(1), 44–58.

Flasiński, M. (2016). *Introduction to artificial intelligence*. Springer. doi:10.1007/978-3-319-40022-8

Fleming, A. D., Goatman, K. A., Philip, S., Prescott, G. J., Sharp, P. F., & Olson, J. A. (2010). Automated grading for diabetic retinopathy: A large-scale audit using arbitration by clinical experts. *The British Journal of Ophthalmology*, *94*(12), 1606–1610. doi:10.1136/bjo.2009.176784 PMID:20858722

Floridi, L., & Chiriatti, M. (2020). GPT-3: Its Nature, Scope, Limits, and Consequences. *Minds and Machines*, *30*(4), 681–694. Advance online publication. doi:10.1007/s11023-020-09548-1

Fok, R., & Weld, D. S. (2023). What Can't Large Language Models Do? The Future of AI-Assisted Academic Writing. In In2Writing Workshop at CHI.

Ford, J., & Sutphen, R. D. (1996). Early intervention to improve attendance in elementary school for at-risk children: *A pilot program. Children & Schools*, *18*(2), 95–102. doi:10.1093/cs/18.2.95

Forrester, C., Boothe, K., & Generative, A. I. (n.d.). *Academic Writing*. Ethical Recommendations.

Fountaine, T., McCarthy, B., & Saleh, T. (2019). Building the AI-powered organization. *Harvard Business Review*, *97*(4), 62–73.

Francke, E., & Bennett, A. (2019, October). The potential influence of artificial intelligence on plagiarism: A higher education perspective. In *European Conference on the Impact of Artificial Intelligence and Robotics (ECIAIR 2019)* (pp. 131-140). Academic Press.

Fricke, S. (2018). Semantic scholar. *Journal of the Medical Library Association: JMLA*, *106*(1), 145. doi:10.5195/jmla.2018.280

Friedler, S. A., Scheidegger, C., Venkatasubramanian, S., Choudhary, S., Hamilton, E. P., & Roth, D. (2019, January). A comparative study of fairness-enhancing interventions in machine learning. In *Proceedings of the conference on fairness, accountability, and transparency* (pp. 329-338). 10.1145/3287560.3287589

Fuchs, K. (2023, May). Exploring the opportunities and challenges of NLP models in higher education: Is ChatGPT a blessing or a curse? *Frontiers in Education*, *8*, 1166682. doi:10.3389/feduc.2023.1166682

Fyfe, P. (2023). How to cheat on your final paper: Assigning AI for student writing. *AI & Society*, *38*(4), 1395–1405. doi:10.1007/s00146-022-01397-z

Gao, C. A., Howard, F. M., Markov, N. S., Dyer, E. C., Ramesh, S., Luo, Y., & Pearson, A. T. (2022). Comparing scientific abstracts generated by ChatGPT to original abstracts using an artificial intelligence output detector, plagiarism detector, and blinded human reviewers. BioRxiv, 2022-12. doi:10.1101/2022.12.23.521610

Gao, B. (2022). Research and implementation of intelligent evaluation system of teaching quality in universities based on artificial intelligence neural network model. *Mathematical Problems in Engineering*, *2022*, 1–10. doi:10.1155/2022/5448359

Garbuio, M., & Lin, N. (2021). Innovative idea generation in problem finding: Abductive reasoning, cognitive impediments, and the promise of artificial intelligence. *Journal of Product Innovation Management*, *38*(6), 701–725. doi:10.1111/jpim.12602

Garcia-Vidal, C., Sanjuan, G., Puerta-Alcalde, P., Moreno-García, E., & Soriano, A. (2019). Artificial intelligence to support clinical decision-making processes. In EBioMedicine (Vol. 46, pp. 27–29). doi:10.1016/j.ebiom.2019.07.019

Gaube, S., Suresh, H., Raue, M., Merritt, A., Berkowitz, S. J., Lermer, E., Coughlin, J. F., Guttag, J. V., Colak, E., & Ghassemi, M. (2021). Do as AI say: Susceptibility in deployment of clinical decision-aids. *NPJ Digital Medicine*, *4*(1), 31. doi:10.1038/s41746-021-00385-9 PMID:33608629

Gayed, J. M., Carlon, M. K. J., Oriola, A. M., & Cross, J. S. (2022). Exploring an AI-based writing Assistant's impact on English language learners. *Computers and Education: Artificial Intelligence, 3*(100055), 100055. doi:10.1016/j.caeai.2022.100055

Gayevska, O., & Shvidkiy, D. (2023). Implementation of the Scientific Research Project Method Using Artificial Intelligence in Teaching Japanese Language to Philology Students. *Scientific Bulletin of Uzhhorod University. Series: "Pedagogy. Social Work*, (2 (53)), 34–39.

Gendron, Y., Andrew, J., & Cooper, C. (2022). The perils of artificial intelligence in academic publishing. *Critical Perspectives on Accounting, 87*, 102411. doi:10.1016/j.cpa.2021.102411

Gevrey, M., Dimopoulos, I., & Lek, S. (2003). Review and comparison of methods to study the contribution of variables in artificial neural network models. *Ecological Modelling, 160*(3), 249–264. doi:10.1016/S0304-3800(02)00257-0

Ghotbi, N. (2023). Ethics of Artificial Intelligence in Academic Research and Education. In *Handbook of Academic Integrity* (pp. 1355–1366). Springer International Publishing. doi:10.1007/978-3-031-54144-5_143

Ghufron, M. A., & Rosyida, F. (2018). The role of Grammarly in assessing English as a Foreign Language (EFL) writing. *Lingua Cultura, 12*(4), 395–403. doi:10.21512/lc.v12i4.4582

Gilal, F. G., Zhang, J., Paul, J., & Gilal, N. G. (2019). The role of self-determination theory in marketing science: An integrative review and agenda for research. *European Management Journal, 37*(1), 29–44. doi:10.1016/j.emj.2018.10.004

Gilat, R., & Cole, B. J. (2023). How will artificial intelligence affect scientific writing, reviewing and editing? The future is here.... *Arthroscopy, 39*(5), 1119–1120. doi:10.1016/j.arthro.2023.01.014 PMID:36774329

Ginting, P., Batubara, H. M., & Hasnah, Y. (2023). Artificial intelligence powered writing tools as adaptable aids for academic writing: Insight from EFL college learners in writing final project. *International Journal of Multidisciplinary Research And Analysis, 6*(10), 4640–4650. doi:10.47191/ijmra/v6-i10-15

Giray, L. (2023). Prompt engineering with ChatGPT: A guide for academic writers. *Annals of Biomedical Engineering, 51*(12), 2629–2633. doi:10.1007/s10439-023-03272-4 PMID:37284994

Golan, R., Reddy, R., Muthigi, A., & Ramasamy, R. (2023). Artificial intelligence in academic writing: A paradigm-shifting technological advance. *Nature Reviews. Urology, 20*(6), 327–328. doi:10.1038/s41585-023-00746-x PMID:36829078

Gorchynskyi, S. V., Sofilkanych, M. I., & Gorbenko, I. F. (2023). The quality of Ukrainian education and academic integrity: the impact of the use of artificial intelligence. *Academic Visions, (20).* https://academy-vision.org/index.php/av/article/view/407

Gozalo-Brizuela, R., & Garrido-Merchan, E. C. (2023). ChatGPT is not all you need. A State of the Art Review of large Generative AI models. *arXiv preprint arXiv:2301.04655.*

Green, M. (2023). Ethical Considerations and Bias Mitigation in the Use of ChatGPT for Scientific Research. Ethics in AI Conference Proceedings, 45-58.

Griffiths, T. L., & Steyvers, M. (2004). Finding scientific topics. *Proceedings of the National Academy of Sciences of the United States of America, 101*(suppl_1), 5228–5235. doi:10.1073/pnas.0307752101 PMID:14872004

Grzebyk, M., Pierscieniak, A., & Stec, M. (2021). Assessment of Management Efficiency in Local Administrative Offices: Case Study Poland. *Lex Localis, 19*(2), 329–351. doi:10.4335/19.2.329-351(2021)

Gundersen, O. E., Gil, Y., & Aha, D. W. (2018). On reproducible AI: Towards reproducible research, open science, and digital scholarship in AI publications. *AI Magazine, 39*(3), 56–68. doi:10.1609/aimag.v39i3.2816

Gunning, D., Stefik, M., Choi, J., Miller, T., Stumpf, S., & Yang, G. Z. (2019). XAI—Explainable artificial intelligence. *Science Robotics*, *4*(37), eaay7120. doi:10.1126/scirobotics.aay7120 PMID:33137719

Gupta, V., & Gupta, C. (2023). Leveraging AI technologies in libraries through experimentation-driven frameworks. *Internet Reference Services Quarterly*, *27*(4), 1–12. doi:10.1080/10875301.2023.2240773

Gureeva, M. Y. (2021). Enterprise management in the context of digitalization of the economy based on the use of artificial intelligence. Master's thesis of specialty 073 "Management", educational program "Business Administration", Poltava University of Economics and Trade.

Haber, R. N., & Schindler, R. M. (1981). Error in proofreading: Evidence of syntactic control of letter processing? *Journal of Experimental Psychology. Human Perception and Performance*, *7*(3), 573–579. doi:10.1037/0096-1523.7.3.573

Haenlein, M., & Kaplan, A. (2019). A brief history of artificial intelligence: On the past, present, and future of artificial intelligence. *California Management Review*, *61*(4), 5–14. doi:10.1177/0008125619864925

Hagendorff, T. (2020). The ethics of AI ethics: An evaluation of guidelines. *Minds and Machines*, *30*(1), 99–120. doi:10.1007/s11023-020-09517-8

Hajkowicz, S., Naughtin, C., Sanderson, C., Schleiger, E., Karimi, S., Bratanova, A., & Bednarz, T. (2022). Artificial intelligence for science–Adoption trends and future development pathways. Academic Press.

Hajkowicz, S., Reeson, A., Rudd, L., Bratanova, A., Hodgers, L., Mason, C., & Boughen, N. (2016). Tomorrow's digitally enabled workforce: Megatrends and scenarios for jobs and employment in Australia over the coming twenty years. Academic Press.

Hakopyants, N. M. (2023). Using ChatGPT in the process of learning English: advantages and opportunities. *Bulletin of the National Technical University "KhPI". Series: Actual problems of the development of Ukrainian society*, (1), 69-72.

Hammad, M. (2023). The impact of artificial intelligence (AI) Programs on writing scientific research. *Annals of Biomedical Engineering*, *51*(3), 459–460. doi:10.1007/s10439-023-03140-1 PMID:36637603

Hariri, W. (2023). Unlocking the Potential of ChatGPT: A Comprehensive Exploration of its Applications. *Technology*, *15*(2), 16.

Hasan, A. R. (2021). Artificial Intelligence (AI) in accounting & auditing: A Literature review. *Open Journal of Business and Management*, *10*(1), 440–465. doi:10.4236/ojbm.2022.101026

Heger, T., Aguilar-Trigueros, C. A., Bartram, I., Braga, R. R., Dietl, G. P., Enders, M., Gibson, D. J., Gómez-Aparicio, L., Gras, P., Jax, K., Lokatis, S., Lortie, C. J., Mupepele, A.-C., Schindler, S., Starrfelt, J., Synodinos, A. D., & Jeschke, J. M. (2021). The Hierarchy-of-Hypotheses Approach: A Synthesis Method for Enhancing Theory Development in Ecology and Evolution. *Bioscience*, *71*(4), 337–349. Advance online publication. doi:10.1093/biosci/biaa130 PMID:33867867

Henning, V., & Reichelt, J. (2008, December). Mendeley-a last. fm for research? *In 2008 IEEE fourth international conference on eScience* (pp. 327-328). IEEE.

HernandezJ. A.CondeJ.ReviriegoP.de ArcauteG. M. R. (2023). Is ChatGPT capable of solving classical Communications and Networking problems? Authorea Preprints.

Hoffman, S. G. (2017). Managing ambiguities at the edge of knowledge: Research strategy and artificial intelligence labs in an era of academic capitalism. *Science, Technology & Human Values*, *42*(4), 703–740. doi:10.1177/0162243916687038

Hong, B., Malik, A., Lundquist, J., Bellach, I., & Kontokosta, C. E. (2018). Applications of machine learning methods to predict readmission and length-of-stay for homeless families: The case of win shelters in New York City. *Journal of Technology in Human Services*, *36*(1), 89–104. doi:10.1080/15228835.2017.1418703

Hong, Q. N., & Pluye, P. (2019). A conceptual framework for critical appraisal in systematic mixed studies reviews. *Journal of Mixed Methods Research*, *13*(4), 446–460. doi:10.1177/1558689818770058

Horoshaylo, O. S., & Kochergina, S. S. (2023). The use of artificial intelligence to improve the quality of teaching foreign languages in a higher educational institution. *Scientific journal of the M. P. Drahomanov NPU. Series 5. Pedagogical sciences: realities and prospects*, 123—127.

How to Copy and Paste Without Plagiarizing In 2022. (2022, October 18). Retrieved from Opportunities. http://opportunities. alumdev.columbia.edu/how-to-copy-an-essay-without-plagiarizing.php

Howat, A. M., Mulhern, A., Logan, H. F., Redvers-Mutton, G., Routledge, C., & Clark, J. (2021). Converting Access Microbiology to an open research platform: Focus group and AI review tool research results. *Access Microbiology*, *3*(4). Advance online publication. doi:10.1099/acmi.0.000232 PMID:34151179

Hristovski, D., Rindflesch, T., & Peterlin, B. (2013). Using literature-based discovery to identify novel therapeutic approaches. *Cardiovascular & Hematological Agents in Medicinal Chemistry (Formerly Current Medicinal Chemistry-Cardiovascular & Hematological Agents)*, *11*(1), 14-24.

Hsu, H. P. (2023). Can Generative Artificial Intelligence Write an Academic Journal Article? Opportunities, Challenges, and Implications. *Irish Journal of Technology Enhanced Learning*, *7*(2), 158–171. doi:10.22554/ijtel.v7i2.152

Huang, Z., & Winkel, W. (n.d.). Automated Feedback: An AI-powered Tool to Scale Micro-level Feedback for Better Academic Writing.

Huang, J., & Tan, M. (2023). The role of ChatGPT in scientific communication: Writing better scientific review articles. *American Journal of Cancer Research*, *13*(4), 1148. PMID:37168339

Huang, Y., Lv, S., Tseng, K. K., Tseng, P. J., Xie, X., & Lin, R. F. Y. (2023). Recent advances in artificial intelligence for video production system. *Enterprise Information Systems*, *17*(11), 2246188. doi:10.1080/17517575.2023.2246188

Hunt, E. B. (2014). *Artificial intelligence*. Academic Press.

Hwang, G. J., Xie, H., Wah, B. W., & Gašević, D. (2020). Vision, challenges, roles and research issues of Artificial Intelligence in Education. *Computers and Education: Artificial Intelligence*, *1*, 100001. doi:10.1016/j.caeai.2020.100001

IEEE Corporate Advisory Group (CAG). (2016). IEEE guide for terms and concepts in intelligent process automation. The Institute of Electrical and Electronics Engineers Standards Association. https://ieeexplore.ieee.org/iel7/8070669/8070670/08070671.pdf

Ifelebuegu, A. O., Kulume, P., & Cherukut, P. (2023). Chatbots and AI in Education (AIEd) tools: The good, the bad, and the ugly. *Journal of Applied Learning and Teaching*, *6*(2).

Ilieva, R., & Tonchev, A. (2022). Adapting the Teaching of Academic Writing to the Emergence of Natural Language Generators. In 2022 V International Conference on High Technology for Sustainable Development (HiTech) (pp. 1–4). IEEE. 10.1109/HiTech56937.2022.10145549

Illia, L., Colleoni, E., & Zyglidopoulos, S. (2023). Ethical implications of text generation in the age of artificial intelligence. *Business Ethics, the Environment & Responsibility*, *32*(1), 201–210. doi:10.1111/beer.12479

Inozemtsev, V., Ivleva, M., & Ivlev, V. (2017, June). Artificial intelligence and the problem of computer representation of knowledge. In *2nd International Conference on Contemporary Education, Social Sciences and Humanities (ICCESSH 2017)* (pp. 1151-1157). Atlantis Press. 10.2991/iccessh-17.2017.268

Ip, K. (2023). Revolutionising content recommendation: The impact of AI in marketing. *Journal of AI. Robotics & Workplace Automation*, *2*(4), 382–389.

Ippolito, D., Yuan, A., Coenen, A., & Burnam, S. (2022). Creative writing with an ai-powered writing assistant: Perspectives from professional writers. *arXiv preprint arXiv:2211.05030.*

Ishchenko, O., & Chernysh, A. (2022). Essay as a Priority Genre of Academic Writting. *Philological Treatises*, *14*(2), 47–55.

Jaiswal, A., & Arun, C. J. (2021). Potential of Artificial Intelligence for transformation of the education system in India. *International Journal of Education and Development Using Information and Communication Technology*, *17*(1), 142–158.

Jarrah, A. M., Wardat, Y., & Fidalgo, P. (2023). Using ChatGPT in academic writing is (not) a form of plagiarism: What does the literature say. *Online J. Commun. Media Technol.*

Jarrah, A. M., Wardat, Y., & Fidalgo, P. (2023). Using ChatGPT in academic writing is (not) a form of plagiarism: What does the literature say. *Online Journal of Communication and Media Technologies*, *13*(4), e202346. doi:10.30935/ojcmt/13572

Järvelä, S., Nguyen, A., & Hadwin, A. (2023). Human and artificial intelligence collaboration for socially shared regulation in learning. *British Journal of Educational Technology*, *54*(5), 1057–1076. doi:10.1111/bjet.13325

Javaid, M., Haleem, A., Singh, R. P., Khan, S., & Khan, I. H. (2023). Unlocking the opportunities through ChatGPT Tool towards ameliorating the education system. *BenchCouncil Transactions on Benchmarks. Standards and Evaluations*, *3*(2), 100115.

Javaid, M., Haleem, A., Singh, R. P., Suman, R., & Rab, S. (2022). Significance of machine learning in healthcare: Features, pillars and applications. *International Journal of Intelligent Networks*, *3*, 58–73. doi:10.1016/j.ijin.2022.05.002

Jeff Searlei. (2016). Kant on genius. https://jeffsearle.blogspot.com/2017/11/kant-on-genius.html

Jeyaraman, M., Ramasubramanian, S., Balaji, S., Jeyaraman, N., Nallakumarasamy, A., & Sharma, S. (2023). ChatGPT in action: Harnessing artificial intelligence potential and addressing ethical challenges in medicine, education, and scientific research. *World Journal of Methodology*, *13*(4), 170–178. doi:10.5662/wjm.v13.i4.170 PMID:37771867

Jiang, J. A., Wade, K., Fiesler, C., & Brubaker, J. R. (2021). Supporting serendipity: Opportunities and challenges for Human-AI Collaboration in qualitative analysis. *Proceedings of the ACM on Human-Computer Interaction, 5*(CSCW1), 1-23. 10.1145/3449168

Jobin, A., Ienca, M., & Vayena, E. (2019). The global landscape of AI ethics guidelines. *Nature Machine Intelligence*, *1*(9), 389–399. doi:10.1038/s42256-019-0088-2

Joyner, R. L., Rouse, W. A., & Glatthorn, A. A. (2018). *Writing the winning thesis or dissertation: A step-by-step guide.* Corwin Press.

Kabudi, T., Pappas, I., & Olsen, D. H. (2021). AI-enabled adaptive learning systems: A systematic mapping of the literature. *Computers and Education: Artificial Intelligence*, *2*(1), 1–12. doi:10.1016/j.caeai.2021.100017

Kalla, D., & Smith, N. (2023). Study and Analysis of ChatGPT and its Impact on Different Fields of Study. *International Journal of Innovative Science and Research Technology*, *8*(3).

Kamila, M. K., & Jasrotia, S. S. (2023). Ethical issues in the development of artificial intelligence: recognizing the risks. *International Journal of Ethics and Systems*.

Kang, Y., Cai, Z., Tan, C. W., Huang, Q., & Liu, H. (2020). Natural language processing (NLP) in management research: A literature review. *Journal of Management Analytics*, *7*(2), 139–172. doi:10.1080/23270012.2020.1756939

Kasneci, E., Seßler, K., Küchemann, S., Bannert, M., Dementieva, D., Fischer, F., Gasser, U., Groh, G., Günnemann, S., Hüllermeier, E., Krusche, S., Kutyniok, G., Michaeli, T., Nerdel, C., Pfeffer, J., Poquet, O., Sailer, M., Schmidt, A., Seidel, T., ... Kasneci, G. (2023). ChatGPT for good? On opportunities and challenges of large language models for education. *Learning and Individual Differences*, *103*, 102274. doi:10.1016/j.lindif.2023.102274

Kennelly, I., & Donnelly, R. (2023). AI Supporting Student Academic Writing in Higher Education.

Kenwright, B. (2024). Is it the end of undergraduate dissertations?: Exploring the advantages and challenges of generative ai models in education. In *Generative AI in teaching and learning* (pp. 46–65). IGI Global.

Khabib, S. (2022). Introducing artificial intelligence (AI)-based digital writing assistants for teachers in writing scientific articles. *Teaching English as a Foreign Language Journal*, *1*(2), 114–124. doi:10.12928/tefl.v1i2.249

Khalil, M., & Er, E. (2023). Will ChatGPT get you caught? Rethinking of plagiarism detection. *arXiv preprint arXiv:2302.04335*. doi:10.1007/978-3-031-34411-4_32

Khang, A., Shah, V., & Rani, S. (Eds.). (2023). *Handbook of Research on AI-Based Technologies and Applications in the Era of the Metaverse*. IGI Global. doi:10.4018/978-1-6684-8851-5

KhanM. J.MahadeA. Investigation to Improve Decision Support Systems with the Help of Artificial Intelligence in Higher Education. *Available at* SSRN 4530480. doi:10.2139/ssrn.4530480

Khan, M., Mehran, M. T., Haq, Z. U., Ullah, Z., Naqvi, S. R., Ihsan, M., & Abbass, H. (2021). Applications of artificial intelligence in COVID-19 pandemic: A comprehensive review. *Expert Systems with Applications*, *185*, 115695. doi:10.1016/j.eswa.2021.115695 PMID:34400854

Kherson Chamber of Commerce. (2017). Pylypenko Yury Vladimirovich https://www.tpp.ks.ua/rus/khersonshchina-v-litsakh/784-pilipenko.html

Kherson Region News. (2017). Joseph Konpadovych Pachockiy https://kherson-news.info/main-news/hersonshina-krai-talantlivyh-ychenyh/

KhlaifZ. N. (2023). Ethical Concerns about Using AI-Generated Text in Scientific Research. Available at SSRN 4387984. doi:10.2139/ssrn.4387984

Khlaif, Z. N., Mousa, A., Hattab, M. K., Itmazi, J., Hassan, A. A., Sanmugam, M., & Ayyoub, A. (2023). The Potential and Concerns of Using AI in Scientific Research: ChatGPT Performance Evaluation. *JMIR Medical Education*, *9*, e47049. doi:10.2196/47049 PMID:37707884

Kim, J., Merrill, K., Xu, K., & Sellnow, D. D. (2020). My teacher is a machine: Understanding students' perceptions of AI teaching assistants in online education. *International Journal of Human-Computer Interaction*, *36*(20), 1902–1911. doi:10.1080/10447318.2020.1801227

Kim, S. G. (2023). Using ChatGPT for language editing in scientific articles. *Maxillofacial Plastic and Reconstructive Surgery*, *45*(1), 13. doi:10.1186/s40902-023-00381-x PMID:36882591

Kim, Y., Soyata, T., & Behnagh, R. F. (2018). Towards emotionally aware AI smart classroom: Current issues and directions for engineering and education. *IEEE Access : Practical Innovations, Open Solutions*, *6*, 5308–5331. doi:10.1109/ACCESS.2018.2791861

King, M. R. (2023). A Conversation on Artificial Intelligence, Chatbots, and Plagiarism in Higher Education. *Cellular and Molecular Bioengineering*, *16*(1), 1–2. doi:10.1007/s12195-022-00754-8 PMID:36660590

Kiron, D. (2017). Lessons from becoming a data-driven organization. *MIT Sloan Management Review*, *58*(2).

Kiselyova, A., & Zavalska, L. (2023). Basics of academic writing: teaching method manual. National Odesa University law academy.

Klobukova, L. P. (1998) Scientific discussion as an act of communication (linguistic aspect). Language, cognition, communication: Sat. of articles.

Kodiyan, A. A. (2019). An overview of ethical issues in using AI systems in hiring with a case study of Amazon's AI-based hiring tool. *Researchgate Preprint*, 1-19.

Koene, A., Clifton, C., Hatada, Y., Webb, H., & Richardson, R. (2019). A governance framework for algorithmic accountability and transparency. Academic Press.

Komova, G. V., Rubtsova, V. V., & Salionovych, L. M. (2018). PBL as a means of forming written academic competence. *Scientific Bulletin of Kherson State University. Ser.: Translation studies and intercultural communication*, 27-31.

Kooli, C. (2023). Chatbots in education and research: A critical examination of ethical implications and solutions. *Sustainability (Basel)*, *15*(7), 5614. doi:10.3390/su15075614

Korinek, A. (2023). Generative AI for economic research: Use cases and implications for economists. *Journal of Economic Literature*, *61*(4), 1281–1317. doi:10.1257/jel.20231736

Kornienko, O. P. (2008). Terminological specificity of English texts of the sublanguage of architecture and construction. *Proceedings of the Russian State Pedagogical University*, 63-100.

Koubaa, A., Boulila, W., Ghouti, L., Alzahem, A., & Latif, S. (2023). Exploring ChatGPT Capabilities and Limitations: A Survey. *IEEE Access*. kssNvYB7y66y. (2023b, September 5). *Online Summarizing Tool | Flashcard Generator & Summarizer | Scholarcy*. Scholarcy | the Long-form Article Summariser. https://www.scholarcy.com/

Kozlenkova, I. V., Samaha, S. A., & Palmatier, R. W. (2014). Resource-based theory in marketing. *Journal of the Academy of Marketing Science*, *42*(1), 1–21. doi:10.1007/s11747-013-0336-7

Kuleto, V., Ilić, M., Dumangiu, M., Ranković, M., Martins, O. M., Păun, D., & Mihoreanu, L. (2021). Exploring opportunities and challenges of artificial intelligence and machine learning in higher education institutions. *Sustainability (Basel)*, *13*(18), 10424. doi:10.3390/su131810424

Kung, J. Y. (2023). Elicit. *The Journal of the Canadian Health Libraries Association*, *44*(1), 15.

Kung, T. H., Cheatham, M., Medenilla, A., Sillos, C., De Leon, L., Elepaño, C., Madriaga, M., Aggabao, R., Diaz-Candido, G., Maningo, J., & Tseng, V. (2023). Performance of ChatGPT on USMLE: Potential for AI-assisted medical education using large language models. *PLOS Digital Health*, *2*(2), e0000198. doi:10.1371/journal.pdig.0000198 PMID:36812645

Kurian, N., Cherian, J. M., Sudharson, N. A., Varghese, K. G., & Wadhwa, S. (2023). AI is now everywhere. *British Dental Journal*, *234*(2), 72–72. doi:10.1038/s41415-023-5461-1 PMID:36707552

Kurzweil, R. (1985). What Is Artificial Intelligence Anyway? As the techniques of computing grow more sophisticated, machines are beginning to appear intelligent—But can they actually think? *American Scientist*, *73*(3), 258–264.

Kushwaha, A. K., & Kar, A. K. (2021). MarkBot – A Language Model-Driven Chatbot for Interactive Marketing in Post-Modern World. *Information Systems Frontiers*. Advance online publication. doi:10.1007/s10796-021-10184-y

Kusters, R., Misevic, D., Berry, H., Cully, A., Le Cunff, Y., Dandoy, L., Díaz-Rodríguez, N., Ficher, M., Grizou, J., Othmani, A., Palpanas, T., Komorowski, M., Loiseau, P., Moulin Frier, C., Nanini, S., Quercia, D., Sebag, M., Soulié Fogelman, F., Taleb, S., ... Wehbi, F. (2020). Interdisciplinary research in artificial intelligence: Challenges and opportunities. *Frontiers in Big Data*, *3*, 577974. doi:10.3389/fdata.2020.577974 PMID:33693418

Kuular, M. Ch. (2021). Terminological Analysis of the Concept "Monography". *Bibliosphere*, (3), 72–82. doi:10.20913/1815-3186-2021-3-72-82

Kuziemski, M., & Misuraca, G. (2020). AI governance in the public sector: Three tales from the frontiers of automated decision-making in democratic settings. *Telecommunications Policy*, *44*(6), 101976. doi:10.1016/j.telpol.2020.101976 PMID:32313360

Kuznetsova, N. G., Zaitseva, I. E., & Stepicheva, O. N. (2016). The Professional Language of Architects: A Systematic Approach to the Dictionary (Based on English, German and French). *Philological Sciences. Questions of theory and practice, 6-2*(60), 98-107.

Leavy, S., Meaney, G., Wade, K., & Greene, D. (2020). Mitigating gender bias in machine learning data sets. *Bias and Social Aspects in Search and Recommendation: First International Workshop, BIAS 2020, Lisbon, Portugal, April 14 Proceedings*, *1*, 12–26.

Lebedeva, N. A. (2018). Teaching English in the field of knowledge "Public management and administration" in an agrarian higher educational institution. *European dimension of reforming public administration in Ukraine: materials of the International Scientific and Practical Conference*. Kyiv "Publishing House "Personal", 60-62.

Lebedeva, N. A., & Pasechko, V. V. (2017). Ukrainian-Russian-English dictionary of livestock terms. *Scientific forum: Innovative science: collection. Art. based on materials of the VII international. scientific-practical conf. No. 6(7).* https://nauchforum.ru/conf/philology/x/26238 https://nauchforum.ru/files/2017_10_26_inno/6%287%29.pdf

Lebedeva, N. A. (2022). Consequences of the Pandemic for Ukrainian Agriculture in the Context of Public Administration. In A. Pego (Ed.), *Handbook of Research on Global Networking Post COVID-19* (pp. 173–188). IGI Global. doi:10.4018/978-1-7998-8856-7.ch009

Lebedeva, N. A. (2022). Teaching of Foreign Language in the Educational Process of Public Administration Personnel in Ukraine. In O. Kulaç, C. Babaoğlu, & E. Akman (Eds.), *Public Affairs Education and Training in the 21st Century* (pp. 294–310). IGI Global. doi:10.4018/978-1-7998-8243-5.ch019

Lebedeva, N. A. (2023). *Improving the Lexical and Grammatical Skills of Students Specializing in Hydraulic Engineering and Water Resources by Means of Writing. Cases on Error Analysis in Foreign Language Technical Writing*. IGI Global. doi:10.4018/978-1-6684-6222-5.ch007

Lecler, A., Duron, L., & Soyer, P. (2023). Revolutionizing radiology with GPT-based models: Current applications, future possibilities and limitations of ChatGPT. *Diagnostic and Interventional Imaging*, *104*(6), 269–274. doi:10.1016/j.diii.2023.02.003 PMID:36858933

Letham, B., Rudin, C., McCormick, T. H., & Madigan, D. (2015). Interpretable classifiers using rules and Bayesian analysis: Building a better stroke prediction model. Academic Press.

Liang, W., Yuksekgonul, M., Mao, Y., Wu, E., & Zou, J. (2023). GPT detectors are biased against non-native English writers. *arXiv preprint arXiv:2304.02819.*

Liao, H. T., Wang, Z., & Liu, Y. (2020, April). Exploring the cross-disciplinary collaboration: A scientometric analysis of social science research related to Artificial Intelligence and Big Data application. []. IOP Publishing.]. *IOP Conference Series. Materials Science and Engineering*, *806*(1), 012019. doi:10.1088/1757-899X/806/1/012019

Liao, Q. V., Gruen, D., & Miller, S. (2020, April). Questioning the AI: informing design practices for explainable AI user experiences. In *Proceedings of the 2020 CHI conference on human factors in computing systems* (pp. 1-15). 10.1145/3313831.3376590

Liao, Q. V., Subramonyam, H., Wang, J., & Wortman Vaughan, J. (2023, April). Designerly understanding: Information needs for model transparency to support design ideation for AI-powered user experience. In *Proceedings of the 2023 CHI conference on human factors in computing systems* (pp. 1-21). 10.1145/3544548.3580652

Liapis, A., Yannakakis, G., & Togelius, J. (2013). Designer modeling for personalized game content creation tools. In *Proceedings of the AAAI Conference on Artificial Intelligence and Interactive Digital Entertainment* (Vol. 9, No. 2, pp. 11-16). Academic Press.

Liebling, D. J., Lahav, M., Evans, A., Donsbach, A., Holbrook, J., Smus, B., & Boran, L. (2020, April). Unmet needs and opportunities for mobile translation AI. *Proceedings of the 2020 CHI conference on human factors in computing systems*. 10.1145/3313831.3376261

Liebrenz, M., Schleifer, R., Buadze, A., Bhugra, D., & Smith, A. (2023). Generating scholarly content with ChatGPT: Ethical challenges for medical publishing. *The Lancet. Digital Health*, *5*(3), e105–e106. doi:10.1016/S2589-7500(23)00019-5 PMID:36754725

Li, J., Larsen, K., & Abbasi, A. (2020a). TheoryOn: A design framework and system for unlocking behavioral knowledge through ontology learning. *Management Information Systems Quarterly*, *44*(4), 1733–1772. doi:10.25300/MISQ/2020/15323

Lingard, L. (2023). Writing with ChatGPT: An illustration of its capacity, limitations & implications for academic writers. *Perspectives on Medical Education*, *12*(1), 261–270. doi:10.5334/pme.1072 PMID:37397181

Listverse (2023, March 22). Controversies. https://listverse.com/2023/03/22/ten-controversial-news-stories-surrounding-ChatGPT/

Li, T., Sahu, A. K., Talwalkar, A., & Smith, V. (2020b). Federated learning: Challenges, methods, and future directions. *IEEE Signal Processing Magazine*, *37*(3), 50–60. doi:10.1109/MSP.2020.2975749

Littman, M. L., Ajunwa, I., Berger, G., Boutilier, C., Currie, M., Doshi-Velez, F., . . . Walsh, T. (2022). Gathering strength, gathering storms: The one-hundred-year study on artificial intelligence (AI100) 2021 study panel report. *arXiv preprint arXiv:2210.15767*.

Liu, H., Azam, M., Bin Naeem, S., & Faiola, A. (2023). An overview of the capabilities of ChatGPT for medical writing and its implications for academic integrity. *Health Information and Libraries Journal*, *40*(4), 440–446. doi:10.1111/hir.12509 PMID:37806782

Liu, N., Shapira, P., & Yue, X. (2021). Tracking developments in artificial intelligence research: Constructing and applying a new search strategy. *Scientometrics*, *126*(4), 3153–3192. doi:10.1007/s11192-021-03868-4 PMID:34720254

Liu, Y., Han, T., Ma, S., Zhang, J., Yang, Y., Tian, J., He, H., Li, A., He, M., Liu, Z., Wu, Z., Zhao, L., Zhu, D., Li, X., Qiang, N., Shen, D., Liu, T., & Ge, B. (2023). Summary of chatgpt-related research and perspective towards the future of large language models. *Meta-Radiology*, *1*(2), 100017. doi:10.1016/j.metrad.2023.100017

LiuZ.YaoZ.LiF.LuoB. (2023). Check me if you can: Detecting ChatGPT-generated academic writing using CheckGPT. Retrieved from http://arxiv.org/abs/2306.05524

Li, Z., Sharma, V., & Mohanty, S. P. (2020). Preserving data privacy via federated learning: Challenges and solutions. *IEEE Consumer Electronics Magazine*, *9*(3), 8–16. doi:10.1109/MCE.2019.2959108

Loai, A. T., Mehmood, R., Benkhlifa, E., & Song, H. (2016). Mobile cloud computing model and big data analysis for healthcare applications. *IEEE Access : Practical Innovations, Open Solutions*, *4*, 6171–6180. doi:10.1109/ACCESS.2016.2613278

Luan, H., Geczy, P., Lai, H., Gobert, J., Yang, S. J., Ogata, H., Baltes, J., Guerra, R., Li, P., & Tsai, C. C. (2020). Challenges and future directions of big data and artificial intelligence in education. *Frontiers in Psychology*, *11*, 580820. doi:10.3389/fpsyg.2020.580820 PMID:33192896

Luckin, R., & Holmes, W. (2016). Intelligence unleashed: An argument for AI in education. Academic Press.

Lund, B. D., Wang, T., Mannuru, N. R., Nie, B., Shimray, S., & Wang, Z. (2023). ChatGPT and a new academic reality: Artificial Intelligence-written research papers and the ethics of the large language models in scholarly publishing. *Journal of the Association for Information Science and Technology*, *74*(5), 570–581. doi:10.1002/asi.24750

Lund, T. (2022). Research Problems and Hypotheses in Empirical Research. *Scandinavian Journal of Educational Research*, *66*(7), 1183–1193. doi:10.1080/00313831.2021.1982765

Lu, Y. (2019). Artificial intelligence: A survey on evolution, models, applications and future trends. *Journal of Management Analytics*, *6*(1), 1–29. doi:10.1080/23270012.2019.1570365

MacCarthyM. (2019). An examination of the Algorithmic Accountability Act of 2019. *Available at* SSRN 3615731. doi:10.2139/ssrn.3615731

Make Use Of. (2023). Key Challenges. https://www.makeuseof.com/openai-ChatGPT-biggest-probelms/

Malik, A. R., Pratiwi, Y., Andajani, K., Numertayasa, I. W., Suharti, S., Darwis, A., & Marzuki. (2023). Exploring Artificial Intelligence in Academic Essay: Higher Education Student's Perspective. *International Journal of Educational Research Open*, *5*, 100296. doi:10.1016/j.ijedro.2023.100296

Malik, A., Budhwar, P., & Mohan, H., & NR, S. (2023). Employee experience–the missing link for engaging employees: Insights from an MNE's AI-based HR ecosystem. *Human Resource Management*, *62*(1), 97–115. doi:10.1002/hrm.22133

Malik, P., Mittal, V., Nautiyal, L., & Ram, M. (2022). NLP techniques, tools, and algorithms for data science. *Artificial Intelligence for Signal Processing and Wireless Communication*, *11*, 123–148. doi:10.1515/9783110734652-006

Maney, K. (2003). *The maverick and his machine: Thomas Watson, Sr. and the making of IBM*. John Wiley & Sons.

Manning, C. D., & Schütze, H. (1999). Lexical acquisition. *Foundations of statistical natural language processing, 999*, 296-305.

Marchandot, B., Matsushita, K., Carmona, A., Trimaille, A., & Morel, O. (2023). ChatGPT: The next frontier in academic writing for cardiologists or a pandora's box of ethical dilemmas. *European Heart Journal Open*, *3*(2), oead007. doi:10.1093/ehjopen/oead007 PMID:36915398

Marr, B. (2023). The Evolution Of AI: Transforming The World One Algorithm At A Time. Retrieved from https://bernardmarr.com/the-evolution-of-ai-transforming-the-world-one-algorithm-at-a-time/

Maruashvili, E. (2023). Criteria For Academic Writing. Georgian Academy of Business Sciences. *MOAMBE*, *1*, 60–64.

Marzuki, W., Widiati, U., Rusdin, D., Darwin, & Indrawati, I. (2023). The impact of AI writing tools on the content and organization of students' writing: EFL teachers' perspective. *Cogent Education*, *10*(2), 2236469. doi:10.1080/2331186X.2023.2236469

Matta, A. (2023) How AI in travel and hospitality is enhancing experiences and optimising operations. Available at https://www.forbesindia.com/article/take-one-big-story-of-the-day/how-ai-in-travel-and-hospitality-is-enhancing-experiences-and-optimising-operations/87027/1

Matveeva, K. V. (2023). The use of artificial intelligence tools in writing scientific research: an ethical aspect. *XIII International scientific and technical conference of students, postgraduates and young scientists "Scientific Spring 2023"*, 246-248.

Mazzone, M., & Elgammal, A. (2019, February). Art, creativity, and the potential of artificial intelligence. In Arts (Vol. 8, No. 1, p. 26). MDPI. doi:10.3390/arts8010026

McClure, E. C., Sievers, M., Brown, C. J., Buelow, C. A., Ditria, E. M., Hayes, M. A., Pearson, R. M., Tulloch, V. J. D., Unsworth, R. K. F., & Connolly, R. M. (2020). Artificial intelligence meets citizen science to supercharge ecological monitoring. *Patterns (New York, N.Y.)*, *1*(7), 100109. doi:10.1016/j.patter.2020.100109 PMID:33205139

McGee, R. W. (2023). Is ChatGPT biased against conservatives? an empirical study. An Empirical Study.

Mhlanga, D. (2023). Open AI in education, the responsible and ethical use of ChatGPT towards lifelong learning. Education, the Responsible and Ethical Use of ChatGPT Towards Lifelong Learning.

Miao, F., Holmes, W., Huang, R., & Zhang, H. (2021). *AI and education: A guidance for policymakers.* UNESCO Publishing.

Michel-Villarreal, R., Vilalta-Perdomo, E., Salinas-Navarro, D. E., Thierry-Aguilera, R., & Gerardou, F. S. (2023). Challenges and opportunities of Generative AI for higher education as explained by ChatGPT. *Education Sciences*, *13*(9), 856. doi:10.3390/educsci13090856

Mijwil, M. M., Hiran, K. K., Doshi, R., Dadhich, M., Al-Mistarehi, A. H., & Bala, I. (2023). ChatGPT and the future of academic integrity in the artificial intelligence era: A new frontier. *Al-Salam Journal for Engineering and Technology*, *2*(2), 116–127. doi:10.55145/ajest.2023.02.02.015

Miller, T. (2019). Explanation in artificial intelligence: Insights from the social sciences. *Artificial Intelligence*, *267*, 1–38. doi:10.1016/j.artint.2018.07.007

Module: Reference Management . (2023). Retrieved from eqpoint.info: http://eqpoint.info/Reference_Management/Reference_Management_Overview.pdf

Mohammadkarimi, E. (2023). Teachers' reflections on academic dishonesty in EFL students' writings in the era of artificial intelligence. *Journal of Applied Learning and Teaching*, *6*(2).

Mohammed, L. T., AlHabshy, A. A., & ElDahshan, K. A. (2022, June). Big data visualization: A survey. In *2022 International Congress on Human-Computer Interaction, Optimization and Robotic Applications (HORA)* (pp. 1-12). IEEE.

Mohammed, O., Sahib, T. M., Hayder, I. M., Salisu, S., & Shahid, M. (2023). ChatGPT Evaluation: Can It Replace Grammarly and Quillbot Tools? *British Journal of Applied Linguistics*, *3*(2), 34–46. doi:10.32996/bjal.2023.3.2.4

Mondal, S., Das, S., & Vrana, V. G. (2023). How to bell the cat? A theoretical review of generative artificial intelligence towards digital disruption in all walks of life. *Technologies*, *11*(2), 44. doi:10.3390/technologies11020044

Moor, J. (2006). The Dartmouth College artificial intelligence conference: The next fifty years. *AI Magazine*, *27*(4), 87–87.

Morley, J., Machado, C. C., Burr, C., Cowls, J., Joshi, I., Taddeo, M., & Floridi, L. (2020). The ethics of AI in health care: A mapping review. *Social Science & Medicine*, *260*, 113172. doi:10.1016/j.socscimed.2020.113172 PMID:32702587

Morrison, F. M. M., Rezaei, N., Arero, A. G., Graklanov, V., Iritsyan, S., Ivanovska, M., Makuku, R., Marquez, L. P., Minakova, K., Mmema, L. P., Rzymski, P., & Zavolodko, G. (2023). Maintaining scientific integrity and high research standards against the backdrop of rising artificial intelligence use across fields. *Journal of Medical Artificial Intelligence*, *6*, 6. doi:10.21037/jmai-23-63

Moss, E., Watkins, E. A., Metcalf, J., & Elish, M. C. (2020, April). Governing with algorithmic impact assessments: six observations. In *Watkins, Elizabeth and Moss, Emanuel and Metcalf, Jacob and Singh, Ranjit and Elish, Madeleine Clare, Governing Algorithmic Systems with Impact Assessments: Six Observations (May 14, 2021). AAAI/ACM Conference on Artificial Intelligence, Ethics, and Society (AIES).* 10.2139/ssrn.3584818

Moustakas, C. (1994). *Phenomenological research methods.* Sage Publications. doi:10.4135/9781412995658

Moya, B., Eaton, S. E., Pethrick, H., Hayden, K. A., Brennan, R., Wiens, J., ... Lesage, J. (2023). Academic integrity and artificial intelligence in higher education contexts: A rapid scoping review protocol. *Canadian Perspectives on Academic Integrity*, *5*(2), 59–75.

Naik, A. R. (2022). How ITC is Using Machine Learning. Available at: https://analyticsindiamag.com/how-itc-is-using-machine-learning/

Nair, K., & Gupta, R. (2021). Application of AI technology in modern digital marketing environment. *World Journal of Entrepreneurship, Management and Sustainable Development*, *17*(3), 318–328. doi:10.1108/WJEMSD-08-2020-0099

Naqvi, Z. (2020). Artificial intelligence, copyright, and copyright infringement. *Marq. Intell. Prop. L. Rev.*, *24*, 15.

Natale, S., & Ballatore, A. (2020). Imagining the thinking machine: Technological myths and the rise of artificial intelligence. *Convergence (London)*, *26*(1), 3–18. doi:10.1177/1354856517715164

Nazari, N., Shabbir, M. S., & Setiawan, R. (2021). Application of Artificial Intelligence powered digital writing assistant in higher education: Randomized controlled trial. *Heliyon*, *7*(5), e07014. doi:10.1016/j.heliyon.2021.e07014 PMID:34027198

Ng, D. T. K., Luo, W., Chan, H. M. Y., & Chu, S. K. W. (2022). Using digital story writing as a pedagogy to develop AI literacy among primary students. *Computers and Education: Artificial Intelligence*, *3*, 100054. doi:10.1016/j.caeai.2022.100054

Nicholson, K., & Slonim, A. (Eds.). (2022). *Artificial intelligence: your questions answered.* Australian Strategic Policy Institute.

Nikolenko, K. V., Protas, O. L., & Yarmolenko, T. A. (2023). Innovative technologies of artificial intelligence to ensure academic integrity in educational institutions of Ukraine. *Perspectives and innovations of science ("Pedagogy" Series, "Psychology" Series, "Medicine" Series)*, (30), 393-406.

Nolan, A. (2024). Artificial intelligence in science: Challenges, opportunities, and the future of research. Academic Press.

Ntoutsi, E., Fafalios, P., Gadiraju, U., Iosifidis, V., Nejdl, W., Vidal, M. E., Ruggieri, S., Turini, F., Papadopoulos, S., Krasanakis, E., Kompatsiaris, I., Kinder-Kurlanda, K., Wagner, C., Karimi, F., Fernandez, M., Alani, H., Berendt, B., Kruegel, T., Heinze, C., ... Staab, S. (2020). Bias in data-driven artificial intelligence systems—An introductory survey. *Wiley Interdisciplinary Reviews. Data Mining and Knowledge Discovery*, *10*(3), e1356. doi:10.1002/widm.1356

Nurshatayeva, A., Page, L. C., White, C. C., & Gehlbach, H. (2020). Proactive student support using artificially intelligent conversational chatbots: The importance of targeting the technology. *EdWorking paper, Annenberg University https:// www. edwor kingp apers. com/sites/defau lt/files/ai20-208. pdf.*

Odrakiewicz, P., Orlykovskyi, M., & Gaylord, M. (2022). Integrity, Sustainability, And Intellectual Capital Challenges in Management Education in The Era of Artificial Intelligence. *Mest Journal, 10*(1).

OECD. (2021). Database of national AI policies. Organisation for Economic Cooperation and Development, Artificial Intelligence Policy Observatory. OECD.

Ollivier, M., Pareek, A., Dahmen, J., Kayaalp, M. E., Winkler, P. W., Hirschmann, M. T., & Karlsson, J. (2023). A deeper dive into ChatGPT: History, use and future perspectives for orthopaedic research. *Knee Surgery, Sports Traumatology, Arthroscopy : Official Journal of the ESSKA, 31*(4), 1190–1192. doi:10.1007/s00167-023-07372-5 PMID:36894785

Olujimi, P. A., & Ade-Ibijola, A. (2023). NLP techniques for automating responses to customer queries: A systematic review. *Discov Artif Intell, 3*(1), 20. doi:10.1007/s44163-023-00065-5

Oravec, J. A. (2023). Artificial Intelligence Implications for Academic Cheating: Expanding the Dimensions of Responsible Human-AI Collaboration with ChatGPT. *Journal of Interactive Learning Research, 34*(2), 213–237.

Oshiro, J., Caubet, S. L., Viola, K. E., & Huber, J. M. (2020). Going Beyond "Not Enough Time": Barriers to Preparing Manuscripts for Academic Medical Journals. *Teaching and Learning in Medicine, 32*(1), 71–81. doi:10.1080/10401334.2019.1659144 PMID:31530189

Ostapovych, O., Ostapovych, N., & Mazurenko, Yu. (2023). ChatGPT in the training of philologists and translators. challenges and prospects. *Scientific notes of the National University "Ostroh Academy": Series. Philology, 17*(85), 200–205.

Ouchchy, L., Coin, A., & Dubljević, V. (2020). AI in the headlines: The portrayal of the ethical issues of artificial intelligence in the media. *AI & Society, 35*(4), 927–936. doi:10.1007/s00146-020-00965-5

Panda, G., Upadhyay, A. K., & Khandelwal, K. (2019). Artificial intelligence: A strategic disruption in public relations. *Journal of Creative Communications, 14*(3), 196–213. doi:10.1177/0973258619866585

Parikh, P. M., Shah, D. M., & Parikh, K. P. (2023). Judge Juan Manuel Padilla Garcia, ChatGPT, and a controversial medicolegal milestone. *Indian Journal of Medical Sciences, 75*(1), 3–8. doi:10.25259/IJMS_31_2023

Park, J. (2023). Artificial intelligence–assisted writing: A continuously evolving issue. *Science Editing, 10*(2), 115–118. doi:10.6087/kcse.318

Partadiredja, R. A., Serrano, C. E., & Ljubenkov, D. (2020, November). AI or human: the socio-ethical implications of AI-generated media content. In *2020 13th CMI Conference on Cybersecurity and Privacy (CMI)-Digital Transformation-Potentials and Challenges (51275)* (pp. 1-6). IEEE. 10.1109/CMI51275.2020.9322673

Pasko, O., Staurskaya, N., Tokareva, O., Cebral, P., Lebedeva, N., & Majiid, S. M. (2020). *Analysis of the Vegetation State of the Territory of Central Iraq Using Landsat Data. Handbook of Research on Agricultural Policy, Rural Development, and Enterpreneurship in Contemporary Economies. IGI Global.*

Pataranutaporn, P., Danry, V., Leong, J., Punpongsanon, P., Novy, D., Maes, P., & Sra, M. (2021). AI-generated characters for supporting personalized learning and well-being. *Nature Machine Intelligence, 3*(12), 1013–1022. doi:10.1038/s42256-021-00417-9

Pavlenko, T. B. (2021). Academic integrity of a student. Electronic data School of leadership for postgraduate students of KhNMU.

Pavlik, J. V. (2023). Collaborating with ChatGPT: Considering the implications of generative artificial intelligence for journalism and media education. *Journalism & Mass Communication Educator, 78*(1), 84–93. doi:10.1177/10776958221149577

Pepper, T. (2023, April 25). *A Beginner's Guide to Working With An AI Writing Assistant.* Retrieved from peppercontent.io: https://www.Peppercontent .io/blog/a-beginners-guide-to-working-with-an-ai-writing-assistant/

Perkins, M. (2023). Academic Integrity considerations of AI Large Language Models in the post-pandemic era: ChatGPT and beyond. *Journal of University Teaching & Learning Practice, 20*(2), 07.

Perry, W. L., McInnis, B., Price, C. C., Smith, S. C., & Hollywood, J. S. (2013). Findings for Practitioners, Developers, and Policymakers. *In Predictive Policing: The Role of Crime Forecasting in Law Enforcement Operations*, 115-38. Available at https://www.jstor.org/stable/10.7249/j.ctt4cgdcz.13

Petare, P. A. (2023). 13 Artificial Intelligence Tools for Education: Exploring The New Horizons For Teaching Learning Process. *Exploring New Horizons*, 77.

Phillips, T., Saleh, A., Glazewski, K. D., Hmelo-Silver, C. E., Mott, B., & Lester, J. C. (2022). Exploring the use of GPT-3 as a tool for evaluating text-based collaborative discourse. *Companion Proceedings of the 12th*, 54.

Pi, Y. (2021). Machine learning in governments: Benefits, challenges, and future directions. *JeDEM-eJournal of eDemocracy and Open Government, 13*(1), 203-219.

Pietikäinen, M., & Silven, O. (2022). Challenges of Artificial Intelligence—From Machine Learning and Computer Vision to Emotional Intelligence. *arXiv preprint arXiv:2201.01466.*

Pigola, A., Scafuto, I. C., da Costa, P. R., & Nassif, V. M. J. (2023). Artificial Intelligence in academic research. *International Journal of Innovation, 11*(3), e25408–e25408. doi:10.5585/2023.25408

Poba-Nzaou, P., Galani, M., Uwizeyemungu, S., & Ceric, A. (2021). The impacts of artificial intelligence (AI) on jobs: An industry perspective. *Strategic HR Review, 20*(2), 60–65. doi:10.1108/SHR-01-2021-0003

Pryhodii, M. A., Hurzhii, A. M., Radkevych, O. P., Kononenko, A. H., & Humennyi, O. D. (2022). *The technology of creating a digital portfolio of vocational (vocational and technical) and professional prehigher education: methodical recommendations.* Institute of Vocational Education of the National Academy of Educational Sciences of Ukraine.

Qasem, F. (2023). ChatGPT in scientific and academic research: Future fears and reassurances. *Library Hi Tech News, 40*(3), 30–32. doi:10.1108/LHTN-03-2023-0043

Radford, A. (2019). Language Models are Few-Shot Learners. arXiv preprint arXiv:1905.08144

Radford, A., Narasimhan, K., Salimans, T., & Sutskever, I. (2018). Improving language understanding by generative pre-training. Academic Press.

Radford, A., Wu, J., Child, R., Luan, D., Amodei, D., & Sutskever, I. (2019). Language models are unsupervised multitask learners. *OpenAI blog, 1*(8), 9.

Rahman, M. A., Terano, H. J., Rahman, N., Salamzadeh, A., & Rahaman, M. S. (2023). ChatGPT and Academic Research: A review and recommendations based on practical examples. Journal of Education. *Management and Development Studies, 3*(1), 1–12. doi:10.52631/jemds.v3i1.175

Ramachandran, L., Gehringer, E. F., & Yadav, R. K. (2017). Automated assessment of the quality of peer reviews using natural language processing techniques. *International Journal of Artificial Intelligence in Education, 27*(3), 534–581. doi:10.1007/s40593-016-0132-x

Ramarao-Milne, P., Jain, Y., Sng, L. M., Hosking, B., Lee, C., Bayat, A., Kuiper, M., Wilson, L. O. W., Twine, N. A., & Bauer, D. C. (2022). Data-driven platform for identifying variants of interest in the COVID-19 virus. *Computational and Structural Biotechnology Journal, 20*, 2942–2950. doi:10.1016/j.csbj.2022.06.005 PMID:35677774

Ramesh, T. R., Lilhore, U. K., Poongodi, M., Simaiya, S., Kaur, A., & Hamdi, M. (2022). Predictive analysis of heart diseases with machine learning approaches. *Malaysian Journal of Computer Science*, 132–148.

Randhawa, G. K., & Jackson, M. (2020, January). The role of artificial intelligence in learning and professional development for healthcare professionals. *Healthcare Management Forum*, *33*(1), 19–24. doi:10.1177/0840470419869032 PMID:31802725

Rane, N. L., Choudhary, S. P., Tawde, A., & Rane, J. (2023). ChatGPT is not capable of serving as an author: Ethical concerns and challenges of large language models in education. *International Research Journal of Modernization in Engineering Technology and Science*, *5*(10), 851–874.

Ray, P. P. (2023). ChatGPT: A comprehensive review on background, applications, key challenges, bias, ethics, limitations and future scope. *Internet of Things and Cyber-Physical Systems*.

Razack, H. I. A., Mathew, S. T., Saad, F. F. A., & Alqahtani, S. A. (2021). Artificial intelligence-assisted tools for redefining the communication landscape of the scholarly world. *Science Editing, 8*(2), 134-144.

Razack, H. I. A., Mathew, S. T., Saad, F. F. A., & Alqahtani, S. A. (2021). Artificial intelligence-assisted tools for redefining the communication landscape of the scholarly world. *Science Editing*, *8*(2), 134–144. doi:10.6087/kcse.244

Reguig, Y., & Mouffok, A. I. (2023). *Comparative Analysis of Current Word Processing Applications That Use Artificial Intelligence Case of Study: The Use of Grammarly and Quillbot Amongst Third Year BA Students at Ibn Khaldoun University of Tiaret* (Doctoral dissertation, Université IBN KHALDOUN-Tiaret).

Remian, D. (2019). Augmenting education: ethical considerations for incorporating artificial intelligence in education. Academic Press.

Resnik, P., & Lin, J. (2010). Evaluation of NLP systems. The handbook of computational linguistics and natural language processing, 271-295.

Ribeiro, M. T., Singh, S., & Guestrin, C. (2016, August). " Why should I trust you?" Explaining the predictions of any classifier. In *Proceedings of the 22nd ACM SIGKDD international conference on knowledge discovery and data mining* (pp. 1135-1144). 10.1145/2939672.2939778

Ribera, M., & Lapedriza, A. (2019, March). Can we do better explanations? A proposal of user-centered explainable AI. *CEUR Workshop Proceedings*.

Rice, S., Crouse, S. R., Winter, S. R., & Rice, C. (2023). The advantages and limitations of using ChatGPT to enhance technological research. *Technology in Society*, 102426.

Richardson, M., & Clesham, R. (2021). Rise of the machines? The evolving role of Artificial Intelligence (AI) technologies in high stakes assessment. *London Review of Education*, *19*(1), 1–13. doi:10.14324/LRE.19.1.09

Roberts, L. W. (2023). Addressing the Novel Implications of Generative AI for Academic Publishing, Education, and Research. *Academic Medicine*, 10–1097. PMID:38451086

Roe, J., Renandya, W. A., & Jacobs, G. M. (2023). A Review of AI-Powered Writing Tools and Their Implications for Academic Integrity in the Language Classroom. *Journal of English and Applied Linguistics*, *2*(1), 22–30. doi:10.59588/2961-3094.1035

Rosyanafi, R. J., Lestari, G. D., Susilo, H., Nusantara, W., & Nuraini, F. (2023). The dark side of innovation: Understanding research misconduct with chat gpt in nonformal education studies at universitas negeri surabaya. *Jurnal Review Pendidikan Dasar: Jurnal Kajian Pendidikan dan Hasil Penelitian, 9*(3), 220-228.

Rouhiainen, L. (2018). *Artificial Intelligence: 101 things you must know today about our future*. Lasse Rouhiainen.

Roumeliotis, K. I., & Tselikas, N. D. (2023). ChatGPT and Open-AI Models: A Preliminary Review. *Future Internet*, *15*(6), 192. doi:10.3390/fi15060192

Rudolph, J., Tan, S., & Tan, S. (2023). War of the chatbots: Bard, Bing Chat, ChatGPT, Ernie and beyond. The new AI gold rush and its impact on higher education. *Journal of Applied Learning and Teaching*, *6*(1), 364–389.

Rudych, O. O., Ostapenko, E. M., & Cherednyk, L. M. (2023). Artificial intelligence and academic integrity: challenges, risks and opportunities for fraud prevention. Innovative pedagogy, 59, 250-254.

Rusmiyanto, R., Huriati, N., Fitriani, N., Tyas, N. K., Rofi'i, A., & Sari, M. N. (2023). The Role of Artificial Intelligence (AI) In Developing English Language Learner's Communication Skills. *Journal of Education*, *6*(1), 750–757.

Russell, S. J., & Norvig, P. (2016). *Artificial intelligence: a modern approach*. Pearson.

Russell, S. J., & Norvig, P. (2010). *Artificial intelligence a modern approach*.

Sabuncuoglu, A. (2020, June). Designing one year curriculum to teach artificial intelligence for middle school. In *Proceedings of the 2020 ACM conference on innovation and technology in computer science education* (pp. 96-102). 10.1145/3341525.3387364

SalahM.AlhalbusiH.IsmailM. M.AbdelfattahF. (2023). Chatting with ChatGPT: Decoding the mind of Chatbot users and unveiling the intricate connections between user perception, trust and stereotype perception on self-esteem and psychological well-being. Research Square, 1-26. doi:10.21203/rs.3.rs-2610655/v2

Salvagno, M., Taccone, F. S., & Gerli, A. G. (2023). Can artificial intelligence help for scientific writing? *Critical Care*, *27*(1), 75. doi:10.1186/s13054-023-04380-2 PMID:36841840

Sanderson, C., Douglas, D., Lu, Q., Schleiger, E., Whittle, J., Lacey, J., Newnham, G., Hajkowicz, S., Robinson, C., & Hansen, D. (2023). AI ethics principles in practice: Perspectives of designers and developers. *IEEE Transactions on Technology and Society*, *4*(2), 171–187. doi:10.1109/TTS.2023.3257303

Savage, N. (2022). Breaking into the black box of artificial intelligence. Academic Press.

Savage, T. M., & Vogel, K. E. (2013). *An introduction to digital multimedia*. Jones & Bartlett Publishers.

Savaget, P., Chiarini, T., & Evans, S. (2019). Empowering political participation through artificial intelligence. *Science & Public Policy*, *46*(3), 369–380. doi:10.1093/scipol/scy064 PMID:33583994

Scantamburlo, T., Charlesworth, A., & Cristianini, N. (2018). Machine decisions and human consequences. *arXiv preprint arXiv:1811.06747*.

Scheel, A. M., Tiokhin, L., Isager, P. M., & Lakens, D. (2021). Why Hypothesis Testers Should Spend Less Time Testing Hypotheses. *Perspectives on Psychological Science*, *16*(4), 744–755. doi:10.1177/1745691620966795 PMID:33326363

Schiff, D., Borenstein, J., Biddle, J., & Laas, K. (2021). AI ethics in the public, private, and NGO sectors: A review of a global document collection. *IEEE Transactions on Technology and Society*, *2*(1), 31–42. doi:10.1109/TTS.2021.3052127

Schintler, L. A., McNeely, C. L., & Witte, J. (2023). A Critical Examination of the Ethics of AI-Mediated Peer Review. *arXiv preprint arXiv:2309.12356*.

Schmohl, T., Watanabe, A., Fröhlich, N., & Herzberg, D. (2020). How can Artificial Intelligence Improve the academic writing of students? *The Future of Education*, 12–14. https://thesiswriter.zhaw.ch/

Schmohl, T., Watanabe, A., Fröhlich, N., & Herzberg, D. (2020). *How can Artificial Intelligence Improve the academic writing of students?* The Future of Education.

Secinaro, S., Calandra, D., Secinaro, A., Muthurangu, V., & Biancone, P. (2021). The role of artificial intelligence in healthcare: A structured literature review. *BMC Medical Informatics and Decision Making*, *21*(1), 1–23. doi:10.1186/s12911-021-01488-9 PMID:33836752

Selbst, A. D. (2017). Disparate impact in big data policing. *Ga. L. Rev.*, *52*, 109.

Semantic Scholar | AI-Powered Research Tool. (n.d.-b). https://shorturl.at/ghHX8

SEO AI. (2023). Multilingual. https://seo.ai/blog/how-many-languages-does-ChatGPT-support/

Seufert, S., Burkhard, M., & Handschuh, S. (2021). Fostering Students' Academic Writing Skills: Feedback Model for an AI-enabled Support Environment. In Association for the Advancement of Computing in Education (pp. 49–58). AACE.

Shahriar, S., & Hayawi, K. (2023). Let's have a chat! A Conversation with ChatGPT: Technology, Applications, and Limitations. *arXiv preprint arXiv:2302.13817.*

Sharabchiev, Yu. T. (2016). How to become a scientist and achieve success in science: creative talent and activation of scientific creativity. *Medical news. No. 5 (260).* https://cyberleninka.ru/article/n/kak-stat-uchenym-i-dobitsya-uspeha-v-nauke-tvorcheskaya-odarennost-i-aktivatsiya-nauchnogo-tvorchestva

Shemshack, A., & Spector, J. M. (2020). A systematic literature review of personalized learning terms. *Smart Learning Environments*, *7*(1), 1–20. doi:10.1186/s40561-020-00140-9

Shergalin, E. E. (2020). Friedrich Eduardovich Falz-Fein (1863-1920) - member of the Russian ornithological committee (on the 100th anniversary of his death*). Rus. ornithol. Journal, 1895.* https://cyberleninka.ru/article/n/fridrih-eduardovich-falts-feyn-1863-1920-chlen-russkogo-ornitologicheskogo-komiteta-k-100-letiyu-so-dnya-smerti

Shevchenko, M. A., & Mitchell, P. D. (2013). Training of military translators in a civilian university (experience of the National Research Tomsk State University). *Language and Culture*, (1(21)), 125–131.

Shokrollahi, Y., Yarmohammadtoosky, S., Nikahd, M. M., Dong, P., Li, X., & Gu, L. (2023). A comprehensive review of generative AI in healthcare. *arXiv preprint arXiv:2310.00795.*

Shringi, K. (2023). Matt Frisbie on Browser Extensions. *IEEE Software*, *40*(4), 118–120. doi:10.1109/MS.2023.3265374

ShrivastavaV. (2023). Skilled Resilience: Revitalizing Asian American and Pacific Islander Entrepreneurship Through AI-Driven Social Media Marketing Techniques. *Available at* SSRN 4507541. doi:10.2139/ssrn.4507541

Sikarskie, A. (2020). *Digital research methods in fashion and textile studies.* Bloomsbury Publishing.

Silva, T., Ma, J., Yang, C., & Liang, H. (2015). A profile-boosted research analytics framework to recommend journals for manuscripts. *Journal of the Association for Information Science and Technology*, *66*(1), 180–200. doi:10.1002/asi.23150

Simmons, A. B., & Chappell, S. G. (1988). Artificial intelligence-definition and practice. *IEEE Journal of Oceanic Engineering*, *13*(2), 14–42. doi:10.1109/48.551

Singh, H., & Singh, A. (2023). ChatGPT: Systematic review, applications, and agenda for multidisciplinary research. *Journal of Chinese Economic and Business Studies*, *21*(2), 193–212. doi:10.1080/14765284.2023.2210482

Singh, R. P., Hom, G. L., Abramoff, M. D., Campbell, J. P., & Chiang, M. F. (2020). Current challenges and barriers to real-world artificial intelligence adoption for the healthcare system, provider, and the patient. *Translational Vision Science & Technology*, *9*(2), 45–45. doi:10.1167/tvst.9.2.45 PMID:32879755

Skidan, V. V., & Yefimchuk, G. V. (2019). Innovative educational approaches in teaching technical disciplines in institutions of higher education. *Scientific notes*, (65), 238-242.

Smith, J. (2022). Knowledge Synthesis with ChatGPT: Connecting Diverse Perspectives in Scientific Research. *Journal of AI Research*, *15*(2), 123–145.

Smith, J. A., & Nizza, I. E. (2022). *Essentials of interpretative phenomenological analysis*. American Psychological Association. doi:10.1037/0000259-000

Smith, J. A., & Osborn, M. (2003). Interpretative Phenomenological Analysis. *Qualitative Psychology*.

Somasundaram, M., Junaid, K. M., & Mangadu, S. (2020). Artificial intelligence (AI) enabled intelligent quality management system (IQMS) for personalized learning path. *Procedia Computer Science*, *172*, 438–442. doi:10.1016/j.procs.2020.05.096

Soroka, V. V. (2023). ChatGPT: Opportunities for education. Science and education in the conditions of war. *Hlukhiv National Pedagogical University named after Oleksandr Dovzhenko: materials of the reporting scientific-practical conference*, 275.

Soubhari, T., Nanda, S. S., Lone, T. A., & Beegam, P. S. (2023). Digital hacks, creativity shacks, and academic menace: The ai effect. In *Sustainable Development Goal Advancement Through Digital Innovation in the Service Sector* (pp. 208–232). IGI Global. doi:10.4018/979-8-3693-0650-5.ch014

Spring, M., Faulconbridge, J., & Sarwar, A. (2022). How information technology automates and augments processes: Insights from Artificial-Intelligence-based systems in professional service operations. *Journal of Operations Management*, *68*(6-7), 592–618. doi:10.1002/joom.1215

Stahl, B. C., & Stahl, B. C. (2021). Ethical issues of AI. Artificial Intelligence for a better future: An ecosystem perspective on the ethics of AI and emerging digital technologies, 35-53.

Stokel-Walker, C. (2023). What is the future of artificial intelligence? *New Scientist*, *258*(3439), 1–9. doi:10.1016/S0262-4079(23)00886-2

Stokel-Walker, C., & Van Noorden, R. (2023). What ChatGPT and generative AI mean for science. *Nature*, *614*(7947), 214–216. doi:10.1038/d41586-023-00340-6 PMID:36747115

Straume, I., & Anson, C. (2022). Amazement and trepidation: Implications of AI-based natural language production for the teaching of writing. *Journal of Academic Writing*, *12*(1), 1–9. doi:10.18552/joaw.v12i1.820

Straw, I., & Callison-Burch, C. (2020). Artificial Intelligence in mental health and the biases of language based models. *PLoS One*, *15*(12), e0240376. doi:10.1371/journal.pone.0240376 PMID:33332380

Strobel, G., Schoormann, T., Banh, L., & Möller, F. (2023). Artificial Intelligence for Sign Language Translation–A Design Science Research Study. *Communications of the Association for Information Systems*, *52*(1), 33. doi:10.17705/1CAIS.05303

Strobl, C., Ailhaud, E., Benetos, K., Devitt, A., Kruse, O., Proske, A., & Rapp, C. (2019). Digital support for academic writing: A review of technologies and pedagogies. *Computers & Education*, *131*, 33–48. doi:10.1016/j.compedu.2018.12.005

Strubell, E., Ganesh, A., & McCallum, A. (2019). Energy and policy considerations for deep learning in NLP. *arXiv preprint arXiv:1906.02243*. doi:10.18653/v1/P19-1355

Susilawati, E., Lubis, H., Kesuma, S., Pratama, K., & Khaira, I. (2022). The Mediating Role of Moral Self-Regulations between Automated Essay Scoring Adoption, Students' Character and Academic Integrity among Indonesian Higher Education Sector. *Eurasian Journal of Educational Research*, *102*(102), 54–71.

Sutherland-Smith, W. (2008). *Plagiarism, the Internet, and student learning: Improving academic integrity*. Routledge. doi:10.4324/9780203928370

Swisher, K. (2022). The Right to (Human) Counsel: Real Responsibility for Artificial Intelligence. *South Carolina Law Review*, *74*, 823.

Taddeo, M., & Floridi, L. (2018). How AI can be a force for good. *Science*, *361*(6404), 751–752. doi:10.1126/science.aat5991 PMID:30139858

TajikE.TajikF. (2023). A comprehensive Examination of the potential application of ChatGPT in Higher Education Institutions. TechRxiv. *Preprint*, 1-10.

Takanova, O. V. (2008). Vocational-oriented teaching of a foreign language in non-linguistic universities. *Agroengineering*, (6), 49–51.

Tereshchuk, V. I., Ilchenko, A. M., & Semenyshina, I. V. (2023). Innovative learning technologies in institutions of higher education. *Academic visions*, (16), 234-238.

The Britannica Dictionary. (2024). https://www.britannica.com/dictionary/talent

The Ticker. (2023). Public Outreach. https://theticker.org/9831/opinions/ChatGPT-will-benefit-the-public-if-regulated/

Thompson, K., Corrin, L., & Lodge, J. M. (2023). AI in tertiary education: Progress on research and practice. *Australasian Journal of Educational Technology*, *39*(5), 1–7. doi:10.14742/ajet.9251

Toğaçar, M. (2022). The Contribution of AI-Based Approaches in the Determination of CO. *Artificial Intelligence for Renewable Energy and Climate Change*, 173.

Toney, A., & Flagg, M. (2020). *US Demand for AI-Related Talent. Center for Security and Emerging Technology*. CSET. doi:10.51593/20200027

Topol, E. J. (2019). High-performance medicine: The convergence of human and artificial intelligence. *Nature Medicine*, *25*(1), 44–56. doi:10.1038/s41591-018-0300-7 PMID:30617339

Torshin, S. P. (2018). To the 175th anniversary of the birth of K.A. Timiryazev. *Agrochemical Bulletin. No. 3.* https://cyberleninka.ru/article/n/k-175-letiyu-so-dnya-rozhdeniya-k-a-timiryazeva

Tretyakova, I. V., & Akymova, A. S. (2018). Academic writing: genres and features. *Dnevnyk nauki, 5,* 1-6.

TS2 Space. (2023). Collaboration. https://ts2.space/en/collaborative-ai-ChatGPT-5s-role-in-facilitating-remote-work-and-team-communication

Tyagi, A. K., & Chahal, P. (2022). Artificial intelligence and machine learning algorithms. In Research Anthology on Machine Learning Techniques, Methods, and Applications (pp. 421-446). IGI Global. doi:10.4018/978-1-6684-6291-1.ch024

Uc-Cetina, V., Navarro-Guerrero, N., Martin-Gonzalez, A., Weber, C., & Wermter, S. (2022). Survey on reinforcement learning for language processing. *Artificial Intelligence Review*, 1–33. doi:10.1007/s10462-022-10205-5

Uekusa, S. (2022). Overcoming disaster linguicism: Using autoethnography during the COVID-19 pandemic in Denmark to explore how community translators can provide multilingual disaster communication. *Journal of Applied Communication Research*, *50*(6), 673–690. doi:10.1080/00909882.2022.2141067

Ulyanova, G. O., & Baadzhi, N. P. (2023). Academic integrity as the basis of academic success. *Legal position, 4(37),* 98–103.

US Treasury. (2021). *Request for Information and Comment on Financial Institutions' Use of Artificial Intelligence, Including Machine Learning*. Department of the Treasury, United States Government.

Vakulenko, V. L., & Boyarchuk, S. V. (2022). Key aspects of academic integrity: preventing plagiarism. *Scientific journal "Humanities studies: pedagogy, psychology, philosophy", 13(4),* 26-34.

Van De Schoot, R., De Bruin, J., Schram, R., Zahedi, P., De Boer, J., Weijdema, F., Kramer, B., Huijts, M., Hoogerwerf, M., Ferdinands, G., Harkema, A., Willemsen, J., Ma, Y., Fang, Q., Hindriks, S., Tummers, L., & Oberski, D. L. (2021). An open source machine learning framework for efficient and transparent systematic reviews. *Nature Machine Intelligence*, *3*(2), 125–133. doi:10.1038/s42256-020-00287-7

Van der Velden, B. H., Kuijf, H. J., Gilhuijs, K. G., & Viergever, M. A. (2022). Explainable artificial intelligence (XAI) in deep learning-based medical image analysis. *Medical Image Analysis*, *79*, 102470. doi:10.1016/j.media.2022.102470 PMID:35576821

Van Dis, E. A., Bollen, J., Zuidema, W., van Rooij, R., & Bockting, C. L. (2023). ChatGPT: Five priorities for research. *Nature*, *614*(7947), 224–226. doi:10.1038/d41586-023-00288-7 PMID:36737653

Van Esch, P., & Stewart Black, J. (2021). Artificial intelligence (AI): Revolutionizing digital marketing. *Australasian Marketing Journal*, *29*(3), 199–203. doi:10.1177/18393349211037684

Van Roy, V., Rossetti, F., Perset, K., & Galindo-Romero, L. (2021). *AI watch-national strategies on artificial intelligence: A European perspective* (No. JRC122684). Joint Research Centre (Seville site).

Voorhees, C. M., Brady, M. K., Calantone, R., & Ramirez, E. (2016). Discriminant validity testing in marketing: An analysis, causes for concern, and proposed remedies. *Journal of the Academy of Marketing Science*, *44*(1), 119–134. doi:10.1007/s11747-015-0455-4

Votto, A. M., Valecha, R., Najafirad, P., & Rao, H. R. (2021). Artificial intelligence in tactical human resource management: A systematic literature review. *International Journal of Information Management Data Insights*, *1*(2), 100047. doi:10.1016/j.jjimei.2021.100047

Wade, A. D. (2022, April). The semantic scholar academic graph (s2ag*). In Companion Proceedings of the Web Conference 2022* (pp. 739-739). Academic Press.

Wagner, G., Lukyanenko, R., & Paré, G. (2022). Artificial intelligence and the conduct of literature reviews. *Journal of Information Technology*, *37*(2), 209–226. doi:10.1177/02683962211048201

Wallace, E., Feng, S., Kandpal, N., Gardner, M., & Singh, S. (2019). Universal adversarial triggers for attacking and analyzing NLP. *arXiv preprint arXiv:1908.07125*. doi:10.18653/v1/D19-1221

Wang, F., & Preininger, A. (2019). AI in health: state of the art, challenges, and future directions. *Yearbook of medical informatics, 28*(01), 16-26.

Wang, W., & Siau, K. (2018). Ethical and moral issues with AI.

Wang, C., Liu, S., Yang, H., Guo, J., Wu, Y., & Liu, J. (2023). Ethical Considerations of Using ChatGPT in Health Care. *Journal of Medical Internet Research*, *25*, e48009. doi:10.2196/48009 PMID:37566454

Wang, F., Liu, X., Liu, O., Neshati, A., Ma, T., Zhu, M., & Zhao, J. (2023, April). Slide4N: Creating Presentation Slides from Computational Notebooks with Human-AI Collaboration. In *Proceedings of the 2023 CHI Conference on Human Factors in Computing Systems* (pp. 1-18). 10.1145/3544548.3580753

Wang, H., Fu, T., Du, Y., Gao, W., Huang, K., Liu, Z., Chandak, P., Liu, S., Van Katwyk, P., Deac, A., Anandkumar, A., Bergen, K., Gomes, C. P., Ho, S., Kohli, P., Lasenby, J., Leskovec, J., Liu, T.-Y., Manrai, A., ... Zitnik, M. (2023). Scientific discovery in the age of artificial intelligence. *Nature*, *620*(7972), 47–60. doi:10.1038/s41586-023-06221-2 PMID:37532811

Wang, Q., Saha, K., Gregori, E., Joyner, D., & Goel, A. (2021, May). Towards mutual theory of mind in human-ai interaction: How language reflects what students perceive about a virtual teaching assistant. In *Proceedings of the 2021 CHI conference on human factors in computing systems* (pp. 1-14). 10.1145/3411764.3445645

Wang, X., Li, L., Tan, S. C., Yang, L., & Lei, J. (2023). Preparing for AI-enhanced education: Conceptualizing and empirically examining teachers' AI readiness. *Computers in Human Behavior*, *146*, 107798. doi:10.1016/j.chb.2023.107798

Wanner, J., Herm, L. V., & Janiesch, C. (2020). How much is the black box? The value of explainability in machine learning models. Academic Press.

Weber, N., & Huici, F. (2020, May). SOL: effortless device support for AI frameworks without source code changes. In *2020 20th IEEE/ACM International Symposium on Cluster, Cloud and Internet Computing (CCGRID)* (pp. 736-743). IEEE. 10.1109/CCGrid49817.2020.00-16

Wynants, L., Van Calster, B., Collins, G. S., Riley, R. D., Heinze, G., Schuit, E., Albu, E., Arshi, B., Bellou, V., Bonten, M. M. J., Dahly, D. L., Damen, J. A., Debray, T. P. A., de Jong, V. M. T., De Vos, M., Dhiman, P., Ensor, J., Gao, S., Haller, M. C., ... van Smeden, M. (2020). Prediction models for diagnosis and prognosis of COVID-19: Systematic review and critical appraisal. *BMJ (Clinical Research Ed.)*, 369. doi:10.1136/bmj.m1328 PMID:32265220

Xiao, W., Zhao, H., Pan, H., Song, Y., Zheng, V. W., & Yang, Q. (2019, July). Beyond personalization: Social content recommendation for creator equality and consumer satisfaction. *In Proceedings of the 25th ACM SIGKDD International Conference on Knowledge Discovery & Data Mining* (pp. 235-245). 10.1145/3292500.3330965

Xu, Y., Liu, X., Cao, X., Huang, C., Liu, E., Qian, S., Liu, X., Wu, Y., Dong, F., Qiu, C.-W., Qiu, J., Hua, K., Su, W., Wu, J., Xu, H., Han, Y., Fu, C., Yin, Z., Liu, M., ... Zhang, J. (2021). Artificial intelligence: A powerful paradigm for scientific research. *Innovation (Cambridge (Mass.))*, *2*(4), 100179. doi:10.1016/j.xinn.2021.100179 PMID:34877560

Yan, D. (2023). Impact of ChatGPT on learners in a L2 writing practicum: An exploratory investigation. *Education and Information Technologies*, *28*(11), 1–25. doi:10.1007/s10639-023-11742-4

Yang, D., Zhao, W. G., Du, J., & Yang, Y. (2024). Approaching Artificial Intelligence in business and economics research: A bibliometric panorama (1966–2020). *Technology Analysis and Strategic Management*, *36*(3), 563–578. doi:10.1080/09537325.2022.2043268

Yao, X., Zhou, J., Zhang, J., & Boër, C. R. (2017, September). From intelligent manufacturing to smart manufacturing for industry 4.0 driven by next generation artificial intelligence and further on. In *2017 5th international conference on enterprise systems (ES)* (pp. 311-318). IEEE.

Yeo, M. A. (2023). Academic integrity in the age of Artificial Intelligence (AI) authoring apps. *TESOL Journal*, *14*(3), 716. doi:10.1002/tesj.716

Yigitcanlar, T., Desouza, K. C., Butler, L., & Roozkhosh, F. (2020). Contributions and risks of artificial intelligence (AI) in building smarter cities: Insights from a systematic review of the literature. *Energies*, *13*(6), 1473. doi:10.3390/en13061473

Yildirim, T. M., Khoramnia, R., Masyk, M., Son, H. S., Auffarth, G. U., & Mayer, C. S. (2020). Aesthetics of iris reconstruction with a custom-made artificial iris prosthesis. *PLoS One*, *15*(8), e0237616. doi:10.1371/journal.pone.0237616 PMID:32790803

Yu, H., Shen, Z., Miao, C., Leung, C., Lesser, V. R., & Yang, Q. (2018). Building ethics into artificial intelligence. *arXiv preprint arXiv:1812.02953*. doi:10.24963/ijcai.2018/779

Yu, H., & Guo, Y. (2023, June). Generative artificial intelligence empowers educational reform: Current status, issues, and prospects. *Frontiers in Education*, *8*, 1183162. doi:10.3389/feduc.2023.1183162

Zawacki-Richter, O., Marín, V. I., Bond, M., & Gouverneur, F. (2019). Systematic review of research on artificial intelligence applications in higher education–where are the educators? *International Journal of Educational Technology in Higher Education*, *16*(1), 1–27. doi:10.1186/s41239-019-0171-0

Zdravkova, K. (2022). The potential of artificial intelligence for assistive technology in education. In Handbook on Intelligent Techniques in the Educational Process: Vol 1 Recent Advances and Case Studies (pp. 61-85). Cham: Springer International Publishing. doi:10.1007/978-3-031-04662-9_4

Zehir, C., Karaboğa, T., & Başar, D. (2020). The transformation of human resource management and its impact on overall business performance: big data analytics and AI technologies in strategic HRM. *Digital Business Strategies in Blockchain Ecosystems: Transformational Design and Future of Global Business*, 265-279.

Zhang, B., Anderljung, M., Kahn, L., Dreksler, N., Horowitz, M. C., & Dafoe, A. (2021). Ethics and governance of artificial intelligence: Evidence from a survey of machine learning researchers. *Journal of Artificial Intelligence Research*, *71*, 591–666. doi:10.1613/jair.1.12895

ZhangB.DafoeA. (2019). Artificial intelligence: American attitudes and trends. *Available at* SSRN 3312874.

Zhang, K., & Aslan, A. B. (2021). AI technologies for education: Recent research & future directions. *Computers and Education: Artificial Intelligence*, *2*, 100025. doi:10.1016/j.caeai.2021.100025

Zhang, L., Basham, J. D., & Yang, S. (2020). Understanding the implementation of personalized learning: A research synthesis. *Educational Research Review*, *31*, 100339. doi:10.1016/j.edurev.2020.100339

Zhang, Y., & Wang, X. (2021). Leveraging ChatGPT for Automated Literature Review. *Proceedings of the International Conference on Artificial Intelligence.*

Zheng, H., & Zhan, H. (2023). ChatGPT in scientific writing: A cautionary tale. *The American Journal of Medicine*, *136*(8), 725–726.e6. doi:10.1016/j.amjmed.2023.02.011 PMID:36906169

Zhou, M., Duan, N., Liu, S., & Shum, H. Y. (2020). Progress in neural NLP: Modeling, learning, and reasoning. *Engineering (Beijing)*, *6*(3), 275–290. doi:10.1016/j.eng.2019.12.014

Zhu, J., Zhang, J., & Feng, Y. (2022). Hard budget constraints and artificial intelligence technology. *Technological Forecasting and Social Change*, *183*, 121889. doi:10.1016/j.techfore.2022.121889

Zlateva, P., Steshina, L., Petukhov, I., & Velev, D. (2024). A Conceptual Framework for Solving Ethical Issues in Generative Artificial Intelligence. In Electronics, Communications and Networks (pp. 110-119). IOS Press. doi:10.3233/FAIA231182

Zohery, M. (2023). ChatGPT in Academic Writing and Publishing: A Comprehensive Guide 2023. Artificial Intelligence in Academia, Research and Science: ChatGPT as a Case Study, 10–61. doi:10.5281/zenodo.7803703

About the Contributors

Anugamini Priya Srivastava, is an Assistant Professor at Symbiosis Institute of Business Management Pune, Symbiosis International Deemed University, Pune India. She is a distinguished academic, blends her organizational behaviour, HRM, and AI expertise to spearhead transformative research endeavours. With a Ph.D. from the esteemed Indian Institute of Technology Roorkee and executive education from Johns Hopkins University and Rice University, her credentials underscore her commitment to academic excellence and innovation. Dr Srivastava's prolific publication record included esteemed journals such as the Journal of Cleaner Production and the International Journal of Manpower, with multiple contributions indexed in Scopus and recognized in ABDC rankings. Her research explores the intersection of authentic leadership, sustainability, and technology, elucidating novel insights for organizational dynamics and employee behavior. In addition to her scholarly contributions, Dr. Srivastava has presented her work at prestigious international conferences, showcasing the practical applications of AI in HRM and marketing contexts. Her involvement in editorial roles for esteemed journals, including Emerald and Elsevier, reflects her standing as a trusted reviewer and thought leader in the academic community. Furthermore, Dr. Srivastava's achievements, including the IBM Digital Badge for Data Science and the Outstanding Reviewer Recognition by Elsevier, underscore her commitment to excellence and recognition within her field. Her international collaborations and guest lectures at institutions like Global Business and Research Centre, DY Patil, Pune, demonstrate her ability to disseminate knowledge and foster academic discourse on a global scale. Dr. Srivastava's dedication to advancing research is further exemplified through her role as an FDP facilitator, simplifying the research journey for aspiring scholars. By leveraging her expertise in AI and statistical analysis, she empowers researchers to navigate complex methodologies and unlock new avenues of inquiry. In conclusion, Dr. Anugamini Priya Srivastava's multifaceted expertise, international collaborations, and commitment to knowledge dissemination position her as a leading figure in AI-driven research exploration. As an editor, she can guide scholars in harnessing AI for transformative research explorations, examinations, and expressions, thereby advancing the frontiers of academic inquiry.

* * *

Sucheta Agarwal is an Associate Professor at the Institute of Business Management, GLA University, Mathura, India. She pursued PhD in Entrepreneurship from the Department of Management Studies, Indian Institute of Technology, Roorkee, India. Her areas of interest include qualitative research, education, entrepreneurship, human resource management, industrial relations and organizational behaviour. Her citations as per the google scholar is 1200+, h-index: 16 and i10 index: 19. She successfully handled the responsibilities of editorial guests in Journal of Enterprising Communities: People and Places in the

Global Economy (Emerald), Journal of Family Business Management (Emerald), International Journal of Educational Management (Emerald) and two guest editorial presently in the running stage of Journal of Family and Economic Issues (Springer, SSCI, IF-2.4) and The Electronic Journal of Information Systems in Developing Countries (Wiley, IF 1.3). She has authored/co-authored several publications and has contributed several research papers to SCOPUS abstracted and ABDC ranked journals of international and national repute. Her recent publications were in the Business Strategy and the Environment, Environment, Development and Sustainability Journal of Cleaner Production, International Journal of Social Economics (Emerald, UK), Journal of Asia Business Studies (Emerald, UK), to name a few. She has also presented many papers in national and international conferences in India and abroad. She is the recipient of the "Young Research Scholarship Award" at AIT Bangkok by GRDS and the "Young Woman Management Researcher Award" by AIMS International. She also received the "Outstanding Reviewer Award" by Elsevier. She is a supervisor for doctoral scholars as well as many master's students.

Vivek Agrawal is a Professor at the Institute of Business Management, GLA University, Mathura, India. He pursued PhD from GLA University. His interest areas include e-service quality, education, entrepreneurship, supply chain management and e-learning. He has several publications to his credit and has contributed several research papers to SCOPUS, SCI and ABDC ranked journals of international repute like, Journal of Cleaner Production, Environment, Development and Sustainability, Electronic Commerce Research, Business Strategy and Development, Indian Journal of Engineering and Materials Sciences, Benchmarking: An International Journal etc. He is the recipient of the "Outstanding Reviewer Award" by Elsevier. He is a supervisor for doctoral scholars as well as many masters' students.

Preethi Ananthachari received her PhD from Periyar University, Salem, TN, India. Currently she is working as an Assistant Professor in AI & Bigdata department, Endicott College of International Studies, Woosong University, Daejeon, South Korea. She has been awarded distinction in her M.Phil (Computer Science). She worked as an Assistant Professor in VIT Bhopal University, MP, India. She worked as a Guest Lecturer in the Department of Computer Science in Periyar University, Salem for a year from 2011-2012. She joined as a Project Fellow in the same department under UGC Major Research Project from the year 2012. Her research interests are Mobile Computing, Sensor Techniques, Wireless Technology, Big Data Analytics, Machine Learning and Robotics. Dr.Preethi has published a book on Python in the year 2020 with Woosong publishers. She received the best paper award in an International Conference on Advances in Engineering and Technology (ICAET) held in E.G.S. Pillai Engineering college, Nagapattinam, Tamil Nadu, India. She served as an invited speaker in many FDP programs and conferences.

Abdul Azeez (Senior Member, IEEE) received his Bachelor of Engineering and M.Tech Degrees in Electronics and Communication Engineering and Digital Electronics and Communication Engineering from Visvesvaraya Technological University (VTU), Belgaum, India in 2005 and 2007 respectively, and the Ph. D Degree in Wireless Communication Engineering from Visvesvaraya Technological University (VTU), Belgaum, India. He has been associated with HKBK college of Engineering where he is currently working as Associate Professor in Department of Electronics and Communication Engineering. He is an active IEEE Member in IEEE COMSOC society, IEEE ITS Society, IEEE Computer Society, IEEE Signal Processing Society, IEEE Photonics Society. He is serving as a treasurer for IEEE ITS Society

Bangalore Section. He is pioneer in starting IEEE ITS Student Branch and IEEE Computer Society student branch in the college. His research interests includes Wireless Communication, Signal Processing, Information Theory and Coding, Evolutionary algorithms. He has served as a Reviewer for various IEEE conferences. He has published several research papers in refereed and international conferences.

Shivam Bhardwaj, a seasoned professional with over 13 years of comprehensive work experience, including 9 years in academia, serves as an Assistant Professor at GLA University, Mathura (India). Currently engaged in pursuing a Ph.D. in entrepreneurship, Shivam has made noteworthy contributions to academic literature. His expertise extends to case writing, with five cases featured in Case Centre (UK), showcasing his ability to provide valuable insights into real-world scenarios. In addition to his academic pursuits, Shivam has demonstrated a flair for communication and thought leadership by crafting over 70 editorials for newspapers. Furthermore, he has authored research articles, highlighting his commitment to advancing knowledge and contributing to scholarly discourse in his field.

Preeti Bhaskar is a prominent faculty and lecturer in University of Technology and Applied Sciences. She has published numerous research papers in ABDC ranking journals and also reviewer to so many other journals. She is also invited as a keynote speaker to conferences and seminars. Her areas of research are HRM, Technology Adoption, Employee job performance, E-Government, and IPA technique.

Jitendra Kumar Dixit is an Associate Professor at the Institute of Business Management of GLA University, Mathura, India. He did PhD in Management. He has more than 12 years of teaching experience. He has attended and presented papers in various national and international conferences. He has also authored research papers in reputed SCOPUS and ABDC journals like Environment, Development and Sustainability, Electronic Commerce Research, Business Strategy and Development etc. His academic and research areas include consumer psychology and behaviour, education, entrepreneurship, sustainable development and econometrics.

Vadivu G. has a B.E., M.Tech., and PhD. With more than 25 years of academic experience, she is a professor currently employed by SRM University's Department of Data Science and Business Systems. Data Analytics, Machine Learning, Data Mining, and Semantic Web are her areas of interest. She has completed numerous certifications, including those from NVIDIA, Udemy, Coursera, NPTEL, and Oracle. She is also a yearly member of the IET, ISC, ACM-W, CSI, and ISC. In 2012, she was awarded a research grant from Dalhousie University in Canada. She also has a number of publications and an active researcher.

Olabode Gbobaniyi is a senior academic currently with Business & Management Faculty of Global Banking School. Research interest aligns mainly towards strategy and leadership in international business and higher education.

Minisha Gupta is an academician and researcher in the area of Human Resource Management. Her areas of expertise are Creativity and Innovation Management, Talent Management, Women Entrepreneurship and Empowerment, Talent Management, Green HRM, Organizational Sustainability, and Artificial Intelligence. She has published papers in Scopus Indexed Journals and also presented her research work into the conferences of national and international repute. She also give lectures on Training and Development, Personality Development and Performance Appraisal. She has been into academics from more than five years. She likes to write her own blog and expand her research work in interdisciplinary research areas.

Hari Kishan Kondaveeti received his B.Tech degree in Information Technology from Acharya Nagarjuna University, India in 2009. He completed his M.Tech, in Computer Science and Engineering from the JNTUK University, India in 2012 and then joined the Department of CS & SE, AUCE (A), Andhra University, India and got a Doctor of Philosophy (Ph.D.) in the field of Computer Science and Engineering. He worked as Research Associate in a research project funded by Naval Science and Technological Laboratory, India when he was at Andhra University. Currently, he is working as Associate Professor at the School of Computer Science and Engineering, VIT-AP University, Andhra Pradesh, India, and acting as a Coordinator of Engineering Clinics. He is an IBM Certified Data Science Professional and NASSCOM Associate Analyst certified faculty and handling multiple Data Analytics courses. His research interests include Digital Image Processing, Machine Learning, Data Analytics, Remote Sensing, and IoT. In recent years, he is focusing on collaborating actively with researchers in several other disciplines and trying to develop interdisciplinary projects.

Samparthi V. S. Kumar received his B.Tech degree in Information Technology from JNTUH University, India in 2006. He completed his M.Tech in Computer Science and Engineering from the NIT Jalandhar University, India in 2010. Currently, he is a Research Scholar at the School of Computer Science and Engineering, VIT-AP University, Andhra Pradesh, India, and pursuing his Ph.D. work in the field of image processing. His main areas of research include image processing, machine learning, and deep learning.

Valli Kumari Vatsavayi is a professor of computer science and systems engineering at Andhra University. She is an active consultant to several government/public sector/private organizations. She successfully completed six consultant projects for Naval Science and Technological Laboratories and two projects for DST, Govt of India. She has successfully managed the computerization of the Integrated Common Entrance Test (ICET) for MCA/ MBA in AP State, on behalf of Convener and APSCHE from 2009 to 2011, and Education Common Entrance Test (EdCET) from 2012 to 2014. She is a member of IEEE, ACM, CRSI, and CSI. She is the founder and Vice-Chair of IEEE Vizag Bay Subsection. She is also the Executive Member of Andhra Pradesh State Knowledge Mission and state nodal officer for Digital India Week, 2015.

Nadezhda Anatolievna Lebedeva is a Doctor of Philosophy in the field of Cultural Studies, professor of International Personnel Academy (Ukraine) and a full member of the Eurasian Academy of Television and Radio. She worked at the Kherson State Agrarian University as the Head department of Humanitarian Disciplines Chair. Currently, Nadezhda Lebedeva is the Chairwoman of the Editorial Board of the international scientific project "Scientific Forum". She also the Main Editor of the international journal "Universum: Philology & Arts", a reviewer and member of the editorial board of scientific collections of international conferences and scientific journals ("Journal of Social, Humanity, and Education", "Journal of Sustainable Tourism and Entrepreneurship" - Indonesia), the author of more than a hundred publications, including Scopus, has recommendations and certificates of honour for successful scientific activity). Experienced in project cinematography management and developed lecture courses in a foreign language for students of state administration. Also she led ESP classes for future architectures and hydraulic engineering and water resources students.

Abinaya M. earned a B.Tech degree from Sairam Institute of Technology in 2017 and an M.Tech degree from SASTRA Deemed to be University in 2019. She is currently pursuing a Ph.D. degree with the Department of Data Science and Business Systems at SRM Institute of Science and Technology in India under Visvesvaraya Ph.D. Scheme for Electronics and Information Technology, which is funded by the Ministry of Electronics and Information Technology. Her areas of interest in research include Augmented Reality, Virtual Reality, Machine Learning, and Mixed Reality.

Mujtaba M. Momin is an Assistant Professor in College of Business Administration at the American University of Middle-East, Kuwait (In Affiliation with Purdue University Indiana USA).

Sachin Kumar Mangla is working in the field of Green and Sustainable Supply Chain and Operations; Industry 4.0; Circular Economy; Decision Making and Simulation. He has a teaching experience of more than five years in Supply Chain and Operations Management and Decision Making, and currently associated in teaching with various universities in UK, Turkey, India, China, France, etc. He is the director of Research Centre for "Digital Circular Economy for Sustainable Development Goals (DCE-SDG), O.P. Jindal Global University, India. He is committed to do and promote high quality research. He has published/presented several papers in repute international/ national journals (Journal of Business Research; International Journal of Production Economics; International Journal of Production Research; Computers and Operations Research; Production Planning and Control; Business Strategy and the Environment;; Annals of Operations Research; Transportation Research Part-D; Transportation Research Part-E; Renewable and Sustainable Energy Reviews; Resource Conservation and Recycling; Information System Frontier; Journal of Cleaner Production; Management Decision; Industrial Data and Management System) and conferences (POMS, SOMS, IIIE, CILT – LRN, MCDM, GLOGIFT). He has an h-index 70, i10-index 150, Google Scholar Citations of 15000. He is involved in several editorial positions and editing couple of Special issues as a Guest Editor in top tier journals. Currently, he is working as an Associate Editor at Journal of Cleaner Production, International Journal of Logistics Management, Sustainable Production and Consumption, Corporate Social Responsibility and Environmental Management, and IMA Journal of Management Mathematics journals. He is also involved in several research projects on various issues and applications of Circular economy, Industry 4.0 and Sustainability. Among them, he contributed to the knowledge-based decision model in "Enhancing and implementing knowledge-based ICT solutions within high risk and uncertain conditions for agriculture production systems (RUC-APS)", European Commission RISE scheme, €1.3M. Recently, he has also received a grant as a PI from British Council – Newton Fund Research Environment Links Turkey/UK – Circular and Industry 4.0 driven solutions for reducing food waste in supply chains. He is also working in several projects on Food Waste and Circular Economy and Industry 4.0 issues, sponsored by AICTE, ICSSR, Government of India. He received project funding for Food Waste Management in Circular Economy from the USERC, Government of India.

Sunil Mishra is Professor in Medi-caps University, Department of Management Studies. He is having 15 plus years of experience. His specialization is Human Resource Management

Ankita Pathak is working as an Assistant Professor in GLA University, Mathura. Her area of specialization is Human Resource Management and Marketing. She holds total 8 years of experience.

Neeraj Pathak is an Assistant Professor in GLA University, Mathura, India and pursuing a Ph.D. at Jiwaji University, Gwalior, India. His area of interest is technology and marketing.

Majdi Anwar Quttainah earned his Ph.D. degree in Management from Rensselaer Polytechnic Institute, Lally School of Management & Technology (USA); MBA degree with merits from the Business School & Entrepreneurship at Newcastle University (UK), and bachelor's degree in International Business from the American International University in London (UK). Dr. Quttainah is an associate professor of management in the College of Business Administration at Kuwait University. His research and teaching interests are corporate governance and strategies, entrepreneurship & small businesses, and organizational development. In addition, as a recognition of his research, he was awarded the Best Young Researcher academic year 2016/2017 Kuwait University. He is an active scholar, presently working as senior editor of FIIB Business Review (Scopus, WoS, Published by the Sage Publishing). His research won several recognition and awards including the Best Paper Award at the 76th Annual Meeting of the Academy of Management Anaheim, CA, the Best Paper Award at the AGBA's 12th Annual World Congress, Kuantan City (State of Pahang), Malaysia, and the Best Paper Award of the Gorontalo International Conference of Project Management (ICPM) - Gorontalo/Indonesia. Also, at the home country level the best paper award for the Kuwait Economic Researcher Award by the Central Bank of Kuwait; May 2019 and 2022.

Veland Ramadani is a Professor of Entrepreneurship and Family Business at the Faculty of Business and Economics, South-East European University, North Macedonia. His primary areas of research focus on entrepreneurship, family businesses, innovation, and sustainability. Dr. Ramadani has an extensive body of work to his name, having authored or co-authored over 140 research articles, 80 book chapters, 12 textbooks, and 28 edited books. His research contributions are notably featured in prestigious academic journals, including the Journal of Business Research, Technological Forecasting and Social Change, Technology in Society, International Journal of Entrepreneurial Behavior & Research, Review of Managerial Science, among others. He received the Award for Excellence in 2016 for an Outstanding Paper published by Emerald Group Publishing, a testament to his outstanding contributions to the field. In addition to his research, Dr. Ramadani has been invited as a keynote speaker at numerous international conferences and as a guest lecturer at President University (Indonesia), Telkom University (Indonesia), University of Trás-os-Montes and Alto Douro (Portugal), and Universum International - UNI (Kosovo). Furthermore, his research influence is underscored by his consistent inclusion among the World's Top 2% of the most influential researchers, as determined by Elsevier and Stanford University for the last four consecutive years. Between 2017 and 2021, Dr. Ramadani served as a member of the Supervisory Board of the Development Bank of North Macedonia, where he also took on the role of Chief Operating Officer for 10 months. Dr. Ramadani has remained actively engaged in various projects, including those funded by the European Union and universities in Saudi Arabia, Kuwait, and the United Arab Emirates. Additionally, he has offered consultancy services to private companies.

Rupayan Roy, an Assistant Professor at the National Institute of Fashion Technology in Kannur, India, specializes in fibrous structures, nonwoven structures, fibre orientation, and fibrous composites. He obtained his Ph.D. in Textile and Fibre Engineering from IIT Delhi, where a wide range of fibrous structures for various applications was explored. His doctoral research primarily focused on the development of highly efficient air filter media utilizing needle-punched nonwovens. With 3 years of experience in academics, Dr. Roy has authored more than 25 research papers and delivered presentations at over 10 conferences of International repute. His primary interest involves advancing the field of fibrous material design for high-end applications. His current research interest includes technical textiles with natural materials.

Rashmi Rani Samantaray presently serves as an Assistant Professor at HKBK College Of Engineering in Bangalore, bringing with her a wealth of experience with 12 years dedicated to teaching undergraduate courses. She earned her M.Tech degree in Electronics from BMS College of Engineering (VTU) and is currently immersed in her Ph.D. pursuit at BMS College Of Engineering under VTU. Her research is centered around wireless communication, specifically delving into the contemporary landscape of 5G, 6G, and Filter bank Multicarrier modulation. Alongside her academic focus, Rashmi exhibits a profound interest in Artificial Intelligence (AI) and Machine Learning (ML) techniques .Her valuable contributions to academia extend to publishing and presenting papers in various IEEE /Springer conferences and journals, which are indexed in Scopus Additionally, Rashmi holds a lifetime membership with the ISTE (Indian Society for Technical Education).

Ankit Saxena, currently serving as an Associate Professor at the Institute of Business Management, GLA University, Mathura, stands as a Director Medalist from Dayalbagh Educational Institute, Dayalbagh, Agra (India), and achieved NET-JRF qualification in 2005. With academic interests encompassing the business paradigms of taxation, financial management, financial derivatives, and Research Methodology, Dr. Saxena has made significant contributions to his field, publishing numerous research papers and contemporary business case studies, including those featured in the UK Case Centre. Beyond academia, he extends his expertise to corporate consultancy, aiding entities in developing strategies for business processes. Dr. Ankit Saxena actively engages in knowledge dissemination by visiting academic institutions, where he imparts insights into emerging education paradigms and motivates individuals to understand the relevance of education in their career building. A sought-after resource person, he has played a key role in 19 Faculty Development Programs (FDPs) and workshops on research methods and teaching pedagogy, organized by various universities, educational bodies, as well as the AICTE Training and Learning (ATAL) Academy. Dr. Saxena's profile reflects a blend of academic excellence and a commitment to bridging the gap between theory and practical application in both educational and corporate contexts.

Mayank Sharma is a seasoned academician and researcher specializing in Marketing and International Management. With over 13 years of experience in teaching and research, he is currently associated with Technische Hochschule in Rosenheim, Germany. Dr. Sharma holds a Ph.D. in Marketing and has diverse qualifications, including PGDIPR Laws, UGC-NET, PGDM, BBA, B.Ed, and CTET. His research interests encompass various areas such as Sales & Distribution Management, Strategic Marketing Management, International Business Management, Marketing of Services, and more. Dr. Sharma's doctoral research focused on the impact of Ingredient Branding on Customer Satisfaction for High Involvement

Products in Delhi/NCR region. Apart from his academic roles, Dr. Sharma is a faculty subject expert for CBSE, New Delhi, involved in drafting skill courses in Marketing & Commercial Applications. He has authored three books for students and actively engages in NBA accreditation work, serving on the Board of Examiners for various universities. Dr. Sharma is a certified auditor for Educational Organizations Management System (EOMS) 21001:2018 and ISO 9000QMS standards. He is also recognized as an Entrepreneurship & Skill Trainer by Wadhwani Foundations – National Entrepreneurship Network (NEN). His contributions extend to international publications, including a co-authored book chapter, and he has presented papers at numerous national and international conferences. Dr. Mayank Sharma's profile is marked by a commitment to education, extensive research, and valuable contributions to the field of Marketing and International Management.

Swati Shetye is a research scholar pursuing her PhD from Symbiosis International deemed university. Her expertise is in the field of Human resource management, policy development and leadership.

Shalini Srivastava has her doctorate in organizational behaviour and has published several research papers on several topics like higher education, self-efficacy etc. She is currently working at Global Banking School in Manchester, UK as a lecturer.

Index

T

U

W

Z

www.ingramcontent.com/pod-product-compliance
Lightning Source LLC
LaVergne TN
LVHW062146300926
849161LV00010B/2641